RECONSIDERING REGIONS IN
AN ERA OF NEW NATIONALISM

Reconsidering Regions in an Era of New Nationalism

Edited by
ALEXANDER FINKELSTEIN
AND ANNE F. HYDE

University of Nebraska Press
LINCOLN

© 2023 by the Board of Regents of the University of Nebraska

All rights reserved

The University of Nebraska Press is part of a land-grant institution with campuses and programs on the past, present, and future homelands of the Pawnee, Ponca, Otoe-Missouria, Omaha, Dakota, Lakota, Kaw, Cheyenne, and Arapaho Peoples, as well as those of the relocated Ho-Chunk, Sac and Fox, and Iowa Peoples.

Library of Congress Cataloging-in-Publication Data

Names: Finkelstein, Alexander, editor. | Hyde, Anne Farrar, 1960– editor.
Title: Reconsidering regions in an era of new nationalism / edited by Alexander Finkelstein and Anne F. Hyde.
Description: Lincoln: University of Nebraska Press, 2023 | Includes bibliographical references and index.
Identifiers: LCCN 2023012260
ISBN 9781496228109 (hardback)
ISBN 9781496237323 (paperback)
ISBN 9781496238399 (epub)
ISBN 9781496238405 (pdf)
Subjects: LCSH: Regionalism—United States—History. | Group identity—United States—History. | National characteristics, American. | Politics and culture—United States—History. | United States—Race relations—History. | BISAC: HISTORY / United States / State & Local / General | SOCIAL SCIENCE / Regional Studies
Classification: LCC E179.5 .R43 2023 | DDC 320.540973—dc23/eng/20230503
LC record available at https://lccn.loc.gov/2023012260

Set in Minion Pro by Scribe Inc.

CONTENTS

List of Illustrations   vii

Introduction: Why Regions?   ix
Anne F. Hyde and Alexander Finkelstein

Part 1. Culture

1. Many Southerners, Many Souths: The New Beginnings of a Regional History   3
Jennifer Ritterhouse

2. Get Farther East Than You Are   31
Flannery Burke

3. Where in the World Is Hawai'i? Shifting Geographies of the Fiftieth State   57
Sarah Miller-Davenport

4. Sounds of Black Internationalism: Reimagining Regions through Anti-apartheid   85
Mickell Carter

Part 2. Space

5. The Significance of Climate in American History: Inventing, Imagining, and Erasing Regions   111
Lawrence Culver

6. A Blueprint for the Border: The Water Treaty of 1944, the International Boundary and Water Commission, and Regional Planning in the Borderlands   133
Sean Parulian Harvey

7. The Formation of Midwestern Regional Identity   152
Jon K. Lauck

8. Spatial Survivance: Haudenosaunee Active Presence in the U.S.-Canadian Borderlands   175
Taylor Spence

Part 3. Institutions

9. Growing Up American: The Children's Aid Society and the American West   203
Courtney E. Buchkoski

10. Where the East Peters Out: Dallas, Fort Worth, and Regional Branding in the Great Southwest   224
Jimmy L. Bryan Jr.

11. Local Identities and National Highways: How Roads Deepened and Diluted Historical Regionalism   253
Alexander Finkelstein

Contributors   279

Index   283

ILLUSTRATIONS

1. A girl in Hawai'i celebrates statehood   72
2. Fact-based region making in the American West   124
3. *Indian Episodes of New York State* (1935)   180
4. Cadwallader Colden map (1725)   183
5. The Haudenosaunee Diaspora (ca. 1700–present)   185
6. Fort Worth and railroads map (1873)   229
7. "Gateway to the Southwest" (1910)   231
8. "A Greeting and a Pledge" (1923)   237
9. *Billy Rose Presents The Last Frontier* (1936)   239
10. USDA national highway map (1926)   262
11. Proposed interregional highway map (1944)   269

INTRODUCTION

Why Regions?

ANNE F. HYDE AND ALEXANDER FINKELSTEIN

Historical actors and those analyzing the past have divided the United States into regions, yet few agree on what those regions are or why they matter. In 1763 anxious British officials divided their chunk of North America into two regions—one for Indigenous subjects and one for Euro-Americans. But that political Proclamation of 1763 failed to keep people apart or stop wars.[1] Nearly a century later, railroads and telegraph lines created a new western region centered on Chicago with hinterlands supporting it.[2] A few decades after that, regional conflict burst into civil war as a seemingly irreconcilable South, North, and West pulled apart delicate national threads over the issues of freedom and slavery.[3] Americans, just a few decades later, reconfigured their conceptions of region to understand a world redefined by the continental United States and its colonies abroad in the aftermath of the Spanish-American War.[4] While a national culture in the twentieth century promised to unite the country, that culture's racial and ethnic divisions created a new definition of region with sharp divides around citizenship and belonging.[5] In the late 1960s, political realignments created new regions based on voting patterns.[6] Then Senator Barack Obama pushed against those categories. Hoping to build a national coalition beyond partisan regional generalizations, he challenged the idea that "red states" and "blue states" divided the country and its people.[7] Despite such proclamations, regions have long mattered in U.S. history.

What are regions? Are regions the sky you look at, the hurricanes or tornados you face, or how religion and language help you understand those storms? Regions are not historical or geographical monoliths but encapsulate all the divisions and contradictions of context that range from very local to global. Do notions of region emerge from worldview and shared custom or from creating and policing borders? Do notions of region foster competitive unity within a cohesive nation or foment dissent and inequity? Do regions act as nations, sometimes harmfully exclusionary, while also bridging geographic and ideological divides? Are regional identities and ideologies carried along when people move? How do regional identities change when we incorporate nonhuman narratives? Can regions be geographically discontinuous?

These questions about the how, why, and what of regions motivated this volume. *Reconsidering Region* brings together eleven essays that explore the creation and significance of regions within and beyond the United States. The scholars here suggest that regions derive from an amalgamation of space, culture, and institutions and are continuously reconstructed by identity, class, politics, language, ethnicity, and history. *Reconsidering Region* does not propose final answers about employing region as an effective category of analysis, but it does argue that region should not be ignored. *Reconsidering Region*'s authors do not propose a single definition of region because regions are dynamic and subjective. In North America, regions are not simply a product of early nationhood and expansion that created sharp divisions leading to Indian Removal, U.S. war with Mexico, and civil war. Regions have changed and endured. Regions have functioned as an outlet for Americans to assert political and social difference within a unified nation. Historians, literary scholars, and social scientists use region to explain and challenge ideas about local cultures and national belonging. These observers of regions, though, must contextualize these regions so as not to perpetuate the assumptions built into colonial structures.

This project and the many questions about how region is defined emerged from the editors' personal struggles to understand where they lived. Oklahoma—like all U.S. states—is a place that defies simple regional categorization. Oklahoma has been labeled as Indian Country, South, West, Midwest, Plains, Bible Belt, Borderlands, Heartland, and Flyover Country. Such contradictory labels fail to grasp the complexity of people and place. Historian Richard White calls Oklahoma part of a "southern wedge into the West."[8] The state carries marks of both when it celebrates Confederate history and settler colonialism that displaced Indigenous power.[9] Yet *southern* and *western* fail to encapsulate the other ways that regional identities have shaped both Oklahomans and outsiders who puzzle over the question of belonging. Should we use a regional lens to see Oklahoma's interracial socialist uprising of tenant farmers, tribal nations who turned down creating New Deal governments to protect oil, massacres of Black people who had achieved material and cultural wealth, a reverence for the military and its spending—none of which fit mythic West or imagined South?[10] This project broadened beyond a struggle to see Oklahoma when we recognized that every state and space contains contradictions that require explanation. Regions can promise to transcend state borders and offer clearer views of what connects people and places, yet they prove just as elusive to define.

This volume, then, questions the often too simple analytical categories used to see region. By considering the fraught ways region has been employed in the past, this collection suggests that new methodologies offer groundwork for sharper and more creative uses. In the last three decades historians have seriously reexamined various pasts with race, gender, class, and environment in mind to frame histories with more nuance. New methodologies, paired with attention to spatial organization, yielded scholarship that expands how we can understand regions through, for example, environmental, political, familial, economic, imaginative, and religious perspectives.[11]

Although region is difficult to deploy precisely and even harder to define, scholars have offered up components of an evolving definition designed to provoke important questions. In 1941, W. J. Cash, struggling to define a new South, called it "a complex of established relationships and habits of thought, sentiments, prejudices, standards, and values, and association of ideas."[12] As a North Carolina newspaperman, Cash offered a rendering of white Southerners' minds to delineate what he labeled a Southern perspective. Because historians and contemporary observers have long employed Cash's framework for regional definition, it offers a useful starting place. Cash's framework evokes many questions about how regions evolve. What constitutes "established" relationships and ideas? Can these regional relationships change with new technologies or populations? Do these relationships emerge from shared custom and ideology, or do these views and customs emerge from politicking spaces and people?

In the 1990s, historians renewed the debate over whether regions mattered. The resounding answer has been "yes, regions matter," yet this renewed debate forced clarification about why and to whom. Historians contend that regions have shaped individuals' identities and structured systems that organize experience. The authors of *All Over the Map*, examining the South, West, and Northeast, added to Cash's definition by demonstrating how regions have been created and renewed by both insiders and outsiders.[13] In 1996, Ed Ayers, Patricia Limerick, Peter Onuf, and Stephen Nissenbaum argued that regional identity is fueled by externalities like government and economy, which in turn feed sets of internally constructed myths. Stephen Nissenbaum demonstrated how New England "style" was nationalized, building on Cash's framework by showing how regional customs and ideals become established internally and externally. By presenting three canonical regions, the study challenged notions about how—or if—other regions might form and on what scale. However, their efforts begged the question of whether regions defined themselves in relation to one another or whether they could be created by their own attributes without comparison to other regions. Do regional identities exist in isolation without any external comparative markers? Similarly, does that view of region consider people who migrate between locales, whose movement both changes the composition of regional culture and enables people to identify with multiple regions?

INTRODUCTION   xiii

In 2011, historians Michelle Nickerson and Darren Dochuk, in their analysis of the Sunbelt's rise and impact, offered a subtle definition of region: "As politically and economically created spaces, regions represent landscapes with nebulous and constantly shifting boundaries drawn by institutional and individual actors who, over time, create patterns that mark geography as distinct—as a recognizable pattern."[14] This definition broadens our understanding of region but also provokes questions. Must regions be organized around geography? What about rural or recently emigrated peoples as coherent regional blocs? What about regions like the Backcountry or Indian Country that shift with conquest, treaties, and reclaiming sovereignty? And what about regions that overlap—using the same space or people contemporaneously or at different moments? Moreover, who "recognizes" the region—those in or those out? Do humans, as opposed to nonhuman and climatic forces, solely shape regions?

More recently, historian Jon Lauck pushed back on broad definitions of region, demanding other, more dynamic scales so that place would not be "flattened and standardized into monotonous and forgettable dots." Using the example of the shifting line between the Midwest and Great Plains, he claims that more localized regions illuminate "a robust and multidimensional civic life."[15] Such a construction of region offers insight about the challenges of finding the right scale and the risk of obscuring or erasing peoples and places if you go too big, but it too provokes questions. How small and distinct should a space be before it becomes a locale and not a region? Why and how have certain regions retained their prominence in the American imagination and geopolitical system? Such a historical question reaffirms how this book reveals the material consequences of regional construction because the stories we tell about ourselves, about others, and about space itself affect how people live their lives.

Other scholars push back in another direction, reminding us that regions are part of larger national and international networks far beyond the bounds of the nation-state. Empire and its intertwined finance and information mechanisms, for example, structure complex relationships between people and place. As such, historians who track transnational movements of people, ideas, and commodities ought to employ region as a category of analysis. This approach could offer a sharper sense of how conceptions of space and identity have evolved over time and how they affect individual decisions. In a world created and inhabited by people of diasporas, the linkages between people and place become important. Region, as a category of analysis, works on a global scale when thinking about migration, solidarity, geopolitical alignment, and imperial projects.

Some scholars and cultural critics have held out region as the brighter, lighter form of nation building, but it also operates as both a derivative and a driver of nationalism. Nationalism has proven a powerful and enduring ideology in the modern world, and scholars of nationalism have invoked the concept critically yet productively to offer deeper historical insight. Studying fractures and dissent within nations along regional lines provides a fuller understanding of how and why internal competition and difference foster (or undermine) nationalist sentiment. Many scholars of nationalism demonstrate the constructed quality of sentiments like patriotism and national identity. That critique ought to push scholars of region to be attentive to how region is intertwined with and subsumed by nation.[16] Scholars of nationalism, like scholars of region, debate if nationalism arises from ideas or structural factors like natural resources or political systems. Indeed, much theorization of nations and nationalism provides scholars of regions useful starting places.[17] Nationalism, many scholars argue, can unite a nation by overshadowing internal dissent from the "exaltation of the nation, if not necessarily as the highest good, then as a transcendent good, a cause at least the equal of any other, superior by far to most."[18] Prasenjit Duara argues, "The symbolic power of nationalism to subordinate and discipline all manner of difference to a greater cause is, of course, important not only for imperialism but for domestic projects as well."[19] Scholars of region can look to studies of nationalism for models of critical analysis that bridges geographical, political, demographic, ideological, and other models of development and identity formation.

Nationalism and regionalism often function in concert, yet they have also been oppositional. The questions of how nationalism is cultivated and who cultivates it shed light on the same processes within regions. Stefan Berger, for example, uses the reunification of Germany to elucidate the competing claims over German national identity, and he concludes that historical narratives played a central role in fostering such an identity.[20] Scholars of region could build on these insights into nationalism's framing of differences within the nation. They can be squashed, subsumed, or elevated by juxtaposing competing and cooperative projects on regional and national scales. Studies of region likewise can offer a lens into the durability of nationalist sentiment and imperial projects. Considering, for instance, how regionalism functions outside of the geographic and chronological scope of the United States by including U.S. territories and Indigenous spaces enables us to represent a long swatch of historical change. Approaching region as scholars have approached nationalism has allowed the contributors of this volume to showcase the simultaneously competitive and cooperative nature of peoples, resources, and places within different regions. The sharply competitive nature of regions has not yet torn the country apart because the bonds and norms of a larger nation temper those sometimes fiercely limned differences.

Modernity too challenges historians to think more acutely about the intersection of space, time, and identity. How do we examine identity and nation in a world connected by the internet, global news, and intertwined financial systems? For nearly a century, highways and airplanes have flattened physical distance. The advent of the telephone and internet produced a more interconnected world, sometimes making geographic distance obsolete. Such technologies have changed—and will continue to change—how people interact, understand themselves, and explain the world around them. Such forces were supposed to end region in an interconnected and uniform society. Instead, interstate highways, air travel, public education, mass culture, fast food, and the consolidation of industries have amplified regional differences, both material and imaginary. Jeffrey Pilcher's global history of the taco, for example, reveals how mass marketing of the taco initially nationalized ideas of regional cuisine and authenticity, but people adapted each taco's taste and meaning based on local ingredients, customs, and business opportunities.[21]

Nefarious or beneficial, region can be a useful way to see power—to illuminate its structures and subjective relationships in particular places. Regional identifications can show how we navigate projects of both conquest and survival. Several of our essays consider how local elites and national institutions built regions to serve both economic and racial agendas. Historians have demonstrated how region enhances analysis of race and migration in relation to power and culture. For example, Peggy Pascoe's history of miscegenation laws across the United States illustrates regional actors understanding and implementing racial supremacy based on perceived threats within particular regions, such as for Asian and Indigenous people in the West.[22] Scholars of immigration have laid out how making immigration a national "problem" criminalized immigrants and expanded the carceral state everywhere.[23] The ideology of racial supremacy evolved across the country adjusting to varying demographic realities and patterns of migration. Historians of race and migration ought to employ a regional lens to better understand the power of such phenomena in their contexts. Historical actors have constructed regions as projects of exclusion and supremacy but with significant efforts dedicated to inclusion and solidarity.

Five core ideas link these essays and the questions that remain. First, regions matter and ought to be analyzed. Second, geographic spaces can hold multiple simultaneously competing and cooperating regional identities. Third, regions in the United States allow for dissent and competition within the nation while maintaining broader national allegiances—even though that balance has often failed. Fourth, mapping regions both obscures and enhances our understandings of them. Fifth, regional associations that serve to advance a specific vision about nation and nationalism require careful probing. Despite sharing core ideas about the importance of historicizing regions, this group of scholars does not agree on what constitutes regions or how various people have regarded their place inside or outside of them. We hope that showcasing disagreements illuminates new approaches and tools.

Region, we conclude, remains a vital category of analysis when fully explicated and contextualized. When we reveal who is defining the category and the purposes for which they are defining it, region becomes useful. This volume expands conversations about region by questioning the canonical regions in U.S. history (e.g., West and South and North) to find complexity in how blocs form and how they understand themselves as historical forces. *Reconsidering Region* brings together scholars who study diverse people and places, and our collective expertise allows us to highlight the many ways regionalist analysis has been undertaken. Historicizing region varies across subjects—time, place, people, and methodologies—so the authors' diversity here fosters a conversation about how to think through the complexity of region. The authors' topics and approaches highlight three distinct yet sometimes overlapping ways to understand how regions form and why they change: culture, space, and institutions. These three categories do not provide neat boxes for regional analysis because region defies easy categorization. The strength of this volume, in part, is the weakness of these categories; each of the essays show how space, culture, and institutions overlap and intertwine.

The first way we define region is culture. In the tradition of W. J. Cash's intellectual definition of region, we assert that contemporary observers began delineating common customs and ideologies between people—notions that scholars should later extend and critique. Indeed, Cash, at the beginning of the U.S. entry into World War II, sought to explain a uniquely uniform Southern identity that explained the region's past and contributed to national development. This cultural view of regions operates without respect to space or geography but pays close attention to individual actors and their beliefs. One strength of this cultural approach to regions is that individuals can take on multiple regional identifications, thereby expanding our ability to understand people's worldviews.

Jennifer Ritterhouse's piece on the South's complexity, with diverse actors and ideals, challenges Cash directly by insisting that historians treat region intersectionally, so that Southern historians consider gender, race, and region in a dynamic relationship. Flannery Burke's chapter uses four major authors of the American West—Bernard DeVoto, Wallace Stegner, Era Bell Thompson, and Louise Erdrich—to illustrate the ways these western writers delineated and defined an East as part of a political project based on their view of the nation. Sarah Miller-Davenport's careful examination of Hawai'i's paradoxical relationship to the continental United States illuminates the contingency of Hawai'i's regional identity on global geopolitics that ensnared Hawai'i and its residents as symbols in various American projects. Mickell Carter's piece argues that Black internationalism forged an international movement rooted in a common struggle against racism. That movement manifested in a transnational identification with protest against South African apartheid, illuminating culture's transcendence over borders.

The second way we organize region is by considering spatial boundaries. This view of region privileges the space people occupy as the paramount tool for drawing connections. The space-based regional view asserts that something inherent to specific places, such as climate or local historical precedent, binds people who live within a recognizable border. This view of region often relies on borders as defined by the nation-state, but rivers, mountains, heat, or ice can also act as borders. A strength of this approach is employing mapping tools to visualize and convey information about people and phenomena within a space. The approach, however, subsumes people within the space, which can often ignore marginalized people within said borders. Spatial organization can also flatten local complexities or irregularities and sometimes fail to respect complexity. Such failure can perpetuate inequalities or unbalanced power relations, especially considering that both humans and nonhumans move.

In this volume, Sean Harvey points out how the realities of managing a river and its resources, compounded by the complexities of local and international politics, shaped the way the Rio Grande contributed to the development of a binational region based on a shared resource. Lawrence Culver's piece shows how economic desires about developing western spaces informed national conceptions of climate and region at the expense of local environmental realities. Thus, during the era of U.S. expansion in the nineteenth century, debate over development made climate a cultural, political, scientific, and technological actor. Jon Lauck's detailed examination of the long history of a single region illuminates "the Midwest's" struggle to find adequate explanatory power. Sometimes, real and meaningful fissures do not correspond to borders and boundaries, as in Taylor Spence's analysis of the evolving Haudensaunee world and its shifting relationship to the U.S.-Canada border.

The final way we construct and organize regions is by looking at state formation, especially efforts to develop institutions that expand state power. The institutional approach to regions can explicate hidden relationships between nationalist sentiment and regional utility. This approach offers insight into how state and nonstate actors have cooperated and competed over development. Defining national and regional developments by state and institutional actors' projects can obfuscate the contingent nature of regional development and the challenges to these projects. This approach can perpetuate harmful or exclusionary visions of nation and region in the service of holding on to power.

Courtney Buchkoski's chapter examines the Children's Aid Society's effort to develop and propagate a particular eastern vision of the American West that, in theory, served as a safety valve for the East's corruption. This example highlights how the imagined reality about one region can reveal anxieties and assumptions about another. Similarly, Jimmy Bryan's close analysis of how white founders and business interests in Dallas and Fort Worth employed the media to attract investors and residents built new myths and images for the region. Alexander Finkelstein's chapter explores how U.S. states used road building both to connect a nation and to cement regional identity. Roads, like airports, required institutions and policies that constructed a regional identity that often erased meaningful objections and dissenters.

Regional identification and borders change over time, for regions and their residents contain multitudes. Historians must recognize who gets to define region and for what purpose. Are regions defined by contemporary actors or subsequent analysts? As a tool of analysis, subjects' proclaimed self-identification with regions can omit connections only later made visible by scholars with the benefit of hindsight. For example, historical actors may not have thought of themselves as part of a "Pacific World," "Atlantic World," or "Borderlands," but scholars are able to identify and connect common characteristics that fit people into a coherent region that often evolves with shared experiences or ideologies. In part, the historian's job is to elucidate connections that help explain that changing context and how people live in it. In recent "Western" scholarship, for example, historians have drawn connections between settler societies across the globe, even when people in Perth and Portland didn't recognize the common intellectual and economic worlds in which they lived.[24] While such analysis illuminates broader patterns and connections, it sometimes requires us to see connections that would have been entirely foreign to—and possibly outright rejected by—the subjects. Such uncomfortable connections can enable analysis beyond explicit contemporary subjectivities.

Because of the difficulties in classifying people, scholars who construct regional identifications must think about their goals. How is our understanding of the past and present enhanced by using region as a category of analysis? More sharply asked, Is region an important analytical tool like gender, race, and class, or is region a vanity project in legitimizing a dominant discourse based on local and national power structures? Can it be both simultaneously? Historians, as Nancy Shoemaker reminds us, "don't invent their categories of analysis." Shoemaker continues, "These systems of marked and unmarked categories—whether race, gender, or region—are ways of thinking that are drawn from society at large."[25] Regional identification is ripe for historical analysis because it is so pertinent to collective and personal identity.

Notes

1. Calloway, *Scratch of a Pen*.
2. Cronon, *Nature's Metropolis*.
3. Nelson, *Three-Cornered War*.
4. Immerwahr, *How to Hide an Empire*.
5. Brundage, *Southern Past*.
6. Kruse and Zelizer, *Fault Lines*.
7. "Barack Obama's Remarks to the Democratic National Convention," *New York Times*, July 27, 2004, https://www.nytimes.com/2004/07/27/politics/campaign/barack-obamas-remarks-to-the-democratic-national.html.
8. White, *"It's Your Misfortune and None of My Own,"* 589.
9. Chang, *Color of the Land*; Field, *Growing Up with the Country*.
10. Green, *Grass-Roots Socialism*; Krehbiel, *Tulsa, 1921*; Crowder, "More Valuable Than Oil."
11. Manganiello, *Southern Water, Southern Power*; Kamerling, *Capital and Convict*; Hyde, *Empires, Nations, and Families*; Robbins, *Colony & Empire*; Wrobel, *Promised Lands*; Dochuk, *From Bible Belt to Sunbelt*.
12. Cash, *Mind of the South*, xlviii.
13. Ayers et al., *All Over the Map*.
14. Nickerson and Dochuk, *Sunbelt Rising*, 14.
15. Lauck, *Interior Borderlands*, xxvi.
16. Hobsbawm, *Nations and Nationalism since 1780*; Berger, *Search for Normality*.
17. Breuilly, *Oxford Handbook of the History of Nationalism*; Berger and Storm, *Writing the History of Nationalism*; Greenfeld, *Nationalism*; Billig, *Banal Nationalism*; Gellner and Breuilly, *Nations and Nationalism*.
18. Pessen, "American Nationalism and American Historians."
19. Duara, *Sovereignty and Authenticity*, 13.
20. Berger, *Search for Normality*.
21. Pilcher, *Planet Taco*.
22. Pascoe, *What Comes Naturally*.
23. Hernández, *Migra!*; Ngai, *Impossible Subjects*; Benton-Cohen, *Inventing the Immigration Problem*.
24. Belich, *Replenishing the Earth*; Wrobel, *Global West, American Frontier*.
25. Shoemaker, "Regions as Categories of Analysis."

Bibliography

Ayers, Edward L., Patricia Nelson Limerick, Stephen Nissenbaum, and Peter S. Onuf. *All Over the Map: Rethinking American Regions*. Baltimore: Johns Hopkins University Press, 1996.

Belich, James. *Replenishing the Earth: The Settler Revolution and the Rise of the Anglo-World, 1783–1939*. Oxford: Oxford University Press, 2009.

Benton-Cohen, Katherine. *Inventing the Immigration Problem: The Dillingham Commission and Its Legacy*. Cambridge MA: Harvard University Press, 2018.

Berger, Stefan. *The Search for Normality: National Identity and Historical Consciousness in Germany since 1800*. Providence RI: Berghahn, 1997.

Berger, Stefan, and Eric Storm. *Writing the History of Nationalism*. London: Bloomsbury Academic, 2019.

Billig, Michael. *Banal Nationalism*. London: SAGE, 1995. http://public.ebookcentral.proquest.com/choice/publicfullrecord.aspx?p=1024116.

Breuilly, John, ed. *The Oxford Handbook of the History of Nationalism*. 1st ed. Oxford: Oxford University Press, 2013.

Brundage, W. Fitzhugh. *The Southern Past: A Clash of Race and Memory*. Cambridge MA: Belknap Press of Harvard University Press, 2005.

Calloway, Colin G. *The Scratch of a Pen: 1763 and the Transformation of North America*. New York: Oxford University Press, 2007.

Cash, W. J. *The Mind of the South*. New York: Vintage, 1991.

Chang, David A. *The Color of the Land: Race, Nation, and the Politics of Landownership in Oklahoma, 1832–1929*. Chapel Hill: University of North Carolina Press, 2010.

Cronon, William. *Nature's Metropolis: Chicago and the Great West*. New York: W. W. Norton, 1991.

Crowder, James L. "'More Valuable Than Oil': The Establishment and Development of Tinker Air Force Base, 1940–1949." *Chronicles of Oklahoma* 70, no. 3 (Fall 1992): 228–57.

Dochuk, Darren. *From Bible Belt to Sunbelt: Plain-Folk Religion, Grassroots Politics, and the Rise of Evangelical Conservatism*. New York: W. W. Norton, 2011.

Duara, Prasenjit. *Sovereignty and Authenticity: Manchukuo and the East Asian Modern*. Lanham MD: Rowman & Littlefield, 2003.

Field, Kendra Taira. *Growing Up with the Country: Family, Race, and Nation after the Civil War*. New Haven CT: Yale University Press, 2018.

Gellner, Ernest, and John Breuilly. *Nations and Nationalism*. Ithaca NY: Cornell University Press, 2009.

Green, James R. *Grass-Roots Socialism: Radical Movements in the Southwest, 1895–1943*. Baton Rouge: Louisiana State University Press, 1980.

Greenfeld, Liah. *Nationalism: Five Roads to Modernity*. Cambridge MA: Harvard University Press, 1995.

Hernández, Kelly Lytle. *Migra! A History of the U.S. Border Patrol*. Berkeley: University of California Press, 2010.

Hobsbawm, E. J. *Nations and Nationalism since 1780: Programme, Myth, Reality.* 2nd ed. Cambridge: Cambridge University Press, 2012.

Hyde, Anne F. *Empires, Nations, and Families: A New History of the North American West, 1800–1860.* Lincoln: University of Nebraska Press, 2011.

Immerwahr, Daniel. *How to Hide an Empire: A History of the Greater United States.* New York: Random House, 2019.

Kamerling, Henry. *Capital and Convict: Race, Region, and Punishment in Post–Civil War America.* Charlottesville: University of Virginia Press, 2017.

Krehbiel, Randy. *Tulsa, 1921: Reporting a Massacre.* Norman: University of Oklahoma Press, 2019.

Kruse, Kevin Michael, and Julian E. Zelizer. *Fault Lines: A History of the United States since 1974.* New York: W. W. Norton, 2020.

Lauck, Jon K. *The Interior Borderlands: Regional Identity in the Midwest and Great Plains.* Sioux Falls SD: Center for Western Studies, 2019.

Manganiello, Christopher J. *Southern Water, Southern Power: How the Politics of Cheap Energy and Water Scarcity Shaped a Region.* Chapel Hill: University of North Carolina Press, 2015.

Nelson, Megan Kate. *The Three-Cornered War: The Union, the Confederacy, and Native Peoples in the Fight for the West.* New York: Scribner, 2020.

Ngai, Mae M. *Impossible Subjects: Illegal Aliens and the Making of Modern America.* Princeton NJ: Princeton University Press, 2004.

Nickerson, Michelle M., and Darren Dochuk, eds. *Sunbelt Rising: The Politics of Place, Space, and Region.* Philadelphia: University of Pennsylvania Press, 2011.

Pascoe, Peggy. *What Comes Naturally: Miscegenation Law and the Making of Race in America.* New York: Oxford University Press, 2011.

Pessen, Edward. "American Nationalism and American Historians." *OAH Magazine of History* 2, no. 4 (Fall 1987): 4–7.

Robbins, William G. *Colony & Empire: The Capitalist Transformation of the American West.* Lawrence: University Press of Kansas, 1994.

Shoemaker, Nancy. "Regions as Categories of Analysis." *Perspectives on History*, November 1996. https://www.historians.org/publications-and-directories/perspectives-on-history/november-1996/regions-as-categories-of-analysis.

White, Richard. *"It's Your Misfortune and None of My Own": A New History of the American West.* Norman: University of Oklahoma Press, 1993.

Wrobel, David M. *Global West, American Frontier: Travel, Empire, and Exceptionalism from Manifest Destiny to the Great Depression.* Albuquerque: University of New Mexico Press, 2013.

———. *Promised Lands: Promotion, Memory, and the Creation of the American West.* Lawrence: University Press of Kansas, 2002.

RECONSIDERING REGIONS IN
AN ERA OF NEW NATIONALISM

PART 1
Culture

ONE

Many Southerners, Many Souths

The New Beginnings of a Regional History

JENNIFER RITTERHOUSE

A friend of mine has a gay pride- and inclusivity-themed T-shirt with the words "All Y'all" written in rainbow letters on the front. When I asked her where she got it, she lit up. She enthusiastically recommended a website and podcast that she explained as part of a wide-ranging response to J. D. Vance's 2016 book *Hillbilly Elegy* from southerners who wanted to challenge stereotypes and emphasize the diversity of people and opinions to be found within Appalachia and the wider South.

Fortunately, Google autocorrects. It turns out that what I had heard as "the Better Southerner" is actually "the Bitter Southerner," as in bittersoutherner.com. *Of course it is*, I instantly thought. I was not surprised, but I was disappointed, even chagrined. Although I did find the Bitter Southerner's content interesting and some of it heartening, I realized that at some deep, unconscious level, I had been hoping for a whole new view—a redefinition of regional identity around better-ness—to counter familiar, entrenched ideas about the bad old (bad Old and bad New) South. But even those who would like to throw off the net of a southern exceptionalism that blames the South for all of America's racial and economic problems often just wriggle through it. They stew and fume about being overlooked or misunderstood, ensuring that a "sense of grievance" remains "at the heart of southern identity," as John Shelton Reed claimed in 1993.[1]

Three decades on from Reed's observation, a Venn diagram of identities generally understood to be "southern" would show two large, overlapping circles: one for those embittered by the decline of white nationalism and another for those embittered by non-southerners' insistence that white nationalism is all that southern identity (actually) means. If they got included in such a diagram at all, the circles of Black-southern, feminist-southern, queer-southern, and progressive-southern identities would be much smaller and more marginal because that is how they appear in popular consciousness. This is a shame, because it is precisely by studying such "marginal," "hyphenated," *intersectional* southerners that historians have, over the last half century, written a truer and more useful history of the American South that, in turn, provides a more usable past for the nation as a whole. In the process, the realization that *everyone is intersectional*—that elite white male is a hyphenated identity—has become a commonplace in theory, even if the implications of this truth are not always fully explored in scholarly practice. Insights originating with Black feminists—from Anna Julia Cooper to Alice Walker and Kimberlé Crenshaw to a first generation of Black feminist historians such as Deborah Gray White, Evelyn Brooks Higginbotham, and Elsa Barkley Brown—have informed scholarship in southern history without a thorough accounting of the debt (a subject I'll come back to).[2] The relationship between intersectionality and region as a category of analysis has also been too little explored.

In this essay, I argue that recent intersectional approaches to southern history have offered some especially dynamic models for writing about regions. Like other interpretive gains of the past few decades, this outcome has resulted primarily from historians listening to previously unheard voices. Marginalized, "different," and dissident southerners often wrestled with questions about "the South" and "southernness" themselves, enabling their most astute historians to see both subjective and structural ways region operated in their and their contemporaries' lives. Like Cooper—whose 1892 book *A Voice from the South by a Black Woman of the South* defined her identity as simultaneously Black, female, southern, and American—those who confronted the multiplicity of their identities developed a "heritage" nestled in consciousness. They became "able," as she put it, "to grasp the deep significance of the possibilities of the crisis" that is and has been life in the South—and the United States—for those kept down, those pushed aside, or more broadly (though I do not mean to draw any false equivalencies), those unable to feel comfortable morally, politically, or personally at the centers of power as currently constituted, even if their social positions and self-presentations allowed access to them.[3] "One ever feels his twoness," wrote W. E. B. Du Bois.[4] Those who felt region ambivalently, as a force tearing them asunder rather than a mythology building them up, have a lot to teach us. It almost goes without saying that politics and culture have always defined their South—really, their Souths, plural—far more than geography.

But this is also true of the Souths of politically and culturally powerful white men, whose identities are equally as intersectional even though they are not always "marked" equally clearly.[5] The key point is that by situating region in what Barkley Brown taught us to think of as the *simultaneity* of identity, by listening to our historical subjects as they embrace and contest and are shaped by ideas about region along with other formative ideologies, historians are encouraged to give up—not on region itself, as some erstwhile southern historians have provocatively suggested, but on trying to pin down the category in favor of learning what they can from its elusiveness.[6] As cultural constructions with shifting and contested boundaries, regions show the ground of ideological struggle, which is no less important than actual ground, landscape, or jurisdictions plotted on a map.

"There is something there, in regions, which holds insight for us as historians," as Laura Edwards argues.[7] But regional approaches cannot help us sharpen our historical vision unless we treat region with the same dynamism as the analytical categories of gender, race, and class. Scholars who manage to keep all these balls in the air gain fresh insights by watching their intercircling motions. "Ideologies looked different when I considered their southern sources," writes Glenda Gilmore, articulating just part of the promise of a more consciously intersectional regionalism.[8] As her work and that of other recent southern historians show, relationships between region, nation, and globe end up looking different as well.

The Disappearing South

"For as long as people have believed there was a South, they have also believed it was disappearing," Edward Ayers wrote in 1996 in *All Over the Map*. He reminded us then that some who lived in Virginia and the Carolinas "thought the South was dying as early as the 1830s, when too much easy money in the Cotton Kingdom pulled people to raw places such as Alabama and Mississippi, which knew nothing of true Southern gentility."[9] Emancipation, Reconstruction, industrialization, and the arrival of mass culture in such forms as radio and film also stirred South-watchers, and the acceleration of change from the New Deal through World War II and the civil rights era seemed all the more certain to bring regional distinctiveness to an end. "The time is coming, if indeed it has not already arrived, when the Southerner will begin to ask himself whether there is really any longer very much point in calling himself a Southerner," C. Vann Woodward famously wrote in 1958. Perhaps "the Southern heritage" was swiftly becoming "an old hunting jacket that one slips on comfortably while at home but discards when he ventures abroad in favor of some more conventional or modish garb."[10]

Many southerners of the late 1950s might well prefer to wrap themselves in the fashions of an undifferentiated Americanness because, especially in the moment of massive resistance to the *Brown v. Board of Education* decision, defending segregation was widely understood to be the sine qua non of southern regional identity. "Once more the South finds itself with a morally discredited Peculiar Institution on its hands," observed Woodward. "The last time this happened, about a century ago, the South's defensive reaction was to identify its whole cause with the one institution that was most vulnerable." Those who rejected the "cardinal test of loyalty" to slavery were "forced to reject the whole heritage" (which, Woodward found it unnecessary to mention, was only on offer to white southerners in the first place). The Confederate unity thus achieved became stronger in defeat as defiance against Yankee meddling and supposed "Negro rule" became the new cardinal test of loyalty and as white women along with white men made a civic religion out of the ideology of the Lost Cause. Yet by the 1950s, even "the consoling security of Reconstruction as the common historic grievance" had been rendered less secure by the "rude hands" of Du Bois and other revisionist historians, who had also challenged both popular and Dunning school narratives about the benevolence of slavery. And so Woodward was optimistic about racial change that might change attitudes toward region. "Historical experience with the first Peculiar Institution ought strongly to discourage comparable experiments with the second," he wrote. "If Southernism is allowed to become identified with a last ditch defense of segregation, it will increasingly lose its appeal among the younger generation. Many will be tempted to reject their entire regional identification, even the name 'Southern,' in order to dissociate themselves from the one discredited aspect."[11]

If Woodward's optimism sounds oddly cautionary, it is because he hoped to preserve some aspects of southern distinctiveness as antidotes to *American* exceptionalism. Could "a hard-won immunity from the myths and illusions of Southern sectionalism provide some immunity to the illusions and myths of American nationalism?" he asked. "Or would the hasty divestment merely make the myth-denuded Southerner hasten to wrap himself in the garments of nationalism?" Leery of an ascendant, often arrogant Cold War superpower with a national culture that encouraged conformity, acquisitiveness, and a false sense of innocence, Woodward highlighted the alternative lessons of southern history, including "a long and quite un-American experience with poverty" and "large components of frustration, failure, and defeat." Such a sobering heritage "affords the Southern people no basis for the delusion that there is nothing whatever that is beyond their power to accomplish." Because limitation and lack of power are "more common among the general run of mankind" than perpetual abundance and success, surely this must be a part of southern heritage "worth cherishing."[12]

So too was white southern guilt. Despite reams of apologia, southern intellectuals had "failed to convince" even themselves that the region's "peculiar evil was actually a 'positive good,'" Woodward argued. "The South's preoccupation was with guilt, not with innocence, with the reality of evil, not with the dream of perfection." Profoundly sadder, southern history must surely be capable of making southerners wiser than other Americans—or so Woodward hoped. Surely the "modern Southerner" could be "secure enough in his national identity" to challenge national myths by holding fast to the elements of regional experience that had been instructive and improving those that had made southerners and the South *better* than they used to be.[13]

Unfortunately, no—at least not in the aggregate. In Woodward's case and that of the historical subfield he cultivated, it has been not merely the preponderance of bitter rather than better (sadder but wiser) southerners but also the durability of national myths that prevented the realization of such a vision. In a country whose regional identifiers began to emerge before the nation-state[14]—a country that did, after all, have a civil war—it has been all too easy to ignore scholars' (various, not solely Woodwardian) reasons for writing about "the South" while clinging to southern exceptionalism in its traditional form as a mythology that exonerates the nation by positioning the region as a not-quite-American "other." The South has served as "the repository for problems that were really 'American' all along and that were only thought to be peculiar to the region and antithetical to mainstream American values," explain Larry Griffin and Don Doyle.[15] "The South plays a key role in the nation's self-image," Ayers concurs, "the role of evil tendencies overcome, mistakes atoned for, progress yet to be made." But the shaping of this role "is not something that is only done *to* the South by malevolent, insensitive non-Southerners," he adds. "The North and the South have conspired to create each other's identity as well as their own."[16]

Drawing on the theoretical work of Edward Said, geographer David Jansson has usefully applied the concept of "internal Orientalism" to explain this collaborative process. Much as Europeans "othered" the Orient to define themselves, would-be Americans—including southerners with conflicted regional and national loyalties—spilled a Suwannee River's worth of ink on the distinctive, "colonial," even "gothic" nature of the South and the "ethnic" characteristics of southern identity.[17] Natalie Ring argues that both a discourse of southern backwardness and the modernizing efforts of reformers from within as well as beyond the region were "central to the development of early twentieth-century liberalism and part of the process of nation-state formation" in the long period from 1880 to 1930.[18] For a more recent era, even nonsoutherners' homegrown racism and conservatism have often been attributed to a supposed "southernization of America"— an idea that has taken on a life of its own since John Egerton wrote about it and the "Americanization of Dixie" in 1974.[19] A quick fast-forward to the 2020s finds sociologist and MacArthur award winner Tressie McMillan Cottom explaining that the South "warehouses our nation's war with itself about citizenship, class, race, gender, immigration, history and future."[20]

While the popularity of blaming the South for American failings has persisted, Woodward's efforts to project a sadder-but-wiser southernness into the national discourse have arguably produced confusion among scholars. He "outlined an intellectual project of southern exceptionalism as a strategic maneuver to critique the excesses of American empire, the underside of American capitalism, and the myth of American innocence from responsibility for the past," write Matthew D. Lassiter and Joseph Crespino, whose 2009 edited volume *The Myth of Southern Exceptionalism* has been an important intervention in southern historians' ideas about region. Though sympathetic to Woodward's critique, Lassiter and Crespino argue that his intellectual project failed precisely because it tried to mobilize one set of myths against another. Following Woodward, "liberal historians in the postwar decades called for a distinctive southern history based not on a set of empirical differences between region and nation"—or, one might add, between one region and another—"but, rather, on the presumed divergence of a collective southern *identity* from national *myths* and American *ideals*." Such slippery definitions became less and less tenable as Woodward's post–World War II context itself became history. By then, most measurable differences among American regions—differences in voting patterns, levels of urbanization and immigration, church attendance, and participation in unions, for example—were clearly differences not of kind but of degree. "Certainly by the second half of the twentieth century, if not before as well," Lassiter and Crespino write, "focusing on the South's aberrant qualities compared to the rest of the United States obscures much more than it reveals about the fundamental questions of modern American history."[21]

Although Lassiter and Crespino say their "agenda is not to absolve the South but to implicate the nation," their argument's most significant implications may be for scholars' own self-understanding. Under the provocative title "The End of Southern History," they lament an "analytical confusion" that is "the inevitable result of the balancing act involved in a scholarly tradition that has maintained the faith in southern exceptionalism, as the essential foundation that legitimates the subfield of southern history, while simultaneously chronicling all of the ways in which the traditional South keeps fading away." Perhaps, they suggest, "southern" history should fade away instead, not least because much of the most exciting research in recent years has been generated "by scholars who position themselves in other subfields—such as African-American, urban, political, social, gender, labor, cultural, and Latino history."[22]

But is unnaming region really the right answer? Though certainly less invested in "the South" than Woodward and his ilk, the scholars Lassiter and Crespino allude to have not necessarily been as committed to other geographical frameworks—whether urban, suburban, metropolitan, national, or transnational—as they suggest. Often, their focus has been not on place so much as on *people*. Recent scholarly trends "reflect a belated but growing recognition," as Lassiter and Crespino themselves observe, "that for most residents of the South, as for most residents of other sections of the United States, regional status is a less salient measure of personal identity than other categories such as race, ethnicity, class, gender, religion, locality, and especially nationality."[23] In other words, scholars have largely been writing about geography in the context of *identity*, not elevating other geographical frameworks over region or starting with the empirical measures or policymaking powers Lassiter and Crespino suggest might make geographical frameworks more legitimate. Recent scholars have also tended to write about geographical identifications as part of a mix: the intersectional identities people feel within and by which they are both consciously and unconsciously shaped as they go about their lives. The relationship between region and other categories of identity—not the mercurial slipperiness of "the South," nor the question of whether it is slipping away—is what scholars can most beneficially grasp.

"Teaching many classes about the South, I found that my attempts to frame the question ['Is there still a South?'] flopped," Ted Ownby reflects. The concern that had animated so much discussion among scholars for so many years hardly interested his students. "Let's study people, their faces and papers and exam answers seemed to respond."[24] And not just imaginary white men, they may have felt, if not articulated. If only because the majority are female, most twenty-first-century college students are likely to be most interested in southern identities different from the falsely archetypal—but actually white and male—ones that writers such as W. J. Cash, the Nashville Agrarians, and to a lesser extent, even Woodward (whose mind ran to hunting jackets rather than hoop skirts) described. Like my friend with her T-shirt, they are interested in fresher garb.

Let's Study People, or the New Beginnings of Southern History

Fortunately, a multitude of scholars have been providing a whole new wardrobe of historical southern identities without worrying too much about whether "southern" is really their brand. Recent historiographers have offered different explanations for when and why this new scholarship about (if not necessarily *in* or *of*) southern history emerged, with the influence of feminist approaches repeatedly seen as paramount. Writing in 2019, Craig Thompson Friend and Lorri Glover focus on the 1980s as a turning point and stress the impact of postmodernism, especially "a questioning of narratives . . . , a heavy and often Marxist critique of capitalism, diversification of voices and perspectives, self-reflexive analyses of the structures and elements of the discipline as much as factual content, and an emphasis on orality as found in podcasts, digital media, television, and film." They also note the "deconstruction of previously unquestioned binaries—white/black, male/female, heterosexual/homosexual"—and argue that "feminist scholars led the way." The particular contributions of *Black* feminist scholars who helped historians replace binaries with intersections go unmentioned in Friend and Glover's fast-paced account. But they do acknowledge the influence of African American historians more generally, especially the "new generation" who undertook "more complex and nuanced explorations of intersectionality" and uncovered "how ideas about race operated with constructs of gender, sexuality, class, and disability to create systems of power and oppression." Together, African American history and women's and gender history "stood at the vanguard of postmodern shifts in southern historiography" that, by the time Friend and Glover's coedited volume *Reinterpreting Southern Histories* appeared in early 2020, had exerted considerable force on popular understandings of the southern past as well. "Destruction of and debates over Confederate monuments became the most public of postmodernism's impact[s] on southern history and historiography," they write—words that leapt off the page within a few short months as the racial reckoning sparked by the murder of George Floyd resulted most immediately in the removal of dozens of statues.[25]

Published more than a decade earlier than Friend and Glover's brief essay, Laura Edwards's longer and more detailed explanation of the "new wave" in southern history discusses similar trends with less emphasis on theory and more on politics. She puts the intellectual turning point earlier, in the 1960s, though far more books appeared in the 1980s and beyond. Influenced by the civil rights movement, feminism, and the New Left, scholars became newly interested in the lives of non-elite southerners—those "who were not rights-bearing individuals and, therefore, not the subjects of mainstream academic scholarship" written by the previous generation of historians. Whether or not they recognized the debt, post-1960s scholars also embraced and elaborated on dissident views from earlier in the twentieth century, including those of Woodward and Du Bois. Their emphasis on social and economic structures rather than "great men" revealed power dynamics and the interconnected workings of gender, race, and class. "While regional in its focus, this body of scholarship—by highlighting diversity and conflict—exploded the myth of the solid South as a uniquely unified region," Edwards writes.[26]

The longevity and pervasiveness of the solid South myth is, nevertheless, what makes the new southern history regional rather than local in character, despite its often deep engagement with very specific settings and conditions. As Edwards's discussion of the South Carolina nullification movement of 1827–33 suggests, the same historical processes that created Confederate nationalism made southernness a dominant ideology and category of identity that was virtually impossible to ignore. One might embrace it or reject it or question its parameters, but to escape some degree of identification, some kind of relationship, to a region so widely understood to be distinctive was impossible. For the South, the local had long been always-already the regional because of the sheer force, in the rising and falling Confederacy, of what Jimmy Bryan's essay in this volume describes as the "mental and emotional cartographies intentionally drawn by specific groups to seize control of their worlds."[27]

Luckily, mental maps, like historical interpretations, are subject to revision. After decades of post-1960s scholarship, "the historiography now characterizes the South as such a diverse region that it is difficult to use the term *southerner* without adding a modifier to indicate *which* southerners are being referenced," Edwards writes. In contrast to the Venn diagram of popular consciousness, professional historians' South "now appears as a place that nurtured radical political alternatives." It also "offered them up" to the supposedly more advanced national state as "yeoman farmers resisted the forces of capitalist economic change; slaves pushed the nation toward emancipation; southern farmers set aside white supremacy to unite across racial lines at various moments; women worked for political equality and social reform during the Progressive Era; industrial workers organized to fight the oppressive hegemony of the business elite; and African Americans' constant struggle against white supremacy made the civil rights movement possible." Rather than falling behind, Edwards concludes, "these southerners led the way in efforts to realize the nation's ideals."[28]

In short, they were better southerners. They were more admirable, by twenty-first-century lights, than the regional archetypes depicted by the Agrarians or Cash. Many also envisioned and consciously worked for a better South, in stark contrast to those who thought the best South was a past South they lamented or hoped would rise again.

As reformers of various kinds, "better southerners"—who can be described more objectively as southern dissenters or dissidents—have had particular appeal for researchers, many of whom "hope to understand the South better so they can fix problems," as Ownby writes.[29] The ripple effects of studying dissidents and other non-elites, from Ida B. Wells to mid-twentieth-century radical writers Katharine and Grace Lumpkin to the poorest sharecroppers and mill workers, have been profound.[30] Historians have not only discovered the South to be more diverse and divided than previously thought. They have also learned to be more careful about how and when to use region as a category of analysis. The logical fallacy of identifying "the South" with the Confederacy becomes clear if one is writing from the point of view of southern Unionists, for example: here were "southerners" who wanted "the South" to go a different way. The same is true of the perspectives of free and enslaved African Americans, whose views were not only bottom-up but outside-in from the circles of power. However hegemonic, a regime is not a region. If "the South" existed in the years from 1861 to 1865, it was a place of both Confederates and anti- and non-Confederates, roughly four million of whom were Black. Within any space at any moment, there are always those who resist the people in charge, who fight back and form not one but many alternative, often activist traditions. By shifting attention away from the people in power and onto those who resisted and opposed them, recent scholarship in southern history has, as Edwards summarizes, "separated regional interests from the political interests" of the dominant group.[31]

It has also compelled at least one scholar to opt for a whole new name. Glenda Gilmore's *Defying Dixie: The Radical Roots of Civil Rights, 1919–1950* is an especially good illustration of how much scholars can learn by *studying people*, particularly dissidents, while keeping the regional aspects of their intersectional identities in view. Perhaps the most obvious feature of Gilmore's book is her capacious definition of her subject. She is interested in anyone with roots in the South who "defied Dixie" in the period before the civil rights movement as conventionally defined. Drawing in expatriates along with resident southerners, she highlights members of the Communist Party as the *most defiant*, the ones who "brooked no compromise with full racial equality" and "stood up to say that black and white people should organize together, eat together, go to school together, and marry each other if they chose." But Gilmore is also fascinated by tortured moderates like Howard Odum and left-liberals like Frank Porter Graham. Her most richly developed portraits are of Lovett Fort-Whiteman, a Texan who was "the first American-born black Communist" and who died in a Soviet gulag, and Pauli Murray, a gender-nonconforming daughter of North Carolina whose long activist career spanned from the late 1930s, when she challenged segregation by applying for graduate study (with Odum) at Chapel Hill, through the 1960s and 1970s, when she participated in the "classical phase" of the civil rights movement, helped found the National Organization for Women (NOW), and became one of the nation's first female Episcopal priests. "*Defying Dixie* is a history in which ideas are embodied in a collective biography of activist black and white Southerners," Gilmore explains. "To illustrate my points, I have chosen characters and events to provide deep local context for broad historical changes."[32]

The result is a sprawling narrative that stretches from Atlanta to Moscow to Cape Town and progresses from mostly Communist "Incursions" in the 1920s through the development, in the 1930s, of a wider Black-left-liberal "Resistance" to the Jim Crow political and social order. The World War II years were a period of "Rebellion," when southerners "mounted a full-fledged, yet largely forgotten civil rights movement" aimed at fundamental economic as well as social change. The book ends with "Cold War Casualties" as anticommunists succeed in discrediting the movement as "un-American" (not merely un-Southern), resulting in the destruction of many activists' careers and a narrowing of civil rights goals. Gilmore avoids the blame-it-on-*Brown* theme that pulses through some recent scholarship, but she does sadly assert that the 1954 Supreme Court decision "was not all that we could have had or all that was due the South. Before *Brown*, activists dreamed a viable dream of true equality among the races, an equality that encompassed politics, education, economics, housing, personal interactions, and legal access. *Brown* squeaked through in the anti-Communist period, but without a Southern Left to shelter it, it stood alone, under attack, for almost a decade until the Civil Rights Act of 1964."[33]

Readers have agreed and disagreed with Gilmore's argument, but one aspect of it that seems to have gone unnoticed is her use of the word *Dixie*. In her book, "southern history becomes a national, even international story" largely *because* she reframes region to distinguish it from regime.[34] Unwilling to give over "the South" to the segregationists, she renames their social and political vision "Dixie" and writes about people who defied it while continuing to be (by her definition) and usually also to think of themselves as *southerners*.

Gilmore also treats region dynamically and intersectionally. She begins her exploration of the category in her very first sentence.

"When African Americans used the word 'Dixie' in the first half of the twentieth century," she writes, "they pronounced the South another country with its own political and social institutions, upheld by a white supremacist regime." White supremacists thought of the region in much the same way, but the Dixie of Black denunciation was an aspiration—and always *only* an aspiration—for them. The "mythical, isolated nation I thought I grew up in existed *only* as an imagined community," Gilmore writes of her childhood in 1950s North Carolina. "The image of the benighted South with its peculiar ways . . . was a creation of the white supremacists themselves" and one they never could make solid. Generation upon generation tried. "Dixie regularly purged itself of dissenters and counted them out of the polity," Gilmore writes. "Many protestors remained, but to acknowledge only those Southerners who stayed behind produces a distorted view of the place." Much as Cash could present "the mind of the South" only by first excluding all but (imagined) white men, the white supremacists' South "could remain the South only by chasing out some of its brightest minds and most bountiful spirits." Those chased away were still southerners. "Growing up under Jim Crow had shaped their politics," and continuing to think of *Dixie* as the enemy to fight or the problem to be solved was continuously shaping. For the dissenters, as for everyone else, the region was "a state of mind as well as an actual place," and their choice to return to the South "either physically or through their intellectual reach" made them part of southern history. Writing them back in changes the narrative and contributes to other narratives. For southern history, Gilmore's book reveals "an insurgent South" that reared activists who "fought longer and harder than anyone else" to achieve racial equality. For other kinds of history, her approach offers other surprises, such as her suggestion that "so many black North Carolinians settled within a few blocks of one another in New York that the Harlem Renaissance might have been the Raleigh Renaissance, North."[35]

As Lassiter and Crespino suggest, the standard for evaluating historical approaches is not so much whether they are "right" as whether they are revealing. Approaching region dynamically and intersectionally certainly can be. Carol Giardina provides another powerful illustration of this in a 2019 article titled "The Making of a Modern Feminist Vanguard, 1964–1973: Southern Women Whose Leadership Shaped the Movement and the Nation—A Synthetic Analysis." Mainly because she counts Black as well as white women from the South as "southern" and their civil rights–related activism as "feminist," Giardina shows "not only that the South was a hotbed of feminist activism, but also that it produced an outsized number of women who had transformative influence on the national feminist movement." Her claims for Black and white southern feminists are large: "Southern women were architects and engineers of the movement's radical and liberal branches. They were the first to apply the strategy of collective action learned in the southern civil rights movement to organize a mass movement against sexism. They dealt decisive blows to the racist, sexist Jezebel myth. . . . In Mississippi they instituted the earliest sexual harassment policies, and from Georgia, Florida, and Louisiana they achieved precedent-setting court victories against protective labor laws that prohibited women's workplace equality." Giardina also credits Pauli Murray and other southern women who "formulated the concept" of an "NAACP for women" and helped create NOW. And she cites Floridians as the first to issue a written call for an independent, women-only liberation movement and Texans as the ones who crafted the legal arguments that won the Supreme Court decision legalizing abortion in *Roe v. Wade*. "The impact of southern women's founding leadership cuts across feminism's rebirth years no matter where one looks," she concludes, "from the formation of the movement and its structure, theory, and strategy to foundational breakthroughs against sexist and racist laws and traditions."[36]

Unfortunately, Giardina chronicles this leadership without ever defining "the South" or what was "southern" about the women whose activism she describes. We learn that Casey Hayden "understood our movement as southern, a radical response to our region's failings," and that Mississippian Cassell Carpenter dubbed herself the "Magnolia Maverick."[37] But Hayden and Carpenter are white.

Whether or not Black women activists considered themselves "southern"—and what they (and their white feminist counterparts) even meant by the term—is an intriguing question Giardina leaves unexplored.

Nevertheless, like Gilmore's disambiguation of Dixie from the South, Giardina's remapping of the feminist vanguard is important because it changes narratives and "dispels widely held misconceptions." Understanding their origins in the southern civil rights movement provides meaning-altering context for ideas such as "Sisterhood is Powerful" and "The Personal is Political." It "also corrects the fallacy that the 1960s revival of feminism was exclusive to big cities." Perhaps most important, lumping by region allows Giardina to look beyond, without ignoring, feminists' and their historians' tendencies to split by race. This, in turn, helps her challenge "the outrageous inaccuracy that black women were not interested in feminism until several years after white women got it going." To the contrary, her approach, like Gilmore's, highlights the significance of longer Black traditions such as the public protests against rape that, as Danielle McGuire has shown, "galvanized local, national, and even international outrage."[38]

The national and international connections and implications of the kind of southern history Gilmore, Giardina, and others are writing deserve comment. Their studies show that, as salutary as global or transnational turns in scholarship may be, they do not make attention to region any less important. Like that of any other analytical category, the salience of region for historians depends on how and how much it mattered in people's lives. Writing about the global vision of the first few generations of Black historians, Robin Kelley encourages those similarly inclined to remember that these intellectuals' broad perspective did not "grow from the vine of smart scholarship." It grew from their embodied experience as African Americans: "It was a product of a state refusing to grant black people citizenship, an enslaved people whose first response was to find a way home, and a political refusal on the part of many black intellectuals to prop up American nationalism and its national myths. After all, their very lives expose the country's most fundamental national myths—that this is a country founded on freedom, democracy, and equality." Locked out of racist America, Black historians looked abroad for both heritage and help, for "social movements for freedom, justice, and self-determination" that "produced this global vision."[39] In this, they were like the Depression-era Black southerners Gilmore studied, who joined the Communist Party not because it was the Communist Party but because its agenda and organizers prioritized Black empowerment, especially in the South, where the vast majority of African Americans lived.

Giardina attributes the "breakout leadership" of Black and white southern feminists to the catalytic force of Black activism as well. Nevertheless, African Americans and their allies are not the only southerners whose historians have been demonstrating the value of dynamic, intersectional approaches to region in recent years. Along with the growing scholarship on Latinx and Asian immigrants, research on southern Indians has been breaking through the Black-white binary that has long dominated southern history.[40] Meanwhile, my own *Discovering the South: One Man's Travels through a Changing America in the 1930s* attempts to gaze back, with intersectionality ever in mind, at an elite, white, southern man—newspaper editor Jonathan Daniels—while following his gaze as he traveled around the South in 1937. Precisely because of his race, sex, and class privilege (as well as his comparative fame as a writer and the son of a former secretary of the navy), Daniels had a both wide-ranging and limited, partial (both incomplete and biased) view on a place and time that, I argue, saw the start of the nation's long civil rights era.[41]

I mention my work on Daniels to reiterate the point that all people are hyphenated, all identities intersectional and different from one another in historical, relational ways. The fallacy of "great man" scholarship and even the first generation of revisionism was to take parts for wholes rather embracing what pathbreaker Jacquelyn Hall identified back in 1989 as "a historical practice that turns on partiality, that is self-conscious about perspective, that releases multiple voices rather than competing orthodoxies, and that, above all, nurtures an 'internally differing but united political community.'" Such a practice emerged from Black feminist thought in the tradition of Anna Julia Cooper. It gained influence through Alice Walker and her concept of "womanism" as an ideology that encompassed both race and gender, the dualities of Black women's experience. And as Kimberlé Crenshaw began to publish essays on "intersectionality" in law journals, historians such as Elsa Barkley Brown, Deborah Gray White, Evelyn Brooks Higginbotham, and Nancy Hewitt searched for their own words for the same set of ideas, which recent developments in scholarship were newly enabling them to get across. For, as Hall astutely observed, "only after the triumph of the scholarship the Civil Rights movement inspired did feminist historians have room to maneuver. Only then could black feminists make themselves heard when they rejected the monolithic, socially constructed category of race and asserted a more complex, if equally constructed, identity as southern African-American women. Only after they had made that move could black and white scholars join in the project of understanding how gender, class, and race crosscut in the history of the region."[42] Shortly after Hall wrote these wise words, divining the direction scholarship would go for the next three decades, a motherlode of essays by Black and white women's historians theorizing intersectionality and relational difference appeared, educating my own generation of scholars.[43] Many of us have been working in this vein ever since, but the deepest digging into intersectionality has continued to be at the margins: the vital work of releasing, as Hall put it, multiple previously unheard voices.

Drawn to Daniels's sweeping Depression-era journey, I decided to try to dig closer to the center of the power structure while still heeding Hall's call to be self-conscious about perspective. As an elite white man, Daniels may seem an unlikely vehicle to make points about intersectionality, but this is a theme of *Discovering the South* (which might have been better titled *Discovering a South*). The admonition that Barkley Brown issued to women's historians in 1992 is due for an update: scholars need "to recognize that being a woman [or a man or nonbinary] is, in fact, not extractable from the context in which one is a woman [or a man or nonbinary]—that is, race, class, time, and place."[44] This is true even—or perhaps especially—for those setting out to write about elite, white, straight, cisgender men.

An insistence on context, the material, the *real* is what historians most have to offer our colleagues in literary and cultural studies. As Brian Ward explained in a forum titled "What's New in Southern Studies" in 2014, many historians of the South feel a "political, perhaps even a moral, imperative" that outweighs their intellectual readiness to recognize "the South" for "the performed, or imagined, or fictive" construct that it is. Thus, "the most useful explorations of symbolic or virtual Souths must be rooted in the material and social relations of the region—themselves intricately connected to myriad global and hemispheric as well as national and local forces—because these southern imaginaries are born of a southern 'world of real bodies' where deep economic, racial, gender, class, and educational inequalities and injustices, and major environmental issues, need to be addressed."[45]

A final few examples of scholarship that has reflected productively on region from a "world of real bodies" come from LGBTQ history. John Howard was hesitant to make generalizations when he introduced the essay collection *Carryin' On in the Lesbian and Gay South*—the first book on the subject—in 1997. The South had long suffered from "a dangerous intellectual history, a tradition that forwards selected notions of the past as widely shared values," he wrote. This was why "'Southern' heritage frequently amounts to a mythologized, planter-class world imbued with racism and misogyny. These concepts are rarely identified as conservative, white male, heterosexist constructs. Instead, they are made to speak for all."[46]

Even so, starting with region yielded fresh insights. It was obvious that "Southerners, rural people especially, don't fit" the "bicoastal bias" of American gay and lesbian history. But to understand what mattered instead in their lives required research, including sustained and creative efforts to overcome the exclusion of LGBTQ history from traditional archives. Historians' initial discoveries pointed to three general "areas of concern" that Howard called "the three r's: race, religion, and rurality." None was exceptional to the South, but all had distinctly southern accents. The legacies of slavery and Jim Crow; particular forms of religiosity, including among LGBTQ people themselves; and the predominance and persistence of rural life in the South shaped experiences and worldviews. A fourth "r" that became evident once scholars looked was *resilience*—a characteristic that must surely be in place for any group to develop the kind of "politics of location" that Giardina says were southern feminists' "tailwinds."[47]

Almost a quarter century of scholarship building on *Carryin' On* has continued to elucidate the four "r's" while contributing to larger historical narratives. Howard and his fellow essayists "opened the metaphorical city gates to let the queers play in the country," writes Jerry Watkins in a 2017 retrospective. A number of subsequent works in LGBTQ history "articulated rural, anti-urban, and southern distinctiveness." This, in turn, revealed how the discourses of "rural" and "southern" frequently "do each other's conceptual work." Along with Carol Mason's book *Oklahomo: Lessons in Unqueering America*, a 2016 edited collection called *Queering the Countryside* shows the discourse of rurality to be "a kind of shorthand for a set of ideas: patriotism, heteronormativity, free-market capitalism, nationalism, Protestant Christianity, family, faith, and folk-communalism. These imaginaries have come to be associated with the small[-]town South yet have immense power in our current political climate as politicians promise to make the country great, 'again.'" The power of such discourse is, in fact, long-standing. "What was long conceived as a 'Southernization' of American politics during America's culture wars after mid-century should," Watkins concludes, "more rightly be thought of as a ruralization of political narratives."[48]

And so, the South seems once again to have come into historians' view only to fade away, in this case into a rural America that stretches across all of "flyover country." The region's Cheshire cat quality has troubled many a historian, yet the important takeaway from Watkin's assessment of southern LGBTQ history really ought to be that examining an appearance of regional difference has allowed scholars to see broader connections and contexts. From the starting point of "Southerners... don't fit," we reach new ideas such as Mason's valuable notion of "unqueering"—the reversal of "the once quiet accommodation of the queer."[49] Like early Black historians' global vision, this idea grew from people's embodied experiences, but it seems likely to send out a vine of smart scholarship. How many other places in history are historians who look likely to see once-accommodated sexual minorities newly targeted as traditional elites cling to power or try to regain it?

Southern exceptionalism *is* a myth. As Lassiter and Crespino point out, virtually every scholar who has pondered the question "ends up acknowledging that the region exists less as an actual place than as a symbol, an expression of collective identity, an *idea*."[50] But it is the false singularity, not the ephemerality, that makes the South of the mind "dangerous," as Howard put it. There never was a single mind of the South, and there have been many Souths of the mind—Dixies defied and Dixies dreamt—that correlate to individuals' politics and intersectional identities.[51] *All Y'all* whose experiences were shaped or self-consciously framed by some idea of the South need to be counted as part of southern, which is also part of national and global, history.

Notes

1. Reed, *My Tears Spoiled My Aim*, 70. As I draft this essay in July 2020, I see that bittersoutherner.com now prominently features a banner and slogan—"Stand for a Better South"—that were not there when I first visited the site in 2019. Contrary to my friend's explanation, the "About" page places the site's origins in 2013, three years before the publication of *Hillbilly Elegy*. Editor Chuck Reece says he "got pissed off" because a magazine failed to list a single bar in New Orleans or anywhere else in the South among its top fifty bars in the world. He created the site to showcase "our region's drinking secrets," and it grew exponentially from there. In 2014, Reece and his coeditors published a mission statement that includes the promise that "the Bitter Southerner exists to support anyone who yearns to claim their Southern identity proudly and without shame—regardless of their age, race, gender, ethnic background, place of origin, politics, sexual orientation, creed, religion, or lack of religion." After the 2016 presidential election, they "promised to go deeper in [their] coverage, to

call out those who would deny the rights of—or commit violence against—anyone they see as 'the other.'" See the website for the Bitter Southerner, accessed July 22, 2020, https://bittersoutherner.com/we-are-bitter.

2. Unfortunately, a *thorough* accounting of the influence of those who taught historians to think, research, and write intersectionally is beyond the scope of this essay about region as a category of analysis. Michele Mitchell provides an excellent overview in "Turns of the Kaleidoscope." Readers of this volume may be especially interested in her extensive treatment of scholarship on the U.S. West.

3. Cooper, *Voice from the South*, 144.

4. Du Bois, *Souls of Black Folk*, 3.

5. Holt, "Marking." For a similar use of the plural "Souths," see Holloway, *Other Souths*. In 2014, the Society for the Study of Southern Literature also chose the plural—"Other Souths: Approaches, Alliances, Antagonisms"—with the goal of having a "capacious, inclusive theme" for its biennial conference. See Ward, "Grand Theories and Granular Practices," 730.

6. On simultaneity, see Barkley Brown, "Polyrhythms and Improvisation" and "What Has Happened Here."

7. Edwards, "What Constitutes a Region?," 486.

8. Gilmore, *Defying Dixie*, 5.

9. Ayers, "What We Talk about When We Talk about the South," 68–69.

10. Woodward, "Search for Southern Identity," 3.

11. Woodward, "Search for Southern Identity," 11–12, 13.

12. Woodward, "Search for Southern Identity," 13, 17, 19.

13. Woodward, "Search for Southern Identity," 20, 25.

14. James C. Cobb discusses the colonial-era "origins of southern 'otherness'" in the first chapter of his invaluable *Away Down South*.

15. Griffin and Doyle, *South as an American Problem*, 8–9.

16. Ayers, "What We Talk about When We Talk about the South," 66.

17. Jansson, "Internal Orientalism."

18. Ring, *Problem South*, 3.

19. Egerton, *Americanization of Dixie*. See also Greene, "On John Egerton and Southern Intellectual History."

20. Cottom, "Art of the New Old South."

21. Lassiter and Crespino, "End of Southern History," 8, 12.

22. Lassiter and Crespino, "End of Southern History," 7, 11, 12.

23. Lassiter and Crespino, "End of Southern History," 12.

24. Ownby, "New Southern Studies," 872.

25. Friend and Glover, *Reinterpreting Southern Histories*, 7–9, 13. On the removal of statues, see Taylor, "Statues Brought Down since the George Floyd Protests Began."

26. Edwards, "Southern History as U.S. History," 559–60.

27. Bryan, "Where the East Peters Out: Dallas, Fort Worth, and Regional Branding in the Great Southwest: Texas at the Regional Crossroads," chapter 10 in this volume.

28. Edwards, "Southern History as U.S. History," 559–61.

29. Ownby, "New Southern Studies," 874–75. The idea of southern "dissenters" goes back at least as far as Carl N. Degler's *Other South*, to which Holloway nods for her collection's title, *Other Souths*.

30. On the Lumpkin sisters, see Hall, *Sisters and Rebels*. There are now a number of scholarly biographies of Wells, including Giddings, *Ida*; Feimster, *Southern Horrors*; Bay, *To Tell the Truth Freely*; and Schechter, *Ida B. Wells and American Reform*.

31. Edwards, "What Constitutes a Region?," 485n3.

32. Gilmore, *Defying Dixie*, 6, 11. Bayard Rustin described the years from 1954 to 1964 as the "classical phase" of the civil rights movement in "From Protest to Politics." See also Hall's use of the term in her widely influential essay "Long Civil Rights Movement and the Political Uses of the Past."

33. Gilmore, *Defying Dixie*, 9–10.

34. Gilmore, *Defying Dixie*, 5.

35. Gilmore, *Defying Dixie*, 1, 4–5.

36. Giardina, "Making of a Modern Feminist Vanguard," 613, 648.

37. Giardina, "Making of a Modern Feminist Vanguard," 626, 618.

38. Giardina, "Making of a Modern Feminist Vanguard," 648–51; McGuire, *At the Dark End of the Street*. On "remapping," see Allured, *Remapping Second-Wave Feminism*.

39. Kelley, "But a Local Phase of a World Problem," 1077.

40. Giardina, "Making of a Modern Feminist Vanguard," 652. On the Native South, see especially Theda Perdue's call for greater visibility in her 2011 presidential address for the Southern Historical Association, published as "Legacy of Indian Removal"; and Snyder and Perdue, "Native South." A few additional examples of recent scholarship that challenges the Black-white binary include Cole and Ring, *Folly of Jim Crow*; Weise, *Corazón de Dixie*; Bow, *Partly Colored*; and Mohl, Saeki, and Van Sant, *Far East, Down South*.

41. Ritterhouse, *Discovering the South*.

42. Hall, "Partial Truths," 908, 903–4.

43. The year 1992, which happens to be the year I started graduate school, was an especially productive one for historians developing a vocabulary for discussing identity in fluid, intersectional, and politically conscious ways. Unable to do justice, in this essay, to the large topic of how such theoretical work has shaped a whole generation of scholarship, I again refer readers to Mitchell's "Turns of the Kaleidoscope." Although *intersectionality* became the most common term, I concur with Mitchell's observation that Kimberlé Crenshaw's influence was by no means singular or even direct and that "Americanist women's historians did not necessarily employ the actual term 'intersectionality' during the early 1990s" ("Turns of the Kaleidoscope," 47). Indeed, I remember buying and tasting my first pomegranate to try to understand what Deborah Gray White meant by one early 1990s metaphor for the complex and fluid nature of identity, and Elsa Barkley Brown's discussion of "simultaneity" and "relational difference" was the most eye-opening and influential for me

personally. Nancy Hewitt's essay "Compounding Differences" also made an especially lasting impression, and the scholarship Mitchell cites as "contemporaneous statements about U.S. women's history and the politics of difference" (Turns of the Kaleidoscope, 61n5) mirrors my graduate school syllabi and reading lists. See esp. Barkley Brown, "Polyrhythms and Improvisation" and "What Has Happened Here"; Hewitt, "Compounding Differences"; and Higginbotham, "African-American Women's History and the Metalanguage of Race." Hewitt's essay is a reminder that white feminist historians helped spread ideas they learned from Black women, and Mitchell cites contemporaneous essays by Linda Gordon and Kathleen M. Brown, among others. Meanwhile, Hewitt is hardly alone in recognizing that "Alice Walker led the way, coining the term 'womanist' to capture Black women's dual identity" (Compounding Differences, 318). See Walker, *In Search of Our Mother's Gardens*. Of Crenshaw's essays, the best known to historians is "Mapping the Margins."

44. Barkley Brown, "What Has Happened Here," 300.

45. Ward, "Grand Theories and Granular Practices," 727–28. Ward builds on points made by Jon Smith in "Toward a Post-postpolitical Southern Studies."

46. Howard. *Carryin' On*, 5.

47. Howard, *Carryin' On*, 4–5, 9; Giardina, "Making of a Modern Feminist Vanguard," 652.

48. Watkins, "Keep On Carryin' On," 3–4; Mason, *Oklahomo*; Grant, Johnson, and Gilley, eds., *Queering the Countryside*.

49. Watkins, "Keep On Carryin' On," 4.

50. Lassiter and Crespino, "End of Southern History," 11.

51. For "dreamt," see Cox, *Dreaming of Dixie*.

Bibliography

Allured, Janet. *Remapping Second-Wave Feminism: The Long Women's Rights Movement in Louisiana, 1950–1997*. Athens: University of Georgia Press, 2016.

Ayers, Edward L. "What We Talk about When We Talk about the South." In *All Over the Map: Rethinking American Regions*, edited by Edward L. Ayers, Patricia Nelson Limerick, Stephen Nissenbaum, and Peter S. Onuf, 62–82. Baltimore: Johns Hopkins University Press, 1996.

Barkley Brown, Elsa. "Polyrhythms and Improvisation: Lessons for Women's History." *History Workshop* 31, no. 1 (April 1991): 85–90.

———. "'What Has Happened Here': The Politics of Difference in Women's History and Feminist Politics." *Feminist Studies* 18, no. 2 (Summer 1992): 295–312.

Bay, Mia. *To Tell the Truth Freely: The Life of Ida B. Wells*. New York: Hill and Wang, 2009.

Bow, Leslie. *Partly Colored: Asian Americans and Racial Anomaly in the Segregated South*. New York: New York University Press, 2010.

Cobb, James C. *Away Down South: A History of Southern Identity*. New York: Oxford University Press, 2005.

Cole, Stephanie, and Natalie J. Ring, eds. *The Folly of Jim Crow: Rethinking the Segregated South*. Arlington: University of Texas Press, 2012.

Cooper, Anna Julia. *A Voice from the South by a Black Woman of the South*. Xenia OH: Aldine, 1892. https://docsouth.unc.edu/church/cooper/cooper.html.

Cottom, Tressie McMillan. "The Art of the New Old South." Medium. Accessed February 10, 2021. https://tressiemcphd.medium.com/the-art-of-the-new-old-south-3587818a143f.

Cox, Karen L. *Dreaming of Dixie: How the South Was Created in American Popular Culture*. Chapel Hill: University of North Carolina Press, 2011.

Crenshaw, Kimberlé. "Mapping the Margins: Intersectionality, Identity Politics, and Violence against Women of Color." *Stanford Law Review* 43, no. 6 (July 1991): 1241–99.

Degler, Carl N. *The Other South: Southern Dissenters in the Nineteenth Century*. New York: Harper & Row, 1974.

Du Bois, W. E. B. *The Souls of Black Folk: Essays and Sketches*. Chicago: A. C. McClurg, 1903. https://docsouth.unc.edu/church/duboissouls/menu.html.

Edwards, Laura F. "Southern History as U.S. History." *Journal of Southern History* 75, no. 3 (August 2009): 533–64.

———. "What Constitutes a Region?" *Diplomatic History* 36, no. 3 (June 2012): 483–86.

Egerton, John. *The Americanization of Dixie: The Southernization of America*. New York: Harper's Magazine, 1974.

Feimster, Crystal. *Southern Horrors: Women and the Politics of Rape and Lynching*. Cambridge MA: Harvard University Press, 2009.

Friend, Craig Thompson, and Lorri Glover, eds. *Reinterpreting Southern Histories: Essays in Historiography*. Baton Rouge: Louisiana State University Press, 2020.

Giardina, Carol. "The Making of a Modern Feminist Vanguard, 1964–1973: Southern Women Whose Leadership Shaped the Movement and the Nation—A Synthetic Analysis." *Journal of Southern History* 85, no. 3 (August 2019): 611–52.

Giddings, Paula. *Ida: A Sword among Lions*. New York: Amistad, 2008.

Gilmore, Glenda Elizabeth. *Defying Dixie: The Radical Roots of Civil Rights, 1919–1950*. New York: Norton, 2008.

Grant, Mary L., Colin R. Johnson, and Brian Joseph Gilley, eds. *Queering the Countryside: New Frontiers in Rural Queer Studies*. New York: New York University Press, 2016.

Greene, Robert, II. "On John Egerton and Southern Intellectual History." Society for U.S. Intellectual History. Accessed August 5, 2020. https://s-usih.org/2013/11/on-john-egerton-and-southern-intellectual-history/.

Griffin, Larry J., and Don H. Doyle, eds. *The South as an American Problem*. Athens: University of Georgia Press, 1995.

Hall, Jacquelyn Dowd. "The Long Civil Rights Movement and the Political Uses of the Past." *Journal of American History* 91, no. 4 (March 2005): 1233–63.

———. "Partial Truths." *Signs* 14, no. 4 (Summer 1989): 902–11.

———. *Sisters and Rebels: A Struggle for the Soul of America*. New York: Norton, 2019.

Hewitt, Nancy A. "Compounding Differences." *Feminist Studies* 18, no. 2 (Summer 1992): 313–26.
Higginbotham, Evelyn Brooks. "African-American Women's History and the Metalanguage of Race." *Signs* 17, no. 2 (Winter 1992): 251–74.
Holloway, Pippa, ed. *Other Souths: Diversity and Difference in the U.S. South, Reconstruction to Present*. Athens: University of Georgia Press, 2008.
Holt, Thomas C. "Marking: Race, Race-Making, and the Writing of History." *American Historical Review* 100, no. 1 (February 1995): 1–20.
Howard, John, ed. *Carryin' On in the Lesbian and Gay South*. New York: New York University Press, 1997.
Jansson, David R. "Internal Orientalism in America: W. J. Cash's *The Mind of the South* and the Spatial Construction of American National Identity." *Political Geographer* 22, no. 3 (March 2003): 293–316.
Kelley, Robin D. G. "'But a Local Phase of a World Problem': Black History's Global Vision, 1883–1950." *Journal of American History* 86, no. 3 (December 1999): 1045–77.
Lassiter, Matthew D., and Joseph Crespino. "The End of Southern History." In *The Myth of Southern Exceptionalism*, edited by Matthew D. Lassiter and Joseph Crespino, 3–22. New York: Oxford University Press, 2010.
Mason, Carol. *Oklahomo: Lessons in Unqueering America*. Albany NY: SUNY Press, 2015.
McGuire, Danielle. *At the Dark End of the Street: Black Women, Rape, and Resistance—A New History of the Civil Rights Movement from Rosa Parks to the Rise of Black Power*. New York: Vintage, 2011.
Mitchell, Michele. "Turns of the Kaleidoscope: 'Race,' Ethnicity, and Analytical Patterns in American Women's and Gender History." *Journal of Women's History* 25, no. 4 (Winter 2013): 46–73.
Mohl, Raymond A., Chizuru Saeki, and John E. Van Sant, eds. *Far East, Down South: Asians in the American South*. Tuscaloosa: University of Alabama Press, 2016.
Ownby, Ted. "The New Southern Studies and Rethinking the Question, 'Is There Still a South?'" *Journal of American Studies* 49, no. 4 (November 2015): 871–78.
Perdue, Theda. "The Legacy of Indian Removal." *Journal of Southern History* 78, no. 1 (February 2012): 3–36.
Reed, John Shelton. *My Tears Spoiled My Aim and Other Reflections on Southern Culture*. Columbia: University of Missouri Press, 1993.
Ring, Natalie J. *The Problem South: Region, Empire, and the New Liberal State, 1880–1930*. Athens: University of Georgia Press, 2012.
Ritterhouse, Jennifer. *Discovering the South: One Man's Travels through a Changing America in the 1930s*. Chapel Hill: University of North Carolina Press, 2017.
Rustin, Bayard. "From Protest to Politics: The Future of the Civil Rights Movement." *Commentary* 39, no. 2 (February 1965): 25–31.
Schechter, Patricia. *Ida B. Wells and American Reform, 1880–1930*. Chapel Hill: University of North Carolina Press, 2001.

Smith, Jon. "Toward a Post-postpolitical Southern Studies: On the Limits of the 'Creating and Consuming' Paradigm." In *Creating and Consuming the American South*, edited by Martyn Bone, Brian Ward, and William A. Link, 72–94. Gainesville: University Press of Florida, 2015.

Snyder, Christina, and Theda Perdue. "The Native South." In *Reinterpreting Southern Histories: Essays in Historiography*, edited by Craig Thompson Friend and Lorri Glover, 415–44. Baton Rouge: Louisiana State University Press, 2020.

Taylor, Alan. "The Statues Brought Down since the George Floyd Protests Began." *Atlantic*, July 2, 2020. https://www.theatlantic.com/photo/2020/07/photos-statues-removed-george-floyd-protests-began/613774/.

Walker, Alice. *In Search of Our Mother's Gardens: Womanist Prose*. New York: Harcourt, Brace, Jovanovich, 1983.

Ward, Brian. "Grand Theories and Granular Practices: The South and American Studies." *Journal of American Studies* 48, no. 3 (August 2014): 723–33.

Watkins, Jerry. "Keep On Carryin' On: Recent Research on the LGBTQ History of the American South." *History Compass* 15, no. 11 (November 2017): 1–9.

Weise, Julie. *Corazón de Dixie: Mexicanos in the U.S. South since 1910*. Chapel Hill: University of North Carolina Press, 2015.

Woodward, C. Vann. "The Search for Southern Identity." In *The Burden of Southern History*, 3–25. 3rd ed. Baton Rouge: Louisiana State University Press, 1993.

TWO

Get Farther East Than You Are

FLANNERY BURKE

Scholars rarely discuss the East as a region. Instead, more often than not, the East acts as a stand-in for the nation as a whole.[1] Boston serves as the nation's intellectual center, New York its urban exemplar, Washington DC its leadership. This essay outlines the region's location and historical significance in works of literature that describe the East's environment, institutions, and culture. While critics might call the writers profiled in this essay—Wallace Stegner, Bernard DeVoto, Era Bell Thompson, and Louise Erdrich—western or midwestern writers, I do not explore each writer's relationship to their regional identity. Rather, I explore how writers imagine regions in their published work. Racial and gender identities intersected with regional identities for these authors, who then each created their own "East." They used their respective "Easts" intermittently and strategically to advance their careers and political endeavors.[2]

Making the East our object of study allows westerners and midwesterners to assume the role of subjects and demonstrates the subjective quality of regions as they are portrayed in American culture. Historians have well described how people outside of the trans-Mississippi American West have imagined the region and the effects of those images on the region itself and the nation broadly.[3] Indeed, the idea of the frontier is perhaps the most explored regionalist idea in U.S. historiography.[4] The frontier was a subjective presentation of regions too, and historians of the American West have necessarily spent considerable time debunking the misunderstandings that have adhered to the Midwest and West and their residents as a result of the idea of the frontier. Rarely, however, have scholars examined how those who called themselves westerners and midwesterners conceived of regions besides their own. A full understanding of the history of the West would include how westerners have understood and defined regions, not just how they have reacted to the regionalism of others.[5]

Once we place westerners and midwesterners in a subject position, they show that they think for themselves. As long as the East stands for the nation as a whole, the political, economic, and cultural needs and desires of westerners remain obscured. In outlining the East as a region, Stegner, DeVoto, Thompson, and Erdrich announced themselves as writers, a challenge in and of itself, to the typically cited source of American literature: the East. They used the published page to broaden the idea of the American experience and its economic, cultural, and ecological future. When they wrote of the East as a region, they did so not necessarily to buttress their own credentials as westerners or midwesterners but to further understanding of political issues of significance to them. They actively sought a reading public's concern for the inequalities that they highlighted. Writers before and after those discussed here have delineated the East with similar aims. Attending closely to exemplary work from diverse authors within the genre of "the eastern" allows scholars to acknowledge the multiple ways that writers may present regions and regional difference and to chart the history of the impact of those presentations.

The "In" Crowd

No historian knows Bernard DeVoto. His work has fallen out of much contemporary academic discussion, and those familiar with his writing are more likely to know of his wife, Avis DeVoto, culinary editor to Julia Child, than they are of her husband.[6] Historians of wilderness, however, might consider the statement a heresy requiring redress. What western historian, they might ask, does not know *The Year of Decision*? What environmental historian does not know of the memorial (or at least its sentiments) in Idaho, just shy of the Montana border, identifying DeVoto as a "conservationist and historian of the West?" What historian born and raised in the West has not clutched a memory of "A Plundered Province" as they toured ivy-covered campuses and cool museum halls on the Eastern Seaboard? But this DeVoto—the DeVoto of the Pulitzer Prize–winning history of the West, the conservationist and historian DeVoto, the DeVoto who bequeathed to western scholars a sense of regional grievance—is the main character of a book: *The Uneasy Chair*, Wallace Stegner's 1974 biography of his dear friend and mentor and a play on DeVoto's long-running column in *Harper's*, "The Easy Chair." The DeVoto historians know is a writer's creation.

Together, DeVoto and Stegner rose to become the most prominent writers associated with the American West in the mid-twentieth century. "To call Stegner and DeVoto compulsive achievers is to understate the case and underestimate both men," observed the scholar John L. Thomas.[7] DeVoto published prolifically between the late 1920s and his death in 1955, taught regularly at the Bread Loaf Writers' Conference in Vermont, and wrote *Harper's* "Easy Chair" column, which Stegner called "a department of the highest prestige, in a magazine with the most intelligent lay audience in America."[8] Stegner shared his friend's ambitions, had a similarly prolific career writing fiction and nonfiction, and accumulated multiple book prizes, including the National Book Award for his novel *The Spectator Bird* and the Pulitzer Prize for his novel *Angle of Repose*. He did so from the West, beginning in 1945 when he took a position as the head of creative writing in Stanford's Department of English. He cultivated in the American West a literary community to rival the one that DeVoto had entered in the American East. As Stegner himself put it in *The Uneasy Chair*, "First by accident and later through his friendship and example, the curve of my life has touched some of the points that Bernard DeVoto's did. We were both boys in Utah, though at different times and in different towns. We were both Westerners by birth and upbringing, novelists by intention, teachers by necessity, and historians by the sheer compulsion of the region that shaped us."[9]

Stegner, an author not known for brevity, succinctly foreshadowed the themes of his biography of his friend: DeVoto's western childhood, his writing career, his success as a historian of the region—themes in DeVoto's life that paralleled his own. The child of a Catholic father and a Mormon mother, DeVoto spent his youth in Utah and sought a writing career first in Chicago and later in Cambridge, Massachusetts. He endeavored to write successful novels, wrote on topics ranging from the U.S. Civil War to urban firefighting in "The Easy Chair," and found his greatest success with a biography of Mark Twain, an edited version of the journals of Lewis and Clark, and his prize-winning popular histories of western settlement: *The Year of Decision 1846*, *Across the Wide Missouri*, and *The Course of Empire*.[10] Stegner also spent his adolescence in Utah, worked in the Midwest, taught at Harvard, and wrote fiction and western history for a wide public audience. Both men were instructors at the Bread Loaf Writers' Conference in Vermont, and their families lived within walking distance of one another in Cambridge in the early 1940s. DeVoto mentored Stegner, and the two became close friends. Stegner secured DeVoto's papers for Stanford's archives following DeVoto's death in 1955, and his biography is as much an homage to his friend as it is to the kind of writing that he and DeVoto published and promoted.

The two men's interest in regionalism grew with their friendship. Among the items in Stanford's archival collection is a letter that DeVoto wrote to Stegner in 1937, early in their relationship, when Stegner was living in Wisconsin. "Teaching is an excellent vocation for [the young writer] if his mind is vigorous enough to resist the academic infection," DeVoto began. "The turnover is large, and if your academic standing is satisfactory you can probably get farther east than you are. These days regional and provincial cultures are extremely promising, and I think will be more important in our literary future."[11] Regional and provincial cultures would be of significance to both men, but in different ways.

While DeVoto sought to establish himself as a writer by finding his own place in the literary establishment of the East, Stegner was interested in presenting the West's cultural cachet as equal or even superior to that of the East.

Stegner made his case in his telling of DeVoto's life. Stegner's image of the West and what he wanted for its literary culture was reflected in *The Uneasy Chair*. He used DeVoto as a character to push against eastern notions of the West as backward, unsophisticated, and unlettered. Near the end of his career, and thirty-five years after DeVoto's death in 1955, Stegner celebrated in the *Los Angeles Times Book Review* what had been, in many respects, his life's work:

> It is exhilarating to me, 60 years after I graduated from a Western university and 45 years after I made the decision to come back West to live and work, to see the country beyond the 100th meridian finally taking its place as a respected and self-respecting part of the literary world. I used to yearn for the day when the West would have not only writers but all the infrastructure of the literary life—a book-publishing industry, a range of literary and critical magazines, good bookstores, a reviewing corps not enslaved by foreign and eastern opinion, support organizations such as PEN, an alert reading public, and all the rest.[12]

By the time he wrote DeVoto's biography in the 1970s, Stegner sought to present himself as a western writer and the West as a place that produced writers and a literary culture representative of the West as a region. For DeVoto, writing the "Easy Chair" column for *Harper's* was proof that westerners could be writers. For Stegner, writing *The Uneasy Chair* was an opportunity to prove that the West's literary culture equaled or even surpassed the East's.

Stegner uses the term *east* or *eastward* as the West's foil at least thirty times in DeVoto's biography. DeVoto's father's Catholicism "was bound to seem eastern, exotic, aristocratic" to a boy from "the gopher hole of a Utah town," and DeVoto learned from his father "a sense that culture existed only farther east."[13] Upon entering Harvard, DeVoto headed toward "the mysterious and intellectual and literary East from which his father had come. Never mind that his father had come from Indiana. To an Ogden boy, anything east of Cheyenne is back East."[14] DeVoto's ambition—particularly his attachment to Harvard, where he was both a student and, later, an instructor—stemmed from his relationship with his father, according to Stegner: "From early in his career he had mythologized his pilgrimage eastward as a quest or a trial, a journey designed to let him prove himself in the intellectual East from which his father had dropped out." After serving stateside in World War I, graduating from Harvard, and returning briefly to Utah, DeVoto taught at Northwestern University between 1922 and 1927, but his time there was merely "a way-station on the road East."[15]

In Stegner's presentation, DeVoto's eastward yearnings delineated his own identity as a western man. Reflecting on his hometown of Ogden "forced him to the perception that for all its advantages, the East was effete, that it lacked the continental view, that its assumptions and prejudices needed a little western fresh air. The literary needed to be told they were sissy."[16] DeVoto's biography of Mark Twain was "a logical outgrowth of his study of the frontier and his irritation with some of the things Easterners had said about it."[17] DeVoto's scorn for the literary elite of the 1920s stemmed from his vision of "the Young Intellectuals as the 'in' crowd, the aesthetes, the expatriates, the ambulance drivers, the effete Easterners."[18] DeVoto's book *Mountain Time* "had also contained, in ways that he could not quite tie down, the West-East conflict, the problems of Westerners who came East toward enlargement and opportunity and were never quite satisfied, were always eaten by the desire to return."[19] That DeVoto never actually returned to live in the West did not stop Stegner from speculating that he wanted to. Stegner's DeVoto is not fiction, but he is Stegner's creation. As a character in one of Stegner's published works, he speaks to Stegner's reading public in Stegner's voice about the importance of westerners and the West to American literature.

While DeVoto the character yearned to return West and build there a literary culture, DeVoto the writer followed a different trajectory. Instead of building cultural institutions in the West, DeVoto built a reputation for himself in the East. He lived in Cambridge; he taught at Bread Loaf; he published with magazines headquartered in New York City. In 1953, when DeVoto pursued a number of travel pieces, the editor of *Argosy: The Complete Man's Magazine* praised DeVoto's work but suggested that he wrote largely for an eastern audience. "An awful lot of that material has reached the same hands, the readers of *Harper's*. It is a highly articulate audience to reach but also a somewhat restricted one. . . . The best thing about [our] audience is the fact that a huge percentage of these people are outdoors people and a big number of these are from the western states," he observed.[20] By 1953, *Argosy*'s editors knew DeVoto's work would be of interest to western readers but that DeVoto did not have a western readership.

Instead, DeVoto addressed the East. For DeVoto the East was also a foil, but not an effete, provincial one as it was for Stegner. It was instead imperial, and in DeVoto's work, its hinterland simmered with resentment. Whereas Stegner wrote to prove the West's literary credentials, DeVoto presented himself as the West's champion, its native-born son who would speak truth to the metropole. DeVoto saw the East as divided into two places: the source of culture and the source of capital. The source of culture remained consistent for DeVoto: New England and Harvard—this was where he made his own home and career. This was the East to which DeVoto was in thrall. The source of capital, however, had a tendency to move around.

Nowhere was this more true than in "A Plundered Province," which DeVoto published in *Harper's* in 1934. Financial organization had not made the West wealthy. "It has, to be brief, made the East wealthy," DeVoto proclaimed.[21] Although years would pass before DeVoto fully emerged as the conservationist memorialized in Idaho, he demonstrated his commitment to protection of the natural world in "A Plundered Province." "The Westerner has seen palaces rise on Fifth Avenue and the endowments of universities and foundations increase with a rapidity that establishes the social conscience of his despoilers. . . . Meanwhile, the few alpine forests of the West were leveled, its minerals were mined and smelted, all its resources were drained off through perfectly engineered gutters of a system designed to flow eastward. It may be empire-building. The Westerner may be excused if it has looked to him like simple plunder."[22] Simple plunder emerged from New York City and Fifth Avenue, but it also originated in Chicago. As DeVoto's polemic continued, he took to task the *Chicago Tribune* as well as the *New York Times*, Illinois as well as Massachusetts, as the agents of the West's despoliation.[23] Chicago could still be the East for the boy from Ogden.[24]

Nonetheless, DeVoto revealed himself as an eastern transplant when he described who he perceived as a typical westerner. "He is a tough, tenacious, over-worked, and cynical person, with no more romance to him than the greasewood and alkali in which he labors. He is the first American who has worked out a communal adaptation to his country, abandoning the hope that any crossroads might become Chicago. The long pull may show—history has precedents—that the dispossessed have the laugh on their conquerors."[25] Designating the East allowed the westerner as a character to emerge, but DeVoto, like many historians in the twentieth century, confused the frontier with the West as a region. As a result, he engaged in a common, erroneous, and colonialist substitution among historians of the frontier. White settlers became "first Americans." Although western historians remember DeVoto as one of their own or, at least, as a popular historian who brought western history to a wide public audience, we might better remember him as a historian of the frontier who satisfied eastern readers' preconceptions about the West. By the time DeVoto completed his historical trilogy about white western settlement, the East had receded in his view.[26] Unlike his friend Stegner, DeVoto never attempted to best the East. He always attempted to belong to it, even when he used his published work to advocate for a different allocation of power between the East and the West.

Era Bell Thompson and Louise Erdrich did not endorse DeVoto's conclusions in their work, although they did have interest in the dispossessed having the laugh on their conquerors. Neither could fully align their race or their gender with American frontier myths to further their own careers, as white men like Stegner and DeVoto could and did. As women of color, they occupied different subject positions than did Stegner and DeVoto. They produced different work, spoke to different publics, and operated from different definitions of regions. Neither fixated on the frontier, and neither drew sharp distinctions between the East's economic and cultural dominance. Neither troubled themselves about the distinction between the West and the Midwest. They built their regions out of different materials, but they still created an East in their published work that the reading public, including westerners and midwesterners, could identify.

My People and Your People

Just as readers meet DeVoto in the pages of *The Uneasy Chair*, they encounter Era Bell Thompson as a character in her own memoir, *An American Daughter*. That *An American Daughter* is Thompson's autobiography does not mean that it is any less of an interpretation than *The Uneasy Chair*. Thompson sought support from the Newberry Library when writing the book, and she emphasized in her book proposal that she wanted to "write about the Midwest" and her own unusual experience growing up as an African American girl on the North Dakota prairies.[27] *An American Daughter*, however, tells a more national story, suggesting Thompson's editorial hand and her career ambitions to be an author of national merit. Like *The Uneasy Chair*, *An American Daughter* is an author's creation, and like Stegner's DeVoto, Thompson's Era Bell is a character.

Born in Iowa in 1905, Thompson moved with her family to North Dakota in 1914, where her father became a farmer. The tragedy of her mother's early death combined with the departure of her brothers for urban work led her father to Bismarck, where he worked for the governor of North Dakota during the Nonpartisan League's brief political dominance in the state. Later, he found work as a chef and ran a secondhand store in Mandan. Following a track career and a difficult bout of pleurisy while a student at the University of North Dakota, Thompson lost her father and then finished school at Morningside College in Sioux City, Iowa, in 1933.

Shortly thereafter, she moved to Chicago permanently. Work was scarce during the Great Depression, especially for Black women, but Thompson found it with the Illinois State employment services offices. A Rockefeller Fellowship in Midwestern Studies from the Newberry Library allowed her to write her 1946 memoir, *An American Daughter*. A year later she began work for *Ebony* magazine, a new enterprise of the Johnson Publishing Company. She made her career with the magazine and traveled throughout the world as *Ebony*'s international editor. Those journeys began with the character Thompson created in her memoir: Era Bell.

Like DeVoto, the young Era Bell had a vague sense of her family's eastern antecedents. When her family acquires a record player, "John Philip Sousa's band became Pop's favorite because he once heard Sousa back East."[28] When Era Bell's mother unexpectedly dies, "that night Pop wrote to a wealthy cousin of Mother's who lived in the East, asking her to take me, but, to my relief, nothing ever came of it."[29] Nonetheless, Era Bell's experience is different from DeVoto's, particularly in Chicago, where she makes her home as an adult and unites her rural upbringing among white farmers with Chicago's Black community.[30] Like DeVoto, Thompson saw Chicago as a city, but rather than an eastern origin point of capitalist exploitation, it was instead the destination of African Americans like herself who were seeking a Black metropolis.[31] Chicago was not easily confused with the East but was instead the Midwest's own.

Thompson's Era Bell champions the Midwest and, over time, delights in Chicago. When she first moves to the city, she has already lived in the Twin Cities, in Mandan, and in rural North Dakota. For Era Bell, Chicago holds the potential to unite the community togetherness that she felt in rural North Dakota and Mandan with the urban closeness of African American communities in the Twin Cities: "Chicago! My eyes grew big and my heart pounded as the yellow cab weaved in and out of the maelstrom of traffic, turned into Michigan Avenue, and started south. . . . A colored woman, another colored man. The crowds and the traffic slowly decreased. All around me now were colored people, lots and lots of colored people, so many that I stared when I saw a white person."[32] Although Era Bell experiences discrimination in Chicago, as she has in every place that she has lived, she grows to love the city, including her jobs with Depression-era employment offices. As the book nears its conclusion, she calls Chicago "the crossroads of America. From the East and West, the North and South, they come—rich man, poor man, black man, white; the foreigner, the old-timer, the young, the intellectual, the illiterate—restless, changing jobs, changings skills and locations, seeking new industries and higher salaries."[33] Thompson too put Chicago at a crossroads, but unlike DeVoto, Thompson did not place Chicago on the edge of a frontier between the East and West, nor did she characterize it as a chimerical model of progress. In *An American Daughter*, the Midwest, composed of the rural and urban places that had formed Thompson's upbringing, is a region unto itself.

Thompson did build an East, but she did so out of different materials than DeVoto did. Era Bell's transformation from a child of the prairies and a young woman of a midwestern metropolis to an American daughter begins in the book's final pages as she embarks on two extensive trips to Canada and throughout the United States: "By vacation time, I had saved a travel fund of fifty dollars—enough to go East, for I had to see more of America; rural and urban Midwest were not enough."[34] Like DeVoto, Era Bell's time in the East is shaped by her western upbringing and midwestern coming-of-age, but she comes to different conclusions. "New York is a wonderful city," Thompson told her readers. "New Yorkers, contrary to western propaganda, turned out to be very friendly people."[35]

Era Bell also proves more willing to revise her preconceptions than DeVoto. In *The Uneasy Chair*, DeVoto scorns New York and locates what he considers "culture" in New England. For DeVoto (or, more accurately, for Stegner's DeVoto), New York is the source of the "effete" and "sissy" young intellectuals who require a western education. Era Bell does not visit New England in *An American Daughter*, and she concurs with Stegner's and DeVoto's preconceptions that *some* New Yorkers are pretentious.[36] When she passes a posh (and likely segregated) apartment building on Riverside Drive, she shares a joke with the building's Black doorman about renting an apartment. She is delighted to turn back and find him "doubled up laughing."[37] Era Bell expects to find pretentious New Yorkers, but she associates that pretension not with their easternness or with an effete intellectualism but with their whiteness.

Narratively and analytically, New York plays a different role for Thompson as well. Like DeVoto, Era Bell associates the East with professional success. "Before I left New York, I had . . . found Sarah Cohn, my Bismarck friend, now a well-paid secretary who divided her evenings between a private pool, where she was a lifeguard, and an orchestra, where she was the only female musician," Thompson wrote. "Sarah had followed through." Sarah had achieved what she had envisioned when the two friends confided their youthful ambitions to one another back in Bismarck. Their reunion also echoed the celebration of the multicultural prairies that appear in earlier chapters of *An American Daughter*, in which Jewish, Scandinavian, and other immigrants made homes for themselves alongside the Thompsons'.[38] In New York, Era Bell is pleased for her friend but also satisfied with her own achievements in Chicago. Immediately after describing Sarah, Thompson wrote, "The last thing I did in New York was to visit a colored newspaper and apply for a job. I wanted to hear 'No,' and know it didn't matter."[39] Unlike DeVoto, Thompson did not engage in any kind of economic critique of the East as an agent of despoliation, nor does Era Bell seek to "get farther east" to prove herself.

Thompson's East extended farther south than did DeVoto's, but not as far south as the nation's capital. "I spent a day in Washington DC, and thought I was deep in the heart of Dixie," Era Bell related with some alarm. "While ascending the narrow stairs of the Capitol on my way to the dome, I was caught between two groups of Southern white people who out-accented Amos and Andy, and I thought my lynching time had come."[40] From childhood, Era Bell associates the South with racist violence, and at the time of her trip, her experience in the region is limited.[41] Her anxious day in Washington is followed almost immediately by a frightening encounter in a Maryland diner when Era Bell refuses to eat in the back in the kitchen. Alone on the bus, awaiting her fellow passengers, her "anger gave way to fear, and all the awful stories I had heard of the South loomed big and terrible. I had defied a white man: black men and women had been lynched for less. When the bus finally drove away, I breathed a prayer of relief. It was a sour ending to a lovely trip."[42] As the target of the South's regime of racial segregation, Era Bell was unable to see it as a region.[43]

Nonetheless, Thompson did not absolve any other region in the United States of racism. In *An American Daughter*, Thompson characterized the South as a more dangerous and extreme version of what she and her family experienced in every other region of the country. The Midwest, East, and West are regions in *An American Daughter*. The North is not. Neither are the East and Midwest simply the North by other names. Equality could prevail throughout the United States, Thompson suggested, not if the North "won" but if all Americans in all regions acknowledged their commonalities. Thompson refused to pit southern white supremacy against northern or even midwestern opportunity.

Neither did Thompson see the country in Black and white. Thompson gently teases her younger self when Era Bell, upon moving from Iowa to North Dakota, eagerly anticipates meeting Indians who will match the children's stories she has read and heard. It was not until her teen years, when she lived in Bismarck and Mandan, however, that Era Bell met or befriended any Indigenous people. In Bismarck, she visits "the Indian school for girls." She acknowledges her childish fantasies as well as a different relationship with them than that of her white neighbors: "There were no wigwams, no squaws, no warriors, only big wooden buildings with little girls in pale blue dresses, their faces stolid and sallow, not red; their bobbed hair straight and black. Some of them ran to blue eyes and blonde tresses, and I was glad they couldn't blame my father for that."[44] In contrasting her childish stereotypes with her adult awareness of Indigenous women's vulnerability, Thompson drew a more complex portrait of Indigenous people's racial experience that acknowledged its differences from her own.[45]

A shadow of Era Bell's childish conclusions still remains, however, when she later observes that "Mandan marks the beginning of the real West. It is here Mountain Time begins, here the Indians come from the reservation to greet the tourist trains and dance at the big rodeo; here, on this side of the river, live the rattlers; and farther to the west, in the Bad Lands, is the town of Medora, once the ranch home of Teddy Roosevelt and his fabulous friend, the French nobleman, the Marquis de Mores."[46] Era Bell's sense of regional distinctiveness grows more precise in the remainder of *An American Daughter*, but Thompson's presentation of Indigenous people is largely restricted to a few encounters in Bismarck and a day in Mandan when the grandmother of a "Sioux" friend visits Era Bell's father's concession stand at the annual rodeo. There are Indians in Thompson's West, but not very many, and none in her Midwest.

It is uncertain, then, who Thompson is addressing in her conclusion to *An American Daughter*. The conclusion follows a second trip, when Era Bell travels to the "Far West" through Montana and into Washington and from there to Victoria, Canada. She returns through California and the Southwest, where "Orientals gave way to Indians." Upon her return to Chicago, having seen a large portion of the United States, she takes up her work again in the employment agency. She concludes with satisfaction after successfully placing a white job seeker, "I know there is still good in the world, that way down underneath, most Americans are fair; that my people and your people can work together and live together in peace and happiness, if they but have the opportunity to know and understand each other. The chasm is growing narrower. When it closes, my feet will rest on a united America."[47] Given Thompson's later success as a travel writer, her embrace of travel as a method of education and understanding is not surprising. In her memoir, Thompson sought to create a reading public for her work. For her, the opportunities to explore all parts of the country were also opportunities for this "American daughter" to know and understand the nation and to share that understanding with others in her publications.

In this final passage of her memoir, however, Thompson invokes not just herself but "my people" and "your people." Her use of the first-person possessive fuses Thompson the writer with Era Bell the character. The transformation is all the more striking because the phrasing recalls Thompson's book proposal, in which she explained that "three times I came down from the prairies to live with 'my people' and twice I returned to my plains."[48] As Thompson settles in Chicago during her third time down from her plains, what has been a story of coming-of-age becomes a story of national understanding. She asks readers to consider who their people are—a question that evokes reflection on regional, racial, and gender identity—and only then to consider what a united America might look like. With the exception of the racial violence that she associates most closely with the South, Thompson does not ask readers to consider any diminishment of racial or regional distinctiveness for the sake of national unity. In fact, her proposal and book read together suggest that it was only when she herself embraced Black cultures that she was able to unite the places and the people she considered her own. Thompson's East is no foil and no agent of capitalist exploitation. It is another piece in the patchwork of a nation that has an unrealized potential to embrace racial equality and unity.

Lively with Ghosts

At first glance, including Louise Erdrich in a group with Bernard DeVoto, Wallace Stegner, and Era Bell Thompson may appear odd. DeVoto, Stegner, and Thompson were contemporaries; DeVoto was born in 1897, Thompson in 1905, and Stegner in 1909. In contrast, Erdrich was born in 1954, just one year before DeVoto died. Nonetheless, Erdrich has similarities with all three authors. Like DeVoto, she attended an Ivy League school "back East," Dartmouth College, and her work is attuned to the natural world. Like Thompson, she has a deep knowledge of the North Dakota and Minnesota prairies, and her work centers female friendship and connection.

Like Stegner, she is a western writer with a wide, national readership and has actively used her writing to bring attention to issues of significance to her.

A member of the Turtle Mountain Band of Chippewa, Erdrich is the author or coauthor of sixteen novels for adults, one collection of short stories, and seven children's books. She is also the author of two works of nonfiction and three collections of poetry. Her first novel, *Love Medicine*, won the National Book Critics Circle Award. Her novel *The Plague of Doves* was a finalist for the Pulitzer Prize, and *The Last Report on the Miracles at Little No Horse* was a finalist for the National Book Award. Several of her novels follow interlocking generations of characters living on a fictional reservation in the northern plains. Her children's book *The Game of Silence* won the Scott O'Dell Award for Historical Fiction and forms part of a series chronicling the day-to-day life of an Ojibwe girl living on Moningwanaykaning, the Island of the Golden-Breasted Woodpecker (also called Madeline Island), in Lake Superior. In its attention to domestic detail, the series is similar to the *Little House on the Prairie* books by Laura Ingalls Wilder but presents Indigenous people as fully formed characters rather than one-dimensional stereotypes. In addition to her successful career as a novelist, Erdrich's Twin Cities bookstore, Birchbark Books, represents the kind of institution that Stegner celebrated when he saw that the West had created a literary culture to compete with that of the East.

As an Indigenous woman who has contributed significantly to literature about the northern plains, Erdrich fits neatly into the category of the western writer, but her East was not formed by westernness. Like Thompson, Erdrich came of age in a region some categorize as the Midwest. Her novels and her career have often centered rural and urban spaces that most authors, including DeVoto and Thompson, would characterize as midwestern, not eastern or western. Like Thompson's work, Erdrich's indicates that midwesterners and westerners both constructed an East. More significantly, Erdrich's work about New England, particularly those stories set at Dartmouth College, place Indigenous people in the East.⁴⁹ The presence of Indigenous people does not signal a western setting in Erdrich's novels as it does in Thompson's memoir and DeVoto's histories. Erdrich's work emphasizes that Indigenous does not mean western and that the East has an Indigenous past, present, and future.⁵⁰

A full accounting of references to the East in Erdrich's work is beyond the scope of this essay, but we can see in her 2020 Pulitzer Prize–winning novel, *The Night Watchman*, the ways in which she has constructed an East as an origin point of expropriation—an expropriation of land and sovereignty. *The Night Watchman* differs from much of Erdrich's work in that it chronicles the changes of a real reservation and describes historical figures, including her grandfather, Aunishenaubay, Patrick Gourneau, the chairman of the Turtle Mountain Band of Chippewa Advisory Committee during the mid-1950s. Gourneau's chairmanship overlapped with the U.S. federal government's efforts to terminate reservations as Indigenous sovereign territory protected by nation-to-nation treaties, an effort that Erdrich, in her author's note, calls "a new front in the Indian Wars" and that Gourneau called "the worst thing for Indians to come down the pike."⁵¹ Based on research that Erdrich conducted with the historian Brenda J. Child, *The Night Watchman* fictionalizes Gourneau's successful resistance to the federal government's termination efforts, efforts concentrated in the American East. The novel acts as a public correction to the archival record, which has often muffled and distorted Indigenous voices by presenting them only as representatives of the U.S. state heard them. In fact, Erdrich concludes her acknowledgments with the statement, "Lastly, if you should ever doubt that a series of dry words in a government document can shatter spirits and demolish lives, let this book erase that doubt. Conversely, if you should be of the conviction that we are powerless to change those dry words, let this book give you heart."⁵² We can read the book, then, as a work that sits more closely to Stegner's biography of DeVoto and Thompson's memoir than it might seem at first glance. Like those volumes, the novel both questions and contributes to the archival record by bringing a broader history to a public audience.

Erdrich never uses the phrase "the East" or "back East" in *The Night Watchman*, but she does convey a place akin to DeVoto's and Thompson's Easts, one that acts as an origin point of power and influence extending westward. That place first emerges in a conversation between Gourneau (called Thomas in *The Night Watchman*) and his father, Biboon, whom Thomas has sought out for advice about how to respond to the federal government's termination effort. Thomas's father suggests a strategy in which the tribe presents itself as an economically vital part of the region that would be lost if federal recognition of the tribe ended: "We're not nothing. People use our work. You got your teachers, nurses, doctors, horse-trading bureaucrats in the superintendent's office. You got your various superintendents. You got your land-office employees and records keepers." Erdrich explains that "all of these jobs and titles could be expressed in Chippewa. It was much better than English for invention, and irony could be added to any word with a simple twist." Biboon concludes, "Make the Washington DC's understand. We just started getting on our feet. Getting so we have some coins to jingle."[53] Erdrich's East is in Thompson's South: Washington DC.

Like DeVoto's and Thompson's Easts, Erdrich's East is intimidating. Overworked, sleep-deprived, and anxious, Thomas frets over the stakes of his plan to bring a delegation to Washington: "What on earth would a person do in Washington? How would they get there? Where would they stay? What if Arthur V. Watkins took him apart? The word was out on Watkins. He raked Indians to pieces with his words and his ways. What if Thomas failed? If he couldn't speak up? If he couldn't argue the case? If they got terminated and everyone lost their land and had to move to the Cities and he had to leave his home behind? What of his family? What of Biboon?"[54] Watkins, a key character in the termination effort, was a senator from Utah, but his westernness makes him no less "a Washington DC" in *The Night Watchman*.[55] As in DeVoto's New York, the East is a potential site of condescension and disempowerment.

Patrice, a fictional character, also draws a line around the East and the Washington DC's. She journeys with the delegation to talk about her work building jewel bearings for military watches and compasses, a task completed by real women from the reservation in the 1950s at the Turtle Mountain Ordnance Plant. Prior to delivering her testimony, Patrice sits in the Ladies Chamber of Congress to acquaint herself with congressional proceedings. While there, she is an eyewitness to the 1954 Capitol shootings by Puerto Rican nationalists. Security guards take Patrice aside for questioning about one of the nationalists, and "it occurred to Patrice then that the woman with the dark hair could have been her sister." Patrice feels a kinship with the woman:

> She realized that here in Washington she'd seen people shot, a thing she'd never seen before, not even on the reservation, a place considered savage by the rest of the country.... It was the woman in the pale brown suit she'd watched, her falcon eyes, her fearless cries, how she held the gun with both hands, how she had tried to unfurl a piece of cloth, red, white, and blue, to snap it out. And how awkward while holding the gun. How Patrice's impulse had been to say "Here, let me help you." To shake out the cloth for her. A flag, certainly a flag of her country.[56]

Patrice resolves to cleanse herself of violent thoughts and meditates on how she can support and protect her home without them. She identifies with the Puerto Rican nationalists, but she does so on the basis of politics, not regionalism, and she rejects violence as a means to her nation's sovereignty.[57] What makes the East is not its location but its relationship to her reservation. When she returns to the jewel-bearing plant after the delegation has successfully defended the Turtle Mountain Chippewa's land, a friend from the reservation asks, "Now you've been to Washington DC, are you too good to talk to me?"[58] The warm conversation that follows is an indication that Patrice still sees the reservation and its community as her source of pride and support. Like Thompson's Era Bell, she does not have to "get farther East" as DeVoto did to see herself as successful or her home as safe.

The starkest presentation of the East in *The Night Watchman* is from the perspective of a ghost. Gourneau attended government boarding schools in Fort Totten, Haskell, and Wahpeton—schools not unlike the one that Era Bell Thompson visited in Bismarck—and Thomas is haunted by the ghost of a boarding school classmate, Roderick, who attended school with him and died when punished with confinement to a cold cellar for several nights. Roderick is trapped between worlds, and his companions among Turtle Mountain Chippewa are few. He accompanies the delegation to Washington DC but can't bring himself to leave when they depart. He repeatedly misses the train and then discovers some of his own among the Smithsonian Museum's collection:

> Oh my! Drawers and cabinets of his own kind of people! Indian ghosts stuck to their bones or scalp locks or pieces of skin.... For centuries, Indians had gone to Washington for the same reasons as the little party from the Turtle Mountains. They had gone in order to protect their families and their land. It was a hazard of travel for Indians to be lynched from streetlamps as a drunken joke. Ghosts with rope necklaces. It turned out the city was packed with ghosts, lively with ghosts. Roderick had never had so much company. And they were glad for somebody new. Glad he stayed behind. They argued with him. Why go back there? Who's waiting for you?[59]

The implication is that Roderick stays. He is not at home, but he is not lonely. His experience uncomfortably recalls Stegner's "Westerners who came East toward enlargement and opportunity and were never quite satisfied, were always eaten by the desire to return." Roderick suggests that not all westerners and midwesterners came East willingly and that "opportunities" did not always provide enlargement.

In sum, *The Night Watchman* shows that Erdrich engages with the idea of region differently than did Stegner, DeVoto, and Thompson. She does not assume a U.S. nation as a governing frame. Speaking with an interviewer in 1988, just four years after the publication of *Love Medicine*, Erdrich reflected on the meaning of region in her work. The interviewer asked, "I grew up in the Southwest where there was virtually no such thing as a full-blooded Indian;

everybody was mixed. Yet, as I grew older, I became aware that there were parts of the country where there was prejudice. Do you think it's a regional question?" Erdrich's answer suggested that she considered regions not as unbroken spaces on a map but from the perspective of human relationships, both political and racial, where borders could create threats for some but not others. "Yes," she said. "I think it is different in different parts of the country. Where Indian land impinges on valuable non-Indian land, or where non-Indians feel threatened, the prejudice is heightened, definitely. There's antagonism when people aren't safe from each other, when non-Indian people feel that something could be taken away."[60] What makes the East the East in *The Night Watchman* is not its place on the map or its standing relative to the West but the desire of its most powerful white figures for Indigenous land.

Stegner, DeVoto, Thompson, and Erdrich placed power and influence in the East. Economic and environmental exploitation of the West along with their own professional success preoccupied Stegner and DeVoto. Thompson shared their assumptions that the East could be pretentious and overbearing, but she was willing to see the region as one more part of a United States that might, with encouragement and reform, stand for universal equality. Erdrich echoes Thompson when she fixates on Washington DC rather than New York City as a potential source of disempowerment, but she does not hold out U.S. national unity as an end goal for her characters or her readers. All four writers used their work and their high profiles to contribute to the archival record and public discussion.

In doing so, they both responded to eastern efforts to define their home regions while asserting the power to define regions for themselves. We might consider each writer a westerner or midwesterner, but their Easts had far more to do with their political and professional commitments than their regional identities. While powerful in shaping U.S. cultural discourse, the East has rarely determined its own regional presentation. Those outside the region have more often marked it. To understand what it means to go back east requires that we listen to what they have to say.

Notes

1. Three critical exceptions are California, Texas, and Florida, which, following World War II, writers also often used as either examples of the nation or unique regional exceptions that stood apart from the West and South.

2. On the intersectional nature of regional identity and region making, see Ritterhouse, "Many Southerners, Many Souths: The New Beginnings of a Regional History," chapter 1 in this volume.

3. Goetzmann and Goetzmann, *West of the Imagination*.

4. Treatments of the frontier's dominance in scholarly interpretation include Cronon, "Trouble with Wilderness"; Grossman, *Frontier in American Culture*; Hyde, *American Vision*; Limerick, *Legacy of Conquest* and *Something in the Soil*; Marx, *Machine in the Garden*; Smith, *Virgin Land*; White, *Eastern Establishment and the Western Experience*; Wrobel, *End of American Exceptionalism*. All respond to Turner, "Significance of the Frontier in American History."

5. Three critical exceptions that influence this essay are Dorman, *Revolt of the Provinces*; Findlay, "Far Western Cityscapes"; and Limerick, "American Landscape."

6. An exception is Schweber's *This America of Ours*, which pairs Bernard DeVoto's conservationism with Avis's more than with Stegner's.

7. Thomas, *Country in the Mind*, 13.

8. Stegner, *Uneasy Chair*, 162.

9. Stegner, *Uneasy Chair*, ix.

10. DeVoto, "Page from a Primer"; "Easy Chair"; *Mark Twain's America*; *Year of Decision*; *Across the Wide Missouri*; *Course of Empire*; *Journals of Lewis and Clark*.

11. DeVoto to Stegner, April 12, 1937, box 5, Bernard Augustine DeVoto Papers.

12. Wallace Stegner, "Out Where the Sense of Place Is a Sense of Motion," *Los Angeles Times*, June 3, 1990, 15. See also Stegner, "Publishing in the Provinces"; Stegner, address to the Western Literature Association, 9th annual meeting, box 166, Wallace Stegner Papers.

13. Stegner, *Uneasy Chair*, 5.

14. Stegner, *Uneasy Chair*, 12.

15. Stegner, *Uneasy Chair*, 45.

16. Stegner, *Uneasy Chair*, 14.

17. Stegner, *Uneasy Chair*, 70.

18. Stegner, *Uneasy Chair*, 111.

19. Stegner, *Uneasy Chair*, 280.

20. Robert Crichton to Carl Brandt, October 4, 1953, box 2, Bernard Augustine DeVoto Papers, M0242.

21. DeVoto, "Plundered Province," 9.

22. DeVoto, "Plundered Province," 12.

23. DeVoto, "Plundered Province," 12–13.

24. Publications following "The West: A Plundered Province" were less likely to target "eastern" capital than they were to target capitalists of all regions. See, for example, DeVoto, "West against Itself."

25. DeVoto, "Plundered Province," 21.

26. DeVoto: *Year of Decision*; *Across the Wide Missouri*; *Course of Empire*.

27. Thompson to Pargellis, May 24, 1944, Stanley McCrory Pargellis Papers.

28. Thompson, *American Daughter*, 91.

29. Thompson, *American Daughter*, 97.

30. Johnson, "This Strange White World."

31. Another Black westerner, Horace Cayton, looked for a similar sense of belonging in Chicago but did not find it and was far more critical of the opportunities that the city afforded African Americans. See Drake and Cayton Jr., *Black Metropolis*.

32. Thompson, *American Daughter*, 193.

33. Thompson, *American Daughter*, 294.

34. Thompson, *American Daughter*, 276.

35. Thompson, *American Daughter*, 278.

36. Thompson did attend the Bread Loaf Writers' Conference in New England as a fellow in 1949 and wrote about the experience for *Negro Digest*. Thompson described DeVoto as "famous" but also "as normal as other people." (Stegner was not in attendance in 1949.) She noted that DeVoto "would rather talk soil conservation any day than tell eager Loafers how to write for a living." See Era Bell Thompson, "BELL's Lettres," drafts, December 1949 and January 1950, box 9, folder 9, Era Bell Thompson Papers.

37. Thompson, *American Daughter*, 278–79.

38. Lansing, "American Daughter in Africa."

39. Thompson, *American Daughter*, 279.

40. Thompson, *American Daughter*, 279.

41. Thompson, *American Daughter*, 280–83.

42. Thompson, *American Daughter*, 279.

43. Ritterhouse, "Many Southerners, Many Souths," chapter 1 in this volume.

44. Thompson, *American Daughter*, 128.

45. Thompson's interest in mixed-race children and social responsibility for them continued. In 1967 she wrote an article about Black and Japanese mixed-race children whose Black American fathers had been stationed in Japan during World War II. See Thompson, "Japan's Rejected."

46. Thompson, *American Daughter*, 145.

47. Thompson, *American Daughter*, 296.

48. Thompson to Pargellis, May 24, 1944. Stanley McCrory Pargellis Papers.

49. Erdrich, *Painted Drum*.

50. Erdrich similarly places Indigenous peoples in the East in her 2009 Dartmouth College commencement keynote address, in which she acknowledges that the college sits on Abenaki land. Erdrich, "Dartmouth Commencement 2009."

Eastern Indigenous presence and Erdrich's work were also themes of the Dartmouth College Native American Alumni Reunion, October 4–7, 1990.

51. Erdrich, *Night Watchman*. On termination policy broadly, see Fixico, *Termination and Relocation*.

52. Erdrich, *Night Watchman*, 451.

53. Erdrich, *Night Watchman*, 119.

54. Erdrich, *Night Watchman*, 336.

55. On Watkins's use of Cold War–era rhetoric, including the terms *free* and *freedom* to describe termination efforts, see Rosier, "They Are Ancestral Homelands," 1301.

56. Erdrich, *Night Watchman*, 394–96.

57. On navigating Indigenous and U.S. nationalist expressions, see Denetdale, "Securing Navajo National Boundaries," 131–48.

58. Erdrich, *Night Watchman*, 436.

59. Erdrich, *Night Watchman*, 440.

60. Bonetti, "Interview," 88.

Bibliography

Bonetti, Kay. "An Interview with Louise Erdrich and Michael Dorris." *Missouri Review* 11, no. 2 (1988): 79–99.

Brinkley, Douglas, and Patricia Nelson Limerick, eds. *The Western Paradox: A Conservation Reader*. New Haven CT: Yale University Press, 2000.

Cronon, William. "The Trouble with Wilderness." In *Uncommon Ground: Rethinking the Human Place in Nature*, edited by William Cronon, 69–90. New York: W. W. Norton, 1985.

Cronon, William, George Miles, and Jay Gitlin. "Becoming West: Toward a New Meaning for Western History." In *Under an Open Sky: Rethinking America's Western Past*, edited by William Cronon, George Miles, and Jay Gitlin, 3–27. New York: W. W. Norton, 1992.

Dartmouth College Native American Alumni Reunion. October 4–7, 1990. DVD. Parts 1–4. Rauner Special Collections Library, Dartmouth College, Hanover NH.

Denetdale, Jennifer Nez. "Securing Navajo National Boundaries: War, Patriotism, Tradition and the Diné Marriage Act of 2005." *Wičazo Ša Review* 24, no. 2 (Fall 2009): 131–48.

DeVoto, Bernard Augustine. *Across the Wide Missouri*. Boston: Houghton Mifflin, 1947.

———. *The Course of Empire*. Boston: Houghton Mifflin, 1952.

———. "The Easy Chair." *Harper's* 186, no. 1113 (February 1, 1943): 333–36.

———, ed. *The Journals of Lewis and Clark*. Boston: Houghton Mifflin, 1953.

———. *Mark Twain's America*. New York: Little, Brown, 1932.

———. "Page from a Primer." *Harper's* 175 (June 1, 1937): 445–48.

———. Papers, 1885–1974. Collection number M0242. Department of Special Collections, Stanford University Libraries, Stanford CA.

———. "The West: A Plundered Province." In Brinkley and Limerick, *Western Paradox*, 3–21.
———. "The West against Itself." In Brinkley and Limerick, *Western Paradox*, 45–73.
———. *The Year of Decision 1846*. New York: Little, Brown, 1943.
Dorman, Robert. *Revolt of the Provinces: The Regionalist Movement in America, 1920–1945*. Chapel Hill: University of North Carolina Press, 1993.
Drake, St. Clair, and Horace R. Cayton Jr., eds. *The Black Metropolis: A Study of Negro Life in a Northern City*. New York: Harcourt, Brace, 1947.
Erdrich, Louise. "Dartmouth Commencement 2009: Keynote Address by Louise Erdrich." Dartmouth. June 16, 2009. YouTube video. https://www.youtube.com/watch?v=4RqB98UxvZE.
———. *The Night Watchman*. New York: HarperCollins, 2020.
———. *The Painted Drum*. New York: HarperCollins, 2005.
Findlay, John M. "Far Western Cityscapes and American Culture since 1940." *Western Historical Quarterly* 22, no. 1 (February 1991): 19–43.
Fixico, Donald. *Termination and Relocation, Federal Indian Policy, 1945–1960*. Albuquerque: University of New Mexico Press, 1986.
Goetzmann, William H., and William N. Goetzmann. *The West of the Imagination*. New York: W. W. Norton, 1986.
Grossman, James, ed. *The Frontier in American Culture: Essays by Richard White and Patricia Nelson Limerick*. Berkeley: University of California Press, 1994.
Hyde, Anne. *An American Vision: Far Western Landscapes and American Culture, 1820–1920*. New York: New York University Press, 1990.
Johnson, Michael K. "'This Strange White World': Race and Place in Era Bell Thompson's American Daughter." In *African Americans on the Great Plains: An Anthology*, edited by Bruce A. Glasrud and Charles A. Braithwaite, 184–203. Lincoln: University of Nebraska Press, 2009.
Lansing, Michael J. "An American Daughter in Africa: Land of My Fathers; Era Bell Thompson's Midwestern Vision of the African Diaspora." *Middle West Review* 1, no. 2 (Spring 2015): 1–28.
Limerick, Patricia Nelson. "The American Landscape Discovered from the West." In *Something in the Soil*, 186–213.
———. *Legacy of Conquest: The Unbroken Past of the American West*. New York: W. W. Norton, 1987.
———. *Something in the Soil: Legacies and Reckonings in the New West*. New York: W. W. Norton, 2000.
Marx, Leo. *The Machine in the Garden: Technology and the Pastoral Ideal in America*. Oxford: Oxford University Press, 1964.
Pargellis, Stanley McCrory. Papers, 1904–68. Box 4, file 136. Office of the President, RG 03, subgroup 05, series 03, Administrative Subject File, 1942–62. Newberry Library, Chicago.

Rosier, Paul. "'They Are Ancestral Homelands': Race, Place, and Politics in Cold War Native America, 1945–1961." *Journal of American History* 92, no. 4 (March 2006): 1300–1326.

Schweber, Nate. *This America of Ours: Bernard and Avis DeVoto and the Forgotten Fight to Save the Wild.* Boston: Mariner, 2022.

Smith, Henry Nash. *Virgin Land: The American West as Symbol and Myth.* Cambridge MA: Harvard University Press, 1950.

Stegner, Wallace. Papers. MS 676. Special Collections and Archives, J. Willard Marriott Library, University of Utah, Salt Lake City.

———. "Publishing in the Provinces." *Delphian Quarterly* 22, no. 3 (Summer 1939): n.p.

———. *The Uneasy Chair: A Biography of Bernard DeVoto.* Garden City NY: Doubleday, 1974.

Thomas, John L. *A Country in the Mind: Wallace Stegner, Bernard DeVoto, History and the American Land.* New York: Routledge, 2000.

Thompson, Era Bell. *American Daughter.* St. Paul: Minnesota Historical Society. 1946. Reprint, Chicago: University of Chicago Press, 1986.

———. "Japan's Rejected: Teen-agers Fathered by Negro Soldiers Face a Bleak Future in a Hostile Land." *Ebony,* September 1967, 42–54.

———. Era Bell Thompson Papers, 1896–1986. Box 9, folder 9. Vivian G. Harsh Research Collection of Afro-American History and Literature, Chicago Public Library.

Turner, Frederick Jackson. "The Significance of the Frontier in American History." In *The Frontier in American History.* 1920. Reprint, Tucson: University of Arizona Press, 1986.

White, G. Edward. *The Eastern Establishment and the Western Experience: The West of Frederic Remington, Theodore Roosevelt, and Owen Wister.* Austin: University of Texas Press, 1969.

Wrobel, David M. *The End of American Exceptionalism: Frontier Anxiety from the Old West to the New Deal.* Lawrence: University Press of Kansas, 1993.

THREE

Where in the World Is Hawai'i?

Shifting Geographies of the Fiftieth State

SARAH MILLER-DAVENPORT

Since its annexation as a U.S. overseas colony in 1898, Hawai'i has had a paradoxical relationship to the continental United States. The problem is rooted both in geography and in contradictory ideas of U.S. nationhood, which were thrown into stark relief with the advent of America's overseas colonial empire. Hawai'i is ostensibly "American" yet thousands of miles away from North America. And for more than six decades, Hawai'i was part of the United States without being a state. As an "incorporated territory" it was eligible for statehood in theory but held back because of its majority nonwhite population. Hawai'i's regional identity has been similarly complex and contingent in the years since the first American settlers arrived in 1820. At various points in its history, it has been identified as an archipelago of Polynesia, as an outpost of New England, as an extension of the U.S. West Coast, as America's "bridge to Asia," and as part of a larger "sea of islands" in the indigenous Pacific—often inhabiting multiple designations at once.

Regions and geography are compelling because of their apparent solidity and legibility. But as the essays in this collection suggest, regions are created and continuously re-created by historical actors themselves. An examination of Hawai'i's place in the United States shows how unstable the very idea of "region" is, as perceptions of Hawai'i's physical location within the United States, or distance from it, were tied to historically contingent ideas about race, culture, citizenship, and the U.S. role in the world. They also depended on the interests and perspectives of those doing the locating—whether they be U.S. settlers, continental Americans, or people living in Hawaiʻi.

Hawaiʻi's transformation from territory to state is an especially powerful example of the protean nature of Hawaiʻi's geographical, cultural, and legal status and demonstrates the slipperiness of these categories in U.S. history more broadly. Statehood came at a moment when U.S. Cold War interests in Asia demanded that the United States "decolonize" its overseas possessions in order to combat the impression that it was an imperial power and, at the same time, demonstrate its commitment to racial tolerance. Statehood served both purposes: it was supposed to solve the problem of U.S. colonialism in Hawaiʻi, and because of the islands' majority Asian population, it would prove to the people of the decolonizing world that the United States was a benevolent global power that celebrated racial and ethnic difference. In the wake of statehood, policymakers in Honolulu and Washington sought to capitalize on Hawaiʻi's newfound status by promoting the fiftieth state as a "bridge to Asia" that brought the United States closer, culturally and geographically, to the peoples of the Pacific. This represented a remarkable development after decades of virulent anti-Asian racism in U.S. law and culture. After statehood was achieved in 1959, its supporters presented it as a natural progression from territorial status—one that affirmed America's commitment to self-government. But this framing erased the ways in which statehood was a product of colonialism in Hawaiʻi and of the racialization of Hawaiʻi's people. Neither of these dilemmas would be solved by statehood; rather, they would reappear as sites of critique in the ethnic studies and Hawaiian sovereignty movements in the later twentieth century.

Until recently, Hawaiʻi's regional positionality has not received much attention from U.S. historians. Indeed, Hawaiʻi is something of an outlier in U.S. historiography generally. It has often been studied in isolation from broader U.S. history or only in the context of U.S. overseas colonialism—although even in this literature, Hawaiʻi is often absent.[1] Moreover, region does not figure prominently as an analytical framework in colonial historiography.

Instead, U.S. colonies are understood as constituting a kind of conceptual region whose location in geographic space is solely defined by their distance from the contiguous United States. For instance, in his recent synthetic work on the U.S. territorial empire, Daniel Immerwahr uses the term "Greater United States" to describe the U.S. relationship to its colonies.[2] Such phrasing provides a useful way of bringing the colonies into U.S. history while acknowledging their subordinate status. But—quite purposefully—it overlooks geographic specificity in favor of a general analytical framework. In doing so, such an approach tends to downplay how colonies are often integrated, in complex ways, into specific regions of the continental United States as well as how people within U.S. territories have pursued regional identities outside of American empire. To those living in U.S. colonies, and to many continental Americans looking outward to those overseas territories, their geographical identities have mattered very much.

Meanwhile, regional U.S. history is dominated by studies on the West and the South. Although it is both the farthest west and most southern of U.S. states, Hawai'i has largely been left out of discussions of the West, and it is altogether missing from Southern history. The case for its integration into the latter is obviously somewhat challenging, although the islands' plantation economy and the migration of many white southerners to Hawai'i certainly open the way for potential inclusion. Historians of the West, however, have begun to acknowledge that scholarship on Hawai'i should be part of the field, particularly when it comes to how we understand Asian immigration to the United States and the role Hawai'i played in continental expansion by connecting the U.S. West to Pacific trade routes.[3]

As Hawai'i's newfound inclusion in U.S. West historiography suggests, regional categories are sites of change and contestation among scholars. There is much debate on how to define "the West" and other regions and on the utility of any such definition at all.[4] For my purposes here, I am less interested in wading into these discussions to assert how Hawai'i does or does not fit into regional histories. Rather, I use a cultural history approach to examine how

Hawai'i's geographic place in the United States has been historically constructed and how Hawai'i's perceived regional location has changed over time. Like the continental North American West, Hawai'i has long held mythic status in American cultural representations. Those myths are by nature evasive and political. But they are nonetheless revealing of the politics they seek to enact.

Hawai'i spent most of its history as an archipelago organized by a complex system of competing but mutually dependent chiefdoms, with a population settled over the course of the first millennium CE by migrants from what is now called French Polynesia.[5] After British navy captain James Cook and his crew landed in Kaua'i in 1778 and introduced firearms and disease to the islands, Chief Kamehameha conquered and united the archipelago and established Hawai'i as an independent kingdom.[6]

With European contact, Hawai'i became an object of imperial rivalry, wherein the kingdom's regional location depended on the perch from which various powers surveyed their imperial ambitions. The British and French approached Hawai'i from their expanding empires in the South Pacific, relying on Hawai'i as a port of call during long whaling expeditions and as a source of sandalwood, a valuable commodity in the Canton market. Americans too were engaged in whaling and trade with Hawai'i in the early nineteenth century, but their presence on the islands soon came to resemble a continuation of settlement patterns in the contiguous United States. Looking westward from their ever-shifting frontier, many Americans began to imagine Hawai'i as an extension of the United States, despite its distance of 2,500 miles from the North American continent. Initially following the model established by U.S. missionaries who moved onto Cherokee Nation territory in the early nineteenth century, American missionaries traveled to Hawai'i with similar intentions of spreading the gospel to heathen peoples.[7] Ultimately, their actions also led to the same result—that of turning Indigenous lands into a site for white American settlement and eventually into a part of the United States itself.

Missionary settlers, who had set sail from Boston Harbor, resisted any acculturation to Hawaiian ways. They sought to convert Native Hawaiians to both Christianity and New England legal codes, particularly those relating to private property, family, and bodily regulation.[8] Early missionaries, tied to their identities as Calvinist Christians and New Englanders, may not have seen themselves as agents of U.S. imperialism, but as Sally Engle Merry argues, their interventions ultimately set the stage for Hawai'i's eventual annexation to the United States in 1898 by bolstering the power of settler elites, who served as advisors to the Hawaiian government, and by introducing property and labor laws that allowed for the rise of an American-owned plantation economy.[9]

As missionaries were seeking to carve out a replica of New England in the middle of the Pacific, other Americans had more ambitious plans for Hawai'i. Well before the era of "high imperialism" in the 1890s, the United States was eyeing Hawai'i as a key node in its plans for a maritime empire. As early as 1840, the navy sent Commodore Charles Wilkes to survey the islands for the U.S. government, with Wilkes reporting back that Pearl Harbor, if deepened, "would afford the best and most capacious harbor in the Pacific."[10] In 1842 President John Tyler extended the principles of the Monroe Doctrine and the "no-transfer" policy to Hawai'i. The first declared that any external intervention in the Americas constituted a hostile act against the United States, while the second—which had originally been applied to Cuba—asserted that should Hawai'i lose its sovereignty, it would be the responsibility of the United States to assert its "right of conquest."[11] As Tyler's statement makes clear, American influence over Hawai'i was coming to be seen as a way for the United States to insert itself into an accelerating global competition for imperial dominion. With Hawai'i's strategic location in the mid-Pacific and its growing white settler population—constituting nearly 7 percent of Hawai'i residents by 1878—many globally minded Americans came to see Hawai'i as the United States' "gateway" to the Pacific and the lucrative China trade.[12] In 1875 this aspiration was formalized in the form of a reciprocity treaty that gave the United States exclusive access to Pearl Harbor in exchange for lifting U.S. tariffs on sugar and other commodities from Hawai'i.[13]

While those advocating a closer relationship between Hawai'i and the United States could agree that the islands were a gateway *to* Asia, there was debate over whether Hawai'i should also serve as gateway *for* Asia—or, more specifically, for Asians. By the late nineteenth century, as the missionary generation gave way to a larger American settler population, Hawai'i's white elite was split between a powerful planter class that relied on imported Asian labor to work in the sugar fields and those who wanted to ensure that white culture and demographic numbers would prevail in the islands. Their disagreement spoke to different visions of Hawai'i's place in the world and in the United States. Nonplanter settlers—lawyers, newspaper publishers, and others in Hawai'i's growing professional class—argued for the islands' annexation to the United States. They appealed to the idea of a white republic made up of "a multitude of small farmers, each of whom will . . . possess sufficient property to make him a conservative supporter of stable government"—the same claim used to promote white settlement across the continental United States.[14] Planters, with an eye to the Asian labor market and in possession of a commodity—sugar—with the potential for global trade, were less invested in intensifying Hawai'i's formal ties to the United States, especially if that meant adopting U.S. laws excluding Chinese immigrants.

But both sides agreed that Native Hawaiians, who were increasingly asserting their cultural nationalism and whose government gave citizenship and voting rights to a substantial number of nonwhites, should no longer be allowed to rule Hawai'i. In 1887, a group of armed settlers coerced King Kalākaua to pass the Bayonet Constitution, which effectively removed the authority of the monarch while granting full governing power to Hawai'i's white-dominated legislature.[15] The annexationist cause, meanwhile, was bolstered by the McKinley Tariff of 1890, which ended preferential treatment of Hawaiian sugar exports to the United States.[16] Three years later, with Queen Lili'uokalani promising to enact a new constitution and restore the power of the monarchy, a coalition of settlers, backed by U.S. marines, overthrew the queen and installed a settler-led government. The new Republic of Hawaii worked to (unsuccessfully) reduce Asian immigration, limited citizenship and voting rights to whites, and outlawed the Hawaiian language, all with the goal of becoming a territory of the United States—though anti-imperialist president Grover Cleveland prevented immediate annexation.[17] While waiting for a more sympathetic administration, the settler government launched a propaganda campaign in the United States aimed at convincing Americans that whites had effectively civilized and Americanized Hawai'i and turned it into an ideal place for mass white settlement. A major exhibition at the 1893 World's Columbian Exposition in Chicago—organized by Lorrin A. Thurston, publisher of the *Honolulu Advertiser* and a leading annexationist—narrated the settlers' triumph over both the islands' Kīlauea volcano and its heathen Natives. It also offered visitors literature on moving to Hawai'i.[18]

To annexationists, Hawai'i's whiteness and Americanness collapsed the distance between Hawai'i and the United States. Even though it took a week on a steamship to traverse the thousands of miles to Hawai'i from the West Coast, the islands, according John Stevens—an annexationist and U.S. minister to Hawai'i—would soon come to resemble "Southern California . . . thus bringing everything here into harmony with American life and prosperity."[19] And indeed, after Hawai'i was annexed to the United States in 1898, at the height of American imperialist fervor during the Spanish-American War, it was the only one of the new U.S. colonies to be made an "incorporated" territory and thus eligible for statehood. This was because Congress believed that Hawai'i's white-dominated government meant that it might one day be responsible enough to join the United States on a fully equal basis.[20]

But despite the claims of the annexationists, Hawai'i was neither American—at least not before 1898—nor particularly white. Although Hawai'i became a tourist playground for wealthy Americans, in the decades before World War II, the efforts to make Hawai'i significantly whiter, driven by the nonplanter elite, were largely unsuccessful, mainly due to the perceived demands for nonwhite labor to work the plantations. While the white population did nearly triple between 1900 and 1940, the number of Native Hawaiians grew by 70 percent, and the Asian population, already a majority, almost doubled, with whites making up a quarter of Hawai'i residents in 1940 and Asians 58 percent.[21] And instead of the United States making Hawai'i more white, Hawai'i threatened to make the United States more Asian. The plantation economy relied first on Chinese laborers, and then, once Hawai'i became a territory of the United States—and thus subject to the Chinese Exclusion Act—planters began recruiting workers from Japan. The new colony became a major conduit for Japanese immigrants, many of whom settled in Hawai'i or eventually made their way to the North American continent, where they faced virulent anti-Asian racism and were accused of stealing jobs from white workers.[22]

The campaign for Hawai'i statehood cast into stark relief the fiction that Hawai'i was a thoroughly Americanized white territory—and that the only feature distinguishing it from the union of states in North America was its arbitrary location in the middle of the Pacific. When the Sugar Act of 1934 limited Hawai'i's sugar exports to the continental United States, the territory's ruling class joined together to lobby for statehood to gain voting representation in Congress (previously not a priority for them, as they were generally allowed to govern Hawai'i as they liked). But while Hawai'i met the constitutional criteria for statehood in terms of population size and administrative infrastructure, Congress refused to grant statehood because of the territory's supposedly unassimilable Asian residents—with those of Japanese descent a particular target for racist suspicions of "disloyalty" as Japan's military incursions in Asia intensified during the 1930s.[23]

Immediately after World War II, the campaign for Hawai'i statehood resumed with new vigor. And yet although statehood had the support of the American public and most members of Congress, opponents deployed various political maneuvers, such as preventing bills from reaching a floor vote or threatening to filibuster, to delay statehood for more than a decade. Southern Democrats formed the base of opposition to statehood. They worried that Hawai'i's senators would ensure the success of the civil rights agenda and objected to the inclusion of a majority nonwhite state. But overtly racist objections to statehood were difficult to sustain in the 1950s, as racial liberalism became increasingly mainstream in U.S. politics and culture. Moreover, given the widely celebrated service record of Hawai'i's Japanese American 100th Infantry Battalion—whose performance in Italy during World War II made it one of the most decorated units in U.S. military history—it was no longer possible to credibly accuse Hawai'i's Japanese population of disloyalty.[24] Statehood opponents turned to subtler rhetorical maneuvers to their case, instead highlighting Hawai'i's distance from the continental United States and proximity to Asia.

Such arguments, however, were ultimately revealed to conflate geographical and racial difference. For example, Nicholas Murray Butler, the former president of Columbia University and a leading voice in the antistatehood movement, claimed that "to add any outlying territory hundreds or thousands of miles away, with what certainly must be much different interests than ours and very different background," could lead to "the beginning of the end of the United States as we have known it."[25] Similarly, representative Woodrow Jones of the segregated state of North Carolina insisted that the U.S. tradition of "restricting statehood to those territories which were a part of the mainland, and which were contiguous to each other" had led to "a unified country with every citizen in all parts of our Nation having pretty generally common views" and "bound together by great and lasting blood and racial ties." To Jones—who willfully ignored the large nonwhite population in the continental United States when invoking blood and race to make the case against statehood—the "oriental" people of Hawai'i could not possibly "be imbued with the national spirit prevalent on the mainland."[26] Another statehood opponent, retired admiral Ellis Zacharias, pointed to Hawai'i's relative closeness to Asia as a reason to deny statehood, predicting that if Hawai'i were made a state, its politicians would face "enormous pressures from Asia" to promote "gambling and narcotics rings" in the United States.[27]

Even as Hawai'i was easier to get to than ever before due to "flying boat" service from the West Coast, Hawai'i's perceived racial difference from the rest of the United States amplified its geographic remove to statehood opponents.

Even many Americans less actively hostile to Hawai'i found it difficult to overcome the notion that it was a foreign land. The territory's main lobbying group for statehood, the Hawaii Statehood Commission, worked to correct this impression wherever it might come up. In one case, it protested the decision of the University of Minnesota in 1947 to reject applicants from Hawai'i because of their supposedly "foreign" status. Suggesting that perhaps "by chance [they] have mistakenly referred to Hawaii as a 'foreign' area," the Statehood Commission gently pointed out that "Hawaii is an incorporated Territory of the United States and an integral part thereof." The university's letter in response was remarkably obtuse, indicating that Hawai'i could not be both noncontiguous with the United States *and* American. After explaining that overenrollment had forced the school to cut back on all nonresident admissions, the letter added, "We have found that students coming from all countries 'outside the continental United States' require to a large extent the same kind of adjustment as those who come from all foreign countries."[28] To many in Hawai'i, the impression that the territory was somehow "outside" the United States threatened to derail statehood. To allay any misunderstandings, the Statehood Commission worked to correct anyone who might deny Hawai'i's American credentials, however meager their influence might be. After a territorial resident alerted the commission to the fact that *National Livestock Producer* and *National Rabbit Raiser* did not offer subscription service to Hawai'i due to its "foreign" status, the Statehood Commission wrote to the publishers, explaining that "the people of Hawaii are particularly sensitive about being designated as a 'foreign' area," as the territory was "on the threshold of attaining the status of a state."[29]

As such examples make clear, many Americans could not comprehend that Hawai'i was a constituent part of the United States, even after the bombing of Pearl Harbor and in the face of straightforward explanations of Hawai'i's territorial status. This was at least partly due to the fact that Hawai'i and other overseas territories were often literally left off U.S. maps, with the United States instead represented as a free-floating continental nation devoid of colonies. The Rand McNally atlas identified Hawai'i and other U.S. territories as "foreign" well into the 1940s. The mapmakers went so far as to insist that Hawai'i "is foreign to our continental shores and therefore cannot logically be shown in the United States proper" in response to a letter from a group of seventh-grade girls in Michigan who had asked how Hawai'i could be "foreign" if the Japanese bombing of Pearl Harbor was considered an attack on the United States.[30] Hawai'i was "foreign," of course, in that its Asian residents were "foreigners," even if most were U.S.-born citizens by World War II. Asian exclusion laws, going back to the Chinese Exclusion Act of 1882, constructed Asian immigrants and their descendants as inherently unassimilable and created the category of the "illegal alien." Unlike white immigrants, though they also faced discrimination, Asian immigrants were barred from becoming U.S. citizens until the overturning of racialized naturalization laws during and after World War II. This made Asians in the United States perpetual aliens, even well after they became citizens.[31]

U.S. maps devoid of Hawai'i and other U.S. colonies were also geographical representations of imperial denial. After the excitement of the Spanish-American War waned, U.S. political and cultural discourse largely forgot about Hawai'i and the colonies acquired from Spain. This was partly a result of profound debate and ambivalence over whether the United States should be a colonial empire in the first place. U.S. anti-imperialists, whether motivated by racism against colonized peoples or by a moral aversion to colonialism, shadowed any triumphalist narratives of U.S. overseas conquest.[32] But rather than bringing critical attention to U.S. empire, anti-imperialists helped obscure it. While the ideology of white republicanism had served as an alibi for the colonialist appropriation of Native lands in North America, anti-imperialists' objection to overseas colonialism was likewise rooted in the notion that the United States was, in essence, a continental republic—albeit one that had recently lost its way. As citizens of a nation that glorified its revolutionary origins, many Americans were invested in the belief that the United States could still be a force for anti-imperialism. This widespread discomfort with U.S. colonialism ultimately produced a colonial order in which the United States offered "benevolent assimilation" to its colonies while promising to tutor them in the ways of eventual self-rule, which the United States alone had the power to bestow.[33] Americans could thus have their empire and anti-imperialism too.

The dissonances, contradictions, and erasures that characterized U.S. colonialism—what Amy Kaplan has called the "anarchy of empire"—shaped the debates around Hawai'i statehood.[34] Although imperial facts belied foundational nationalist ideology, Americans' refusal to reckon with this dilemma inflected the arguments on all sides of the statehood debate. Opponents like Butler and Jones claimed that Hawai'i statehood would be an aberration from the tradition of contiguous expansion in service of white republicanism. Meanwhile, statehood advocates initially attempted to refute this charge by insisting that Hawai'i was already fundamentally American and, later, that its racial diversity portended a more enlightened American democracy. The two camps, united in imperial innocence, ignored the fact that both the territory of Hawai'i and the continental United States were products of settler colonialism.

Statehood opponents equated Americanness with whiteness. Many statehood advocates also struggled to decouple race and national identity, despite Hawai'i's demographic realities. The leadership of the Statehood Commission—made up mostly of white men, especially in its early years—was often drawn from the same ranks as the annexationists of the late nineteenth century. One chairman, Lorrin P. Thurston, was the publisher of the family-owned *Honolulu Advertiser* and the son of Lorrin A. Thurston, who orchestrated the movement to overthrow of Queen Lili'uokalani.[35] But while the elder Thurston and his fellow annexationists had sought to turn Hawaiʻi into a white republic, the Statehood Commission of the post–World War II years was forced to confront the fact of Hawaiʻi's Asianness.

This proved difficult for early Statehood Commission leaders, even though Hawaiʻi's plantation economy had long been powered by Asian labor. But Hawaiʻi society had acculturated them to white supremacy: Hawaiʻi's class lines were defined in overtly racial terms—with different plantation jobs assigned by ethnic group—and whites constituted only a small fraction of the territory's laborers.[36] In the late 1940s and early 1950s, the Statehood Commission actively worked to "whiten" Hawaiʻi in its advocacy efforts, sometimes through blatant statistical distortion. In a 1947 letter to the editor of the *Worcester Telegram*, the commission's executive secretary, George McLane, downplayed the territory's Asianness: "Many people are under the impression that the Hawaiian legislature is in danger of control by persons of oriental ancestry," but they "do not realize that Hawaii's 519,000 population is composed of well over 85% bonified [sic] United States citizens, and citizens of Caucasian background outnumber citizens of Japanese background."[37] McLane's numbers were likely deliberately dishonest, as they appear to have included military personnel in Hawaiʻi, which during and immediately after World War II gave enough of a boost to the islands' white population to shift the usual balance between whites and Japanese. By 1950, however, Hawaiʻi's Japanese population constituted a plurality similar to prewar figures—37 percent of territorial residents to whites' 23 percent.[38]

Along with numerical manipulation, the Statehood Commission used rhetorical tactics to obscure the prevalence of Asian and Indigenous cultures in Hawaiʻi society by reference to the territory's links to North America. Harkening back to the annexationist myth that Hawaiʻi was a little New England, McLane elsewhere made repeated reference to the legacy of the missionaries who arrived in Honolulu harbor in 1820. For instance, in correspondence with Massachusetts congressman Thomas J. Lane, McLane claimed that, as in Lane's home state, "the heritage of New England is likewise dominant" in Hawai'i and that the territory had Massachusetts missionaries to thank for the fact that American culture was so "firmly entrenched" in the islands.[39]

Ironically, similar arguments informed opposition to statehood within Hawai'i itself, and in one notable case, they came from a surprising source. Alice Kamokila Campbell, a territorial senator representing Maui and an heiress to a wealthy family descended from Hawaiian nobility, was perhaps the most vocal opponent of statehood in Hawai'i. Kamokila Campbell—the only dissenting member of the territorial legislature when it voted on statehood in 1945—is known for being among the few Native Hawaiians to speak out against statehood before the bill passed Congress in 1959. In her words, statehood would mean "forfeit[ing] the traditional rights and privileges of the natives of our islands for a mere thimbleful of votes in Congress." At the same time, however, she emphasized Hawai'i's Americanism to make her case and argued in favor of maintaining Hawai'i's territorial status. In hearings in Hawai'i before a visiting congressional delegation in 1946, Kamokila Campbell described the territory as "an American community where civic pride abounds," and she praised the "Americanization" of Hawai'i and many of its residents. But she warned her listeners that the territory's Japanese community, which had achieved "numerical superiority," remained unassimilated, as Shintoism was "still deeply impregnated into their very blood stream." Statehood would further empower the Japanese, who represented a national security threat to the United States and "a serious menace to American good government."[40] Given the unlikelihood of Hawaiian independence, Kamokila Campbell may well have been pandering to her mainland audience by invoking tropes of Americanization and assimilation in a strategic effort to preserve a limited form of Native Hawaiian autonomy, which she thought territorial status provided. But her line of argument nonetheless reveals how U.S. colonialism continued to constrain the terms of debate around statehood.

As the statehood issue dragged on into the 1950s, however, the terms of debate began to evolve. Statehood advocates increasingly moved away from narratives exaggerating Hawai'i's whiteness and Americanness. By the time the statehood bill passed both houses of Congress in 1959, a new justification had emerged: Hawai'i statehood was necessary because of the symbolic and geographical role Hawai'i and its residents of Asian descent could play in the Cold War battle for the allegiance of a decolonizing Asia.

President Dwight Eisenhower's secretary of the interior, Fred Seaton, spoke to this new conception of Hawai'i's role in U.S. foreign policy, calling Hawai'i "the picture window of the Pacific through which the peoples of the East look into our American front room"—one that would showcase Hawai'i's people of "oriental or Polynesian racial extraction." Statehood was seen as part of a larger U.S. project to convince Asians of America's benevolent intent in the Pacific. Including the nonwhite people of Hawai'i as fully equal citizens of the United States, Seaton argued, would lend legitimacy to U.S. anticolonial rhetoric, so that "the peoples of those eastern lands washed by the waters of the Pacific" would see that "we do, indeed, practice what we preach."[41] As Seaton's statement indicates, with statehood Hawai'i was meant to serve as a kind of liminal space between the United States and Asia. Other statehood supporters made similar claims while also suggesting that the people of Hawai'i themselves were not merely to be put on display in America's "front room" but could serve as mediators or brokers to help Americans navigate Asian culture. According to Jack Burns, Hawai'i's territorial congressional delegate and later governor of the fiftieth state, "the citizen of Hawaii, that new man of the Pacific, will be our most effective bridge to the Asian world."[42]

This shift in argument—from emphasizing Hawai'i's Americanness to highlighting its Asianness—was due to the intersection of developments on the global stage and within the United States. The communist victory in China, North Korea's breach of the 38th parallel, and the movement for decolonization in Asia drew U.S. focus to the Pacific, where the United States and the Soviet Union were battling for ideological allegiance. With both superpowers accusing each other of imperialist intent, Soviet propagandists

FIG. 1. A girl in Hawai'i celebrates statehood. Courtesy of Hawai'i State Archives.

pointed to Jim Crow and Asian exclusion laws in the United States as compelling evidence of U.S. hypocrisy. Meanwhile, activists in the United States used Soviet critiques of segregation to push for civil rights. All this combined to exert increasing pressure on the United States to both reform its laws and launch its own propaganda campaign to project an image to the world of a racially egalitarian nation.[43] Hawai'i statehood could thus serve several ends at once: as a declaration of U.S. support for self-government, an example of racial equality, and an assertion of America's presence in the Pacific.

With statehood, Hawai'i's regional position in relation to the United States—always dependent on racialized representations of Hawai'i's people—was again revised, its geographic location serving a new national purpose. Earlier arguments for statehood had borrowed 1890s annexationist discourse that sought to minimize the distance between Hawai'i and the United States by insisting on Hawai'i's whiteness; now, in the context of the Cold

War and a decolonizing Asia, statehood supporters believed Hawai'i and its majority Asian population would bring the United States closer to Asia.

This aspiration was encapsulated in the framing of Hawai'i as a "bridge to Asia," a favorite catchphrase of statehood advocates. The idea of Hawai'i as a bridge to Asia drew on older understandings of Hawai'i as a gateway to the Pacific, and many statehood supporters used the terms interchangeably. But it is notable that the bridge metaphor was mainly a post–World War II phenomenon, and it is worth taking a moment to parse the different meanings of the two phrases. While *gateway* suggests a barrier to entry as well as an opening, *bridge* implies movement and connection. And indeed, the notion of a bridge spoke to the image of Hawai'i, and of the United States, that liberal U.S. policymakers wanted to project to Cold War Asia: as a place that was welcoming to people of Asian descent and open to Asian cultural influences.

After statehood, the U.S. government, together with the State of Hawai'i, worked to institutionalize the idea of Hawai'i as a bridge to Asia through the creation of the East-West Center—a graduate school at the University of Hawai'i—and the Peace Corps's largest volunteer training program, based on the Big Island. While the first was focused on bringing Asian students to the United States and the latter on schooling Americans in Asian culture, both initiatives proclaimed their commitment to fostering "mutual understanding" between the United States and Asia and between Americans and Asians. But in seeking to bind the United States and Asia closer together, these programs obscured and, in many cases, aided American imperialism in Asia. While proclaiming their intent to promote peace and equality between Asia and the United States, the East-West Center and the Peace Corps were nonetheless based on an impulse to spread U.S.-style modernity to people in the decolonizing world in order to secure their opposition to communism and the Soviet Union. Meanwhile, the U.S. invasion of Vietnam—executed by the U.S. Pacific Command in Hawai'i, which represented the consolidation of America's longstanding military presence in Asia and the Pacific—showed what could happen if nations in Asia resisted American capitalist ideology. Hawai'i did become a cultural and geographical meeting ground that brought Asia and the United States closer together, but usually not in ways that bridged the profound asymmetries of power between the two.[44]

Hawai'i statehood was more than a merely symbolic gesture, however, and it was part of a larger historical transformation that changed popular liberal conceptions of citizenship and American identity—of who and what constituted the U.S. nation. Statehood was accompanied by a transformation in the legal status of Asian immigrants, who finally became eligible for naturalized citizenship through the elimination of long-standing Asian exclusion policies, first with the end of Chinese exclusion in 1943 and then with the repeal of all anti-Asian immigration and naturalization laws in 1952.[45] This came at a time when racial liberals were promoting the idea of the United States as an ethnically diverse and racially tolerant nation, even if that promise was not yet fully realized.[46] Asian Americans in particular were held up as examples of the potential for racial minorities to achieve equality and social mobility in the United States—though the concept of Asians as a "model minority" overlooked continuing anti-Asian racism and served to discipline African Americans by suggesting that they too could overcome racism through pluck and hard work.[47]

Against this background, many continental Americans in the post–World War II decades extolled Hawai'i's majority-Asian, multiethnic society as a center for Asian culture and racial harmony. Just as policymakers sought to use Hawai'i as a way to gain entry into Asia, Hawai'i in the postwar years came to be celebrated as a conduit for Asian and Pacific island influences to enter the continental United States. Nowhere was there more enthusiasm for Hawai'i than in California. Once the stronghold of the national anti-Asian movement, California became a major consumer of cultural exports from Hawai'i in the years before and after statehood, with many Californians coming to view the new state as an extension of the West Coast. The luau was perhaps the most popular "Hawaiian" cultural practice imported by Californians.

According to the *Los Angeles Times*, luaus had become so prevalent in Southern California in the 1960s that the "number and variety of luaus . . . seem[ed] to be infinite."[48] Luaus combined the performance of westernized versions of Hawaiian traditions, such as hula dancing, with a variety of Asian cuisines.[49] Their adherents viewed them both as ways to express their racial liberalism and appreciation for nonwhite culture and as vehicles for sexual liberation. With its informality and relaxed cultural and sexual mores, the luau meshed particularly well with the "California lifestyle." *Sunset* magazine, with a circulation of eight hundred thousand in 1965 and as a major chronicler and promoter of life in California and the U.S. West, was a key purveyor of the idea that California and Hawai'i shared a deep cultural connection.[50] The magazine, which boasted what it called a "second home" office in Honolulu, carried at least one article on Hawai'i in every issue, urging readers to travel to Hawai'i and experiment with luaus and other Asian and Pacific cultural practices that would help them become more worldly and sophisticated.

As Californians and other continental Americans were embracing Hawai'i as both a "bridge to Asia" and a multicultural paradise within the United States, new debates emerged in Hawai'i itself over the islands' cultural, geographical, and legal relationship to the United States. In the late 1960s, excitement over statehood waned as the persistence of Hawai'i's long-standing problems of racism and inequality became clear. Local activists, often inspired by critiques of U.S. imperialism both abroad and at home—in the form of the Black Power movement and Third World Liberation Front—increasingly challenged the idea that being a fully equal part of the United States benefited people living in Hawai'i. This critique of statehood and of Hawai'i's connection to the United States more broadly was at the heart of the ethnic studies movement at the University of Hawai'i in the 1960s and 1970s. Where state boosters claimed that Hawai'i represented America's best self—a racial paradise that embodied national ideals of democracy and racial egalitarianism—ethnic studies activists insisted that Hawai'i was in many ways exceptional to U.S. norms.

Although Hawai'i was prone to the racism and inequality found elsewhere in the United States, it was also a place with its own particular racial dynamics, which were a result of its long-standing links to Asia, its indigenous history and former status as a sovereign kingdom, and its relative geographic isolation. Hawai'i, they argued, "occupies a unique position in the Nation as a whole with its mixed population."[51] The ethnic studies curriculum should therefore ensure that "Hawaii's people are the focal point," and emphasis should be given to how ethnicity worked in Hawai'i specifically, not in the United States more broadly. U.S. history or present-day trends should be "drawn upon only if they contribute to a better understanding of Hawaii's situation."[52]

Ethnic studies activists also insisted on the need to study Hawai'i from the perspective of Native Hawaiians rather than white Americans, who were "colonizers telling the native they colonized what his/her problems are and what his/her history has been."[53] The push for rejecting the colonial gaze and analyzing Hawai'i on its own terms was a fundamental rebuke to popular ideas of Hawai'i's current and historical relationship to the United States. It spoke to a widely held belief among Native Hawaiians that Hawai'i was not and never had been an integral part of the United States but was a separate and unequal community whose autonomy had been stolen but not forgotten.

This was a radical revision of U.S.-Hawai'i history that would eventually evolve into the modern Hawaiian sovereignty movement of the late twentieth century and today. Sovereignty advocates point to the illegality of the overthrow of Queen Lili'uokalani and Hawai'i's subsequent annexation to the United States as the basis for their call for international recognition of Native Hawaiians' ongoing claim to lands seized by the United States in 1898.[54] One of the goals of many within the sovereignty movement is to disentangle Hawai'i's history and culture from that of the United States and to study it on its own terms. As per the mission statement of the University of Hawai'i's Center for Hawaiian Studies, for instance, its goal is to present from a Native Hawaiian perspective "the interplay of history, culture, politics, and the importance of interconnectedness of all knowledge, both contemporary and ancestral, in order that students will understand Kanaka Maoli [Native Hawaiian] experiences in the context of world indigenous peoples."[55] Committed explicitly to advancing the cause of Hawaiian sovereignty, Hawaiian studies teaching focuses not only on interdisciplinary research but on the study of the Hawaiian language and the revitalization of Indigenous cultural practices.

A related school of activist scholarship seeks to situate Hawai'i in a larger ocean world and focuses on the ocean itself as a place—one that people live in and with and that binds Pacific Islanders together despite great distances between them—rather than an obstacle to overcome or a conduit for colonial conquest.[56] Such works center the perspective of islanders themselves and emphasize the islands of the Pacific as important objects of analysis in their own right, not merely as waystations in Western imperial dramas. They foreground Hawaiians' connections to the peoples of Melanesia, Micronesia, Polynesia, and Australia and New Zealand rather than the United States or Asia.

In many ways this scholarship is a form of regional history, in that it takes Oceania as its geographic starting point and demands recognition of the historical, geographical, and cultural links among its peoples. As with past attempts to incorporate Hawai'i into various regional imaginaries, the call to locate Hawai'i and other Pacific islands in Oceania is partly a political project—in this case, to reclaim the region as "our sea of islands" rather than "islands in a far sea" on the periphery of European and U.S. empires.[57] But the concept of Oceania can also be seen as a rejection of region as an analytical category, at least as it has been constituted by U.S. and European imperial powers.

Fijian-Togan scholar Epeli Hau'ofa argues that Oceania is inherently expansive. Contrary to Western ideas of islands as small and inconsequential, the people of the Pacific islands have traditionally understood their homelands as part of a vast sea—"a large world in which peoples and cultures moved and mingled, unhindered by boundaries of the kind erected much later by imperial powers." As Hau'ofa writes, "Their universe comprised not only land surfaces, but the surrounding ocean as far as they could traverse and exploit it, the underworld with its fire-controlling and earth-shaking denizens, and the heavens above with their hierarchies of powerful gods and named stars and constellations that people could count on to guide their ways across the seas." Today, as Pacific Islanders have spread out around the world, they too are no longer confined to national boundaries, and Oceania "is growing bigger every day."[58] Perhaps, as Hauʻofa suggests, we can hold in tension the contradictions between the implied rootedness of region—and the work it can do for Indigenous solidarities—and its historical instability. An unrooted region can also carry emancipatory possibility.

Notes

1. Two of the biggest edited volumes on U.S. empire—Kaplan and Pease's *Cultures of United States Imperialism* and McCoy and Scarano's *Colonial Crucible*—leave out Hawaiʻi entirely.

2. Immerwahr, *How to Hide an Empire*.

3. One sign of Hawaiʻi's inclusion in the historiography of the U.S. West is the Western History Association's creation of an award in 2014 for books on the history of the Pacific West, which includes Hawaiʻi, Alaska, and U.S. possessions in the Pacific. For works that link Hawaiʻi to U.S. continental and Pacific expansion, see Cumings, *Dominion from Sea to Sea*; and Igler, *Great Ocean*.

4. Johnston, "Beyond 'The West.'"

5. For a history of Hawaiʻi before Cook, see Chang, *World and All the Things upon It*, 1–23; and Finney, "Other One-Third of the Globe."

6. For a survey of Hawaiʻi's history beginning with Cook's arrival, see Daws, *Shoal of Time*. There is much debate on Native Hawaiian population numbers before Western contact, but nearly all agree that the introduction of new diseases led to a population decline of over 80 percent. For a helpful summary of these debates, see Okihiro, *Columbia Guide to Asian American History*, 45–55. For a political history of the Hawaiian Kingdom, see Osorio, *Dismembering Lāhui*.

7. Conroy-Krutz, *Christian Imperialism*, 120–29.

8. For a summary account of Hawaiʻi's relationship to the U.S. from the time of the first American settlements, see Okihiro, *Island World*. On missionaries, see Grimshaw, *Paths of Duty*. On the introduction of New England legal codes, see Osorio, *Dismembering Lāhui*; and Merry, *Colonizing Hawaiʻi*.

9. Merry, *Colonizing Hawaiʻi*, 258–68.

10. Naval History and Heritage Command, "Pearl Harbor."

11. Loveman, *No Higher Law*, 143; Anderson, *Heathen Nation Evangelized*, 206.

12. Schmitt, *Demographic Statistics of Hawaii*, 12.

13. On the reciprocity treaty, see Osorio, *Dismembering Lāhui*, 162–71.

14. Skwiot, *Purposes of Paradise*, 34.

15. Osorio, *Dismembering Lāhui*, 240–42.

16. Skwiot, *Purposes of Paradise*, 36–37.

17. On the overthrow of Liliʻuokalani and annexation, see Pratt, *Expansionists of 1898*; LaFeber, *Cambridge History of American Foreign Relations*; Coffman, *Nation Within*; and Silva, *Aloha Betrayed*.

18. Skwiot, *Purposes of Paradise*, 37–41. See also Saranillio, *Unsustainable Empire*, 31–66.

19. Skwiot, *Purposes of Paradise*, 38.

20. Skwiot, *Purposes of Paradise*, 45.

21. U.S. Census Bureau, *Statistics for Hawaii, 1910*, 9; Schmitt, *Demographic Statistics of Hawaii*, 12.

22. Takaki, *Strangers from a Different Shore*, 147–48.

23. For an overview of the statehood campaign, see Bell, *Last among Equals*. See also Miller-Davenport, *Gateway State*, 19–49.

24. On the 100th Infantry Battalion, see Odo, *No Sword to Bury*, 221–52.

25. Associated Press, "Dr. Butler Opposes Hawaii Statehood," *New York Times*, March 13, 1947.

26. Jones quoted in Cong. Rec., 83 Cong., 1 sess. (1953), 1782.

27. Cong. Rec., 83 Cong., 2 sess. (1954), 3485.

28. Correspondence between the Hawaii Statehood Commission and the University of Minnesota, May–July 1947, Collection COM-18: Records of the Hawaii Statehood Commission, Hawaiʻi State Archives (hereafter COM-18), box 4.

29. Letter from George McLane to Henderson Publishing, February 20, 1950, COM-18, box 7.

30. Immerwahr, *How to Hide an Empire*, 12.

31. Ngai, *Impossible Subjects*.

32. On anti-imperialism, see Cullinane, *Liberty and American Anti-Imperialism*; Sexton and Tyrrell, *Empire's Twin*.

33. Kramer, *Blood of Government*; Rafael, *White Love*.

34. Kaplan, *Anarchy of Empire*.

35. Chaplin, *Presstime in Paradise*.

36. Okihiro, *Cane Fires*.

37. Letter from George McLane to the editor of the *Worcester Telegram*, March 19, 1947, COM-18, box 4.

38. Census figures printed in Senate Committee on Interior and Insular Affairs, *Hearings on Statehood for Hawaii*, 83 Cong., 1 and 2 sess. (1953 and 1954), 205. The same census reported that Hawaiians (including part-Hawaiians) made up 17 percent of the population; Chinese, 6.5 percent; and Filipinos, 12 percent. Other groups—including Puerto Ricans and Koreans—made up the remaining 4 percent.

39. Letter from George McLane to Thomas J. Lane, April 28, 1947, COM-18, box 4.

40. House Committee on the Territories, *Hearings on Statehood for Hawaii*, 79 Cong., 2 sess. (1946), 481–85.

41. Senate Committee on Interior and Insular Affairs, *Hearings on Statehood for Hawaii*, 86 Cong., 1 sess. (1959), 3.

42. Senate Committee on Interior and Insular Affairs, *Hearings on Statehood for Hawaii*, 85 Cong., 1 sess. (1957), 10.

43. See Borstelmann, *Cold War and the Color Line*; Dudziak, *Cold War Civil Rights*; Klein, *Cold War Orientalism*; Von Eschen, *Satchmo Blows Up the World*; and Parker, *Hearts, Minds, Voices*.

44. Miller-Davenport, *Gateway State*, 79–115.

45. For immigration reform after World War II, see Ngai, *Impossible Subjects*.

46. For more racial liberalism, see Gerstle, *American Crucible*.

47. Wu, *Color of Success*.

48. "Hostesses Seeking Far Out Cuisine," *Los Angeles Times*, August 25, 1968.

49. Although the Hawaiian spelling is *lūʻau*, here I am using the anglicized *luau*, as the type of party the latter describes only nominally resembles a traditional Hawaiian lūʻau.

50. For more on *Sunset*'s influence on the culture of the U.S. West, see Starr, *Sunset Magazine*, 52.

51. Third World Liberation Front to Richard Takasaki, proposal for a School of Ethnic Area Studies, April 7, 1969, Office of the Vice President for Academic Affairs, Manoa Campus Program, University Archives at the University of Hawaiʻi-Manoa (hereafter UAUH), box 2.

52. Cleveland's speech before the Hawaiian Civic Club, quoted in memo from Nancy Young to Stuart Brown et al., February 16, 1973, Faculty Senate Executive Committee, UAUH, box 22.

53. Larry Kamakawiwoole, speech on ethnic studies, February 16, 1972, Faculty Senate Executive Committee, UAUH, box 22.

54. For more on the Hawaiian sovereignty movement, see Trask, *From a Native Daughter*; Kauanui, *Hawaiian Blood*; Kaʻōpua, Hussey, and Wright, *Nation Rising*; and Kauanui, *Paradoxes of Hawaiian Sovereignty*.

55. Mission statement of the School of Hawaiian Knowledge, accessed May 12, 2023, https://manoa.hawaii.edu/hshk/kamakakuokalani/mission-op/.

56. Two of the foundational scholarly works on Oceania are Wendt, "Towards a New Oceania"; and Hauʻofa, "Our Sea of Islands." See also Teaiwa, "L(o)osing the Edge"; Teaiwa, "On Analogies"; Mar, *Decolonisation and the Pacific*; Ingersoll, *Waves of Knowing*; and Anderson, Johnson, and Brookes, *Pacific Futures*.

57. Hauʻofa, "Our Sea of Islands," 152.

58. Hauʻofa, "Our Sea of Islands," 154, 152, 151.

Bibliography

Anderson, Rufus. *A Heathen Nation Evangelized: History of the Sandwich islands Mission*. London: Hodder and Staughton, 1872.

Anderson, Warwick, Miranda Johnson, and Barbara Brookes, eds. *Pacific Futures: Past and Present*. Honolulu: University of Hawai'i Press, 2018.

Bell, Roger. *Last among Equals: Hawaiian Statehood and American Politics*. Honolulu: University of Hawai'i Press, 1984.

Borstelmann, Thomas. *The Cold War and the Color Line: American Race Relations in the Global Arena*. Cambridge MA: Harvard University Press, 2001.

Chang, David. *The World and All the Things upon It: Native Hawaiian Geographies of Exploration*. Minneapolis: University of Minnesota Press, 2016.

Chaplin, George. *Presstime in Paradise: The Life and Times of The Honolulu Advertiser, 1856–1995*. Honolulu: University of Hawai'i Press, 1998.

Coffman, Tom. *Nation Within: The Story of America's Annexation of the Nation of Hawai'i*. Kāne'ohe HI: EPICenter, 1998.

Conroy-Krutz, Emily. *Christian Imperialism: Converting the World in the Early American Republic*. Ithaca NY: Cornell University Press, 2015.

Cullinane, Michael Patrick. *Liberty and American Anti-Imperialism*. New York: Palgrave Macmillan, 2012.

Cumings, Bruce. *Dominion from Sea to Sea: Pacific Ascendancy and American Power*. New Haven CT: Yale University Press, 2009.

Daws, Gavan. *Shoal of Time: A History of the Hawaiian Islands*. New York: Macmillan, 1974.

Dudziak, Mary. *Cold War Civil Rights: Race and the Image of American Democracy*. Princeton NJ: Princeton University Press, 2002.

Finney, Ben. "The Other One-Third of the Globe." *Journal of World History* 5, no. 2 (Fall 1994): 273–97.

Gerstle, Gary. *American Crucible: Race and Nation in the Twentieth Century*. Princeton NJ: Princeton University Press, 2001.

Grimshaw, Patricia. *Paths of Duty: American Missionary Wives in Nineteenth-Century Hawaii*. Honolulu: University of Hawai'i Press, 1989.

Hau'ofa, Epeli. "Our Sea of Islands." In *A New Oceania: Rediscovering Our Sea of Islands*, edited by Vijay Naidu, Eric Waddell, and Epeli Hau'ofa, 2–16. Suva, Fiji: School of Social and Economic Development, University of the South Pacific, 1993.

Igler, David. *The Great Ocean: Pacific Worlds from Captain Cook to the Gold Rush*. New York: Oxford University Press, 2013.

Immerwahr, Daniel. *How to Hide an Empire: A History of the Greater United States*. New York: Farrar, Straus and Giroux, 2019.

Ingersoll, Karin Amimoto. *Waves of Knowing: A Seascape Epistemology*. Durham NC: Duke University Press, 2016.

Johnston, Robert. "Beyond 'The West': Regionalism, Liberalism and the Evasion of Politics in the New Western History." *Rethinking History* 2, no. 2 (1998): 239–77.

Ka'ōpua, Noelani Goodyear, Ikaika Hussey, and Erin Kahunawaika'ala Wright, eds. *A Nation Rising: Hawaiian Movements for Life, Land, and Sovereignty*. Durham NC: Duke University Press, 2004.

Kaplan, Amy. *The Anarchy of Empire in the Making of U.S. Culture*. Cambridge MA: Harvard University Press, 2005.

Kaplan, Amy, and Donald Pease. *Cultures of United States Imperialism*. Durham NC: Duke University Press, 1993.

Kauanui, J. Kēhaulani. *Hawaiian Blood: Colonialism and the Politics of Sovereignty and Indigeneity*. Durham NC: Duke University Press, 2008.

———. *Paradoxes of Hawaiian Sovereignty: Land, Sex, and the Colonial Politics of State Nationalism*. Durham NC: Duke University Press, 2018.

Klein, Christina. *Cold War Orientalism: Asia in the Middlebrow Imagination, 1945–1961*. Berkeley: University of California Press, 2003.

Kramer, Paul. *The Blood of Government: Race, Empire, the United States, & the Philippines*. Chapel Hill: University of North Carolina Press, 2006.

LaFeber, Walter. *The Cambridge History of American Foreign Relations*. Vol. 2, *The American Search for Opportunity, 1865–1913*. New York: Cambridge University Press, 1993.

Loveman, Brian. *No Higher Law: American Foreign Policy and the Western Hemisphere Since 1776*. Chapel Hill: University of North Carolina Press, 2010.

Mar, Tracey Banivanua. *Decolonisation and the Pacific: Indigenous Globalisation and the Ends of Empire*. New York: Cambridge University Press, 2016.

McCoy, Alfred, and Francisco A. Scarano. *Colonial Crucible: Empire and the Making of the Modern American State*. Madison: University of Wisconsin Press, 2009.

Merry, Sally Engle. *Colonizing Hawai'i: The Cultural Power of Law*. Princeton NJ: Princeton University Press, 2000.

Miller-Davenport, Sarah. *Gateway State: Hawai'i and the Cultural Transformation of American Empire*. Princeton NJ: Princeton University Press, 2019.

Naval History and Heritage Command. "Pearl Harbor: Its Origin and Administrative History Through World War II." 2015. https://www.history.navy.mil/research/library/online-reading-room/title-list-alphabetically/u/the-us-navy-and-hawaii-a-historical-summary/pearl-harbor-its-origin-and-administrative-history.html.

Ngai, Mai. *Impossible Subjects: Illegal Aliens and the Making of Modern America*. Princeton NJ: Princeton University Press, 2005.

Odo, Franklin. *No Sword to Bury: Japanese Americans in Hawai'i during World War II*. Philadelphia: Temple University Press, 2004.

Okihiro, Gary Y. *Cane Fires: The Anti-Japanese Movement in Hawaii, 1865–1945*. Philadelphia: Temple University Press, 1992.

———. *The Columbia Guide to Asian American History*. New York: Columbia University Press, 2005.

———. *Island World: A History of Hawai'i and the United States*. Berkeley: University of California Press, 2008.

Osorio, Jonathan Kay Kamakawiwoʻole. *Dismembering Lāhui: A History of the Hawaiian Nation to 1887*. Honolulu: University of Hawaiʻi Press, 2002.
Parker, Jason. *Hearts, Minds, Voices: U.S. Cold War Public Diplomacy and the Formation of the Third World*. New York: Oxford University Press, 2016.
Pratt, Julius. *Expansionists of 1898: The Acquisition of Hawaii and the Spanish Islands*. Baltimore: Johns Hopkins University Press, 1936.
Rafael, Vicente. *White Love and Other Events in Filipino History*. Durham NC: Duke University Press, 2000.
Saranillio, Dean Itsuji. *Unsustainable Empire: Alternative Histories of Hawaiʻi Statehood*. Durham NC: Duke University Press, 2018.
Schmitt, Robert C. *Demographic Statistics of Hawaii: 1778–1965*. Honolulu: University Press of Hawaii, 1968.
Sexton, Jay, and Ian Tyrrell, eds. *Empire's Twin: U.S. Anti-imperialism from the Founding Era to the Age of Terrorism*. Ithaca NY: Cornell University Press, 2015.
Silva, Noenoe K. *Aloha Betrayed: Native Hawaiian Resistance to American Colonialism*. Durham NC: Duke University Press, 2004.
Skwiot, Christine. *The Purposes of Paradise: U.S. Tourism and Empire in Cuba and Hawaiʻi*. Philadelphia: University of Pennsylvania Press, 2010.
Starr, Kenneth. *Sunset Magazine: A Century of Western Living, 1898–1998*. Stanford CA: Stanford University Libraries, 1998.
Takaki, Ronald T. *Pau Hana: Plantation Life and Labor in Hawaii, 1835–1920*. Honolulu: University of Hawaiʻi Press, 1984.
———. *Strangers from a Different Shore: A History of Asian Americans*. New York: Penguin, 1989.
Teaiwa, Teresia K. "L(o)osing the Edge." *Contemporary Pacific* 13, no. 2 (2001): 343–57.
———. "On Analogies: Rethinking the Pacific in a Global Context." *Contemporary Pacific* 18, no. 1 (2006): 71–87.
Trask, Haunani-Kay. "The Birth of the Modern Hawaiian Movement: Kalama Valley, O'ahu." *Hawaiian Journal of History* 21 (1987): 126–53.
Von Eschen, Penny. *Satchmo Blows Up the World: Jazz Ambassadors Play the Cold War*. Cambridge MA: Harvard University Press, 2004.
Wendt, Albert. "Towards a New Oceania." *Mana Review: A South Pacific Journal of Language and Literature* 1, no. 1 (1976): 49–60.
Wu, Ellen. *The Color of Success: Asian Americans and the Origins of the Model Minority*. Princeton NJ: Princeton University Press, 2013.

Published Government Sources

House Committee on the Territories. *Hearings on Statehood for Hawaii*. 79 Cong., 2 sess. (1946). Washington: U.S. Government Printing Office, 1946.
Senate Committee on Interior and Insular Affairs. *Hearings on Statehood for Hawaii*. 83 Cong., 1 and 2 sess. (1953 and 1954). Washington: U.S. Government Printing Office, 1954.

———. *Hearings on Statehood for Hawaii.* 85 Cong., 1 sess. (1957). Washington: U.S. Government Printing Office, 1957.

———. *Hearings on Statehood for Hawaii.* 86 Cong., 1 sess. (1959). Washington: U.S. Government Printing Office, 1959.

U.S. Census Bureau, *Statistics for Hawaii, 1910.* Washington DC: Government Printing Office, 1913.

FOUR

Sounds of Black Internationalism

Reimagining Regions through Anti-apartheid

MICKELL CARTER

During the 1980s, African decolonization propelled the continent into the global spotlight. After hundreds of years, the world began to see an increase of global Black representation in government as many African countries, such as Kenya, Nigeria, and Ghana, gained their independence.[1] While numerous countries in Africa obtained political freedom, South Africa's government continued an oppressive system of legalized racism—apartheid. Although established in 1948, apartheid remained in effect well into the late twentieth century. It disenfranchised Black communities and segregated the Black majority from the white minority. Amid apartheid, international movements emerged and demanded change in South Africa. Consequently, in 1979, a lavish, Las Vegas–style casino resort called Sun City was developed to create a positive image of South African race relations for its international audience. The apartheid government portrayed Sun City as a racial utopia for Black South Africans.

In 1985, fifty-four artists collaborated to produce a musical record that would raise global awareness of apartheid and oppose the unjust South African system while simultaneously critiquing the Sun City resort. Rock star Steven Van Zandt, also known as Little Steven, explained that the artists' record, *Sun City*, emerged "out of outrage and the desire to educate" and sought to "stimulate awareness, to ask all people everywhere to get involved by singing along and informing themselves about South Africa."[2] Though the song intended to reach all audiences, the song's Black performers functioned as Black internationals who identified common histories of struggle and visions for liberation. This chapter explores how these artists reimagined a Black region that transcended national borders, one that encompassed Africa and linked Black Americans and Black South Africans through a common struggle against racism and oppression. By analyzing the musical record *Sun City* and its title track's music video, this chapter argues that ideological regions can transcend national borders through Black internationalism.

Nations, borders, space, and geography may consist of real or imagined landscapes. However, scholars such as spatial theorist Edward W. Soja suggest both real and imaginary geographies can combine to formulate what he calls the "thirdspace."[3] Other scholars have furthered this concept by suggesting race also contributes to social, political, and cultural constructs of space.[4] Further, Soja suggests the conceptual power of regions can construct ideological landscapes where racial matters are instantaneously vague and transparent.[5] In part, race and space can be utilized to articulate a region as "a place of struggle."[6] Soja sees common struggle an important unifier for groups of people.

Building on Soja's spatial ideas, historians Keisha Blain and Tiffany Gill define Black internationalism as "a global political, intellectual, and artistic movement of African descended people engaged in a collective struggle to overthrow global White supremacy in its many forms."[7] It transcends the nation-state and encompasses "global visions of freedom and work[s] to forge transnational solidarities with people of color across the world."[8] Historian Robeson Frazier describes Black internationalists as individuals within the African diaspora who connect local, national, and global matters. He explains that their efforts seek to improve inequalities (social, economic, and racial) around the globe.[9] Because Black consciousness and common Black struggle operate as the core of Black internationalism, it links these individuals beyond borders, oceans, and boundaries.[10]

Despite its artists residing in two distinct locations, by communicating brotherhood, fraternity, and unity, *Sun City* articulated a form of Black internationalism that utilized artistry to unite people from inside and outside of the African diaspora. As the United States and South Africa are divided by oceans and landscapes, many consider them politically, socially, and culturally separate. However, in 1985, Black American artists reimagined a region that transcended national borders by encompassing Black internationalism (Black peoples' transnational linkages through their shared Black struggle). The *Sun City* musical record and its title track's music video were the result of an ideological region, or thirdspace, constructed and realized through common experiences and battles within a global Black freedom struggle.

When imagining regions, the Black artists involved with the record *Sun City* also communicated Black consciousness that encompassed Pan-African ideologies. Through their lyrics and music video, Black artists formulated a transnational region through Pan-Africanism, which scholar Hakim Adi defines as "a belief in the unity, common history and common purpose of the peoples of Africa and the African diaspora and the notion that their destinies are interconnected."[11] Pan-Africanists seek the liberation and advancement of the African continent, as it is the home of African citizens and the homeland of global African residents throughout the African diaspora.[12] As part of their opposition to South African apartheid, the *Sun City* artists expressed Black internationalism and Pan-Africanism as they fostered an ideological and transnational region that rejected anti-Blackness and welcomed Black liberation.

Apartheid

South Africa has a long history of racial oppression. Tracing back to Dutch colonization and the slave economy of the seventeenth century, anti-Blackness permeated South African society.[13] Rapid African decolonization after World War I and the war economy of World War II (which created economic opportunities for Black people in South Africa) threatened white social and economic superiority. Consequently, such threats led to the rise of apartheid or codified racism. To regain economic and social power, by the 1950s white South Africans elected the National Party government, which formed the system of apartheid and established legalized racial segregation related to where Black South Africans lived, went to school, worked, and so on. Under this system, Black South Africans received poor education, low-paying jobs, and inadequate living conditions.[14] Laws such as the Population Registration Act, the Group Areas Act, and the Bantu Authorities Act furthered the implementation of segregation. These laws facilitated the division of South Africans into four races—white, Black, Colored (mixed-race), and Asian—established where individual races could live (separate from one another), and relocated Black South Africans to impoverished lands based on their tribal origins, or Bantus.[15]

Quest for Liberation

Apartheid did not come without resistance. Black South Africans' quest to liberate themselves from apartheid's racial caste system and anti-Blackness resulted in rebellion. During the 1950s and 1960s, several opposition movements formed, such as the African National Congress (ANC), the Pan-Africanist Congress (PAC), the Azanian People's Liberation Army (APLA), and so on. Although many Black activists sought justice in South Africa peacefully, oppression, discrimination, and anti-Black violence remained. For instance, in 1960 white police forces murdered sixty-nine peaceful protestors in the Sharpeville Massacre. This event convinced many that justice could not be obtained through nonviolence but that freedom would only come by force.[16] Activists founded an armed wing of the ANC, Umkhonto we Sizwe ("Spear of the Nation"), that would fight for freedom and democracy by any means necessary.[17] Nelson Mandela, one of the ANC's leaders, stated that the African peoples' history of nonviolence had only led to "nothing but more and more repressive legislation, and fewer and fewer rights."[18] Fighting peacefully for equality and justice had proven to be ineffective. If equality for Black South Africans could be attained by armed resistance, Mandela expressed his will to die for it.[19] Similarly, during the civil rights and Black Power movements, some

Black Americans also embraced armed self-defense and Black self-determination.

Transformative international politics of the 1950s and 1960s, such as the increase of independent African states and the U.S. civil rights and Black Power movements, led to a rise in global Black consciousness. Black consciousness advocated for Black pride, self-awareness, and self-determination.[20] Black people gained inspiration from the idea of an independent African continent and viewed themselves as actors in a common Black struggle. However, the rise of Black consciousness contributed to an even stricter apartheid system with more restrictive sanctions. Nonetheless, this stirred Black youth uprisings and sparked the anti-apartheid movement to grow both inside South Africa and throughout the African diaspora.[21] While country after country in Africa gained independence, apartheid in South Africa only seemed further entrenched.

Anti-apartheid movements continued to grow even during the 1970s, in part due to Black South African worker strikes. Because so many international firms owned businesses in South Africa, the South African worker strikes brought international attention to Black people's working conditions.[22] Global criticism grew and continued to heighten, and by the 1980s, South Africa's apartheid government received "international pressure [which] reached an all-time peak."[23] For instance, Britain had one of the largest anti-apartheid movements that included thousands of people. These activists held demonstrations for sanctions to stop the apartheid regime and a full boycott of South African goods. Further, activists called for the release of ANC leader Nelson Mandela (sentenced to life in prison on accounts of sabotage).[24] In Canada, a large anti-apartheid movement emerged that held boycotts and organized groups such as the Toronto Committee for the Liberation of Southern Africa.[25] Additionally, anti-apartheid movements could be found in both Australia and New Zealand, where a large number of inhabitants were South African.[26] Although anti-apartheid movements emerged in various countries, each incorporated different ideologies such as anticolonialism, Black Power, and antiracism.[27]

In the United States, civil rights and Black Power advocates rallied behind antiracism and anti-oppression. Although the movements took place on different soil, the civil rights and Black Power movements in the United States and the anti-apartheid movement in South Africa resembled one another. Both Black Americans and Black South Africans faced and fought against segregation, political disenfranchisement, underresourced education, and lower-paying jobs. Each movement also incorporated music to create a "common identity" and push the movement forward globally.[28] The Negro spiritual "Keep Your Eyes on the Prize," for instance, inspired hope to protestors during the civil rights movement, and "Senzeni Na?" (What Have We Done?) acted as a nonviolent protest song sung by South Africans during their quest for liberation during apartheid.[29] Using music as a form of protest or to inspire hope continued into the 1980s, the peak of apartheid.

Transnational Musical Activism

Even preceding *Sun City*, in January 1985, two of the biggest artists of the decade, Lionel Richie and Michael Jackson, wrote and produced the song "We Are the World," a powerful example of musical activism. More than forty rock, pop, and soul artists collaborated on the song, calling themselves USA for Africa. The record brought global attention to the Ethiopian famine, which began just months prior, and it also raised approximately $22 million for relief.[30] The record was an "international phenomenon," reaching number one in Britain, Australia, and the Netherlands and number two in Japan.[31] The same year, rock artists performed a major concert known as Live Aid, considered "the largest rock-music festival ever."[32] Like "We Are the World," the concert intended to bring global awareness to and raise funds for the Ethiopian famine. Unfortunately, it helped conceal the politics behind the famine. In part, a right-wing military dictatorship's attempt to starve out an insurgent liberation movement sparked the famine. Instead, media disguised the blame, placing it on a "natural" phenomenon caused by a drought. More than just apolitical, "We Are the World" and

Live Aid did not criticize government roles or U.S. policy (which denied Ethiopia food aid), thereby contributing to the famine.[33]

Nonetheless, musical activism such as Live Aid proved successful, as the concert lasted for ten hours. Televised worldwide, Live Aid performed in two countries (the United States and Britain) and raised more than $16 million. Though both "We Are the World" and Live Aid were similar forms of musical activism, they varied from the *Sun City* project. Van Zandt explained, "Just as many of us [musical artists] sung out on behalf of the victims of Africa's famine so we are singing out also for those hungry for freedom."[34] In other words, Van Zandt articulates the difference between "We Are the World" and Live Aid and what would become Sun City. While some artists came together to raise awareness for the victims of famine, the Artists United Against Apartheid had a bigger aim: to inform global citizens about the atrocities of apartheid while aiding Black South Africans' quest for liberation.

The Making of "Sun City"

In 1985, rock star Steven Van Zandt wrote and released the musical record *Sun City* and its title track's music video. Van Zandt credits his multiple visits to South Africa, speaking with several South African groups, and realizing Black South Africans had "neither freedom nor human rights" for his inspiration to produce "Sun City."[35] The artists who collaborated on the project, as seen in the appendix, called themselves Artists United Against Apartheid. The fifty-four artists who contributed to the record were from diverse backgrounds; they were white, Black, men, women, and artists from outside of the United States. *Sun City* consisted of well-known artists such as Bruce Springsteen, Run-DMC, Bob Dylan, David Ruffin, Ringo Star, Afrika Bambaataa, George Clinton, Grandmaster Melle Mel, and Kurtis Blow. International performers who participated in the record included Australian rock group Midnight Oil member Peter Garrets, Nigerian musician Sonny Okosuns, and even South African groups Via Afrika and the Malopoets.[36]

Despite the possibility of retaliation or imprisonment by apartheid forces, the South African musical group the Malopoets expressed their commitment to the *Sun City* project "even if it meant death to them."[37] The musical record and its music video sought to protest the apartheid system and raise global awareness about injustices in South Africa. The song itself acted as a political statement and an anthem of unity, justice, and equality. Further, the anthem acted as a vehicle that exemplified notions of solidarity through Black internationalism and Pan-Africanism. Through their engagement with artistry and activism, Black musicians supported revolution and embraced the idea of a new Black region.

Reminiscent of Black international leaders of the past such as Marcus Garvey, W. E. B. Du Bois, and Malcolm X, the artists that performed on the *Sun City* record used culture to "articulate a global critique of racism."[38] Lines such as "Freedom is a privilege nobody rides for free" and "Somebody tell me why are we always on the wrong side" suggest that collective freedom from racism, oppression, and injustice will only be obtained if all global subjects fight for it.[39] Additionally, the artists condemned imperialist nations, like the United States, and their common histories of subjugation by expressing, "We [are] always on the wrong side."[40]

Musical expression acts to communicate common struggles and convey goals of Black internationalism, such as universal emancipation.[41] Artists United Against Apartheid acted as a medium for persons of African descent in the United States and abroad to imagine a global Black region through revolution in a fight for universal liberation. *Sun City*'s incorporation of Black and white artists fostered the concept that Black internationalism not only went beyond borders but also worked through race to confront racism. Black internationalism is not confined to a sense of racial pride; however, global emancipation is at its core. Aspirations of liberation resulted in an imagined thirdspace; as both Black and white artists used their music to protest discrimination against Black people in South Africa, they made the statement that the Black struggle was everyone's struggle.

Additionally, *Sun City*'s incorporation of hip-hop, soul, and rock was an attempt to appeal to both Black and white communities globally. Also, the combination of diverse musical styles intended to appeal to young, old, Black, and white audiences. Regardless of their U.S. location, they sang against racism in South Africa, crossing national boundaries and raising consciousness to other Black and white people around the globe through lines such as "It's time for some justice / it's time for the truth." Artists United Against Apartheid communicated a common struggle for justice and liberation among those of African descent and created unity between Black and white people despite national borders.

Sun City's title track "Sun City" begins with high energy percussion sounds similar to African rhythms. It incorporates these rhythms with jazz legend Miles Davis's trumpet melody, which sets an aggressive and sorrowful tone. The opening bars include the chanting of the phrases "Sun City" and "South Africa" in the background.[42] The "Sun City" chants reference the Las Vegas–style casino resort (also named Sun City) located in Bophuthatswana, one of the "independent" homelands created under the Bantu Authorities Act. The Bantus policy intended to segregate the Black South Africans from the white South Africans by using forced removal to lands called Bantustans. The homelands separated families, forced labor upon Black South Africans, and left Black communities impoverished.[43] Consequently, to create a positive image of Bantustans for its international audience, the apartheid government "showcased" the Sun City resort as a paradise for Black South Africans.[44]

The "Sun City" and "South Africa" chants yield an instant connection between the artists and South Africa. It is not simply the chants that produce this connection but also the chants' easily identifiable African accent. The melody transitions from an up-tempo African beat to a genre that is a combination of rock and pop. This progression from African beats to pop expresses a sonic attempt to link together two continents to fight against apartheid. It strategically balances the instrumentation to the vocals of the song. Though the instrumentation is loud and up-tempo, it does not overpower the artists' vocals. This makes "Sun City's" message even more powerful. Both the instrumentation and vocals go hand in hand by portraying the feelings of frustration and anger.[45] The artists verbalize unified diversity in the song's opening bars by singing, "We're rockers and rappers united and strong."[46] This line recognizes the diversity of genres on the record, including well-known rock, soul, and reggae and the newer genre of hip-hop.

Scholar Tricia Rose explains that hip-hop music, or rap, is "a black cultural expression that prioritizes black voices from the margins of urban America," as rap artists "speak with the voice of personal experience."[47] Scholar Miles White describes hip-hop music as "the sound of the urban street . . . rising from the black ghetto."[48] During the 1980s, hip-hop music became a verbal expression of rage and frustration and expressed hardcore realism.[49] Distinct from "We Are the World," "Sun City's" inclusion of hip-hop communicated frustration. By incorporating rap artists, the Artists United Against Apartheid articulated a form of unity that included the perspectives of youthful, urban, Black performers. Additionally, "Sun City's" inclusion of hip-hop set it apart from other forms of musical activism of the decade such as "We Are the World" and USA for Africa. While these forms of musical activism conveyed messages of sympathy and hope, "Sun City" communicated anger and incorporated hip-hop to further articulate artists' rage. Hip-hop and the rage it expressed quickly gained popularity in the United States and abroad. Soon the genre sprouted in South Africa.[50] As rap artists employed hip-hop across the globe to express local identities, "Sun City" artists instead used hip-hop as a vehicle to communicate a global diasporic Black identity and region through Black internationalism.[51]

"Sun City's" use of hip-hop to articulate a diasporic Black region distinguished it from earlier forms of musical activism such as "We Are the World" and Live Aid. Furthermore, unlike "We Are the World" and Live Aid, the incorporation of hip-hop widened "Sun City's" audience beyond strictly white and middle-class Black people to also include Black youth. Also, "Sun City" conveyed rage and protest, different from the kindness and sympathy expressed by "We Are the World" and Live Aid. "Sun City's" elements of hip-hop helped personify rage at the injustices against Black people in an ideological diasporic region that included South Africa.

"Sun City" and Political Activism

Sun City artists criticized state actors responsible for abhorrent crimes against Black South Africans. Hip-hop and the *Sun City* record were overtly political, as opposed to other genres and forms of activism such as Live Aid, which were actively antipolitical (receiving little backlash). For instance, the *Sun City* record called out not only the anti-apartheid government but also the U.S. president, Ronald Reagan, and U.S. policy. Through lines from the record's title track such as "Quiet diplomacy ain't nothing but a joke," Artists United Against Apartheid labeled the U.S. government's anti-apartheid tactics as insufficient.[52] By 1986, TV personality Phil Donahue described the record as "the most politically aggressive movement in rock 'n' roll."[53]

Aggression and outrage seep through "Sun City's" opening verses as hip-hop artists rap, "It's time for some justice / it's time for some truth."[54] This line specifically speaks of apartheid in South Africa and calls the system unjust. As the song continues, artists George Clinton and Joey Ramone sing specifically about Ronald Reagan's ties to the apartheid government in the lines "Our government tells us we're doing all we can / Constructive Engagement is Ronald Reagan's plan."[55] When the United Nations pushed to impose sanctions on South Africa, intending to isolate it, the Reagan administration advocated for "constructive engagement" instead, arguing that South Africa needed incentives to encourage a gradual shift from apartheid.[56] Artists United Against Apartheid protested not only the South African government but also the Reagan administration.

The election of President Reagan drastically changed government policy concerning South Africa. While his predecessor, President Jimmy Carter, expressed that the nation should advocate racial and ethnic equality, President Reagan believed that the

United States "had to oppose communism and protect its strategic interest in the region" and considered South Africa an "anti-Communist ally."[57] His administration did not criticize white South Africans and openly expressed South Africa was a comrade to the United States and the South African government would not be deserted. Despite the numerous international anti-apartheid movements, President Reagan kept close relations with the South African government and endorsed constructive engagement.[58] Although unpopular among the Black American community, in 1984 Reagan received 59 percent of the nation's votes for reelection. In the 1984 election, he received 66 percent of the white vote while only receiving 9 percent of the Black vote.[59]

Unlike the United States, the majority of the South African population was unable to vote. Such complete disenfranchisement led to global outrage and helped fuel the anti-apartheid movement in both the United States and South Africa. "Sun City" clearly voiced the importance of the voting issue. Artists Eddie Kendrick and Bruce Springsteen sang, "23 million can't vote because they're black / we're stabbing our brothers and sisters in the back."[60] The multiple apartheid acts and laws, whose intentions were to segregate, left the Black majority population with no political voice.

The United States and South Africa share a similar past of discrimination. Similarities between the South African anti-apartheid movement and the Black American civil rights movement enhanced the connection between Black people in the United States, Black people of South Africa, and the white people who committed to helping bring an end to racial injustice. As early as the 1960s, the Black American community had already drawn parallels between Jim Crow laws and apartheid laws.[61] Both the civil rights movement and the anti-apartheid movement shared a common history of discrimination and violence and a common cause: overcoming white supremacy. This cause also inspired the work of Artists United Against Apartheid, as they used it to fuel and convey a Black region with liberation at its core.

"Sun City" Music Video

Following the record, the "Sun City" music video provided viewers with a visual depiction of solidarity while also highlighting the injustices in southern Africa. The video begins with a Sun City casino promotional video that shows the lavish resort and describes it as "part of the realities of the apartheid." The promotional video neglects to show the real conditions of the Black people who resided in Bophuthatswana. Quickly interrupted by a loud gunshot and "real" video footage from South Africa, the video portrays Black South Africans running from law enforcement and the police brutality against them. As "Sun City" lyrics begin, the video interchangeably shows clips of Black South Africans' struggles and the lavishness of the Sun City resort, with clips such as white visitors lounging around its swimming pools. By juxtaposing Black South African struggles and white comfort, the video expresses that injustices against Black South Africans, in part, went unnoticed and Sun City comforts came at the expense of Black discomfort and struggle. The video depicts these struggles and anti-apartheid protests framed against white comfort, the Sun City casino resort, and the record's artists.[62]

The video attempted to show the true nature of apartheid and its Bantustans by incorporating many violent and negative images. One image was that of a newspaper article that read, "Sun City-Fantasy Island in the midst of Hell." The video also included images of Nelson Mandela reminding the world of his imprisonment and showed clips of the civil rights movement and Martin Luther King Jr. This drew the connection between the civil rights movement and the anti-apartheid movement and articulated a notion of a real and imagined "thirdspace" constructed by a common struggle and Pan-African solidarity.[63]

Scholar Regina Bradley articulates how hip-hop music encompasses regional sentiments and that it can also move beyond geographic borders or "pushes past the geographic and cultural boundaries of the region."[64] The hip-hop artists in the "Sun City" music video articulated the notion that although Black Americans and Black South Africans lived in two regions of the globe, they were still part of a global Black region. This Black global region included a common history and shared goal of social, economic, and racial justice. While the "Sun City" music video articulated a Black region beyond U.S. borders, it also furthered the notion that all persons who did not protest apartheid were part of the problem. Additionally, the video preached unity to overcome oppression and injustices. The video depicted unity through multigenre and multiethnic artists as they walked, marched, sang, and rapped side by side. Further, the video showed viewers scenes of white artists singing lines that alluded to Black South Africans as their "brothers and sisters." Artists United Against Apartheid referenced the oppressed South Africans as "brothers and sisters," which also displayed their effort to go beyond national borders by creating a connection between American and South African persons. Images of white-Black unity portrayed an imagined region that transcends not only borders but also races. It demonstrated a multiethnic region created through fraternity and solidary.[65]

Representations of solidarity became more evident throughout the video. The white artists articulated solidarity with oppressed Black people nationally but also internationally. The artists declared that due to a similar past of oppression of Black Americans, they too shared concern for the South Africans' struggle.[66] As the video continued, more images and video clips depicted unity and solidarity among Black and white persons. For example, the artists were together toward the beginning of the music video, often seen in pairs or small groups. However, toward the end of the music video, the artists gathered in large groups of both Black and white individuals, depicting diversity and inclusion. Diverse instruments also portrayed notions of inclusion.

Toward the end of the video, crowds of people protested while artists played instruments such as drums and saxophones. Interestingly, while individuals dressed in common American-style clothing of the era, others, including white persons, wore African-inspired clothing and headwear.[67] As scholar Monica Miller explains, Black style is both "personal and political, about individual image and group regard"; the Black subjects wearing African-inspired clothing expressed a stylized Pan-African Black identity.[68] Additionally, by depicting African-inspired attire on white bodies, the "Sun City" music video portrayed unity and solidarity. This message of solidarity became more evident throughout the music video.

The last scenes of the music video depicted Black and white artists with different backgrounds, genres, and attire enjoying one another's company in what looked to be a festive event or outdoor party portraying an image of Black joy. This articulated a notion that all persons, despite their differences, can and should be accepted and embraced and may live harmoniously. Depictions of anti-apartheid protests followed scenes of harmonious diversity. The final scene of the video portrayed a massive group of Black South Africans singing in unison while others held a sign that read "MANDELA MUST BE RELEASED." Consequently, this scene articulated that harmonious and multiethnic unity could not be realized if apartheid continued to exist.[69] Thus, in its expression of a global Black region, "Sun City" also acted as a vehicle of opposition against apartheid and white supremacy.

Cultural Boycott

The Sun City resort became a controversial site as international empathy for the Black South Africans' struggle grew. Consequently, multiple anti-apartheid movements surfaced around the globe, and the Sun City casino resort in Bophuthatswana gained global attention. In 1979, white South African business tycoon Solomon (Sol) Kerzner created the resort and described it as "a place all South Africans could enjoy irrespective of their race"; others, such as the Artists United Against Apartheid, rejected this description.[70] The Artists United Against Apartheid not only raised awareness of the cruelties of the apartheid government but also urged other celebrities not to perform at the Sun City resort. This could be seen in the lines "You can't buy me I don't care what you pay / Don't ask me Sun City because I ain't gonna play."[71]

The ANC, and later the United Nations, called for a cultural boycott to protest apartheid, which gained massive media coverage and large international support from activists, politicians, celebrities, and musical performers.[72] The Artists United Against Apartheid encouraged this cultural boycott, as the artists urged entertainers not to play at Sun City. This led to division among celebrities. While some accepted "Sun City's" plea for resisting the resort's offers to perform, others instead went willingly.[73] The casino's lavishness and offers of large payments lured many athletes and celebrities to the Sun City casino resort.[74] Nevertheless, entertainers, athletes, and organizations led the charge to boycott South Africa. Johnathan Freedman revealed that pressure to no longer perform at Sun City intensified as critics, such as Mfanafuthi Johnstone (Johnny) Makatini (ANC observer to the United Nations), compared Black artists who traveled to South Africa to "Jews entering Hitler's Nazi troops during the Holocaust."[75]

Performers who traveled to or performed in South Africa received sharp media criticism and negative publicity and were denied opportunities.[76] Also, the ANC and the Special Committee Against Apartheid monitored international and foreign entertainers who appeared in South Africa and placed them on an international sanctions list.[77] Black celebrities such as Harry Belafonte argued that by performing at Sun City, one supported the apartheid system. While many Black artists such as Sammy Davis Jr. and Natalie Cole did not perform at Sun City regardless of money propositions, other Black artists such as Millie Jackson, the O'Jays, and Tina Turner accepted offers. After performing at Sun City, some artists did criticize the apartheid regime and vowed not to perform there until segregation had ceased.[78] However, others such as the Black American musical group the Commodores kept their contracts with the Sun City resort closely guarded. When news leaked about Black entertainers who performed at Sun City, many would pull out, while others, such as Ray Charles, refused to apologize for their encounters with the resort.[79] Some believed celebrities who encouraged the boycott of South Africa to be hypocrites, as they could afford not to perform in South Africa compared to their other celebrity counterparts. Furthermore, Alfred Jones explained that when celebrities who support the cultural boycott "are willing to divest themselves of their wealth, put on military fatigues and pick up the gun to go into the bush with the ANC (African National Congress) as freedom fighters, they can call me and I will do the same. Until that time, don't tell me what to believe or where I can or cannot go."[80]

Some white celebrities also refused to support the cultural boycott. Despite portrayals of anti-apartheid protests, Black South African struggles, and messages of solidary that the Artists United Against Apartheid conveyed in their "Sun City" record and music video, some still chose to perform or visit. For example, after hearing the "Sun City" record and watching its music video, Lanny Wadkins, a white U.S. golfer, decided to "see for himself" the segregation and oppression in Bophuthatswana.[81] After returning from a golfing tournament in Bophuthatswana, Wadkins stated the "Sun City" music video was unrealistic, as he saw racial integration throughout the homeland. Nevertheless, others rejected Wadkins's observations and did not support his decision to go to Bophuthatswana. Black American golfer Lee Elder told *Jet* magazine that he believed Wadkins should not have traveled to Bophuthatswana at all.[82]

Consequently, the owners of the Sun City casino resort requested both Black and white celebrities, such as Wadkins, to not make statements that could cause controversy while in Bophuthatswana, and in return, they would receive white South African privileges. By carefully selecting Black performers who were not known for political activism, the South African government would declare the Black performers "honorary Whites," providing them with access to facilities such as hotels and restaurants that were typically denied to Black people.[83] Although the Artists United Against Apartheid imagined and expressed a transnational Black region, the cultural boycott debates demonstrate the limitations of ideological regions. Nevertheless, Artists United Against Apartheid used music to communicate solidarity and urge fans and celebrities to take action against the racist apartheid system. Van Zandt explained the artists hoped that "once informed, we all might take a closer look at our own consciousness and the disease of racism in our own culture."[84]

"Sun City" aided in spreading awareness of Black South Africans' struggle. For instance, in 1986 Sheldon W. Rice from Hampton, Virginia, wrote to *Ebony* magazine after watching the "Sun City" music video:

> Recently, I had the opportunity to see a music video entitled *Sun City*. . . . I was appalled at the mistreatment of the people. How could such cruelty be allowed to continue, and for so long? Yet, this situation has been going on for years and years. Being born in the early '60s, I was too young to remember what South Africa was about, or for that matter, where it was. My parents' generation could more or less sympathize with the South African situation. However, their plight has gotten much worse, and sympathy just doesn't "cut it."[85]

Rice demonstrates the influence of "Sun City" and how it created a global space for Black solidarity. The record and music video helped inform global citizens while simultaneously sparking outrage to produce tangible change, as "sympathy just doesn't 'cut it.'"[86]

Despite Artists United Against Apartheid's efforts to inform and display solidarity with oppressed people, the "Sun City" record did not get as much airplay in the United States.[87] The song did, however, reach number twenty-one on the U.K. music charts and[88] number ten on the Canadian charts[89] and achieve its ultimate goal of bringing global awareness to the apartheid struggle in South Africa.[90] Further, the record's and video's royalties supported the Africa Fund and South African political prisoners, their families, and the needs of South African exiles.[91] By supporting these organizations and individuals, the artists demonstrated that the quest to dismantle apartheid transcended national borders. The artists conveyed that Black liberation lay in a diasporic Black region, and through multiethnic solidarity, universal freedom could be realized. In part, the artists' international ideas of Black liberation influenced the dismantling of apartheid.

In the 1980s, as Black South Africans gained international support through a worldwide cultural boycott and global anti-apartheid movements, Black South Africans took center stage. Like other artists before them, the Artists United Against Apartheid used music to increase international attention to the injustices Black South Africans faced at the hands of the apartheid government. "Sun City's" Black artists, regardless of national boundaries, rejected borders and oceans as dividers. Instead, they expressed unity between Black Americans and Black South Africans. Further, due to shared experiences and common struggles, the Black artists in Artists United Against Apartheid acted as Black internationalists and demonstrated their interconnectedness with Africa. Black musical artists constructed a borderless, global Black region through their record. Also, even though not of African descent, the record's white artists expressed solidarity with Black South Africans. Beyond race, they portrayed solidarity toward Black people's oppression both nationally and internationally. The *Sun City* record itself expressed that Black internationalism could also unite people outside of the African diaspora by conveying brotherhood, fraternity, and unity in a universal way. It shows us that common struggles against racism, oppression, and imperialism can formulate international, ideological, and Pan-African Black regions. It further demonstrates how music (or culture in general) can be utilized as a means to unify and organize multiethnic communities to seek racial justice, transformation, and transnational change.

Notes

1. Whitaker, "Independent Nations of the World," 78–80.
2. Marsh, *Sun City by Artists United Against Apartheid*, 5.
3. Soja, *Thirdspace*, 57.
4. See Stephanie Camp's *Closer to Freedom*; Kathrine McKittrick's *Demonic Grounds*; and others.
5. Soja, *Thirdspace*, 2.
6. Davis, *Southscapes*, 1–3.
7. Blain, Gill, and West, *To Turn the Whole World Over*, 2.
8. Blain and Swan, "Reconceptualizing the History of Black Internationalism," 572.
9. Frazier, "Sketches of Black Internationalism and Transnationalism," 231–32.
10. Martin, West, and Wilkins, *From Toussaint to Tupac*, 1–3.
11. Adi, *Pan-Africanism*, 2.
12. Adi, *Pan-Africanism*, 2.

13. Worger and Clark, *South Africa*, 3–4.
14. Stapleton, *Military History of South Africa*, 152–53.
15. O'Malley the Heart of Hope, "1951."
16. Welsh, *Rise and Fall of Apartheid*, 157–63.
17. African National Congress, "Manifesto of Umkhonto we Sizwe."
18. Mandela, "I Am Prepared to Die."
19. Mandela, "I Am Prepared to Die."
20. Adi, *Pan-Africanism*, 173–75.
21. Stapleton, *Military History of South Africa*, 152–53.
22. Worger and Clark, *South Africa*, 78.
23. Freedman, "Sun City and the Sounds of Liberation," 2–3.
24. See Mandela, "I Am Prepared to Die"; AA Forward to Freedom, "Anti-apartheid Movement in the 1980s."
25. Webb, "Hidden Histories & Political Legacies."
26. Webb, "Hidden Histories & Political Legacies."
27. Limb, Knight, and Root, "Global Antiapartheid Movement," 163.
28. Van Blommestein and Hope, "Language of Songs," 67.
29. Van Blommestein and Hope, "Language of Songs," 65–66.
30. Lynn Van Matre, "'We Are the World' to Turn Overseas," *Chicago Tribune*, April 25, 1985.
31. J. DeKnock, "'We Are the World' Successfully Spinning around the Globe," *Chicago Tribune*, May 3, 1985.
32. Ken Tucker Knight, "Impresarios Will Find It Tough to Top Megabucks 'Live Aid' Rock Concert," *Chicago Tribune*, June 30, 1985.
33. De Waal, *Evil Days*, 4–6; Shepherd, "Ethiopia," 6.
34. Johnson, "Rock Star Says, 'Mama Forgot to Teach Me That I Was White,'" 59.
35. Johnson, "Rock Star Says, 'Mama Forgot to Teach Me That I Was White,'" 58–59.
36. Marsh, *Sun City by Artists United Against Apartheid*, 16.
37. Johnson, "Rock Star Says, 'Mama Forgot to Teach Me That I Was White,'" 58.
38. Freedman, "Sounds of Liberation," 4.
39. Artists United Against Apartheid, "Sun City."
40. Artists United Against Apartheid, "Sun City."
41. Martin, West, and Wilkins, *From Toussaint to Tupac*, 1–3.
42. Artists United Against Apartheid, "Sun City."
43. Evans and Higgs, "Embracing Activism in Apartheid South Africa," 509.
44. Evans, "Resettlement and the Making of the Ciskei Bantustan," 21–22.
45. Artists United Against Apartheid, "Sun City."
46. Artists United Against Apartheid, "Sun City."
47. Rose, *Black Noise*, 2.
48. White, *African American Music in Global Perspective*, 48–52.
49. White, *African American Music in Global Perspective*, 48–52.
50. Kunzler, "South African Rap Music," 28.
51. See Mitchell, *Global Noise*; Perry, "Hip Hop's Diasporic Landscapes of Blackness."

52. Artists United Against Apartheid, "Sun City."
53. Johnson, "Rock Star Says, 'Mama Forgot to Teach Me That I Was White,'" 56.
54. Artists United Against Apartheid, "Sun City."
55. Artists United Against Apartheid, "Sun City."
56. Ungar and Vale, "South Africa."
57. Hill, "Constructive Engagement," 6–25.
58. Hill, "Constructive Engagement," 6–25.
59. Cornell University, "How Groups Voted in 1984."
60. Artists United Against Apartheid, "Sun City."
61. *Ebony*, "Jim Crow South African Style," 123.
62. Artists United Against Apartheid, "Artists United Against Apartheid—Sun City." Lyrics can be found online at SpringsteenLyrics.com, "Sun City," accessed June 15, 2023, https://www.springsteenlyrics.com/lyrics.php?song=suncityaccessed.
63. Soja, *Thirdspace*, 57.
64. Bradley, *Chronicling Stankonia*, 13.
65. Artists United Against Apartheid, "Sun City."
66. Artists United Against Apartheid, "Sun City."
67. Artists United Against Apartheid, "Sun City."
68. Miller, *Slaves to Fashion*, 3.
69. Artists United Against Apartheid, "Sun City."
70. Alan Cowell, "Sol Kerzner, South African Casino Tycoon, Is Dead at 84," *New York Times*, March 27, 2020, https://www.nytimes.com/2020/03/27/business/sol-kerzner-dead.html?auth=login-google.
71. Artists United Against Apartheid, "Sun City."
72. South African History Online, "South Africa's Academic and Cultural Boycott."
73. Freedman, "Sun City and the Sounds of Liberation," 4–6.
74. Freedman, "Sun City and the Sounds of Liberation," 4.
75. Freedman, "Sun City and the Sounds of Liberation," 4.
76. Freedman, "Sun City and the Sounds of Liberation," 4–6.
77. Scott Kraft, "Column One: A Cultural Boycott in Evolution: Foreign Artists Now Can Get the Blessing of Anti-apartheid Groups to Perform in South Africa. Some Chafe at Having to 'Consult.' Transgressions of Others Are Not Forgotten," *Los Angeles Times*, April 18, 1991, https://www.latimes.com/archives/la-xpm-1991-04-18-mn-176-story.html.
78. *Jet*, "Should Famous Blacks Entertain in South Africa?," 54.
79. Freedman, "Sun City and the Sounds of Liberation," 4–6.
80. Alfred Jones, "Boycotting South Africa," *Los Angeles Times*, March 3, 1985, https://www.latimes.com/archives/la-xpm-1985-03-03-ca-32658-story.html.
81. *Jet*, "Lee Elders Raps Golfers Fooled by South Africans," 46.
82. *Jet*, "Lee Elders Raps Golfers Fooled by South Africans," 46.
83. Freedman, "Sun City and the Sounds of Liberation," 4–7.
84. Marsh, *Sun City by Artists United Against Apartheid*, 5.
85. Rice, "South Africa," 9.

86. Rice, "South Africa," 9.
87. *Rolling Stone*, "100 Best Albums of the Eighties."
88. Official Charts, "Sun City."
89. Library and Archives Canada, "RPM100 Singles."
90. *Rolling Stone*, "100 Best Albums of the Eighties."
91. African Activist Archive, "African Activist Archive."

Bibliography

AA Forward to Freedom. "The Anti-apartheid Movement in the 1980s." Accessed November 19, 2015. https://www.aamarchives.org/history/1980s.html.

Adi, Hakim. *Pan-Africanism: A History*. London: Bloomsbury Academic, 2018.

African National Congress. "Manifesto of Umkhonto we Sizwe." December 16, 1961. http://web.archive.org/web/20061217090228/http://www.anc.org.za/ancdocs/history/manifesto-mk.html.

Artists United Against Apartheid. "Sun City." Written by Steven Van Zandt. *Sun City*. EMI Manhattan Records, 1985, MP3.

———. "Artists United Against Apartheid—Sun City." Performed by Artists United Against Apartheid. EMI Manhattan Records, 1985. Music in History. January 26, 2009. YouTube video. https://www.youtube.com/watch?v=aopKk56jM-I.

Blain, Keisha N., Tiffany M. Gill, and Michael Oliver West. *To Turn the Whole World Over: Black Women and Internationalism*. Urbana: University of Illinois Press, 2019.

Blain, Keisha N., and Quito Swan. "Reconceptualizing the History of Black Internationalism." *Journal of African American History* 106, no. 4 (January 2021): 571–76, https://doi.org/10.1086/716558.

Bradley, Regina N. *Chronicling Stankonia: The Rise of the Hip-Hop South*. Chapel Hill: University of North Carolina Press, 2021.

Camp, Stephanie M. H. *Closer to Freedom: Enslaved Women and Everyday Resistance in the Plantation South*. Chapel Hill: University of North Carolina Press, 2006.

Cornell University. "How Groups Voted in 1984." Accessed May 2, 2023. https://ropercenter.cornell.edu/how-groups-voted-1984.

Davis, Thadious M. *Southscapes Geographies of Race, Region, and Literature*. Chapel Hill: University of North Carolina Press, 2014.

de Waal, Alexander. *Evil Days: Thirty Years of War and Famine in Ethiopia*. New York: Human Rights Watch, 1991.

Ebony. "Jim Crow South African Style: American Bucks Apartheid." May 1964, 123–26.

Evans, Laura. "Resettlement and the Making of the Ciskei Bantustan, South Africa, c. 1960–1976." *Journal of Southern African Studies* 40, no. 1 (2014): 21–40.

Evans, Neva, and Catherine Higgs. "Embracing Activism in Apartheid South Africa: The Sisters of Mercy in Bophuthatswana, 1974–94." *Catholic Historical Review* 94, no. 3 (2008): 500–521.

Films On Demand. "The Making of Sun City." 1987. http://digital.films.com/PortalPlaylists.aspx?aid=8690&xtid=53175.

Frazier, Robeson Taj P. "Sketches of Black Internationalism and Transnationalism." *Journal of African American History* 96, no. 2 (2011): 231–35.

Freedman, Jonathan. "Sun City and the Sounds of Liberation: Cultural Resistance for Social Justice in Apartheid South Africa." Master's thesis, University of California, 2014. http://escholarship.org/uc/item/99d3x9rv.

Hill, Shandra D. "Constructive Engagement: Ronald Reagan's Problematic Policy of Appeasement with South Africa." Master's thesis, Georgetown University, 2012.

Jet. "Lee Elders Raps Golfers Fooled by South Africans." January 13, 1986, 46.

———. "Should Famous Blacks Entertain in South Africa?" May 27, 1985, 52–55.

Johnson, Robert E. "Rock Star Says, 'Mama Forgot to Teach Me That I Was White'; Helps Raise Millions to Fight Racism." *Jet*, March 17, 1986.

Kunzler, Daniel. "South African Rap Music, Counter Discourses, Identity, and Commodification Beyond the Prophets of Da City." *Journal of Southern African Studies* 37, no. 1 (2011): 27–43.

Library and Archives Canada. "RPM100 Singles." January 25, 1986. https://www.bac-lac.gc.ca/eng/discover/films-videos-sound-recordings/rpm/Pages/item.aspx?IdNumber=4322&.

Limb, Peter, Richard Knight, and Christine Root. "The Global Antiapartheid Movement." *Radical History Review* 14, no. 119 (2014): 161–77.

Mandela, Nelson. "Transcript: Nelson Mandela Speech 'I Am Prepared to Die.'" SBS News. Accessed June 18, 2023. https://www.sbs.com.au/news/article/transcript-nelson-mandela-speech-i-am-prepared-to-die/acc7mlanu.

Marsh, Dave. *Sun City by Artists United Against Apartheid: The Making of the Record.* New York: Penguin Books, 1985.

Martin, William G., Michael O. West, and Fanon Che Wilkins, eds. *From Toussaint to Tupac: The Black International since the Age of Revolution*. Chapel Hill: University of North Carolina Press, 2009.

McKittrick, Katherine. *Demonic Grounds: Black Women and the Cartographies of Struggle*. Minneapolis: University of Minnesota Press, 2006.

Miller, Monica L. *Slaves to Fashion: Black Dandyism and the Styling of Black Diasporic Identity*. Durham NC: Duke University Press, 2010.

Mitchell, Tony, ed. *Global Noise: Rap and Hip-Hop Outside the USA*. Middletown CT: Wesleyan University Press, 2001.

Official Charts. "Sun City." November 11, 1985. http://www.officialcharts.com/search/singles/sun%20city/.

O'Malley the Heart of Hope. "1951: Bantu Authorities Act No 68." 2015. https://www.nelsonmandela.org/omalley/index.php/site/q/03lv01538/04lv01828/05lv01829/06lv01844.htm.

Perry, Marc D. "Hip Hop's Diasporic Landscapes of Blackness." In West, Martin, and Wilkins, *From Toussaint to Tupac*, 232–58.

Rice, Sheldon W. "South Africa." *Ebony*, December 1986, 9–15.

Rolling Stone. "100 Best Albums of the Eighties." November 16, 1989. http://www.rollingstone.com/music/lists/100-best-albums-of-the-eighties-20110418.

Rose, Tricia. *Black Noise: Rap Music and Black Culture in Contemporary America.* Middletown CT: Wesleyan University Press, 1994.

Shepherd, Jack. "Ethiopia: The Use of Food as an Instrument of U.S. Foreign Policy." *Issue: A Journal of Opinion* 14, no. 2 (1985): 4–9. https://doi.org/10.2307/1262530.

Soja, Edward W. *Thirdspace: Journeys to Los Angeles and Other Real-and-Imagined Places.* Malden MA: Blackwell, 2014.

South African History Online. "South Africa's Academic and Cultural Boycott." Accessed April 24, 2021. https://www.sahistory.org.za/article/south-africas-academic-and-cultural-boycott#:~:text=The%20anc's%20original%20call%20for,the%20following%20year%20in%20london.

Stapleton, Timothy Joseph. *A Military History of South Africa: From the Dutch-Khoi Wars to the End of Apartheid.* Santa Barbara CA: ABC-CLIO, 2010. PDF e-book.

Stephens, Michelle. "Disarticulating Black Internationalisms: West Indian Radicals and the Practice of Diaspora." *Small Axe* 9, no. 1 (2005): 100–111.

Ungar, Sanford J., and Peter Vale. "South Africa: Why Constructive Engagement Failed." *Foreign Affairs* 64, no. 2 (1985): 234–58. https://doi.org/10.2307/20042571.

United States Department of Justice. "History of Federal Voting Rights Act." Updated July 28, 2017. http://www.justice.gov/crt/history-federal-voting-rights-laws.

van Blommestein, Jeremy, and Sarah Hope. "The Language of Songs: The Utilization of Freedom Songs as a Form of Protest in the South African Anti-apartheid and U.S. Civil Rights Movements." *International Journal of Knowledge, Culture & Change in Organizations: Annual Review* 10, no. 1 (2012): 59–68.

Webb, Chris. "Hidden Histories & Political Legacies of the Canadian Anti-apartheid Movement." *Canadian Dimension* 48, no. 2 (March 2014): 19–22.

Welsh, David. *The Rise and Fall of Apartheid.* Johannesburg: Jonathan Ball, 2010.

Whitaker, Charles. "Independent Nations of the World." *Ebony*, 1985, 78–86.

White, Miles. *African American Music in Global Perspective: From Jim Crow to Jay-Z: Race, Rap, and the Performance of Masculinity.* Champaign: University of Illinois Press, 2011.

Worger, William, and Nancy L Clark. *South Africa: The Rise and Fall of Apartheid.* 2nd ed. New York: Routledge, 2011.

PART 2

Space

FIVE

The Significance of Climate in American History

Inventing, Imagining, and Erasing Regions

LAWRENCE CULVER

In 1893, when Frederick Jackson Turner laid out his arguments for the frontier as a potent force in American history, his case rested on it as a vast expanse of open land. Except as open space and a demographic and geographic safety valve, however, all that western land was in his formulation inert, awaiting Anglo-American historical dynamism. The land, like its Native American and Mexican inhabitants, possessed no agency in Turner's worldview.[1]

Actual American settlers, in contrast, had a very different perspective. The environment was an active force in their lives. Good land meant not just food and survival but health and wealth. Bad land meant penury, pestilence, and death. Land was a subset of climate, and climate was a constant preoccupation. Their worldview did not separate land and climate into soil and weather, as twenty-first-century science would. Informed by the evolving natural sciences, folk belief, and climatic ideas from antiquity, which conceived of climate as geography—distinct climatic zones that were fixed places, not changeable weather patterns—settlers "read" climates. In so doing, they made choices about settlement, assumptions about inhabitants of different climates, and predictions about the future of entire regions. Indeed, climate was central to how they defined regions. In turn, regionalism shaped perceptions of climate. Americans of different regions—North and South—could look at the West and draw climatic conclusions that differed widely and projected very different futures for the same region, and indeed also projected different futures for the nation as a whole. While many white nineteenth-century Americans could be classified as nationalists, their nationalism took different regional forms and imagined different national futures. Climate was, in fact, a key example of this. Climatic perceptions and misperceptions were rooted in both regional ideologies and identities. In this way, climate, real and imagined, was deeply intertwined with regionalism and region making in U.S. history.

Economic desires, rather than environmental realities, would dominate national conceptions of climate and region. These could and would change over time, particularly as climate evolved from a matter of survival to an economic or healthful asset and, after 1945, seemingly a mere lifestyle amenity. Yet each of these regional and climatic formulations betrayed an alarming willingness to embrace delusion and to claim imagined climates when preferable to fact. Actual climate often held less importance than economic interest. Every region originates with invention, a claim of distinctiveness or identity, however defined. Yet invention rooted in reality could and did sometimes give way to self-serving fabulation and fantasy, and seeing regionalism though a lens of climate highlights this fact in U.S. history.

The greatest conflict in U.S. history was between regions, North and South. Their fundamental difference, one that predated slavery, was a climatic one: in the hot and humid South you could grow cotton, while in the North you could not. Before the Civil War, supporters and opponents of slavery engaged in a fraught climatic debate. Was the nation's new West a desert or a garden? By examining this climatic confusion and contestation—how individuals and nations perceived and thought about climate—we can uncover a far older and more complex history of climate as a cultural, political, and scientific issue, one that has played a key role in debates in eras long before our own. This essay focuses on one particular moment in this much larger history: the nineteenth-century United States and its ideology of expansion, "Manifest Destiny"; its encounter with a roadblock to that expansion, the arid

West of North America, particularly a large region that came to be called the "Great American Desert"; and a contentious debate over the development of this region. This debate hinged on climate and whether humans had the capacity to overcome climatic problems like aridity through technological means or perhaps even change the climate itself.

European settlers in North America and many other places drew upon a long experience of farming, on the agricultural folk knowledge of their cultures, on old—and sometimes ancient—religious and philosophical ideas about nature, and on the newly emergent natural sciences.[2] Folk belief may seem dubious by the standards of the early twenty-first century, but it had been earned by generations of long and hard agricultural work, of learning nature through labor. When explorers or settlers tried to discern climate, they were first and foremost reading landscapes. In an era before precise measurements of rainfall, humidity, or temperature, and long before regular weather and temperature records were kept, a new landscape held many clues to a region's climate. Were trees abundant or good pasturage? Did streams and rivers seem constant? What kind of flora and fauna occupied the landscape? Did it remind them of productive agricultural landscapes they had seen or heard of in Europe? Did the climate seem healthful and free of disease? Such questions were logical and valid. Settlers lacked modern climate science and—no less importantly—long-term experience with these landscapes. In their native lands in Europe, they had possessed long histories of heat and cold; of floods, droughts, and blizzards; of average times to plant or harvest; of times of feast or famine. Native peoples, of course, knew all these as well and in some cases possessed climatic knowledge stretching back thousands of years, though settlers paid that knowledge little heed.

Manifest Destiny Encounters the Great American Desert

One key moment in the history of perceptions of climate was the Euro-American encounter in North America with the Great Plains and the arid, high-elevation terrain of the Great Basin between the Rocky Mountains and the Sierra Nevada Mountains. This encounter led to a cartographic place name that once appeared prominently on maps of the continent but has now completely disappeared: the Great American Desert. Confronted with the treeless expanse that began west of the Mississippi and Missouri Rivers and stretched across ever-higher terrain all the way to the easternmost ranges of the Rocky Mountains, with deserts continuing westward beyond the mountains, white Americans thought that they had found a barrier and roadblock to their continental ambitions. Indeed, even humid areas with abundant rainfall but limited forests were initially viewed as agriculturally useless. While settlers soon discovered that the eastern prairies—what would later become states like Illinois and Iowa—were in fact productive farmland, the high plains farther west seemed more daunting.[3]

The environmental facts—a treeless landscape—were seen through political and economic prisms. Historians and average Americans alike look back on the westward expansion of the United States across the continent in the nineteenth century and see relentless purpose, a historical "destiny" made manifest. The broad popularity of the ideology of Manifest Destiny—a belief in the spread of the U.S. political and economic system, of the English language and Protestant Christianity—might make it in retrospect seem inevitable. In the words of John L. O'Sullivan, a journalist who originated the term while pushing for the annexation of Texas and the Oregon Country, it meant "the fulfillment of our manifest destiny to overspread the continent allotted by Providence for the free development of our yearly multiplying millions."[4] The adherents of Manifest Destiny blithely assumed that everyone else in North America (namely, Native American Indians and Mexicans) would obligingly retreat, slowly fade away, or—in the darkest genocidal impulses of this mindset—be exterminated. Historians have ably unpacked this ideology, amply illuminating all its problematic racial, religious, and cultural aspects. Yet even many historians still treat it and the expansion of the

United States as inevitable. Moreover, they ignore the ecological assumptions as implicit in Manifest Destiny as its explicit racism and religious chauvinism. The entire continent itself—its climates, its soils and topography, its flora and fauna—was intended to comply with Anglo-American designs. Anything that suggested otherwise was an affront.

Across the nineteenth century, some would attempt just that, asserting that the Great American Desert was no more than a passing mirage. Either that supposed aridity was merely an illusion, or technology and irrigation would defeat it, or even more radically, humans could change an arid climate to a wet one through their own actions. Just as oil and coal industry capitalists and environmentalists and wind and solar energy developers find themselves on opposite sides of a climate divide in the early twenty-first century, politics and economic interests produced a climate divide in antebellum America. In this case, the issue was in the volatile subject of slavery and its potential expansion. Many Northerners saw the Great American Desert and the vast tracts of mountains and wilderness that lay beyond it as ample evidence that slavery would not expand, that the nation had reached its natural limits, and that what lay beyond would best be left to Indians and animals.

No less a national figure than Daniel Webster—New Englander by birth, senator from Massachusetts, and secretary of state under three presidents—railed against the prospect of a federal mail route connecting the Pacific coast to the United States, let alone future annexation:

> What do we want with this vast, worthless area? This region of savages and wild beasts, of deserts, of shifting sands and whirlwinds of dust, of cactus and prairie dogs? To what use could we ever hope to put these great deserts, or those endless mountain ranges, impenetrable, and covered to their very base with eternal snow? What can we ever hope to do with the western coast, a coast of three thousand miles, rock-bound, cheerless, uninviting, and not a harbor on it? What use have we for such

a country? Mr. President, I will never vote one cent from the public treasury to place the Pacific coast one inch nearer to Boston than it now is.[5]

Proslavery Southerners, in contrast, saw the exact opposite—the expansion of slavery as inevitable. They headed west, and as far as they were concerned, the political dominion and humid climes of the United States were destined to go with them. Such ideas would lead them into Mexican Texas and precipitate a war with Mexico. The United States defeated Mexico with relative ease, but then the climatic debate returned. In East Texas, they found a humid, warm climate, much like that of the U.S. South, and cotton production—and slavery—spread rapidly across East Texas. Overwhelming the Tejano Mexican population, Anglo settlers declared Texas an independent "Lone Star Republic" in 1836. Its subsequent annexation by the United States in 1845 triggered a war with Mexico. For Mexico, that war was catastrophic—it ultimately lost more than half of its national territory, and many twenty-first-century Mexicans still refer to the conflict not as a war, or even an invasion, but rather simply as "El Disastre."

For the victorious United States, the war seemed to be a fulfillment of everything Manifest Destiny had promised. They had defeated a weaker nation, to their eyes inherently inferior due to its Catholicism and mixed-race population. Now all that formerly Mexican land lay free for the taking. Slave owners eagerly anticipated expanding their cotton empire to the Pacific. Northerners fretted about the same outcome—the spread of slavery meant the growth of its economic power and political influence. The United States had won the war, but its union was fragile and, in gobbling up more than half of Mexico, nearly undid itself in the Civil War. Manifest Destiny became manifest disaster, and not for the last time.

That looming sectional division was rapidly manifested in differing views of climate. A survey party, commissioned to delineate the new boundary between the two nations, offered a concise example of the sectional and climatic divide. The head of the boundary commission, New Yorker John Russell Bartlett, was sacked after committing two unpardonable crimes: compromising with his Mexican counterpart on the location of the boundary and publicly stating that much of this new American territory appeared to be worthless. As he and his men trudged west from El Paso through the rugged deserts of the future states of New Mexico and Arizona, his faith in the national enterprise began to falter: "As we toiled across these sterile plains, where no tree offered its friendly shade, the sun glowing fiercely, and the wind hot from the parched earth, cracking the lips and burning the eyes, the thought would keep suggesting itself. Is this the land which we have purchased, and are to survey and keep at such a cost? As far as the eye can reach stretches one unbroken waste, barren, wild, and worthless. For fifty-two long miles we have traversed it without finding a drop of water."[6]

He was stripped of his command, and Congress refused to pay for the publishing of his journal, unlike the other surveys they had funded. His replacement, William Emory, while more attuned to the territorial aspirations of the Southern slaveholders who had pushed for war, was nonetheless likewise hard-pressed to paint an overly positive picture of the region. His best hope was that technological development—railroads—and military suppression of the Apache would render the region more amenable to development, preferably through slave agriculture.[7]

Bartlett, a New Yorker, had been undermined by other members of the boundary survey, Southerners whose suspicions of the Yankee Bartlett had been amply confirmed. They reported his actions to Southerners in Congress and thus forced his removal. This action was indicative of far deeper regional divisions—differences based in political, economic, racial, and social outlooks but also no less in climatic perceptions. Slave-owning Southerners hoped to expand their lucrative slave empire into the newly annexed Southwest, perhaps even all the way to the Pacific. They were eager to imagine that the soils and climate that had proven so salubrious in the Southeast would be found farther west as well and were in no mood to hear news to the contrary. In 1845, South Carolinian John C. Calhoun, who had served as vice president and senator, asserted that the states of the South and West occupied a single physiographic region, a "supersized" South, extending from the Atlantic coast to the Gulf coast and from the Mississippi River valley to the valley of the Rio Grande. The arid landscape of West Texas or New Mexico—at that point, still Mexican Nuevo Mexico—was transmogrified in Calhoun's wishful thinking into a place indistinguishable from that of humid and wet South Carolina.[8] False climatic assumptions like these would help lead the United States into war with Mexico. False delusions could have real consequences.[9]

In opposition to this myth of a Southern pastoral garden in the West was another idea, more grounded in fact, even if still a cultural construction in its own way. This was the belief that some portion of the West—perhaps just a narrow strip of land running north and south on the high plains just east of the Front Range of the Rocky Mountains, or perhaps a much larger area encompassing much of the West—was a "Great American Desert." Zebulon Pike's journal of his 1810 expedition cast the plains, treeless and windswept, as a desert as forbidding as the Sahara. The Stephen F. Long expedition reconfirmed this when its report was published in 1823.[10]

Aridity seemed to preclude the possibility of farming—a dire outcome for a nation where the idealized yeoman farm was sacrosanct. The claim that some significant part of the West was what Washington Irving termed the "Great American Desert" in his book *Astoria* (1835), an account of the western fur trade, seemed to throw the entire enterprise of western territorial expansion into doubt. His description certainly struck at any idea of a western "garden" ripe for easy settlement: "It is a land where no man permanently abides; for, in certain seasons of the year there is no food either for the hunter or his steed. The herbage is parched and withered; the brooks and streams are dried up; the buffalo, the elk, and the deer have wandered to distant parts, keeping within the verge of expiring verdure, and leaving behind them a vast uninhabited solitude, seamed by ravines, the beds of former torrents, but now serving only to tantalize and increase the thirst of the traveler."[11]

Irving's book popularized the term, and the "Great American Desert" would appear on maps of the West for decades to come, useless for farming and settlement. Yet Irving, like so many of his era, made more than agricultural assumptions based on aridity. A region unsuitable for farming was unsuitable for civilization and, by inference, civilized people. If anyone did ever live in this forbidding landscape, the Great American Desert might serve as the problematic birthplace of "new and mongrel races, like new formations in geology, the amalgamation of the 'debris' and 'abrasions' of former races, civilized and savage; the remains of broken and almost extinguished tribes; the descendants of wandering hunters and trappers; of fugitives from the Spanish and American frontiers; of adventurers and desperadoes of every class and country yearly ejected from the bosom of society into the wilderness."[12]

In Irving's view, the Great American Desert was more than a disappointment to prospective settlers. It was a permanent impediment to settlement and national ambitions of continental supremacy and might in the future even serve as a homeland for warlike nomads born of a hybrid English, Spanish, and Indian ancestry who would prey on more settled and "civilized" peoples. This literary impression was followed up by many eyewitness accounts and ultimately buttressed by institutional science. Federal surveys, like those led by John Charles Frémont, led to the publication of survey reports full of detail, lavishly illustrated with landscapes, flora, fauna, and maps.

In this era, maps were more than simple visual expressions of geographic information. In the early republic of the United States, they represented national ambition and the confluence of science and art. They represented both real and aspirational geography. As Jimmy L. Bryan Jr., another contributor to this volume, has noted, maps helped make the nation manifest, and mapmakers were not hesitant to present the most positive view of everything from expansionist geographies to climate and natural resources.[13] Further, geographic literacy—the ability to read and create maps and the money to collect them—was proof of social and economic status. Several of the nation's founders, including George Washington and Thomas Jefferson, took pride in their experience and abilities as land surveyors. Not for nothing were so many Americans—the rich and the striving alike—pictured with maps and globes in individual and family portraits. These maps were visual manifestations of individual and collective ambitions. Maps, in short, mattered, and citizens took them seriously.[14]

These published reports made a significant impression on eastern readers. Historians today often see them as landmarks in the scientific exploration of western North America but do not always realize that to many readers of the time, they were more like glossy real estate brochures. The reports, in fact, cost more to print than the surveys themselves cost to complete. These lavish visual representations of a current and future America helped visualize and construct an expansionist nation. That does not mean that these reports were necessarily false. Instead, it meant that many readers were only too eager for them to confirm their most optimistic imaginings about the West.[15] Climate was always perceived through lenses: lenses of economic self-interest, political ideology, or regional identity and ambitions. Inhabitants of existing regions were inventing futures for new regions. While climate served as their central preoccupation in this case, the larger phenomenon is a striking reminder of the importance of regions and regionalism as potent forces in U.S. history.

Utah's Deseret and the Question of Western Climate

Few readers were more interested than members of the Church of Jesus Christ of Latter-day Saints—known to most outsiders as Mormons—a new religious group that had attempted to settle in the Midwest but became targets of violent hostility. Looking for an escape, church leaders pored over Frémont's reports and even hung survey maps on the walls of their temple in Nauvoo, Illinois.[16] Church leaders apparently considered locations in Texas, California, and Vancouver Island but rejected all of them as *too* attractive—they would soon be inundated with settlers, and the Mormons would be hopelessly outnumbered. Instead, they began to focus on a series of valleys in the eastern Great Basin, hoping that somewhere in that vast space they could find a home that would sustain them but not attract too much attention from others.[17] It was, they imagined, a place where "good living will require hard labor," and they were right.[18] Yet mountain snowmelt fed streams and rivers that flowed through the region, converging on the Great Salt Lake, a salty sea with no outlet to the ocean.

That water, channeled into communal irrigation projects that watered the good soils of the Salt Lake Valley and surrounding valleys, led to a successful settlement, the first Anglo-American settlement to succeed and endure in this harsh region. Native Americans, such as the Pueblo Indians, and Mexican settlers in New Spain and the Mexican Southwest had long practiced irrigation, but for Anglo-Americans it was largely new. Brigham Young in particular was fascinated by this mode of agriculture and asked anyone who had returned east on the Santa Fe Trail to describe the irrigation practices of Pueblo and Hispano residents of Nuevo Mexico. Subsequent Latter-day Saint historical accounts would amplify the harshness of Utah, depicting a trackless desert tamed only by hardworking and faithful pioneers. The new Mormon Zion was not an easy place, but it was no wasteland and had advantages in addition to the reliable streams. There were forests in the mountains for timber, ample salt on the shores of the Great Salt Lake, and hot and cold springs for drinking, bathing, and "taking the waters" for health, and the high elevation, aridity, and cold winters kept diseases such as malaria at bay. It was healthier than their former settlements in the Midwest, which had been plagued by malaria. Robert Bliss, who arrived several months after the first wave of settlers, reported that "the atmosphere is pure & there has been no sickness as yet among us to speak of. . . . All are pleased with the climate."[19]

The Mormons, like other European settlers, saw "climate" as synonymous with health, or its absence. They believed that illness was spread by bad air, "miasmas" of fog, mist, or stale atmosphere. Tuberculosis and other respiratory illnesses were most often blamed on this "bad" air, but other illnesses were as well. Swamps or other places of stagnant water were viewed as public health dangers in need of draining, just as a sick person needed bleeding. While their knowledge of pathogens, bacteria, or viruses was primitive or nonexistent, their concerns were well placed—swampy water bred mosquitoes, and mosquitoes were most definitely vectors of contagion. Settlers saw clear connections between their bodies and the surrounding environment, a link that later generations would lose and are only now reconnecting, as twenty-first-century humans worry about contaminants, from heavy metals to artificial hormones, accumulating in ecosystems and in human bodies.[20]

The Mormons officially arrived in Salt Lake Valley in July 1847, and the Gold Rush and the conclusion of the U.S.-Mexico War meant that the United States arrived soon after. They accordingly began petitioning to be admitted to the union as a territory and state, a goal they would not finally achieve until 1896, after formally renouncing their practice of polygamy. The vast territory they tried to claim—essentially all of the Great Basin plus Southern California—meant that their proposal elicited little support in Washington. In fact, however, it was rejected for yet another reason as well—its proposed name, Deseret. According to Mormons, this was an ancient word for the honeybee and connoted the industry and organization that they hoped characterized their society. To eastern ears, however, "Deseret" sounded too much like "desert." The new dominions of the United States might well be arid, but calling a vast swath of them a desert was unacceptable. Though the name lingered in local usage—the Church-owned Salt Lake City newspaper is still called the *Deseret News* today—it was jettisoned in favor of another name, Utah, derived from the Ute Indians who populated the Salt Lake Valley and much of the future state in 1847.

Irrigation and Reclamation

The federal government might have vetoed Deseret, but the arid regions of the West were real enough. In response to arid climate conditions, irrigation seemed the only feasible solution. The success of the Mormon settlement was held up as proof that cooperative irrigation could be successful. While a growing chorus supported private and public irrigation schemes, there were significant divisions within the irrigation movement, or what would come to be called "Reclamation." Two individuals personified this divide: John Wesley Powell and William Ellsworth Smythe.

Powell had made a national name for himself by leading an expedition down the Colorado River, surviving the terrifying rapids in the Grand Canyon and other gorges and surveying geography that had been utterly unknown to whites. Powell later served as the chief geologist for the United States Geographical and Geological Survey of the Rocky Mountain Region and then as director of the United States Geological Survey. His reports combined Victorian travelogues and descriptions of scenery with a clear-eyed and decidedly unromantic view of the limited potential of arid western lands for settlement and agriculture.[21] The culmination of his writings was his *Report on the Lands of the Arid Region of the United States* (1879). Powell argued that the arid West called for a new government approach and a new kind of homesteading. Unlike in the East, homesteading land allocations would have to be much larger, and the government would have to plan large-scale irrigation projects: "To a great extent, the redemption of all these lands will require extensive and comprehensive plans. . . . Individual farmers, being poor men, cannot undertake the task."[22] Powell thought that the arid West, properly settled through careful planning, could be home to a small population of farmers and ranchers. Sean Harvey's chapter in this volume on the Water Treaty of 1944 discusses water infrastructure development on both sides of the border in the twentieth century and is a reminder that government-funded infrastructure did indeed prove key to development in an arid region that had always been a settlement and development problem in earlier Spanish and Mexican eras. Indeed, the United States and Mexico would cooperate on a variety of development schemes in the borderlands yet, at the same time, continue to have contentious disagreements over water. For that matter, U.S. states did and do disagree about their water allotments under the Colorado River Compact, fights that will only become

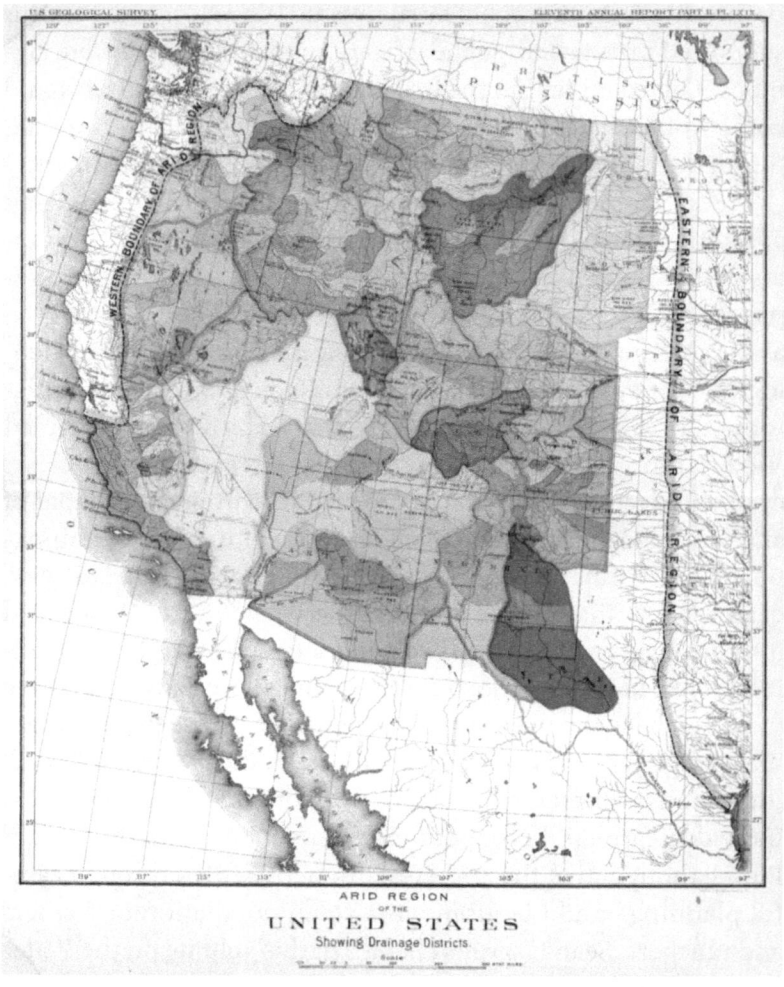

FIG. 2. Fact-based region making in the American West. John Wesley Powell, *Eleventh Annual Report of the Director of the United States Geological Survey, Part 2—Irrigation: 1889–1890* (Washington DC: U.S. Government Printing Office, 1893).

more acrimonious as the entire region becomes drier and hotter in the twenty-first century.

This modest, slow, and carefully planned realistic future did not appeal to some Americans, who thought that irrigation could be transformative—it could utterly remake the West into a place as populous and agriculturally productive as the East. A vociferous champion of this view was William E. Smythe. Smythe agreed with Powell on the importance of irrigation—he even highlighted Powell's views in his own writings. However, he saw irrigation as a deus ex machina, a wondrous solution that could transform the desert into a garden, make farms productive, and create cities as large as any in the East. His magnum opus—printed as a book and in serial or excerpted form in numerous regional and national magazines—was *The Conquest of Arid America* (1900). In it, Manifest Destiny lived on, but instead of divine providence, irrigation technology was now the force that would lead Americans to their continent-conquering destiny. For Smythe, the Mormon settlement in Utah had created one of the "real utopias of the arid West."[23] He likewise praised the growth of Southern California, which had transformed from a rural backwater in the 1870s to a booming urban and agricultural region in the early twentieth century. He toured the country extolling the virtues of irrigation, telling fervent believers that irrigation had freed them from climate. He even claimed that aridity was a virtue because it forced individualistic Americans to work together. Better yet, aridity "compels the use of irrigation. And irrigation is a miracle!"[24]

Ready to believe this miracle, Congress passed the Newlands Reclamation Act in 1902, authorizing the federal funding of dam and irrigation projects. The first project completed under the new law was the Roosevelt Dam on the Salt River in Arizona. Anglo settlers renamed the Salt River Valley the Valley of the Sun and planted lawns and eastern greenery to offset the stark landscape of the Sonoran Desert, and metropolitan Phoenix was born. By 2010, Phoenix—in the middle of one of the driest deserts on earth—had surpassed Philadelphia to become the fifth-largest city in the United States. Powell likely would have found this unsustainable and foolhardy, but his vision of the West had lost, and Smythe's had won.

Yet Powell and Smythe, despite their divergent views, both accepted that the West was indeed fundamentally arid. Their divergence concerned the degree to which irrigation could alter this condition. But what if this fact could be occluded, or even undone?

Could aridity be erased? Was the aridity of the region overstated? Some writers tried to assert that aridity was a mirage. Others would assert that it could be eliminated altogether through human action. Belief in their claims would prove one of the greatest—and most foolhardy—acts of climatic delusion in U.S. history.

Using Climate Fantasy to Fabricate Region

The person most responsible for erasing the Great American Desert—in both name and the aridity that name represented—was William Gilpin. He was both an individual and a representative for a whole type of person—the western booster who sold the lands of the West regardless of reality. Gilpin should have known better—he had traveled to the Far West with John C. Frémont's 1843 expedition, all the way to Fort Vancouver. He fought in the U.S.-Mexico War and in campaigns against the Comanches and Pawnees. During the Civil War, he served as the first territorial governor of Colorado. All that lived experience, however, would prove no impediment to his assertions about the Far West. Wallace Stegner, a twentieth-century author and environmentalist, asserted that Gilpin "looked clear over the continent of facts and into prophecy."[25]

For Gilpin, it was all simply a matter of perspective. He would use climate to invent region, explain civilization, and invent a messianic role for the United States and Anglo-Americans. Yet Gilpin did not begin by simply weaving myth out of whole cloth. His assertions did usually have some basis in fact, but from that fact, his assertions would stray ever further until his claims bordered on the nonsensical.

Gilpin merged avarice, wishful thinking, "science," religion, and Manifest Destiny into a heady mix—if the West seemed daunting to some, he would instead rhetorically refashion it into whatever form he wanted. For Gilpin, the West was first and foremost about the future, and that future was full of vast, even awesome, promise. His expansive geography also matched the acquisitive worldview of Anglo-Americans, interested in spreading their national domain as far as possible. As a region-maker—albeit one utterly divorced from reality—he was without equal. According to Gilpin, the "Plateau of the Table Lands" between the Rockies and Sierras not merely included the Great Basin but extended south to the Valley of Mexico and all the way to the Andes. This territory, he asserted, "appears to me the most interesting, the most crowded with various and attractive features, and the most certainly destined eventually to contain the most enlightened and powerful empire of the world. At present it is no more known or comprehended, *as it is*, by the American people than was America itself to the poet Homer, and is to them as much a myth as the continent of Atalanta."[26]

Gilpin asserted that the Great American Desert, not his West of milk and honey, was in fact the mirage he had come to dispel forever: "The scientific writers of our country adhere with unanimity to the dogmatic location somewhere of '*a great North American desert*'. Yet here is no desert, and none anywhere else exists. This dogmatic *mirage* has recently receded from the basin of the Salt Lake; it is about to be expelled from its last resting place, the basin of the Colorado."[27] Settlers and federal survey reports had sometimes seized on the most positive or optimistic reading of western climate. Gilpin, in a sense, heightened this by seizing on the most optimistic readings of emerging climate science, though his salesman-huckster fabulations went far beyond mere optimism or even exaggeration into a realm of climate fantasy.

Gilpin erased the reality of the high plains (and all climatic and geographic reality) with a fictional landscape of wish fulfillment, erasing all the travails ordinary Americans faced in the post–Civil War era. Good land in the East was taken, the Civil War had wreaked havoc on the economy of the South, and the nation was enduring one of a series of economic crises that lasted from the 1870s through the 1890s. Later "boosters" of climate and region—of Southern California and the Southwest in the 1880s to 1920s, for example—selling an agricultural paradise, homebuyers' Eden, and health refuge, owed something to Gilpin.[28]

Likewise, his own efforts could be read back into the past. If Gilpin served as a premonition of climate-related real estate booms, his writings also preserved the religious, political, and ideological underpinnings of Manifest Destiny by transforming them into "scientific" language and assertions. Gilpin seemed to enter a patriotic and scientific rapture when contemplating the "untransacted destiny" of the American people: "In the current of ages, mysteries become *sciences*."[29]

This "science" of climate, which Gilpin ascribed to both terrain and global temperature gradients, he also applied to assertions about race and civilization. According to Gilpin, the world's great civilizations developed in

> succession along the undulating zone of the northern hemisphere of the globe, within the isothermal belt. They form within it a continuous zodiac from east to west. These *empires* are the Chinese, the Indian, the Persian, the Grecian, the Roman, the Spanish, the British, finally, the *republican empire* of the people of North America. . . . *I repeat again the fact*, that this zone belts the globe around where the continents expand and the oceans contract: it undulates with the axis of warm temperature (52 degrees of mean heat): it contains ninety-five one-hundredths of the white people of the globe, and all its civilization![30]

Civilization had been born of climate, and its final, perfected product was the United States. For Gilpin, America's global destiny would be fulfilled by the construction of a transcontinental railway, in turn only a part of a globe-encircling "Cosmopolitan Railway" that would unite all the world's continents, commerce, and politics and make the United States the hub, the center of the world. His fantasy rested on modern technology, but what he had perhaps unwittingly created was a very old idea: climate as not long-term weather but instead geographic place.

Gilpin may have been the P. T. Barnum, even the Wizard of Oz, of western promotion, but less florid regional boosterism still incorporated similar fabrication, overselling assets and concealing dangers. By the later decades of the nineteenth century, California was

"Our Italy," the "Mediterranean Shores of America," and the most successful real estate campaign in U.S. history had begun to sell Southern California relentlessly. "Semi-Tropical Southern California" was made real by the mass planting of nonnative palm trees, fed by water from elsewhere. California's siren call was climate—climate that nurtured luxury citrus crops, that cured the ailing, and that promised white racial rejuvenation in "the first Mediterranean climate the Anglo-Saxon race has thoroughly mastered."[31]

Yet all that golden boosterism concealed something sinister, even beyond its not-so-implicit racism. California did have a more hospitable climate than most of the Great Basin or interior Southwest. But this promoted paradise was also prone to disaster. Earthquakes might have been the most infamous, but droughts and fires were threats as well. Indeed, the Golden State's climate was a changeable one prone to wild extremes, like the rains and floods of 1861 and 1862, which wiped out surviving Mexican cattle ranchos and meant that governor-elect Leland Stanford had to travel to his inauguration at the state capitol building in Sacramento by boat before relocating the entire state government to San Francisco.

"The Great American Desert" and its erasure were proof of how climatic reality was no match for ideology or economic self-interest. Yet both were products of an era when climate was a life-or-death matter. By the twentieth century, notwithstanding the Dust Bowl or the Galveston Hurricane as terrifying exceptions, climate had become more of a commodity and an aspect of daily life rather than a constant source of concern. With the Sunbelt, it became an amenity. After 1945, FHA (Federal Housing Administration) loans, federal dam projects, the interstate highway system, and especially air-conditioning changed Americans' relationship with nature. They had, it seemed, entered the age of climate control. In the largest internal migration in the nation's history, homebuyers flocked to Florida, Texas, the Southwest, and California. These places differed greatly in climate, but all offered sunshine and warm weather. For people fleeing lake-effect snow in Buffalo or Cleveland, the superficial appeal was obvious, even if the climates underneath were disparate.

The climatic promotion of California was, in key ways, a premonition of the Sunbelt. Sunbelt promotion also obscured dangers and disasters, from fires and droughts in California and the Southwest to hurricanes that killed thousands in Texas and Florida. It was not a region unified by climate, but it *was* a region unified by similar forms of urbanism, often laissez-faire economics and conservative politics, and repeated climatic disasters. Though Sunbelt boosters might still advertise the virtues of small government and suburban living, as a region it was increasingly dependent on vast government expenditures to cope with present and future climate-related disasters. By drawing so many millions to places of peril, the rise of the Sunbelt, like the growing awareness of climate change, means that climate is once again a central preoccupation for Americans. Once more climate highlights contentious ideological fault lines in the United States and may be redefining regions or perhaps even creating new ones. Regionalism has not faded as a potent force, and though Americans might have thought that they were done with climate, climate is not done with them.

Notes

1. Turner, "Significance of the Frontier in American History." This online version reflects Turner's 1893 conference address, while most printed versions are reprints of a heavily revised and expanded version from the 1920s.

2. The classic work on nature in European intellectual traditions remains Glacken's *Traces on the Rhodian Shore*.

3. Jimmy L. Bryan Jr. analyzes both pessimistic and romantic views of North American grasslands in "Our Eyes Ached with the Very Vastness."

4. John L. O'Sullivan elaborated on this view in an article titled "Annexation" in the *United States Magazine and Democratic Review*.

5. Daniel Webster quoted in Connelley, *Doniphan's Expedition*.

6. Albuquerque Museum, *Drawing the Borderline*, 37–38.

7. Greenberg, "Domesticating the Border," 83–112.

8. Smith, *Virgin Land*, 148.

9. Smith's *Virgin Land* examines Southern perceptions and dreams of the West in "The South and the Myth of the Garden," 145–54.

10. Smith, *Virgin Land*, 175–76.

11. Irving, *Astoria*, 167–68.

12. Irving, *Astoria*, 168.

13. Bryan, "Unquestionable Geographies," 593–637.
14. See Schulten, *Mapping the Nation*; Brückner, *Geographic Revolution in Early America*.
15. The classic history of these federal surveys and their place in national history is Goetzmann's *Exploration and Empire*.
16. Abbott, *How Cities Won the West*, 76.
17. Farmer, *On Zion's Mount*, 39–40.
18. Arrington, *Great Basin Kingdom*, 41.
19. Farmer, *On Zion's Mount*, 42–47 (Bliss quote, 45). Donald Worster places the history of Mormon irrigation and agriculture into a larger perspective in *Rivers of Empire*, 74–83.
20. For more on the connections between climate and health, see Valenčius, *Health of the Country*.
21. Martin Padget analyzes the mix of science and more romantic elements in Powell's writing in *Indian Country*.
22. Powell, *Report on the Lands of the Arid Region of the United States*, viii.
23. Smythe, *Conquest of Arid America*, 49.
24. Smythe, *Conquest of Arid America*, 40.
25. Stegner, *Beyond the Hundredth Meridian*, 2.
26. Gilpin, *Mission of the North American People*, 103.
27. Gilpin, *Mission of the North American People*, 49.
28. For the history of western boosterism, see Wrobel, *Promised Lands*.
29. Gilpin, *Mission of the North American People*, 124, 99.
30. Gilpin, *Mission of the North American People*, 106.
31. See chapter 1 of Culver, *Frontier of Leisure*.

Bibliography

Abbott, Carl. *How Cities Won the West: Four Centuries of Urban Change in Western North America*. Albuquerque: University of New Mexico Press, 2008.

The Albuquerque Museum. *Drawing the Borderline: Artist-Explorers of the U.S. Mexico Boundary Survey*. Albuquerque: Albuquerque Museum, 1996.

Arrington, Leonard J. *Great Basin Kingdom: An Economic History of the Latter-Day Saints, 1830–1900*. Cambridge: Harvard University Press, 1958.

Brückner, Martin. *The Geographic Revolution in Early America: Maps, Literacy, and National Identity*. Chapel Hill: University of North Carolina Press, 2006.

Bryan, Jimmy L., Jr. "Our Eyes Ached with the Very Vastness: Reimagining the Great American Desert as the Great American Prairie." *Great Plains Quarterly* 39, no. 3 (Summer 2019): 243–63.

———. "Unquestionable Geographies: The Empirical and the Romantic in U.S. Expansionist Cartography, 1810–1848." *Pacific Historical Review* 87, no. 4 (2018): 593–637.

Connelley, William E. *Doniphan's Expedition and the Conquest of New Mexico and California*. Topeka KS: published by the author, 1907.

Culver, Lawrence. *The Frontier of Leisure: Southern California and the Shaping of Modern America*. Oxford: Oxford University Press, 2012.

Farmer, Jared. *On Zion's Mount: Mormons, Indians, and the American Landscape*. Cambridge MA: Harvard University Press, 2008.

Gilpin, William. *Mission of the North American People, Geographical, Social, and Political: Illustrated by Six Charts Delineating the Physical Architecture and Thermal Laws of All the Continents*. Philadelphia: J. B. Lippincott, 1873.

Glacken, Clarence C. *Traces on the Rhodian Shore: Nature and Culture in Western Thought from Ancient Times to the End of the Eighteenth Century*. Berkeley: University of California Press, 1967.

Goetzmann, William. *Exploration and Empire: The Explorer and the Scientist in the Winning of the American West*. New York: Knopf, 1966.

Greenberg, Amy S. "Domesticating the Border: Manifest Destiny and the 'Comforts of Life' in the U.S.-Mexico Boundary Commission and Gadsden Purchase, 1848–1854." In *Land of Necessity: Consumer Culture in the United States–Mexico Borderlands*, edited by Alexis McCrossen, 83–112. Durham NC: Duke University Press, 2009.

Irving, Washington. *Astoria, or Anecdotes of an Enterprise beyond the Rocky Mountains*. New York: John B. Alden, 1883.

O'Sullivan, John L. "Annexation." *United States Magazine and Democratic Review* 17, no. 1 (July–August 1845): 5–10.

Padget, Martin. *Indian Country: Travels in the American Southwest, 1840–1935*. Albuquerque: University of New Mexico Press, 2004.

Powell, John Wesley. *Report on the Lands of the Arid Region of the United States, with a More Detailed Account of the Lands of Utah*. 2nd ed. Washington DC: Government Printing Office, 1879.

Schulten, Susan. *Mapping the Nation: History and Cartography in Nineteenth-Century America*. Chicago: University of Chicago Press, 2012.

Smith, Henry Nash. *Virgin Land: The American West as Symbol and Myth*. Cambridge MA: Harvard University Press, 1950.

Smythe, William E. *The Conquest of Arid America*. New and revised ed. New York: MacMillan, 1907.

Stegner, Wallace. *Beyond the Hundredth Meridian: John Wesley Powell and the Second Opening of the West*. Boston: Houghton Mifflin, 1954.

Turner, Frederick Jackson. "The Significance of the Frontier in American History." Presented at the American Historical Association, Chicago, 1893. https://www.historians.org/about-aha-and-membership/aha-history-and-archives/historical-archives/the-significance-of-the-frontier-in-american-history.

Valenčius, Conevery Bolton. *The Health of the Country: How American Settlers Understood Themselves and Their Land*. New York: Basic Books, 2002.

Worster, Donald. *Rivers of Empire: Water, Aridity, and the Growth of the American West*. Oxford: Oxford University Press, 1992.

Wrobel, David M. *Promised Lands: Promotion, Memory, and the Creation of the American West*. Lawrence: University Press of Kansas, 2002.

SIX

A Blueprint for the Border

The Water Treaty of 1944, the International Boundary and Water Commission, and Regional Planning in the Borderlands

SEAN PARULIAN HARVEY

"A long our long border we have no armies and no guns," intoned President Gustavo Díaz Ordaz during the groundbreaking ceremony for Amistad Dam (originally called Diablo Dam) on the Rio Grande River. "Instead of fortifications," he continued, "we are building dams . . . [and] doing common work for the good of both countries." After Díaz Ordaz finished speaking, President Lyndon Baines Johnson told the audience how "regional planning and collaboration along the border are absolutely essential." Johnson continued to use the rhetoric of cooperation and bilateralism when he spoke about additional U.S.-Mexican projects such as the construction of joint communications systems, interconnected power grids, and chemical and fertilizer plants. On this day, however, Díaz Ordaz and Johnson had met to commemorate a dam that was jointly financed by both the United States and Mexico. At first glance, such a project seems out of place amid current polemics surrounding the U.S.-Mexico boundary, but the origins of this dam lay in a treaty signed by the United States and Mexico in 1944.[1]

For some, the soaring rhetoric used by Díaz Ordaz and Johnson speaks to how these dams fulfilled a key diplomatic function between two neighboring countries. But the emphasis on "common work," "collaboration," and "regional planning" belies the more quotidian genesis of these dams. For years, farmers and residents in Mexico and the United States hoped to build works that generated electricity and prevented the Rio Grande River from overflowing its banks. Flood prevention and the development of agriculture in the Rio Grande River delta were two of the primary reasons for the passage of the Water Treaty of 1944. This treaty sought to institutionalize a form of regional planning and infrastructural development through an agreement to jointly manage the river and distribute its water.

The Water Treaty of 1944 was a dramatic reversal of how the U.S. government viewed the allocation of the Rio Grande River's waters. At the end of the nineteenth century, U.S. officials refused to honor Mexican requests for a fair share of the river's water. This stance was crafted by U.S. attorney general Judson Harmon and became known as the Harmon Opinion. Harmon's logic rested upon the fact that since Rio Grande water originated within the territorial boundaries of the United States, Mexico had no claim to the river. This unilateral claim caused much hardship among Mexican farmers, but American diplomats and farmers soon discovered that the Harmon Opinion created a precedent that allowed Mexico to claim most of the Rio Grande's water south of El Paso.

Mexican claims upon the majority of the Rio Grande's water downstream from Elephant Butte Dam forced the United States to cooperate in the management of boundary streams. Drawing upon the Harmon Opinion's logic, Mexico claimed most of the Rio Grande along Texas because Mexican aquifers recharged the river's waters along that stretch. Mexico's claim to the majority of the Rio Grande's water forced the United States to negotiate with Mexican diplomats on behalf of growers from Texas. The Water Treaty of 1944 settled this conflict by allotting a set amount of water that U.S. and Mexican consumers could draw from the Rio Grande and two other boundary streams. It also stipulated that the United States and Mexico would build two dams on the Rio Grande—Falcon and Diablo (later renamed Amistad)—to fix the watercourse in place, prevent flooding, and generate electric power. Last, the Water Treaty of 1944 created a binational agency called the International Boundary and Water Commission (IBWC). The IBWC would be responsible for overseeing the border and managing the land and river boundary lines as well as the infrastructure that marked and maintained the U.S.-Mexico divide.[2]

The final Senate vote was 76-10 in favor of the treaty, and the tally revealed no regional or party alignments. If one were to focus their scrutiny solely upon the *Congressional Record*, it seems that the Water Treaty of 1944 encountered very little opposition. As Norris Hundley wrote, the U.S. Senate voted 76 to 10 in favor of the treaty "primarily because of international considerations. . . . The overwhelming vote revealed no regional or party alignments, as the minority consisted of both Republicans and Democrats who came from such diverse states as Florida, California, Minnesota, and Montana." But outside of the Senate chambers, bureaucrats and labor unions engaged in fierce debates over the IBWC and how it undermined American sovereignty. These debates reveal that the treaty represented more than just a division of waters. Instead, the Water Treaty of 1944 suggested that the economic futures of the two countries were closely intertwined.

This essay charts how the river's unpredictability caused policymakers to reenvision the role the Rio Grande played as a boundary line. Instead of thinking of the river as a boundary between the two countries, government officials began to look at the river as the shared resource of a larger binational region. Previous scholars have argued that the United States acquired the capacity to unilaterally regulate its southern boundary as the twentieth century progressed, but the Water Treaty of 1944 demonstrates how environmental, economic, and cultural concerns made it difficult for the U.S. state to use its discretion when enforcing its boundary with Mexico.[3] In particular, this case study reveals how the U.S. federal government responded to the local concerns of Anglo, Mexican American, and Mexican farmers by adopting a policy that treated the Rio Grande River as the shared resource of a binational region.

Regions and regionalism originate in the realms of culture and discourse, but this case study explores how the prerogatives of the state can deny or affirm the boundaries of certain regions. This chapter focuses on the passage of the Water Treaty of 1944. The creation of the IBWC sheds light on how local water users influenced federal water officials and their approach to the problems of managing the Rio Grande River. This essay is interested in exploring how a set of economic and environmental circumstances allowed federal officials to imagine the Rio Grande borderlands as a region that extended into both the United States and Mexico. This case study demonstrates how government officials adopted the view of many water users in the Rio Grande River delta by using the watercourse as the centerpiece of a larger regional development plan. However, acknowledging a binational region also drew concern from labor unions, New Deal officials, and imperially minded Los Angeles boosters about how shared planning and infrastructure would transform the economic and political relationships between the two countries. The treaty would force the U.S. state to share power and authority with a neighboring country whose citizens were nonwhite, and that raised the hackles of many opponents of the treaty.

Regions and their boundaries are often contested. This case study highlights how labor leaders and bureaucrats placed the priorities of the "national economy" and "territorial sovereignty" above the environmental and economic prerogatives of local borderlands residents. Even if the U.S. state's learning curve bent toward local concerns, competing visions of political authority and the growth of a territorially bounded U.S. economy disrupted the unity of the Rio Grande borderlands as a distinct physical region connected by a river, a shared economy, and a set of racialized workers and residents.

Early Pleas for Planning in Borderlands

The United States and Mexico have a long history of binational border commissions. After the United States forcefully seized a third of Mexico's territory in the U.S.-Mexico War, the two countries commissioned binational surveys to map the new boundary between the two countries. Between 1849 and 1856 these surveyors struggled to work in harsh environments and were plagued by incompetence, cronyism, inadequate funding, and imprecise instruments. Despite these setbacks, these joint commissions produced many land and water maps and also erected stone monuments to mark the boundary line across the Desert Southwest.[4]

The water border proved to be equally tricky. The Rio Grande rises in the jagged, snow-capped peaks of the American Rockies and wends its way from the high plateau of Colorado into the hot, dry, and dusty plains of New Mexico and Texas. After descending even farther, the river gently lolls for 1,250 miles across the wide delta of the peculiarly named Rio Grande Valley until it empties into the Gulf of Mexico.[5] The river's volume was never large when compared to other major rivers, but the scarcity of Rio Grande water became a source of increasing tension between the United States and Mexico at the end of the nineteenth century. The difficulty of managing the international stream, though, stimulated calls for a binational solution to the river's problems.

A rash legal decision known as the Harmon Opinion jeopardized any possibility of cooperative planning. In the early 1890s water shortages prompted Mexican farmers to clamor for relief. The Mexican minister in Washington DC, Matías Romero Avendaño, accused American settlers in New Mexico of causing the water shortages.[6] Initially, U.S. secretary of state Walter Q. Gresham responded to Romero's claims by blaming the water shortages on drought but was unsure if this was the wisest defense. Gresham asked U.S. attorney general Judson Harmon to weigh in on the matter.

Harmon's response thoroughly denied Mexican requests to provide relief and suggested that the United States did not owe Mexican farmers any guarantees to Rio Grande water. Harmon's logic rested upon his claim that the management and distribution of natural resources were powers reserved for sovereign states. Harmon drew upon a judicial decision penned by John Marshall to bolster his argument. Borrowing from Marshall, Harmon contended that "the fundamental principle of international law is the absolute sovereignty of every nation, against all others, within its own territory." Since the river's main water source was in the United States, it was part of American territory, and another country's claim to a portion of that river's water "would be inconsistent with the sovereignty of the United States over its national domain."[7]

An observer of the debate commented that Harmon's opinion was unenforceable and would only exacerbate conflict over the Rio Grande River. Increased development along its banks would soon precipitate discord and strife among different water users, since "a large project already under construction on the Salado and ... new projects being launched on the American side" would almost surely lead to new shortages and a "bitter controversy over the use of this water."[8] As a result, many local water users preferred a binational mechanism to control and manage the waters contained within the boundary stream.

Even though Harmon's opinion argued that the United States was the only country that could regulate the Rio Grande River, Texas farmers began to pursue an international treaty to regulate the boundary stream beginning in the early 1900s. Periodic floods and droughts led some Texans to plead for the federal government's help in regularizing the river's flow. J. P. Nicholson made this sentiment clear in 1902, when he wrote to the U.S. secretary of state John Hay about a potential binational arrangement to build irrigation works and levees along the river. "The question of irrigation along the lower Rio Grande," wrote Nicholson, "has long been discussed, and the inestimable benefits of a proper system, not only to the people residing in the valley of said river but also to those of the nations on both sides, are well known." Nicholson observed that any engineering on the Rio Grande River would be impossible "without the aid of governments of both said nations" and suggested that the United States and Mexico cooperate to plan and build flood- and irrigation-works.[9]

A binational agreement that conserved and distributed the Rio Grande would also be beneficial for the economic development of local water users. A Texas irrigator named F. S. Robertson stated that an international agreement would put the Rio Grande borderlands region on a "sound basis" and "begin to attract the more conservative investors who have heretofore been inclined to await a settlement to the difficult problems of water supply."[10] Robertson also suggested that likeminded irrigators on the Mexican side of the border also sought a binational agreement because "a number of influential Mexicans of the Rio Grande country will cooperate in this undertaking."[11]

Texas water users pushed for bilateral management of the river because unilateral management failed to adequately protect border residents from the dangers of flooding. After disastrous floods in 1916, 1917, 1919, and 1922, residents of the lower Rio Grande Valley built levees to curtail future river overflows. Aware that flood management on one side of the river would be inadequate, landowners from Texas called upon the U.S. Department of State to convince Mexico to build a similar set of works on their side of the river. This plea, though, failed to produce any results. In 1932 a disastrous flood spilled over American embankments and further demonstrated how Mexican cooperation was necessary to hold back the waters of the Rio Grande.[12]

A bilateral study commissioned by the United States and Mexico concluded that both countries should jointly build several storage and diversion dams. After the 1932 flood, the United States and Mexico convened a joint panel known as the International Water Commission (IWC) to generate recommendations on how to manage the river. The head of the IWC, Elwood Mead, recommended that both countries cooperate to build a series of storage dams on the river. Mead suggested that binational dams were necessary to "provide flood control facilities unattainable . . . by either nation acting alone." But cooperation would prove to be untenable throughout the 1930s because the U.S. Bureau of Reclamation was tied up with large dam-building projects across the U.S. West.[13]

Adding to the unlikelihood of U.S.-Mexican cooperation on Rio Grande river management was the fact that the Mexican government used the Harmon Opinion as the justification for claiming most the Rio Grande River's water south of El Paso. Most of the acre-footage south of Elephant Butte Dam originated in Mexico. By using Harmon's logic, Mexico was able to claim the Rio Grande south of El Paso as a Mexican river because Mexican aquifers recharged the river. This allowed Mexico City bureaucrats and engineers to begin plans for the construction of unilateral waterworks on their side of the border. Fearful that Mexican irrigation infrastructure could deprive them of their water, growers in Texas pressured the United States to negotiate with Mexico in 1941. After three years of deliberations, both countries approved the International Water Commission's recommendations from the 1930s and began the process of ratifying the subsequent treaty that resulted.[14]

Initially, officials in the U.S. water bureaucracy supported the treaty and its terms because hydroengineering on the Rio Grande River would be economically beneficial for the region. H. H. Bashore, the commissioner for the Bureau of Reclamation (BOR), stated how the treaty created opportunities for economic development and modernization in both the United States and Mexico. The BOR commissioner described how the "majority of the [Rio Grande] water runs off into the Gulf of Mexico" because the river lacked structures that could store the water. Bashore suggested that the residents of the Rio Grande borderlands would benefit if farmers and businesspeople used this water for industrial and consumptive uses. Dams needed to be built on the Rio Grande, according to Bashore, because "hydroelectric power is needed for development."[15] Dams emerged as the primary goal among water users, Bureau of Reclamation officials, and engineers in the International Water Commission and International Boundary Commission. It is no coincidence that so many engineering and water officials touted river engineering as a solution to problems of flooding. The faith in dam building that we see during the 1930s and 1940s is part of a larger constellation of ideas about the environment that circulated among agricultural and economic administrators during the time.

Conservation, Hydroengineering, and the Mexican Claim

Environmental and economic planning that used dams as the key impetus for development were common in both the United States and Mexico during the 1930s and 1940s. The emphasis on dam building is an example of what one historian has called the "New Conservation." Agrarian reformers who took inspiration from the "New Conservation" sought "to rebuild rural life and to raise rural incomes with measures tied directly to conservation objectives," such as "flood control ... and cheap hydropower for farms and new industries."[16] Washington bureaucrats largely swept aside their suggestions during the 1920s, but the New Deal proved to be an excellent vehicle for the types of reforms that agricultural economists and farmers had proposed during the farm depression that followed World War I.

During the 1930s, the federal government began to build a host of dams and other waterworks across the country. Projects like Boulder Canyon Dam (later renamed Hoover Dam) have long captured our attention as feats of engineering and public relief projects. But Boulder Canyon, the Tennessee River Authority, Mississippi River flood control, and the Bonneville Power Administration also represented investments in public infrastructure for future economic planning.[17]

These massive edifices were the key to what Roosevelt called his "Seven Regions Plan." The Tennessee Valley Authority (TVA) served as the primary model for these regional development schemes because of its successful implementation of a series of initiatives that began with hydropower dams. Roosevelt intended the TVA to be the model for regional development schemes all over the country. He suggested that TVA-style plans be implemented in California's Central Valley, the Arkansas River Valley, and the Missouri River Valley. FDR's court packing scheme, however, depleted his political capital in Congress and consigned his "Seven Regions Plan" to the dustbin.[18]

Even though many of the official regional planning commissions failed to materialize, this type of work continued unofficially in many parts of the country. The Grand Coulee and other dams in the Pacific Northwest served as the anchors for less centralized regional development schemes that promoted aerospace manufacturing and other energy-intensive industries. To be sure, FDR had grand ideas for river engineering and economic development in the United States, but these plans also mirrored similar designs in Mexico.

Under Lázaro Cárdenas, Mexico embarked on a similar project of industrial and agricultural reform. Much like Roosevelt,

Cárdenas placed the farmer's underdeveloped purchasing power at the heart of the economic downturn.[19] In order to modernize the economy and equalize the amount of capital that flowed between the countryside and the metropole, Cárdenas undertook a reform program that looked very similar to the goals of the New Conservationists in the United States. New dams rose up all over the country. Both the United States and Mexico recognized how rivers and their latent energy were key to the modernization of both countries.[20] The Water Treaty of 1944 should be seen as an extension of the dam-building impulse that we saw in the United States and Mexico during the 1930s.

Discussion of the Water Treaty of 1944 and the Rio Grande River revealed that many bureaucrats thought that the shared management of the watercourse was critical for the safety and economy of the communities in the Rio Grande borderlands. Even though the Water Treaty of 1944's terms fell far short of the model set by the TVA, it may be worthwhile to consider how the IBWC and its hydroengineering on the Rio Grande River fit the template set forth by regional development plans that centered the development of hydropower. By agreeing to share the financial costs of the dam as well as the water and energy that would result, the IBWC was providing a template for a type of regional planning centered on the Rio Grande River. But this vision for shared resource planning rankled many water users who thought that such an agreement weakened the power of the U.S. state.

Troubling National Sovereignty

Previous studies of the 1944 Water Treaty ultimately argue that World War II motivated people to support or oppose the treaty. But if one looks at the debates outside of the Senate, it becomes clear that support or opposition to the treaty did not hinge solely upon a commitment to Roosevelt's Good Neighbor policy. Instead, it seems much more evident that antagonism to the Water Treaty of 1944 represented opposition to the idea of regional planning for the Rio Grande River and its Mexican and American water users. Senate support for the treaty broke along the lines of those who supported more economic integration with Mexico and those who thought that such integration may hamper the growth and development of the U.S. Southwest.[21]

On one side of the debate stood Southern California. The Metropolitan Water District of Southern California emerged as one of the treaty's staunchest opponents and critics. Instead of touting the treaty as an accord between two partners, Los Angeles water users undermined the validity of the treaty by sowing doubts about Mexico's ability to use Rio Grande water for agriculture. Water authorities across Southern California claimed the treaty would line the pockets of a few great landholders at the expense of Mexican freeholders and American farmers, workers, and city dwellers.[22]

As an "imperial metropolis" with a long history of seizing the natural resources of Mexico to fuel its economic growth, the city of Los Angeles had a lot to lose if the treaty passed. Since Mexico had staked a strong claim to the majority of Rio Grande River waters, Mexican negotiators offered to exchange Rio Grande water for a fair allotment of Colorado River acre-footage. Since the Colorado River provided much of Los Angeles's electricity through the Boulder Canyon Dam (later renamed the Hoover Dam), the treaty threatened to sap the energy required for the city's residential and industrial growth.[23]

The Water Treaty of 1944 also threatened to topple the racist hierarchies that placed Los Angeles's interests above Mexican priorities. Since the mid-nineteenth century, Los Angeles boosters and industrialists thought that the economic interests that extended from Los Angeles into Mexican oil fields and mines should remain "dominated by whites." Putting Mexican interests on an equal footing upended the racial dynamics that characterized the relationship between the United States and Mexico.[24] In a similar vein, Harold Ickes's protests of the treaty also revealed anxiety over how the treaty could transform the economic and political relationships between the United States and Mexico.

On one level, Ickes opposed the Water Treaty of 1944 in order to defend his bureaucratic turf. As head of the Department of the Interior, Ickes oversaw some of the most important recovery and development functions of the New Deal. Over the course of the 1930s, the feisty and irascible Ickes turned the Department of the Interior into the New Deal's premier agency by centralizing a host of different initiatives intended to modernize and balance the consumptive power of Americans in rural and urban settings. Ickes oversaw the creation or expansion of government initiatives like the Works Progress Administration, Civilian Conservation Corps, and Bureau of Reclamation. Ickes contended, however, that the treaty's creation of the International Boundary and Water Commission unnecessarily duplicated the functions of different agencies housed in the Department of the Interior, such as the BOR. But Ickes's fears over the Water Treaty of 1944 and the IBWC extended beyond bureaucratic infighting and revealed anxiety over state power and sovereignty.

Ickes predicted that sharing the Rio Grande's waters would hamper the U.S. government's ability to direct the economic development and growth of the U.S. Southwest. During the 1930s, New Dealers and New Conservationists such as Ickes remade the federal government into the primary engine for producing and sustaining economic growth. According to one historian, "New Dealers . . . sought to create long-term markets by building infrastructure in undeveloped regions of America."[25] Projects like dams led to increased investment in infrastructure and employed people. As a result, New Deal planners saw dams as a way to overcome the economic conditions that led to the Great Depression. The Water Treaty of 1944, however, put this economic panacea in peril.

For Ickes and other treaty opponents, the Water Treaty of 1944 threatened to undermine and weaken the sovereignty of the American nation-state. According to Charles Maier, the twentieth century was the apogee for the shibboleth of national "territoriality." In previous centuries, governments were only concerned with how their authority and power were projected toward other sovereigns, but the middle of the twentieth century witnessed a transformation in the ways that governors understood sovereignty. Instead of facing outward, twentieth-century governments turned inward and sought "bounded geographical space" as a "basis for material resources, political power, and common allegiance." The idea that territory provided a canvas where a sovereign state could control people and things took on added significance in light of the depressed economies of the 1930s. Economic recovery and modernization schemes—such as the New Deal—sought to wring every ounce of efficiency and economic productivity out of marginal soils and undammed rivers. As Maier explained, a sovereign state no longer construed "territory as a passive enclosure to be policed and kept orderly" but was instead "a source of resources, livelihood, output, and energy." Directing the nation's storehouse of resources for economic production proved to be one of the primary characteristics of an independent state.[26]

The Rio Grande borderlands and their promise for a regionally based development plan that spanned the international divide threatened the hyperterritorial economic ambitions of Ickes's New Deal state. The central state's claim to authority was its ability to manage the nation's inventory of physical assets so that they could be used as inputs for the industries contained within the national economy. By offering to share these resources with a neighboring state, the United States was hobbling its economic growth and undermining its claim to sovereignty over its territory and economy. Much like in the case of Hawai'i, which Sarah Miller-Davenport explores in another chapter in this volume, the Rio Grande borderlands troubled ideas of American sovereignty by mixing American territory and institutions with the so-called foreign elements of a majority nonwhite population.

This perceived assault on the sovereignty of the United States and the agency primarily responsible for the management of its resources and territory led the persnickety Ickes to point out the treaty's sour terms for the United States. Ickes highlighted how the treaty hampered the country's future economic potential. "This treaty deals," said Ickes, "in the natural resources of the United States, with what we must conservatively use in order to produce." The treaty's recognition that natural resources should be shared across the international divide called into question the solidity of the country's physical, political, and economic borders.

Much like Ickes sought to preserve the bureaucratic turf of his department, he also sought to preserve the sovereign turf of the administration's economy and territory.[27]

The American Federation of Labor (AFL) also assailed the IBWC and the Water Treaty of 1944 in staunch nationalist and protectionist terms. The AFL argued that the treaty halted development in the U.S. Southwest and threatened to put American laborers out of work. Additionally, the AFL complained that the IBWC was granted far too much power to manage the construction of the Rio Grande River's dams. Specifically, the lack of congressional oversight gave the IBWC the power to allow the "free passage of cheap Mexican labor in to [sic] the U.S. for the construction of such works along boundary sections without any immigration restrictions, passports, or labor requirements." All of these benefits granted to Mexican laborers, the AFL pointed out, did not include American workers, who were shut out of these construction jobs.[28] The AFL was adamant that "the United States gains nothing by the proposed guarantee to Mexico."[29]

The enforcement of a solid border between the United States and Mexico became a preoccupation of labor unions amid growing controversy over the movement of Mexican contract and undocumented workers into the United States. Both Anglo and Mexican American workers resented the influx of Mexican nationals during the 1940s.[30] The Water Treaty of 1944 represented another avenue for Mexican nationals to make inroads into the American economy the enticements of southwestern growers and farmers. Even if many Mexican Americans thought that the IBWC and its dams would be helpful in preventing floods and generating electricity, they also thought that the hydraulic infrastructure called for in the treaty benefited large growers by further intermingling the economies of the United States and Mexico.

The IBWC, however, allowed for more surveillance and control of the border than many workers anticipated. The infrastructure on the river allowed the United States to more effectively monitor the boundary line to prevent the entry of unsanctioned Mexican nationals into the United States. For example, concrete channels alongside the managed river made it easier for Border Patrol agents to identify and apprehend unsanctioned border crossers because there was no brush or terrain to hide migrants. Even if many border residents benefited from the dams, the electricity and irrigation promised by the IBWC and the treaty reinforced the power of Anglo growers on the U.S. side of the river.

The Low Modernism of the IBWC

Though the Senate overwhelmingly approved the treaty and the IBWC in 1944, questions about the agency remained. Congressional budget analysts and reclamation officials continuously suggested that the Bureau of Reclamation should take over the IBWC's functions. But diplomats, local citizens, and congressional allies defended the agency and its mission to control flooding and generate hydropower.

As the junior senator from Texas, Lyndon Baines Johnson became a staunch supporter of the bilateral management of the Rio Grande River. Once Johnson assumed office in 1949, he corresponded regularly with his constituents in the Rio Grande border counties, who told him how the dams called for in the treaty were necessary for flood control. Local businessmen and farmers implored him to support the dam to help build agriculture and local industry. A water user from Edinburg, Texas, thought that the IBWC could help the region prosper because it kept both Mexican and U.S. interests in mind.[31] Johnson was also deeply moved by a series of letters from schoolchildren that described how the dam would protect their towns from flooding. These children, who lived in both Eagle Pass, Texas, and Piedras Negras, Coahuila, implored Johnson to support the IBWC because the people of both border cities "suffered very much in the last flood of 1954."[32] Johnson became convinced that the Rio Grande River and its dams needed to be managed by both countries in order to successfully protect residents from flooding but also to develop the region's economy. His support of the IBWC and its work would continue, and as president he would preside over the groundbreaking for one of these dams alongside his Mexican counterpart. Support for the regional development of the Rio Grande borderlands both preceded and continued long after Roosevelt's Good Neighbor policy made it prudent for the Senate to ratify the Water Treaty of 1944.

Though it fell far short of a comprehensive development blueprint for the region, like the TVA, the Water Treaty of 1944 did cement some goals for local water users. As far back as 1902, residents clamored for binational management of the river to aid the development of the region. The state did not just "see" the river as a naturalized boundary between the two countries but instead "learned" how to envision it as part of a larger binational region.[33] The Water Treaty of 1944 represents the state recognizing those aims and intentions. Even though the AFL claimed that the "U.S. gains nothing from the proposed treaty," local water users firmly contended that their lives and livelihoods were improved by recognizing the shared opportunities that arose from a bilateral scheme to manage the Rio Grande River, which was at the heart of their imagined geography of the Rio Grande borderlands.[34]

At the same time that the river emphasized the similarities between Mexico and the United States, it also heightened the difference. The line that joined the economic and physical space of these countries, though, also magnified the perceived separation between the United States and Mexico. Even though the Water Treaty of 1944 may have joined the territories of both countries and abstracted physical and economic space, the canals and dams built along the river made the movement of Mexican workers and migrants within the region much more visible and fraught.

Notes

1. "Johnson and Díaz Ordaz See Amistad Dam Being Built across the Rio Grande," *New York Times*, December 4, 1966.

2. Hundley, *Dividing the Waters*, 23, 131–35. Diablo Dam would later be renamed Amistad.

3. Adelman and Aron, "From Borderlands to Border," 814–41. For recent works that emphasize the cooperation between the U.S. and Mexican states, see Hernández, *Migra!*; and Cadava, *Standing on Common Ground*.

4. Alvarez, *Border Land, Border Water*, 17; Mueller, *Restless River*, 27, 43; St. John, *Line in the Sand*, 24–38.

5. Phillips, *Reining in the Rio Grande*, 1–11; Mueller, *Restless River*, 1–15; Horgan *Great River*, 1–7.

6. Hundley, *Dividing the Waters*, 21–22; Sandos, "International Water Control," 492.

7. Hundley, *Dividing the Waters*, 25.

8. "Mexico Acts to Divide Border Rivers Waters," *Delta Irrigation News* (McAllen, Texas), July 20, 1927, box 7.222, hereafter NARAFW.

9. J. O. Nicholson to John Hay, March 5, 1902, box 7.222, NARAFW; Hundley, *Dividing the Waters*, 31.

10. "Mexico Acts to Divide Border Rivers Waters," *Delta Irrigation News* (McAllen, Texas), July 20, 1927, box 7.222, NARAFW.

11. F. S. Robertson to Elwood Mead, November 30, 1928, box 7.222, NARAFW.

12. Timm, *International Boundary Commission*, 216.

13. F. S. Robertson to Elwood Mead, November 30, 1928, box 7.222, NARAFW; Hundley, *Dividing the Waters*, 31–45; Walsh, *Building the Borderlands*, 45, 57–64, 95, 102.

14. W. E. Anderson to Elwood Mead, December 17, 1928, box 7.222, NARAFW; Walsh, *Building the Borderlands*, 45, 57–64, 95, 102.

15. "Statement by H. H. Bashore at Hearings of Mexican Treaty," n.d., folder 032.5, box 70, NARADB.

16. Phillips, *This Land, This Nation*, 2.

17. Pisani, *Water and American Government*, 220–21, 227–32; White, *Organic Machine*, 60; and Smith, *Building New Deal Liberalism*, 1–5, 19–20.

18. Ekbladh, *Great American Mission*, 48–49; Schwarz, *New Dealers*, 236; and Kennedy, *Freedom from Fear*, 340, 344.

19. Dwyer, *Agrarian Dispute*, 168–71; Olsson, *Agrarian Crossings*, 41, 53, 56; Hundley, *Dividing the Waters*, 75–76.

20. Dwyer, *Agrarian Dispute*, 170.

21. "Opposition to Mexican Water Treaty Grows as Senate Hearings Are Started," n.d., *Colorado River Aqueduct News* (Metropolitan Water District of Southern California, Los Angeles), folder 032.5, box 70, NARADB; "Six States Agree but California Objects," *Chieftain* (Pueblo CO), December 15, 1944, folder 032.5, box 70, NARADB.

22. Department of Water and Power of the City of Los Angeles to Franklin Roosevelt, January 13, 1945, folder 032.5, box 70, NARADB.

23. Kim, *Imperial Metropolis*.

24. Kim, *Imperial Metropolis*, 1–3, 13.

25. Schwarz, *New Dealers*, 236.

26. Maier, "Consigning the Twentieth Century to History," 818.

27. Harold Ickes to Franklin Delano Roosevelt, March 18, 1944, folder 032.5, box 70, NARADB.

28. "A F of L in National Convention Finds Mexican Treaty to be Grave Threat to Labor," n.d., folder 032.5, box 70, NARADB.

29. *Colorado River Aqueduct News* (Metropolitan Water District of Southern California, Los Angeles), November 30, 1944, folder 032.5, box 70, NARADB; "A F of L in National Convention Finds Mexican Treaty to be Grave Threat to Labor," folder 032.5, box 70, NARADB.

30. Blanton, "Citizenship Sacrifice," 299–320.

31. "Water Group Opposes Rider on Dam Funds," *Valley Morning Star*, May 30, 1946; "Bureau Airs Stand on Water Bill," *Valley Evening Monitor*, May 14, 1946; "Valley Water Association Opposed Reclamation Bureau," *Valley Evening Monitor*, May 14, 1946.

32. Lyle S. Almond to Lyndon Baines Johnson, July 5, 1960, folder 1960, box 807, LBJ; E. S. Wouillard to Lyndon Baines Johnson, June 29, 1960, folder 1960, box 807, LBJ; J. E. Sturrock to Lyndon Baines Johnson, July 1, 1960, folder 1960, box 807, LBJ; Yolanda Jamàs to Lyndon Baines Johnson, March 8, 1960, folder 1960, box 807, LBJ; Susanna Oviedo to Lyndon Baines Johnson, March 8, 1960, folder 1960, box 807, LBJ.

33. For more on "learning like a state" versus "seeing like a state," see Rome, "What Really Matters in History," 303–18; and Scott, *Seeing like a State*, 1–6.

34. "A F of L in National Convention Finds Mexican Treaty to be Grave Threat to Labor," folder 032.5, box 70, NARADB.

Bibliography

Adelman, Jeremy, and Stephen Aron. "From Borderlands to Border: Empires, Nation-States, and the Peoples in between in North American History." *American Historical Review* 104, no. 3 (June 1999): 814–41.

Alvarez, C. J. *Border Land, Border Water: A History of Construction on the U.S.-Mexico Divide*. Austin: University of Texas Press, 2019.

Blanton, Carlos Kevin. "The Citizenship Sacrifice: Mexican Americans, the Saunders-Leonard Report, and the Politics of Immigration, 1951–1952." *Western Historical Quarterly* 4, no. 3 (Autumn 2009): 299–320.

Cadava, Geraldo L. *Standing on Common Ground: The Making of a Sunbelt Borderland*. Cambridge MA: Harvard University Press, 2013.

Dwyer, John W. *The Agrarian Dispute: The Expropriation of American-Owned Rural Land in Postrevolutionary Mexico*. Durham NC: Duke University Press, 2008.

Ekbladh, David. *The Great American Mission: Modernization and the Construction of an American World Order*. Princeton NJ: Princeton University Press, 2010.

Hernández, Kelly Lytle. *Migra! A History of the U.S. Border Patrol*. Berkeley: University of California Press, 2010.

Horgan, Paul. *Great River: The Rio Grande in North American History*. Vol. 1, *Indians and New Spain*. New York: Rinehart, 1954.

Hundley, Norris, Jr. *Dividing the Waters: A Century of Controversy between the United States and Mexico*. Berkeley: University of California Press, 1966.

Kennedy, David. *Freedom from Fear: The American People in Depression and War, 1929–1945*. New York: Oxford University Press, 1999.

Kim, Jessica. *Imperial Metropolis: Los Angeles, Mexico, and the Borderlands of American Empire*. Chapel Hill: University of North Carolina Press, 2019.

LBJ. Lyndon Baines Johnson Senate Papers, 1949–1961. Lyndon Baines Johnson Presidential Library and Museum, Austin TX.

Maier, Charles. "Consigning the Twentieth Century to History: Alternative Narratives for the Modern Era." *American Historical Review* 15, no. 3 (June 2000): 807–31.

Mueller, Jerry E. *Restless River: International Law and the Behavior of the Rio Grande*. El Paso: Texas Western, 1975.

NARADB. Bureau of Reclamation Files, RG 115, National Archives and Records Administration, Denver.

NARAFW. Records of the International Boundary and Water Commission, RG 76, National Archives and Records Administration, Fort Worth TX.

Olsson, Torre. *Agrarian Crossings: Reformers and the Remaking of the U.S. and Mexican Countryside*. Princeton NJ: Princeton University Press, 2017.

Phillips, Fred M., G. Emlen Hall, and Mary E. Black. *Reining in the Rio Grande, People, Land, Water*. Albuquerque: University of New Mexico Press, 2011.

Phillips, Sarah T. *This Land, This Nation: Conservation, Rural America, and the New Deal*. Cambridge: Cambridge University Press, 2007.

Pisani, Donald. *Water and American Government: The Reclamation Bureau, National Water Policy, and the West, 1902–1935*. Berkeley: University of California Press, 2002.

Rome, Adam. "What Really Matters in History: Environmental Perspectives on Modern America." *Environmental History* 7 (April 2002): 303–18.

Sandos, James A. "International Water Control in the Lower Rio Grande Basin 1900–1920." *Agricultural History* 54, no. 4 (October 1980): 490–501.

Schwarz, Jordan. *New Dealers: Power Politics in the Age of Roosevelt*. New York: Knopf, 1994.

Scott, James C. *Seeing like a State: How Certain Schemes to Improve the Human Condition Have Failed*. New Haven CT: Yale University Press, 1998.

Smith, Jason Scott. *Building New Deal Liberalism: The Political Economy of Public Works, 1933–1956*. Cambridge: Cambridge University Press, 2009.

St. John, Rachel. *Line in the Sand: A History of the Western U.S.-Mexico Border*. Princeton NJ: Princeton University Press, 2011.

Timm, Charles August. *The International Boundary Commission, United States and Mexico*. Austin: University of Texas Press, 1941.

Walsh, Casey. *Building the Borderlands: A Transnational History of Irrigated Cotton along the Mexico-Texas Border*. College Station: Texas A&M University Press, 2008.

White, Richard. *The Organic Machine: The Remaking of the Columbia River*. New York: Hill and Wang, 1995.

SEVEN

The Formation of Midwestern Regional Identity
JON K. LAUCK

While World War II was raging, a group of scholars in the Midwest gathered together to think about their region. English professor Howard Troyer, the chairman of the Committee on Faculty Lectures at Lawrence College in Appleton, Wisconsin, assembled an impressive roster of thinkers to come to campus and opine about the Midwest. By the time of the war, Troyer could assert without equivocation or doubt that various American regions had taken root: the Deep South, the Desert Southwest, the Far West of California, the Pacific Northwest, New England, the Eastern Atlantic states, and the Midwest.[1] At the same time as the Wisconsin conference, another prominent historian could confidently say that the people of the "region are conscious of an identity of interests, and of a common outlook upon life, which give to the Old Northwest an individuality as distinct as that possessed by the people of New England, or of the Old South."[2] During the war, when the governor of Iowa was organizing a regional meeting related to economic planning, he invited representatives from the twelve states that were widely thought of as constituting the Midwest.[3] While diminished somewhat since the World War II era by faster communications, mass culture, the global economy, the internet, and other various cosmopolitanisms, Troyer's regional designations still persist and are meaningful sources of identity. The origins of regional consciousness and the emergence of the Midwest as an obvious and identifiable region can be found in the early nineteenth century in the decades after the adoption of the Northwest Ordinance. Crucial steps in the formation of the region include an early North/South split between the western lands on either side of the Ohio River and the subsequent social and political frictions between these regions, the hardening of regional lines during the Civil War era, and the blossoming of various modes of midwestern regional culture and thought premised on a separation from the East. This essay first explores the political conflicts that led to a profound divergence between the Midwest and the South during the first half of the nineteenth century and then outlines the growth of forms of cultural regionalism that cemented Midwest identity in the second half of the century.

From the beginning of the republic, people began to see and talk about the Midwest as a place that was unique and separate. The Northwest Ordinance of 1787 was passed to govern the area north of the Ohio River, and the Southwest Ordinance of 1790 specifically set forth that it was to govern the area south of the river. When Ohioans wrote their first constitution in 1802, they demarcated the beginnings of the Midwest by declaring their state's legitimacy based on the congressional enabling act governing the area "northwest of the river Ohio." When de Tocqueville descended the river, he noted how the Kentucky side was sparsely populated by idle people and its environs were slave-oriented, while the Ohio side was humming with activity and was where "man appears to be in the enjoyment of that wealth and contentment which is the reward of labor."[4] The Midwest also separated from the East. From the time of the colonial era, there were frictions between the more populated and more powerful coastal regions and the "Backcountry."[5] From the "beginning East and West have shown a sectional attitude," said Frederick Jackson Turner, and the "interior of the colonies on the Atlantic was disrespectful of the coast, and the coast looked down upon the upland folk."[6] The sense of marginality in the Backcountry and the fear of being dominated by eastern capital, culture, and political power would persist and grow throughout the nineteenth century and after.

During the first half of the nineteenth century, the starkest regional divergence existed between the Midwest and the South.

The historian Eric Foner explains that the "whole mentality and flavor of southern life . . . seemed antithetical to the North. Instead of progress, the South represented decadence, instead of enterprise, laziness. . . . To those with visions of a steadily growing nation, slavery was an intolerable hindrance to national achievement."[7] In contrast to the vigorous, democratic, and entrepreneurial Midwest, one Wisconsinite, in a typical formulation, saw Southerners as a "set of cowards, full of gasconade, and bad liquor, brought up to abuse negroes and despise the north, too lazy to work; they are not above living on the unrewarded labor of others."[8] In contrast to the Midwest, said one Ohio congressman, the South "builds up no middle class of intelligent farmers, artisans, and mechanics, who constitute the real strength, who make the real wealth, and are justly the pride and glory of the free states."[9] Four million slaves were held in bondage in the South by the time of the Civil War, while the Northwest Ordinance had banned slavery in the Midwest.

Slavery existed at the top of a list of differences that divided the regions into separate cultural spheres. In the South, the Cavalier culture stemming from the region's first immigrants prevailed. The aristocratic pro–Crown and Church of England immigrants of the early Southern colonies contrasted with the more varied culture of the Midwest, made up of anti-Crown dissidents such as the Puritans, the Quakers of Pennsylvania, and upland nonslaveholding Scotch-Irish Southerners.[10] The Southern culture of honor, dueling, militarism, and violence contrasted with the more democratic and entrepreneurial Midwest.[11] One Georgia editor said he was "sickened" by the "free society" of the Midwest and its "conglomeration of greasy mechanics, filthy operatives, small-fisted farmers, and moon-struck theorists" who were "hardly fit for association with a southern gentlemen's body servant."[12] The South was hierarchical and rural, and the "planter ideal stressed values and practices that were frankly old world and sometimes even feudal in origin and tone" and even included "medieval joustings."[13] Self-improvement, uplift, and literacy, meanwhile, were prized in the Midwest and the South's medieval fantasies dismissed. The reform movements and improvement plans of the Midwest "aroused both contempt and fear in the South," in part because abolitionism was fused into them but also because the South remained generally suspicious of "progress" and wedded to reaction.[14] The distinction could be seen in the realm of education. By 1870, nearly 80 percent of midwestern children attended school, while 29 percent of Southern kids did.[15] Regional tensions shaped education policy, since many Southerners associated common schools with meddling reformers and hostile abolitionists.[16]

Given these deep regional differences, sectional frictions steadily mounted throughout the first half of the nineteenth century and manifested themselves in political battles and, finally, in a shooting war. In 1820 the particular issue at hand was the future of Missouri. Tensions were momentarily halted by the Missouri Compromise, which banned the institution of slavery anywhere north of Missouri's southern boundary.[17] This decision contributed to a growing North-South divide by holding slavery below a certain geographic line. Regional tensions were also caused by tariffs, which were favored by midwestern congressmen and commercial interests and bitterly opposed by Southern cotton planters, who wanted more open trade to sell their fiber to Europe. South Carolina leaders denounced the "Tariff of Abominations" and threatened to "nullify" federal tariff laws during the early 1830s. The latter half of the decade also saw a rapid increase in the amount of abolitionist activity, much of it springing from places such as Oberlin College and Lane Theological Seminary in Ohio; Galesburg, Illinois ("the chief city of the Abolitionists in Illinois," according to a St. Louis newspaper); midwestern Quaker enclaves; and various evangelical churches and colleges around the Midwest that embraced the antislavery cause.[18] The annexation of Texas and the war with Mexico during the 1840s were spurred on by Southerners seeking more lands below the Missouri Compromise line, which might allow the extension of slavery and greater slave-state influence in Washington. Midwestern congressmen such as Abraham Lincoln, on the other hand, opposed the war in Mexico because it would strengthen the slave power.[19] The Wilmot Proviso, which antislavery legislators tried to attach to Mexican War legislation, sought to block the extension of slavery to new territories and did so by using the exact same Northwest Ordinance language that banned slavery. (During the famed Webster-Hayne debates of the 1830s, Webster also invoked the Ordinance's ban on slavery.)[20]

The regions diverged beyond the particular issue of slavery. While large plantations dominated Southern agriculture, and cotton was increasingly king during the antebellum era, in the Midwest yeoman farming was the rule, and diversified farms were the norm as midwestern agriculture expanded westward. Midwestern farms mixed wheat, corn, cattle, pigs, chickens, dairy, gardens, orchards, and a variety of economic pursuits. While the planter class dominated politics, and millions of people were excluded from the political process in the South, the ideology of the common man prevailed in midwestern politics, and suffrage rights expanded throughout the nineteenth century. The Midwest, already home to a mix of peoples from various regions, also became home, starting in the 1840s, to a rich mix of new immigrants from Ireland, Germany, Scandinavia, and other places, while the South remained largely unaffected by immigration, and its existing English/Scotch-Irish ethnic patterns prevailed. Education levels were much higher in the Midwest and colleges more widespread. The Midwest also remained home to a wider mix of religions than the South.[21] In a sign of midwestern openness and theological diversity, many utopian societies were also founded in the Midwest, while they largely avoided the South (only two of the over one hundred utopian communities established by reformers were located in the South).[22] During the 1840s, in a harbinger of what was to come, the religions that did transcend region began to divide over slavery, leading to the creation of Southern Baptists, Southern Methodists, a southern wing of Presbyterians, and other sectional religious entities.[23]

The Midwest-South rupture finally came in the 1850s. Perhaps most explosive was the adoption of the Fugitive Slave Act as part of the Missouri Compromise. Such laws, passed along "strikingly sectional" lines, were deeply unpopular in the increasingly antislavery Midwest.[24] They meant the addition of two more potential slave states to the Union and also that the police powers of the federal government and unwilling local officials would be harnessed to capture slaves who escaped over the Ohio River to freedom.[25] Such escapes were featured in the wildly successful novel *Uncle Tom's Cabin*, written by Harriet Beecher Stowe and based on her time in Cincinnati when her husband taught at Lane Theological Seminary (originally intended as an "antislavery fort") and as she embraced local civic affairs, including the activities of the Cincinnati Semi-Colon Club and its stable of regionalists.[26] The book sold millions of copies and caused Ohio towns to debate where Eliza might have traversed the icy river.[27] Throughout the 1850s abolitionists in the Midwest would actively resist efforts to recapture runaway slaves, and Southerners would, in turn, routinely denounce abolitionist hotbeds and the Midwest's active underground railroad network, whose lantern-lit paths routinely helped slaves escape.[28] One Indiana man, for example, guided two thousand fugitive slaves to freedom between 1826 and 1846.[29] Midwestern states such as Michigan and Ohio also passed personal liberty laws designed to frustrate Southern usage of the Fugitive Slave Act, and in Wisconsin the Supreme Court, in a case in which the court freed an abolitionist for rescuing slaves, even declared the fugitive law unconstitutional.[30]

The final spark that would ignite the Civil War came from midwestern territories. The Kansas-Nebraska Act of 1854, following the principle of popular sovereignty, allowed the new Kansas and Nebraska territories to choose to be free or slave states in a space where slavery, by virtue of the long-standing Missouri Compromise, was supposed to be forbidden.[31] When Iowa joined the Union in 1846, for example, it joined as a free state without quarrel, since it had been part of the Louisiana Purchase and thus subject to the antislavery rules of the Missouri Compromise.[32] But after passage of the Nebraska bill in a vote divided by section, upending the Missouri Compromise, such long-standing procedures provided no clarity. Senator Benjamin Wade of Ohio denounced the Nebraska bill as a "declaration of war on the institutions of the North, a deliberate sectional movement by the South for political power, without regard for justice or consequences."³³ The Nebraska bill, as it was then known, split deep along party lines. Every midwestern Whig voted against it, while almost every Southern Whig voted in favor, while Southern Democrats overwhelmingly favored the measure. Senator Wade of Ohio thought the bill would destroy the republic and saw a corresponding total eclipse of the sun as a sign of the coming end.³⁴

The Kansas-Nebraska Act caused a rapid chain reaction in American politics. Antislavery opponents of the Nebraska bill quickly organized themselves and spurred the rapid rise of a major new political party in the Midwest.³⁵ People opposed to the spread of slavery immediately formed the new Republican Party in places like Ripon, Wisconsin; Crawfordsville, Iowa; and Jackson, Michigan. In the latter town various people and factions famously gathered in a grove of oak trees to forge their new anti-Nebraska party.³⁶ The new Michigan Republican Party that resulted adopted a platform denouncing slavery as a "relic of barbarism" and the "slaveholding oligarchs of the South" for their "schemes of aristocracy" and vowed to "cooperate and be known as Republicans until the contest" against the feudal South "be terminated."³⁷ By midsummer anti-Nebraska conventions had convened and organized new state Republican parties "throughout the Middle West."³⁸ The GOP, one historian noted, became the "first willfully sectional party in American history."³⁹ Soon after came the holdings of *Dred Scott v. Sanford* (1857), a case with decidedly midwestern origins. The *Dred Scott* case was a major blow to the Midwest's long-standing ban on slavery and accompanying case law and a major defeat for midwestern abolitionists who had been aiding the escapes of Southern slaves for years. The Court's assault on the Northwest Ordinance, in particular, "outraged Abraham Lincoln and other Midwesterners" and brought regional warfare a step closer.⁴⁰

Lincoln was soon in charge of the Union war effort. Over half of the Union's troops would come from the Midwest, even though the region only constituted a quarter of the country's population.⁴¹ The original five midwestern states sent nearly a million soldiers to war for the Union, and the Midwest provided nearly all of Lincoln's generals and most of his cabinet.[42] Ohio alone produced sixty-four Union generals.[43] Midwestern towns emptied of fighting-age men. Hillsdale College in Michigan saw its entire student body march off to war, along with a quarter of the men in Michigan.[44] Lawrence College in Wisconsin was also quick to "declare itself for the Union" via speeches by the president and other dignitaries. Lawrence professors raised companies to fight, the entire class of 1864 marched off to war, and the college provided a "steadfast wall of blue."[45] These large Union armies led by Ohio generals were fed by midwestern farms, which provided nearly 80 percent of the Union's wheat, corn, and oats while, at the same time, New England's agricultural production shrank.[46] The Ohio and Mississippi River valleys proved to be crucial theaters of the war for the Union cause. The victory of Illinoisan Ulysses S. Grant's midwestern troops over units from Alabama, Mississippi, Arkansas, Louisiana, and Tennessee—in a show of midwestern force over the renegade South at Shiloh—led to Union control of the Mississippi River valley and ultimately secured the western theater for Lincoln.[47]

The heightened sectional conflict of the 1850s and then the Civil War killed the remnants of unity still lingering from an earlier era in the American West. The slaughter at Shiloh and a hundred other places drove home the deep divisions between the Midwest and the South, and the memories kindled in hundreds of midwestern Grand Army of the Republic lodges maintained the regional animosities. The South also mattered less economically to the Midwest. During the first decades of the nineteenth century, much of the Midwest's trade flowed down the Ohio River to the Mississippi and on down to New Orleans, giving the early Midwest a partial Southern economic connection.[48] But with the building of the Erie Canal and other smaller midwestern canals, the greater use of the Great Lakes for commerce, and the coming of a dense railroad network in the Midwest, the region's economic orientation changed from the South to the Northeast.[49] In 1850 the Midwest sent the bulk of its corn down the Ohio River to the South, and it sent quadruple the amount of pork to the South that it did to the East; by 1860, after expanding midwestern and eastern railroads became integrated, the Midwest sent quadruple the amount of corn to the East that it sent to the South and six times the amount of pork.[50] The regions also became deeply divided by economic policy. The Midwest and the North, in general, favored tariffs to protect their burgeoning industrial sectors. So begun a movement for "home manufactures," which declared that the region must choose "either to be in a state of dependence, with foreign manufactures, or be independent, clothed in homespun, the products of our own labor."[51] The South, meanwhile, sought more open trade to sell its growing cotton stores. By the time of the Civil War, Southern cotton constituted two-thirds of American exports.[52] Most of the grains and meat produced on midwestern farms were consumed domestically, so foreign trade was less of a concern in the region. The Midwest and South were also divided over internal improvements such as canals and bridges and efforts to improve harbors on the Great Lakes that midwestern legislators eagerly sought in order to spur economic traffic.[53] Midwesterners thought such improvements boosted economic development, while the South opposed giving greater authority to the central government and feared the loss of goods that once flowed by river to the South to Great Lakes shipping. All these factors diminished a once generic "West" in favor of a clear division between the Midwest and the South.[54] In a sign of the regional reorientation, the number of midwestern newspapers that once had *western* in the title dropped from fifty in the early decades to fifteen in 1840 to one in 1860.[55] The Ohio River had become a stark dividing line between the Midwest and South.[56]

Throughout all of the postwar presidential elections, in which several midwestern Republican candidates ran for president, not one of them won a Southern state. The South remained a rock-solid Democratic bastion. When these Republican presidential candidates were competing, they frequently "waved the bloody shirt," or reminded voters how the South had rebelled and tried to break up the Union, and these reminders became a prominent part of midwestern political culture. For four decades after the

Civil War, waving the bloody shirt "remained relatively effective, especially in the Middle West."[57]

At the same time as midwesterners branded Southerners as treasonous and the Midwest deviated dramatically away from the South, there also grew a self-conscious regionalism that often was directed at separating the Midwest from the feared hegemony of the East. These forces could be detected from the beginning of the Midwest, of course. The Northwest Ordinance signaled that the Midwest would be separate and new and hold the dreams of those founders who sought to overcome the remnants of colonialism in the East.[58] The Appalachian mountain chain served as a symbolic as well as a very real dividing line between the Midwest and the East for many years. Senator Rufus King of New York said in 1786 that "nature has severed the two countries by a vast and extensive chain of mountains, interest and convenience will keep them separate, and the feeble policy of our disjointed Government will not be able to unite them."[59] Migrants into the Midwest, Frederick Jackson Turner noted, "when they crossed the Alleghanies became self-conscious and even rebellious against the rule of the East."[60] Widening the separation, in the 1820s and 1830s, just as abolitionism was intensifying in the Midwest and frictions with the South were growing, midwestern regionalist voices were becoming louder and better organized. These voices were reacting against an eastern domination of American intellectual and cultural life; a "resentment against eastern publishers and periodicals" was building, and the result was a "literary declaration of independence."[61] States in the West, said the *Western Journal* of St. Louis in 1851, were tired of being seen as "Provinces of the East" and were seeking their own identities.[62] They did so via regional publications from the era such as the *Cincinnati Mirror*, the *Western Literary Magazine* out of Columbus, *Chicago Magazine*, *Centinel of the North-Western Territory*, the *Western Spy and Literary Cadet* out of Cincinnati, and the *Western Journal and Civilian* out of St. Louis.[63] The most common form of cultural regionalism—literature—also flowered.[64] The goal of the midwestern regionalists, Terry Barnhart explains, was to produce a "literature and history that would declare its intellectual and cultural independence from the literary establishment in the northeastern United States."[65]

The emergence of regionalist thought in the antebellum Midwest and the continually escalating tensions with the South ushered in a new phase of midwestern identity formation by the 1850s. By this decade people living in the old Northwest Territory "began to think of themselves as different. They were not part of the South, the East, or the Far West or the mountains and plains."[66] During this decade, as Andrew Offenburger has explained, the term *Middle West* came into use.[67] After the Mexican War and the acquisition of a vast territory extending to the Pacific Ocean, what would become the Midwest was no longer the western edge of the country. When railroads were planned for construction to the Far West, what was once West became the middle of the country, or midwestern, and the term *Midwest* began showing up on railroad maps.[68] As the divide with the South expanded, what was once considered the general "West" also split into a free West and a Southern-oriented region. With the deepening of the Midwest's agrarian sympathies and the rise of abolitionism in the region, midwesterners "could hardly picture their Eden populated by fellow humans held in bondage," and thus "they divorced the lands of the Southwest from their Garden, which they confined now to the Upper Mississippi Valley."[69] With the coming of the war, it became customary to "omit the southern part of the Mississippi Valley and to write about a Middle West that lies between the Canadian boundary and the Ohio River and extends westward a greater or less distance beyond the Mississippi River," and this usage became sanctioned by dictionaries, government reports, the census, and conventional wisdom.[70]

A well-defined Midwest, one separate from the South and distinct from what we now see as the West, or the land beyond the 100th meridian, was emerging.[71] The new Midwest was economically strong and, by 1870, had a greater population than New England and the mid-Atlantic states combined, and it was becoming the nation's agricultural and industrial heartland.[72] The region had matured from its "embryonic state" and was rooted and stable and capable of fostering the production of enduring art.[73] It was the kind of regional identity that emerges "wherever people live together long enough to enclose their daily experience in a skein of common memories."[74] By the later 1800s the term *Middle West* "was firmly entrenched and began to appear regularly in capitalized form."[75]

In addition to a clear regional moniker, there arose a successful and recognized regionalist literature by the end of the nineteenth century. Some critics held that prior to the Civil War, the Midwest had "produced no Melville, no Hawthorne, no Whitman, no Emerson," but some intellectual infrastructure in the form of regional magazines had been established.[76] In the years after the war, the payoff came in the form of ascendant writers who "were not freakish flowerings from barren ground" but "products of western soil, prepared for four decades by industrious and forgotten literary pioneers."[77] William Dean Howells, even though he went east, had a deep grounding in Ohio and believed in the decentralization of culture and recognized the rising influence of "the Great Middle West."[78] One of his first works was a campaign biography of the first midwestern Republican president, Abraham Lincoln, who gave him the Venice consulship, and he proudly served as a true blue Ohio Republican, not averse to hoisting the bloody shirt and sharply rejecting the "unrepentant but reconciled rebel leaders who tried to destroy us as a people."[79] James Whitcomb Riley of Indiana was also universally known during the late nineteenth century and cut a wide swath for midwestern writers.[80] When the Indiana Club convened in Chicago in 1902, it could celebrate the several regional authors of the Hoosier state, including Riley and the vocal defender of the Midwest, Booth Tarkington.[81] Regionalist literary groups such as the Society of Midland Authors in Chicago also became prominent.[82] These were signs that a fully formed midwestern identity had been achieved and midwestern voices had arisen. By the late nineteenth century, after decades of intensifying regional differentiation, a "once vague and variously labeled landscape" had become a "distinct and powerful place" known as the Midwest.[83]

Notes

1. Troyer, *Culture of the Middle West*, vi. Troyer had impeccable midwestern credentials. He was born in Indiana, attended Earlham College in Richmond, Indiana, and earned his PhD from the University of Wisconsin, where he taught until joining Lawrence College. Troyer then went on to serve as the dean of the liberal arts college at Cornell College in Mt. Vernon, Iowa, from 1957 to 1969.

2. Quaife, "Significance of the Ordinance of 1787," 415.

3. "Governors Revive Regional Issue," 80. While the configuration can be traced to earlier decades, it is clear that these twelve states were considered the Midwest by about 1900. Shortridge, "Emergence of 'Middle West' as an American Regional Label," 212.

4. De Tocqueville, *Democracy in America*, 376–77. See also Salafia, *Slavery's Borderland*.

5. Nobles, "Breaking into the Backcountry," 644–45, 648, 652–53.

6. Turner, "Significance of the Section in American History," 258.

7. Foner, *Free Soil*, 51.

8. Foner, *Free Soil*, 69.

9. Foner, *Free Soil*, 47–48.

10. Fischer, *Albion's Seed*.

11. McPherson, "Antebellum Southern Exceptionalism," 428–29; Wyatt-Brown, *Southern Honor*.

12. McPherson, "Antebellum Southern Exceptionalism," 422.

13. Degler, "Two Cultures," 102 (quotations); Osterweis, *Romanticism and Nationalism in the Old South*; Nabors, *From Oligarchy to Republicanism*; Genovese, *Political Economy of Slavery*; Bertelson, *Lazy South*; Guelzo, *Fateful Lightning*, 23, 28; O'Connor, *American Sectionalism in the British Mind*, 58–59.

14. McPherson, "Antebellum Southern Exceptionalism," 430.

15. Meyer et al., "Public Education as Nation-Building in America," 597, 600.

16. Morse, "Knowledge Is Power," 2.

17. Wilentz, "Jeffersonian Democracy and the Origins of Political Antislavery in the United States," 375–401. For an earlier divergence, see Cayton, "'Separate Interests' and the Nation-State," 39–67.

18. Muelder, "Moral Lights around Us," 251; Hamm et al., "Great and Good People," 3–25; Siebert, "Quaker Section of the Underground Railroad in Northern Ohio," 479–85. Many Quakers left the South because of slavery and became abolitionists in the Midwest, deepening the divide between the regions. Lantzer, "Forging God's Country," 21. Eastern donors became nervous because midwestern academics and reformers were so ardently abolitionist. Goodheart, "Abolitionists as Academics," 421–33.

19. Etulain, "Abraham Lincoln," 4.
20. Potter, *Impending Crisis*, 21; Guelzo, *Fateful Lightning*, 64; Remini, "Northwest Ordinance of 1787," 15. The Wilmot Proviso votes fell along regional lines. See also Onuf, *Statehood and Union*, 144–45.
21. Butler, "Midwest's Spiritual Landscapes."
22. Degler, "Two Cultures," 98.
23. Mathews, "Methodist Schism of 1844 and the Popularization of Antislavery Sentiment," 3–23; Staiger, "Abolitionism and the Presbyterian Schism," 391–414; McKivigan, *War against Proslavery Religion*; Goen, "Broken Churches, Broken Nation," 21–35; Volpe, *Forlorn Hope*, 19; Harper, "Downwind from the New England Rat," 25–42.
24. Sewell, *House Divided*, 35.
25. The law overruled earlier court rulings that allowed local officials to ignore the demands of slave catchers and even prosecute them for kidnapping. Guelzo, *Fateful Lightning*, 72. See also Farrison, "Flight across Ohio," 272–80.
26. Reynolds, *Mightier Than the Sword*, 92–99; Guelzo, *Fateful Lightning*, 74; Hubbart, *Older Middle West*, 56; Robinson, *When I Was a Child I Read Books*, 177.
27. Koch, "Where Did Eliza Cross the Ohio?," 588.
28. Koch, "Marking the Old 'Abolition Holes,'" 308–10; Soike, *Necessary Courage*; Siebert, "Underground Railroad in Ohio," 44; Sheppard, "Abolition Center," 265–66; Morgans, *John Todd and the Underground Railroad*; Walsh, "Three Antislavery Newspapers," 172–74; Galbreath, "Anti-slavery Movement in Columbiana County," 355–57; Siebert, "Beginnings of the Underground Railroad in Ohio," 70–72.
29. Lantzer, "Forging God's Country," 27.
30. Rosenberg, "Personal Liberty Laws and Sectional Crisis," 25–44; Sewell, *House Divided*, 30.
31. In March 1853, in another manifestation of sectionalism and in a move that could have prevented much bloodshed, all Southern senators (except those from Missouri) had voted to block the creation of what is now Kansas as a free state. The bill had already passed the House of Representatives. Sewell, *House Divided*, 42.
32. Guelzo, *Fateful Lightning*, 77.
33. Guelzo, *Fateful Lightning*, 78.
34. Goodrich, *War to the Knife*, 5. See also Maizlish, *Triumph of Sectionalism*.
35. See Peck, *Making an Antislavery Nation*; Silbey, "After 'The First Republican Victory,'" 4; Hansen, *Making of the Third Party System*; Huston, "Illinois Political Realignment of 1844–1860," 507; Sewell, *Ballots for Freedom*; Nevins, *Emergence of Lincoln*, 12, 27; Blue, "Chase and the Governorship," 197; Green, *Freedom, Union, and Power*, 13; Morrison, *Slavery and the American West*; Hess, *Liberty, Virtue, and Progress*.
36. "Gathering under the Oaks," 562. See also "Early History of the Republican Party in Ohio," 327–31.
37. Holt, "Making and Mobilizing the Republican Party," 29–30; Gienapp, *Origins of the Republican Party*, 104–5.
38. Sewell, *House Divided*, 49; Sewell, *Ballots for Freedom*, 264.

39. Frederickson, *Inner Civil War*, 49; Grant, *North over South*, 5; Edwards, "Domesticity versus Manhood Rights," 176 (calling the GOP a "militantly sectional party").

40. Lantzer, "Forging God's Country," 28.

41. Lantzer, "Forging God's Country," 29; Etcheson, "How the Midwest Won the Civil War," in Lauck, ed., *Oxford Handbook of Midwestern History*.

42. Shriver, "Freedom's Proving Ground," 131; Onuf, "Northwest Ordinance and Regional Identity," 293.

43. Etcheson, "How the Midwest Won the Civil War"; Curry, "Ohio Generals and Field Officers in the Civil War," 306–11.

44. Kestenbaum, "Modernizing Michigan," 129.

45. Plantz, "Lawrence College," 160–61.

46. Etcheson, "How the Midwest Won the Civil War."

47. Woodworth, *Nothing but Victory*; Connelly, *Army of the Heartland*, 178. On the experiences of the only all-western brigade in the eastern theater, see Nolan, *Iron Brigade*. The 2nd Wisconsin Regiment of the Iron Brigade lost more soldiers in battle than any other regiment in the Union army.

48. Gruenwald, "Space and Place on the Early American Frontier," 31–36.

49. McPherson, "Antebellum Southern Exceptionalism," 426; Engle, *Struggle for the Heartland*, 4, 6; Gruenwald, "Space and Place," 38–40.

50. Sewell, *House Divided*, 8. By the time of the war, the "Mississippi had practically ceased to compete with the lake, canal, and railroad routes eastward." Hubbart, *Older Middle West*, 74.

51. Scheiber, "On the Concepts of 'Regionalism' and 'Frontier,'" xi.

52. Sewell, *House Divided*, 6.

53. On the debate over the Harbor and River Bill, which the South opposed, see Hubbart, *Older Middle West*, 21–27. See also Egnal, "Explaining John Sherman," 110.

54. See Phillips, *Rivers Ran Backward*. This also meant that a Kentucky considered western for much of its history became oriented to the South even though it never seceded and was a state of mixed loyalties during the war. Harkins, "Colonels, Hillbillies, and Fightin'," 430; Marshall, *Creating a Confederate Kentucky*; Wall, *How Kentucky Became Southern*; Stanley, *Loyal West*, 130–52.

55. Gruenwald, "Space and Place," 43.

56. Gruenwald, "Space and Place," 44–45. See also Wheeler, "Higher Education in the Antebellum Ohio Valley," 1.

57. Luthin, "Waving the Bloody Shirt," 70; Lauck, *Prairie Republic*, 34–36, 68, 178; Current, "Politics of Reconstruction in Wisconsin," 84. See also Harris, *Across the Bloody Chasm*, chap. 2. On concerns about overuse of bloody shirt tactics by some in the GOP, see Hirshon, *Farewell to the Bloody Shirt*.

58. Whitney, "Upper Midwest as the Second Promised Land."

59. Turner, "Significance of the Section in American History," 260.

60. Turner, "Significance of the Section in American History," 258; Billington, "Historians of the Northwest Ordinance," 410–11.

61. Donald and Palmer, "Toward a Western Literature," 415–16.

62. Turner, "Significance of the Section in American History," 264.

63. Hubbart, *Older Middle West*, 54; Donald and Palmer, "Toward a Western Literature," 422–23; Murray, "Early Literary Developments in Indiana," 327–33; Rhode, "Persistence of Place," 47–59; Habich, *Transcendentalism and the Western Messenger*; Quaife, "Wisconsin's First Literary Magazine," 43–56; Dowler, "John James Piatt," 1–10; Anderson, "Queen City and a New Literature," 8; Wright, *Culture on the Moving Frontier*, 115; Basler, "Pioneering Period," 121–22.

64. Venable, *Beginnings of Literacy Culture in the Ohio Valley*; Venable, "Literary Periodicals of the Ohio Valley," 198–202; Wheeler, "Literature of the Western Reserve," 101–5; Esarey, "Literary Spirit among the Early Ohio Valley Settlers," 143–57.

65. Barnhart, "Common Feeling," 41–42.

66. Ridge, "How the Middle West Became America's Heartland," 13.

67. Offenburger, "U.S. Expansion and the Creation of the Middle West." Forty years ago, the geographer James Shortridge interpreted the term *Middle West* as applying to Kansas/Nebraska, or the place between the Northwest and Southwest on a North-South axis, and downplayed the East/West dynamic that Offenburger has found. Nevertheless, Shortridge agreed that the term *Middle West* was in wide use by about 1900 and applied to the traditional twelve-state understanding of the Midwest. Shortridge, "Emergence of 'Middle West' as an American Regional Label," 211–12.

68. Offenburger, "U.S. Expansion and the Creation of the Middle West."

69. Billington, "Garden of the World," 29.

70. Raney, "People of the Land," 15.

71. Lauck, *Interior Borderlands*.

72. Meyer, "Midwestern Industrialization and the American Manufacturing Belt," 925; Rose, "On the Path toward National Eminence," 157–81.

73. Baldinger, "Middle West Builds a Home," 59.

74. Higham, "Hanging Together," 9 (quotation); Duerkes, "Travel Literature and Midwestern Identity," 53–54; Mathiesen, "Belonging in the Midwest," 119–46.

75. Offenburger, "U.S. Expansion and the Creation of the Middle West."

76. Donald and Palmer, "Toward a Western Literature," 427.

77. Donald and Palmer, "Toward a Western Literature," 428.

78. Steiner, "Birth of the Midwest," 23n31 (quotation); Payne, "Ohio World of William Dean Howells," 127–37; Hogue, "Forgotten Frontier," 231–42.

79. Budd, "Howells, the *Atlantic Monthly*, and Republicanism," 140, 142.

80. Crowder, *Those Innocent Years*.

81. DeSantis and Brooks, "George Cary Eggleston's Explanation for Indiana's Literary Achievements," 59–64; Schumaker, *History of Indiana Literature*; Beer, "Midlander." See also DeMuth, *Small Town Chicago*.

82. Loerzel, "People Are Getting Tired of Broadway and Fifth Avenue."

83. Steiner, "Birth of the Midwest," 8.

Bibliography

Anderson, David D. "The Queen City and a New Literature." *MidAmerica* 4 (1977): 7–17.

Baldinger, Wallace S. "The Middle West Builds a Home: Chicago as a Focus on the Arts." In Troyer, *Culture of the Middle West*, 57–72.

Barnhart, Terry A. "'A Common Feeling': Regional Identity and Historical Consciousness in the Old Northwest, 1820–1860." *Michigan Historical Review* 29, no. 1 (Spring 2003): 39–70.

Basler, Roy P. "The Pioneering Period." *Centennial Review* 2 (1958): 111–24.

Beer, Jeremy. "Midlander: Booth Tarkington's Defense of the Midwest." In Lauck, *Midwestern Moment*, 35–53.

Bertelson, David. *The Lazy South*. New York: Oxford University Press, 1967.

Billington, Ray A. "The Garden of the World: Fact and Fiction." In *The Heritage of the Middle West*, edited by John J. Murray, 27–53. Norman: University of Oklahoma Press, 1958.

———. "The Historians of the Northwest Ordinance." *Journal of the Illinois State Historical Society* 40, no. 4 (December 1947): 261–80.

Blue, Frederick J. "Chase and the Governorship: A Stepping Stone to the Presidency." *Ohio History* 90, no. 3 (Summer 1981): 197–220.

Budd, Louis J. "Howells, the *Atlantic Monthly*, and Republicanism." *American Literature* 24, no. 2 (May 1952): 139–56.

Butler, Jon. "The Midwest's Spiritual Landscapes." in Lauck, Whitney, and Hogan, *Finding a New Midwestern History*, 196–210.

Carrington, Henry B. "Early History of the Republican Party in Ohio." *Ohio Archaeological and Historical Society Publications* 2, no. 2 (September 1888): 327–331.

Cayton, Andrew R. L. "'Separate Interests' and the Nation-State: The Washington Administration and the Origins of Regionalism in the Trans-Appalachian West." *Journal of American History* 79, no. 1 (June 1992): 39–67.

Connelly, Thomas Lawrence. *Army of the Heartland: The Army of Tennessee, 1861–1862*. Baton Rouge: Louisiana State University Press, 1967.

Crowder, Richard. *Those Innocent Years: The Legacy and Inheritance of a Hero of the Victorian Era*. Indianapolis: Bobbs-Merrill, 1957.

Current, Richard N. "The Politics of Reconstruction in Wisconsin, 1865–1873." *Wisconsin Magazine of History* 60, no. 2 (Winter 1976–77): 82–108.

Curry, Colonel W. L. "Ohio Generals and Field Officers in the Civil War." *Ohio Archaeological and Historical Quarterly* 23, no. 3 (1914): 306–11.

Degler, Carl. "The Two Cultures and the Civil War." In *The Development of an American Culture*, edited by Stanley Coben and Lorman Ratner, 94–100. Englewood Cliffs NJ: Prentice-Hall, 1970.

DeMuth, James. *Small Town Chicago: The Comic Perspective of Finley Peter Dunne*. Port Washington NY: Kennikat, 1980.

DeSantis, Vincent P., and Janet Brooks, eds. "George Cary Eggleston's Explanation for Indiana's Literary Achievements." *Indiana Magazine of History* 59, no. 1 (March 1963): 59–66.
de Tocqueville, Alexis. *Democracy in America*. Vol. 1. New York: Vintage, 1945.
Donald, David, and Frederick A. Palmer. "Toward a Western Literature, 1820–1860." *Mississippi Valley Historical Review* 35, no. 3 (December 1948): 413–28.
Dowler, Clare. "John James Piatt, Representative Figure of a Momentous Period." *Ohio History Journal* 45, no. 1 (January 1936): 1–10.
Duerkes, Wayne. "Travel Literature and Midwestern Identity: The Case of Illinois." In Lauck, *Making of the Midwest*, 53–66.
Edwards, Rebecca. "Domesticity versus Manhood Rights: Republicans, Democrats, and 'Family Values' Politics, 1856–1896." In *The Democratic Experiment: New Directions in American Political History*, edited by Meg Jacobs, William J. Novak, and Julian E. Zelizer, 175–97. Princeton NJ: Princeton University Press, 2003.
Egnal, Marc. "Explaining John Sherman: Leader of the Second American Revolution." *Ohio History* 114 (2007): 105–17.
Engle, Stephen D. *Struggle for the Heartland: The Campaign from Fort Henry to Corinth*. Lincoln: University of Nebraska Press, 2001.
Esarey, Logan. "The Literary Spirit among the Early Ohio Valley Settlers." *Mississippi Valley Historical Review* 5, no. 2 (September 1918): 143–57.
Etcheson, Nicole. "How the Midwest Won the Civil War." In Lauck, *Oxford Handbook of Midwestern History*, forthcoming.
Etulain, Richard W. "Abraham Lincoln: Political Founding Father of the American West." *Montana: The Magazine of Western History* 59, no. 2 (Summer 2009): 3–22.
Farrison, W. Edward. "A Flight across Ohio: The Escape of William Wells Brown from Slavery." *Ohio Historical Quarterly* 61, no. 3 (July 1952): 272–80.
Fischer, David Hackett. *Albion's Seed: Four British Folkways in America*. New York: Oxford University Press, 1989.
Foner, Eric. *Free Soil, Free Labor, Free Men: The Ideology of the Republican Party before the Civil War*. New York: Oxford University Press, 1970.
Frederickson, George M. *The Inner Civil War: Northern Intellectuals and the Crisis of the Union*. Urbana: University of Illinois Press, 1965.
Galbreath, C. B. "Anti-slavery Movement in Columbiana County." *Ohio Archaeological and Historical Society Publications* 30, no. 4 (October 1921): 355–95.
"Gathering under the Oaks." *Ohio Archaeological and Historical Society Publications* 13, no. 4 (October 1904): 562.
Genovese, Eugene D. *The Political Economy of Slavery*. New York: Pantheon, 1965.
Gienapp, William E. *The Origins of the Republican Party, 1852–1856*. New York: Oxford University Press, 1987.
Goen, C. C. "Broken Churches, Broken Nation: Regional Religion and North-South Alienation in Antebellum America." *Church History* 52, no. 1 (March 1983): 21–35.

Goodheart, Lawrence B. "Abolitionists as Academics: The Controversy at Western Reserve College, 1832–1833." *History of Education Quarterly* 22, no. 4 (Winter 1982): 421–33.

Goodrich, Thomas. *War to the Knife: Bleeding Kansas, 1854–1861*. Lincoln: University of Nebraska Press, 2004.

"Governors Revive Regional Issue." *Annals of Iowa* 25, no. 1 (Summer 1943): 80–82.

Grant, Susan-Mary. *North over South: Northern Nationalism and American Identity in the Antebellum Era*. Lawrence: University Press of Kansas, 2000.

Green, Michael S. *Freedom, Union, and Power: The Civil War Republican Party*. New York: Fordham University Press, 2004.

Gruenwald, Kim M. "Space and Place on the Early American Frontier: The Ohio Valley as a Region, 1790–1850." *Ohio Valley History* 4, no. 3 (Fall 2004): 31–48.

Guelzo, Allen C. *Fateful Lightning: A New History of the Civil War and Reconstruction*. New York: Oxford University Press, 2012.

Habich, Robert D. *Transcendentalism and the Western Messenger: A History of the Magazine and Its Contributors, 1835–1841*. Cranbury NJ: Fairleigh Dickinson University Press, 1985.

Hamm, Thomas D., April Beckman, Marissa Florio, Kristi Giles, and Marie Hopper. "'A Great and Good People': Midwestern Quakers and the Struggle against Slavery." *Indiana Magazine of History* 100, no. 1 (March 2004): 3–25.

Hansen, Stephen. *The Making of the Third Party System: Voters and Parties in Illinois, 1850–1876*. Ann Arbor: UMI Research, 1980.

Harkins, Anthony. "Colonels, Hillbillies, and Fightin': Twentieth-Century Kentucky in the National Imagination." *Register of the Kentucky Historical Society* 113, nos. 2–3 (Spring/Summer 2015): 421–52.

Harper, Keith. "Downwind from the New England Rat: John Taylor, Organized Missions, and the Regionalization of Religious Identity on the American Frontier." *Ohio Valley History* 9, no. 3 (Fall 2009): 25–42.

Harris, M. Keith. *Across the Bloody Chasm: The Culture of Commemoration among Civil War Veterans*. Baton Rouge: Louisiana State University Press, 2014.

Hess, Earl. *Liberty, Virtue, and Progress: Northerners and Their War for the Union*. New York: Fordham University Press, 1997.

Higham, John. "Hanging Together: Divergent Unities in American History." *Journal of American History* 61, no. 1 (June 1974): 5–28.

Hirshon, Stanley P. *Farewell to the Bloody Shirt: Northern Republicans and the Southern Negro, 1877–1893*. Bloomington: Indiana University Press, 1962.

Hogue, Bev. "Forgotten Frontier: Literature of the Old Northwest." In *The Regional Literatures of America*, edited by Charles L. Crow, 231–42. Malden MA: Blackwell, 2003.

Holt, Michael F. "Making and Mobilizing the Republican Party, 1854–1860." In *The Birth of the Grand Old Party: The Republicans' First Generation*, edited by Robert F. Engs and Randall M. Miller, 5–28. Philadelphia: University of Pennsylvania Press, 2002.

Hubbart, Henry Hyde. *The Older Middle West, 1840–1880: Its Social, Economic and Political Life and Sectional Tendencies before, during and after the Civil War.* New York: D. Appleton-Century, 1936.
Huston, James L. "The Illinois Political Realignment of 1844–1860: Revisiting the Analysis." *Journal of the Civil War Era* 1, no. 4 (December 2011): 506–35.
Kestenbaum, Justin. "Modernizing Michigan: Political and Social Trends, 1836–1866." In *Michigan: Visions of Our Past*, edited by Richard J. Hathaway, 115–32. East Lansing: Michigan State University Press, 1989.
Koch, Felix J. "Marking the Old 'Abolition Holes.'" *Ohio Archaeological and Historical Society Publications* 22, no. 2 (April 1913): 308–18.
——. "Where Did Eliza Cross the Ohio?" *Ohio Archaeological and Historical Society Publications* 24, no. 4 (October 1915): 588–90.
Lantzer, Jason S. "Forging God's Country: The Northwest Territorial Ordinance, the Second Great Awakening, and the Midwestern Vision for America." In Lauck, *Making of the Midwest*, 17–35.
Lauck, Jon K., ed. *The Interior Borderlands: Regional Identity in the Midwest and Great Plains.* Sioux Falls SD: Center for Western Studies, 2019.
——, ed. *The Making of the Midwest: Essays on the Formation of Midwestern Identity, 1787–1900.* Hastings NE: Hastings College Press, 2020.
——, ed. *The Midwestern Moment: The Forgotten World of Early Twentieth-Century Midwestern Regionalism, 1880–1940.* Hastings NE: Hastings University Press, 2017.
——, ed. *Oxford Handbook of Midwestern History.* New York: Oxford University Press, forthcoming.
——. *Prairie Republic: The Political Culture of Dakota Territory, 1879–1889.* Norman: University of Oklahoma Press, 2010.
Lauck, Jon K., Gleaves Whitney, and Joseph Hogan, eds. *Finding a New Midwestern History.* Lincoln: University of Nebraska Press, 2018.
Loerzel, Robert. "'People Are Getting Tired of Broadway and Fifth Avenue': The Origins of the Society of Midland Authors." In Lauck, *Midwestern Moment*, 19–34.
Luthin, Reinhard H. "Waving the Bloody Shirt: Northern Political Tactics in Post–Civil War Times." *Georgia Review* 14, no. 1 (Spring 1960): 64–71.
Maizlish, Stephen F. *The Triumph of Sectionalism: The Transformation of Ohio Politics, 1844–1856.* Kent OH: Kent State University Press, 1983.
Marshall, Anne E. *Creating a Confederate Kentucky: The Lost Cause and Civil War Memory in a Border State.* Chapel Hill: University of North Carolina Press, 2013.
Mathews, Donald G. "The Methodist Schism of 1844 and the Popularization of Antislavery Sentiment." *Mid-America* 51, no. 1 (January 1968): 3–23.
Mathiesen, Henrick Olav. "Belonging in the Midwest: Norwegian Americans and the Process of Attachment, ca. 1830–1860." *American Nineteenth Century* 15, no. 2 (2014): 119–46.
McKivigan, John R. *The War against Proslavery Religion: Abolitionism and the Northern Churches, 1830–1865.* Ithaca NY: Cornell University Press, 1984.

McPherson, James M. "Antebellum Southern Exceptionalism: A New Look at an Old Question." *Civil War History* 50, no. 4 (December 2004): 418–33.

Meyer, David R. "Midwestern Industrialization and the American Manufacturing Belt in the Nineteenth Century." *Journal of Economic History* 49, no. 4 (December 1989): 921–37.

Meyer, John W., David Tyack, Joane Nagel, and Audri Gordon. "Public Education as Nation-Building in America: Enrollments and Bureaucratization in the American States, 1870–1930." *American Journal of Sociology* 85, no. 3 (November 1979): 591–613.

Morgans, John Patrick. *John Todd and the Underground Railroad: Biography of an Iowa Abolitionist*. Jefferson NC: McFarland, 2006.

Morrison, Michael A. *Slavery and the American West: The Eclipse of Manifest Destiny and the Coming of the Civil War*. Chapel Hill: University of North Carolina Press, 1997.

Morse, Scott N. "'Knowledge Is Power': The Reverend Grosvenor Clarke Morse's Thoughts on Free Schools and the Republic during the Civil War." *Kansas History* 31, no. 1 (Spring 2008): 2–13.

Muelder, Hermann R. "'The Moral Lights around Us.'" *Journal of the Illinois State Historical Society* 52, no. 2 (Summer 1959): 248–62.

Murray, Agnes M. "Early Literary Developments in Indiana." *Indiana Magazine of History* 36, no. 4 (December 1940): 327–33.

Nabors, Forest A. *From Oligarchy to Republicanism: The Great Task of Reconstruction*. Columbia: University of Missouri Press, 2018.

Nevins, Allan. *The Emergence of Lincoln*. New York: Charles Scribner's Sons, 1950.

Nobles, Gregory H. "Breaking into the Backcountry: New Approaches to the Early American Frontier, 1750–1800." *William and Mary Quarterly* 46, no. 4 (October 1989): 641–70.

Nolan, Alan T. *The Iron Brigade: A Military History*. New York: Macmillan, 1961.

O'Connor, Peter. *American Sectionalism in the British Mind, 1832–1863*. Baton Rouge: Louisiana State University Press, 2017.

Offenburger, Andrew. "U.S. Expansion and the Creation of the Middle West in the Nineteenth Century." In Lauck, *Oxford Handbook of Midwestern History*, forthcoming.

Onuf, Peter S. "The Northwest Ordinance and Regional Identity." *Wisconsin Magazine of History* 72, no. 4 (Summer 1989): 293–304.

———. *Statehood and Union: A History of the Northwest Ordinance*. Bloomington: Indiana University Press.

Osterweis, Rollin G. *Romanticism and Nationalism in the Old South*. New Haven CT: Yale University Press, 1949.

Payne, Alma J. "The Ohio World of William Dean Howells—Ever Distant, Ever Near." *Old Northwest* 10, no. 1 (Spring 1984): 127–37.

Peck, Graham A. *Making an Antislavery Nation: Lincoln, Douglas, and the Battle over Freedom*. Urbana: University of Illinois Press, 2017.

Phillips, Christopher. *The Rivers Ran Backward: The Civil War and the Remaking of the American Middle Border.* New York: Oxford University Press, 2016.
Plantz, Samuel. "Lawrence College." *Wisconsin Magazine of History* 6, no. 2 (December 1922): 160–61.
Potter, David M. *The Impending Crisis, 1848–1861.* New York: HarperCollins, 1976.
Quaife, Milo M. "The Significance of the Ordinance of 1787." *Journal of the Illinois State Historical Society* 30, no. 4 (January 1938): 415–28.
———. "Wisconsin's First Literary Magazine." *Wisconsin Magazine of History* 5, no. 1 (September 1921): 43–56.
Raney, William F. "The People of the Land." In Troyer, *Culture of the Middle West*, 13–24.
Remini, Robert V. "The Northwest Ordinance of 1787: Bulwark of the Republic." *Indiana Magazine of History* 84, no. 1 (March 1988): 15–24.
Reynolds, David S. *Mightier Than the Sword: Uncle Tom's Cabin and the Battle for America.* New York: W. W. Norton, 2011.
Rhode, Robert T. "The Persistence of Place: Alice Cary's Authentic Rural Settings." *Ohio Valley History* 7, no. 1 (Spring 2007): 47–59.
Ridge, Martin. "How the Middle West Became America's Heartland." *Inland* 2 (1976): 13–18.
Robinson, Marilynne. *When I Was a Child I Read Books: Essays.* New York: Farrar, Straus and Giroux, 2012.
Rose, Gregory S. "On the Path toward National Eminence: Economic Development in the Old Northwest, 1850–1860." In Lauck, *Making of the Midwest*, 157–81.
Rosenberg, Norman L. "Personal Liberty Laws and Sectional Crisis: 1850–1861." *Civil War History* 17, no. 1 (March 1971): 25–44.
Salafia, Matthew. *Slavery's Borderland: Freedom and Bondage along the Ohio River.* Philadelphia: University of Pennsylvania Press, 2013.
Scheiber, Harry N. "On the Concepts of 'Regionalism' and 'Frontier.'" In *The Old Northwest: Studies in Regional History, 1787–1910*, edited by Harry N. Scheiber, vii–xix. Lincoln: University of Nebraska Press, 1969.
Schumaker, Arthur A. *A History of Indiana Literature.* Indianapolis: Indiana Historical Bureau, 1962.
Sewell, Richard H. *Ballots for Freedom: Antislavery Politics in the University States, 1837–1860.* New York: Oxford University Press, 1976.
———. *A House Divided: Sectionalism and Civil War, 1848–1865.* Baltimore: Johns Hopkins University Press, 1988.
Sheppard, Thomas J. "An Abolition Center." *Ohio Archaeological and Historical Society Publications* 18 (1910): 265–68.
Shortridge, James. "The Emergence of 'Middle West' as an American Regional Label." *Annals of the Association of American Geographers* 74, no. 2 (1984): 209–20.
Shriver, Phillip R. "Freedom's Proving Ground: The Heritage of the Northwest Ordinance." *Wisconsin Magazine of History* 72, no. 2 (Winter 1988–1989): 126–31.
Siebert, William H. "Beginnings of the Underground Railroad in Ohio." *Ohio Archaeological and Historical Quarterly* 56, no. 1 (1947): 70–93.

———. "A Quaker Section of the Underground Railroad in Northern Ohio." *Ohio Archaeological and Historical Quarterly* 39, no. 3 (July 1930): 479–502.

———. "The Underground Railroad in Ohio." *Ohio Archaeological and Historical Society Publications* 4 (1895): 44–63.

Silbey, Joel H. "After 'The First Republican Victory': The Republican Party Comes to Congress, 1855–1856." *Journal of Interdisciplinary History* 20, no. 1 (Summer 1989): 1–24.

Soike, Lowell J. *Necessary Courage: Iowa's Underground Railroad in the Struggle against Slavery*. Iowa City: University of Iowa Press, 2013.

Staiger, C. Bruce. "Abolitionism and the Presbyterian Schism of 1837–38." *Mississippi Valley Historical Review* 36, no. 3 (December 1949): 391–414.

Stanley, Matthew E. *The Loyal West: Civil War and Reunion in Middle America*. Urbana: University of Illinois Press, 2017.

Steiner, Michael C. "The Birth of the Midwest." In Lauck, Whitney, and Hogan, *Finding a New Midwestern History*, 3–24.

Troyer, Howard. *The Culture of the Middle West*. Appleton WI: Lawrence College Press, 1944.

Turner, Frederick Jackson. "The Significance of the Section in American History." *Wisconsin Magazine of History* 8, no. 3 (March 1925): 255–80.

Venable, William H. *Beginnings of Literacy Culture in the Ohio Valley: Historical and Biographical Sketches*. Cincinnati OH: Robert Clark, 1891.

———. "Literary Periodicals of the Ohio Valley." *Ohio Archaeological and Historical Society Publications* 1 (June 1887): 201–5.

Volpe, Vernon L. *Forlorn Hope of Freedom: The Liberty Party in the Old Northwest, 1838–1848*. Kent OH: Kent State University Press, 1990.

Wall, Maryjean. *How Kentucky Became Southern: A Tale of Outlaws, Horse Thieves, Gamblers, and Breeders*. Lexington: University Press of Kentucky, 2010.

Walsh, Annetta C. "Three Anti-slavery Newspapers." *Ohio Archaeological and Historical Society Publications* 31, no. 2 (April 1922): 172–212.

Wheeler, Kenneth H. "Higher Education in the Antebellum Ohio Valley: Slavery, Sectionalism, and the Erosion of Regional Identity." *Ohio Valley History* 8, no. 1 (Spring 2008): 1–22.

Wheeler, Robert H. "The Literature of the Western Reserve." *Ohio History Journal* 100 (Summer/Autumn, 1991): 101–28.

Whitney, Gleaves. "The Upper Midwest as the Second Promised Land." In Lauck, Whitney, and Hogan, *Finding a New Midwestern History*, 281–302.

Wilentz, Sean. "Jeffersonian Democracy and the Origins of Political Antislavery in the United States: The Missouri Crisis Revisited." *Journal of the Historical Society* 4, no. 3 (Fall 2004): 375–401.

Woodworth, Steven E. *Nothing but Victory: The Army of the Tennessee, 1861–1865*. New York: Vintage, 2005.

Wyatt-Brown, Bertram. *Southern Honor: Ethics and Behavior in the Old South*. New York: Oxford University Press, 1982.

EIGHT

Spatial Survivance

*Haudenosaunee Active Presence in the
U.S.-Canadian Borderlands*

TAYLOR SPENCE

In 1923, Deskaheh, a.k.a. Levi General, a Cayuga political leader and speaker for the Six Nations (Haudenosaunee) Council, traveled to England to deliver a message he hoped would gain him an audience with the king.[1] Two years earlier, in 1921, the Northwest Mounted Police (the Royal Canadian Mounted Police, or RCMP) had established a permanent post in his home at Grand River in central Ontario. This invasion came after more than forty years of conflict between the Canadian government and the Six Nations and appeared to be part of an intentional campaign to usurp the long-standing relationship forged between the British Empire and the Haudenosaunee over hundreds of years and replace it with its own nationalistic and paternalistic oversight, the ultimate purpose of which appeared to be assimilation, erasure, and land expropriation.

The Six Nations Council charged Deskaheh with the mission to raise the alarm in England and the Continent about Canada's encroachments. In 1922, the Six Nations petitioned the International Court of Justice; in 1923 Deskaheh traveled to England on a newly minted Six Nations passport; and in 1924 he traveled to Geneva, Switzerland (presumably with the same documentation), in an attempt to speak before the League of Nations.[2] These efforts proved fruitless. Yet this junket demonstrated the Haudenosaunee Confederacy's commitment to defending their sovereignty and maintaining a distinct political identity. However, when Deskaheh attempted to return home by way of the United States using his Six Nations passport, Canadian border officials refused him entry, and he remained stuck, just a few hundred miles from his home, lodged in the interstices of the settler nation. He died the next year a guest of the Tuscarora Nation in Lewiston, New York, and a martyr to the cause of Haudenosaunee spatial sovereignty.[3]

Sovereignty and movement are fundamentally linked, and Canada's rejection of Deskaheh's Six Nations passport and, with it, his sovereign political identity demonstrated how the border imbued the officialdom of the settler nation with the power to dictate Indigenous destinies.[4] Nevertheless, the Haudenosaunee were adept at the parry and thrust of settler colonialism and used Deskaheh's experiences to construct a new resistance tradition of crossing the settler nation's borders in order to reinscribe their much older cultural space. They based this mobile sovereignty on their preborder boundaries and requickened it with actions such as rituals of crossing, processions, public performances, cultural exhibitions, and political and legal actions. This use of movement to both survive and resist settler-colonial bordering is *spatial survivance.*

Anishnaabeg literary scholar Gerald Vizenor says that survivance is the "active presence" of Indigenous people resisting "absence, deracination, and oblivion." It is "the continuance of stories, not a mere reaction, however pertinent. Survivance is greater than the right of a survivable name."[5] More than mere survival but not quite full autonomous actualization, survivance pertains to the historical fact of conquest and its ongoing and lived legacies in the lives of Indigenous peoples. Vizenor did not invent the word, nor the idea. Survivance has a similar meaning in the context of French-Canadians who have experienced anglophonic conquest.[6] Yet white Quebeckers were conquered, not mapped out of existence. Indigenous survivance kindles "the active sense of [Indigenous] presence" in every facet of embodied existence in the settler-colonial context. Spatial survivance, the tradition Deskaheh's story represents, pertains to the particular actions of Indigenous people—in this case, the Haudenosaunee—to redraw and thereby reestablish their cultural spaces and occupy them in spite of the national borders that attempted to erase them.[7]

For white settlers, the actuality of the border between the United States and Canada has waxed and waned over the years since the American Revolution. Four treaties—the Treaty of Paris in 1783, Jay's Treaty in 1794, the Treaty of Ghent in 1815, and the Webster-Ashburton Treaty in 1842—testify to the contentious significance of this border in the formation of the settler nation from the vestiges of European imperialism in the eighteenth and nineteenth centuries. This border was the first crucible of an American exceptionalist identity and remained a signifier of U.S. Anglophobia well past the American Civil War, something that might come as a surprise to some North Americans today.[8]

However, seen from the perspective of Indigenous people, the border has been a continual and troubling reality from the beginning. After the Revolution, the Haudenosaunee, whose commons the border divided, recognized the potential significance of the settlers' line and demanded another negotiation with the United States and Great Britain. The resulting 1794 Jay Treaty guaranteed the right of Indians "dwelling on either side of the said Boundary Line to pass and repass." As part of the negotiations to end the War of 1812, the British called for the creation of an Indigenous territory, which would lie between the two settler polities. This proposal upheld the commitments Great Britain had made to its Indigenous allies in the Proclamation of 1763 to protect their territorial sovereignty, but it also aimed to use Indigenous people as a "useful barrier" between British subjects and U.S. citizens.[9]

The United States flatly refused to accept such a buffer state but reaffirmed Indigenous people's right to cross the border.[10] Still, the border was a step toward the erasure of Haudenosaunee cultural space. Nevertheless, as long as the Indigenous peoples—such as the Haudenosaunee, who cherish commons bisected by the international border—continue to resist this imposition, the U.S.-Canadian borderlands will remain an unfinished project of conquest.[11]

Deskaheh's story sifts out a more subterranean tension in post-conquest Haudenosaunee politics, and that is how the international border transformed their political structures.[12] Haudenosaunee political authority is ascending, meaning that it rises from the local, on-the-ground dominion of the clans to the nation and then the League of the Haudenosaunee.[13] The central political ritual for delineating these three branches of government (if you will) is the Condolence Council, in which the clans memorialize a deceased political leader and lift another up in his place. This ritual comes out of the clan's remembrance of specific places, which only they know. Thus, while the loss of land, which began after the American Revolution, appeared to place in jeopardy the entire political structure of the League, it may be that at the level of clan memory, the idea of a unified League continued. Deskaheh moved out of and into this palimpsest of the League's traditional space and sought to return to Six Nations based on the same idea.[14]

Clinton Rickard, the man at whose house Deskaheh lived out his exile, took up the idea of Haudenosaunee spatial sovereignty after the Cayuga chief's death. Rickard founded the Indian Defense League of America (IDLA) the next year "to guarantee unrestricted passage on the continent of North America for Indian people." Rickard "considered [such cross-border movement to be] an inherent right," but in fact his claim was based on long-established settler law.[15] Beginning on July 14, 1928, Haudenosaunee people marched across the Niagara River on the "Peace Bridge" from Hamilton, Ontario, to Buffalo, New York, to reaffirm their rights guaranteed under the provisions of Jay's Treaty. Annually since then, in what has become known as the "Border Crossing Celebration," the IDLA has conducted the same ritual of crossing the border.[16]

However, the arc of settler colonialism is long and persistent and always tilts toward the erasure and assimilation of Indigenous peoples, and so spatial survivance requires constant tending. In recent years, the United States and Canada have demonstrated an increasing tendency to abrogate and ignore long-standing legal commitments to the Haudenosaunee.[17] Historians of the Haudenosaunee contribute to this erasure by allowing the United States and Canadian settler nations to dictate how they understand the historic parameters of Haudenosaunee space, particularly by situating the Haudenosaunee homeland in the state of New York when, in fact, they have long-cherished connections to other sites around Lake Ontario and the upper St. Lawrence River.[18] Historians and other scholars who work with Indigenous communities impacted by the border can do their part by not allowing the settler nation to shape their work. In the case of the Haudenosaunee, this would mean addressing and discussing the entire diaspora as one Indigenous community, not for the purposes of a romantic return to the great days of yore, but as the means of resisting settler nationalism's tendency to divide and conquer. At the same time, the Haudenosaunee themselves are continuing their efforts at reaffirming and reasserting their cross-border spatial identity in rituals of return and border-crossing.

Inner and Outer Commons: Iroquoia and Etino'ëh

Spatial survivance has its origins in colonizers' insecure need "to own" Indigenous peoples to buttress their sense of superiority and power. Arthur C. Parker, a Seneca archeologist and director of the Rochester Museum of Arts and Sciences, understood this orientalist desire to acquire the exoticism and luster of the Haudenosaunee. The more fearsome the Haudenosaunee appeared, the more powerful New Yorkers felt they were. Parker used his position to inculcate in New York's schoolchildren (and their parents) these ideas with colorful and exciting productions that transformed the Haudenosaunee into archetypical "Indians" in an illustrious state history. At the same time, these kinds of maneuvers ensured the continuing spatial sovereignty of the Haudenosaunee in their homelands.

However, a deeper and older spatial awareness predates the advent of the settler nations' borders, which we might understand as the Haudenosaunee inner and outer commons. Historian Allan Greer formulates a useful schema for understanding commons systems in settler colonialism, which enables a clearer understanding of Haudenosaunee spatial sovereignty. An "inner" commons, which in Europe encompassed the resources and space

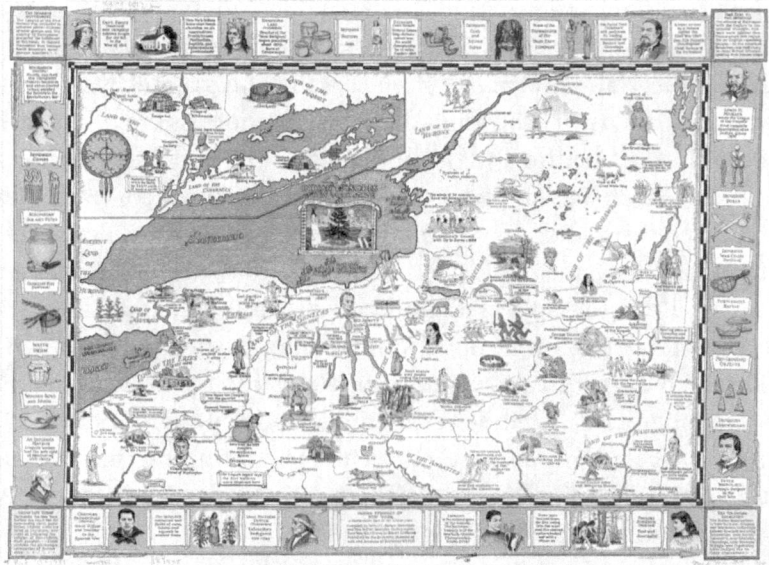

FIG. 3. *Indian Episodes of New York State* (1935), by Arthur C. Parker and Mrs. Herricks (collection of the American Geographical Society), embeds Haudenosaunee history, people, and places in the soil and cultural fabric of the state of New York and New Yorkers.

shared by the residents of a manor or a village, in settler colonialism became the space imperialists claimed for their exclusive use. The "outer" commons, which in Europe included all the resources shared by multiple manors or villages—resources such as rivers, peat bogs, and forest mast—in settler colonialism became the imperial "grazing commons": a joint collective of nascent empires. The act of allowing livestock to graze in Indigenous lands enabled the expropriation of the wealth that greatly benefited settlers and created the conditions for a seemingly blameless conquest based in agricultural practice rather than malicious actions.[19]

Inner and outer commons is also a framework that describes Haudenosaunee spatial conceptualizations. The origins of Haudenosaunee sovereignty lie in generations of clan occupation and resource use in particular locations. Lisa Brooks's notion of the *wlôgan*, or "bowl," is useful in understanding these clan commons. Wlôgan were (and are) Abenaki homeplaces, which emerged over time in locations (sometimes around former beaver ponds) whose geomorphology and available natural resources sustained and became the commons of an extended kinship group. Clan members in the original five Haudenosaunee nations—the Mohawk, Oneida, Onönda'geh, Cayuga, and Seneca—coalesced in bowls that provided ample room to retreat into highlands, to descend into fertile lowlands, and to control access into and out of common spaces.[20] According to linguist Phyllis Bardeau, the nation was "a geo-political unit" where "control over a territory" was its main purpose.[21] Haudenosaunee nations gained control of their space by utilizing natural pinch points and bottlenecks in the geography. These places were the divisions between Haudenosaunee inner and outer commons.

These individual Haudenosaunee wlôgan, when grouped together, became the larger shared commons of the League of the Haudenosaunee. Traditional histories of the formation of the League situate an international pathway at the center of a region riven by a ceaseless cycle of violence and resource competition. A man called "the Peacemaker," an outsider born on the Bay of Quinte on the north shore of Lake Ontario (at the site of another key pinch point, the headwaters of the St. Lawrence), sailed across the lake on a mission to establish peace.[22] He located the pathway warriors frequented as they attacked and counterattacked. A Clan Mother named Yegowaneh lived along this road and offered food and shelter to passing warriors. The Peacemaker convinced her of his vision for a peaceful sharing, and she became a key vector in communicating his message of peace to the nations. In assuming this role, she received a new name, Jegöhsahse—"she [who] has a new face."[23] His skillful diplomacy and her participation transformed a road used for war into one that brought peace and ultimately a shared resource commons.[24] The Peacemaker's central insight was to see that the geography that the nations had adapted to and occupied might sustain a larger outer commons.

As Matthew Dennis understands it, the League made it possible for Haudenosaunee to transform outsider into insider, first in terms of the five and then six nations (the Tuscarora were adopted in 1723) and later in terms of other nations such as the Yendat.[25] The League's inner commons, what might be called "Iroquoia," was situated in the protected drainages of the Alleghenies and Appalachians and in the lowlands between these mountains and Lake Ontario. This stable and productive heartland provided the Haudenosaunee a base from which to martial their unified energies for expansion outward into an outer commons—Etinoëh, "Mother Earth," the waxing and waning wider sphere of Haudenosaunee influence, at times encompassing the entirety of Lake Ontario; the upper St. Lawrence, including the Isle de Montréal; the Ontarian Peninsula; and the Forks of the Ohio.[26] The Haudenosaunee world was thus made up of multiple smaller bowls nested in the great wlôgan of Lake Ontario, or Cataraqui. Haudenosaunee conceptualized the peaceful sharing of resource commons with a roasted beaver tail, which all could eat with their fingers but with "no knife near our dish."[27]

When U.S. and British negotiators at Paris in 1782 looked at a map of the region, they did not see an Indigenous commons but saw a watery pathway snaking toward the Great Northwest and the possibility of the riches of the Far East. The two colonizers agreed to share this pathway and drew a line through the middle of the St. Lawrence River and the Great Lakes, even though no one from either the United States or British Canada was regularly sailing out in the middle of these lakes, nor steaming up the St. Lawrence. One traveled through the forest or along the water's edge.[28] The signatories to the Treaty of Paris knew very well the limits of the Haudenosaunee world. They had been allied with or fighting them for more than two hundred years. The line emanated from imperialist visionaries who aspired to move across and through the space. Drawing a line down the middle of these waterways was a manifestation of expansive intention. The border ensured that no Indigenous nation would have a place between the settler nations. They had used up all the future space.

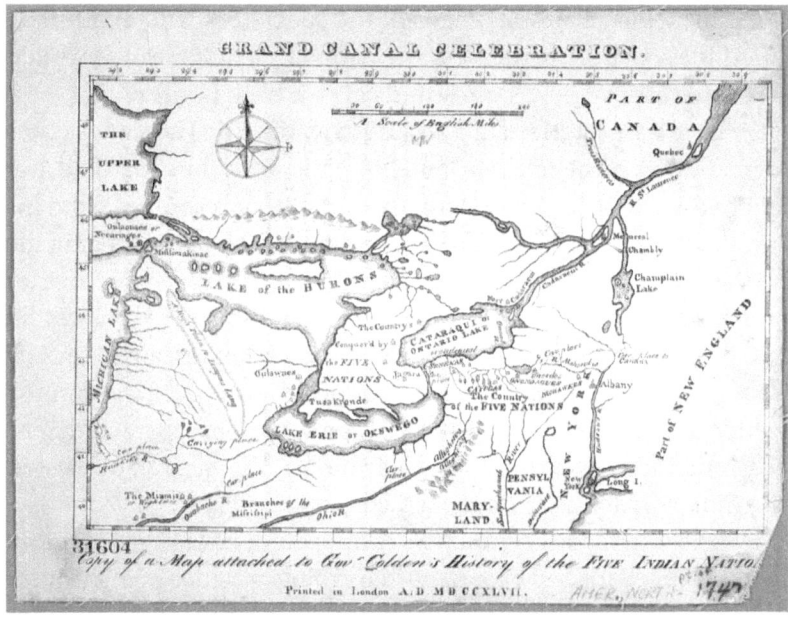

FIG. 4. *Cadwallader Colden: A Map of the Country of the Five Nations Belonging to the Province of New York* (1725), a map that captures the expansiveness of "Etinoëh" (note that Haudenosaunee claims include the Ontarian Peninsula). Cadwallader Colden, *The History of the Five Indian Nations Depending on the Province of New-York in America* (New York: Printed and sold by William Bradford, 1727), frontispiece.

Border-Crossing Rituals

In 1833, two men met in the forest of New York. One man, named Drid, was a member of the Mohawk Nation of Akwesasne, a territory that straddled the international border and the St. Lawrence River. He regularly moved around the Mohawk homeland to hunt. The other was a white man named Peter Foster. Foster had purportedly nursed a "deadly hatred" of Indians since his boyhood. Locals recounted stories "of the numbers slain by him during his long career in the forest." True to his reputation, Foster tracked down Drid, the two men tussled, and Foster shot Drid in the heart. In September of 1834, a Herkimer County Court jury acquitted Foster on all counts. Foster rose up in the courtroom, stretched his arms wide above the heads of the spectators, and exclaimed, "God bless you all! God bless the people!" Drid's family traveled down to retrieve Drid's body and carry it back home.[29]

After the Revolution, in a series of treaties, the Haudenosaunee signed away most of their lands in New York, but that had not stopped Drid, before his death, from claiming resources from his traditional hunting grounds.[30] About half of the people that made up the Six Nations relocated to Upper Canada (present-day Ontario) and resided along the Grand River, creating the Six Nations Grand River Reserve. However, a significant population remained in New York on original homelands. Oneida and Onönda'geh lived in the center of the state, and in the West, both the Tuscarora and Seneca remained on portions of their lands. The Seneca possessed the most territory, split between eleven locations.[31]

As the nineteenth century wore on, Haudenosaunee lost more land in New York and experienced ongoing and increasing trouble crossing "the line," as they called it.[32] In 1867, the Canadian nation-state was formed, and in 1924 the Indian Act in Canada and the Immigration Act in the United States attempted to impose citizenship on the Haudenosaunee and regulate and control border crossing. The Haudenosaunee adapted, developing two linked interpretations of their spatial sovereignty and two sets of spatial survivance traditions. The first, *interior* set of traditions saw Haudenosaunee communities charting their own individuated destinies as reservations and multinational territories. They are the subject of numerous separate histories.

The second, *exterior* tradition is as yet indistinct and not fully formed, but it entails the creation of a spatial network by crossing state, provincial, and international borders based on the older idea of Etinoëh. This old-new tradition began soon after the Revolution. Cayuga chief Peter Wilson explains that when the British paid their annuities, the Haudenosaunee at Six Nations notified the "New York" Haudenosaunee who came to Fort Erie in Upper Canada and obtained their share. Likewise, when the United States paid its annuities, all the Haudenosaunee would congregate at Canandaigua in New York to receive their payment.[33] In October of 1845,

FIG. 5. *The Stretched Longhouse: The Haudenosaunee (Iroquois) Diaspora*, ca. 1700–present. Map by the author.

G. S. Riley, who was a non-Haudenosaunee resident of Rochester, New York, resided at the Tonawanda reservation, where he witnessed diasporic Haudenosaunee gathered together to "condole" a chief. Riley could not understand the Seneca-language ceremony, but he did understand that representatives from all six nations had come, including Mohawks from Canada.[34] On October 9, 1884, "an unusually large delegation of Indians from the various reservations and Canada" convened in Buffalo for what was also probably a Condolence Council, according to the *Milwaukee Sentinel*.[35] In 1936, the anthropologist William N. Fenton attended a Condolence held in Onondaga, New York, with both "New York" and "Canadian" Haudenosaunee representatives.[36]

These cross-border rituals have continued into more recent times. Some forty descendants of the Seneca chief Cornplanter, who live on Seneca lands in northwestern Pennsylvania, welcome hundreds of their descendants for a reunion annually.[37] Each year on November 11, the Ganondagan State Historic Site welcomes Haudenosaunee people and others to commemorate the signing of the Treaty of Canandaigua in 1794, historically significant for its assertion of "nation-to-nation status" between the League and the United States.[38] For nearly thirty years the Iroquois Museum in Howes Cave, New York, has hosted a Haudenosaunee Indian Festival that draws performers from Six Nations and Haudenosaunee people from all across the wider Haudenosaunee diaspora.[39] In 2000, one thousand Haudenosaunee gathered in New York to condole Chief Brian Skidders, which Six Nations member Norman Jacobs considered "really, really something."[40] I attended a powwow at the Oneida Nation of Wisconsin in 2014, where I encountered Haudenosaunee from all over the diaspora. These private and public border-crossings become cultural "hubs" for Haudenosaunee people to reaffirm their clan connections as well as their connections to their homelands.[41]

For some Haudenosaunee, a desire to return to and reclaim land in Iroquoia has been one cause of border-crossing.[42] In 1957 Francis Johnson, called "Standing Arrow," led two hundred Mohawk people to a piece of territory along the Schoharie Creek west of Albany, New York, which lay in traditional Mohawk territory. They made this move after having been dispossessed of their homes due to the widening of the St. Lawrence Seaway in Quebec.[43] They defied eviction along the Schoharie and ended up relocating to one hundred and twenty acres of land nearby, donated by a local farmer the next year.[44] In the fall of 1973, members of the Kahnawake Longhouse of the Mohawk Nation south of the city of Montreal sent out eviction notices to fifteen hundred non-Haudenosaunee residents of their territory, giving them two weeks to vacate their homes and leave. An armed conflict ensued between the provincial police and Haudenosaunee warriors from as far away as Oklahoma who returned to fight. "There we were risking our lives," Louis Hall, Karioniaktajeh, told a reporter, "to defend 2.5 acres when we've got millions in New York State." He and other members of the Longhouse went down to the Adirondack Park in New York and decided to occupy an abandoned Girl Scout camp called

Moss Lake. Julian Delaronde, one of these returners, called his wife, Judy, around May 20, 1974, and told her he had found a house. "You think maybe he found a mansion the way he described it. It was just this little cabin," recounted Judy.[45] In the wake of the American Indian Movement's (AIM) takeover of Wounded Knee, the Mohawk Nation acquired a piece of territory near Altona, New York, in 1977 and set up a clan-based "independent territory" called Ganienkeh.[46]

I called the number on their website and spoke with Kiotenhariyo, who explained to me that rather than being strictly a Mohawk nation, Ganienkeh is a pan-Indian place where Oneida, Onönda'geh, Ojibwe, Mohawk, and others live together under one Longhouse. "Here the people shall live according to the rules of nature," their *Manifesto* reads. "Here the Great Law of the Six Nations Iroquois Confederacy shall prevail. The people shall live off the land. The co-op system of economy shall prevail. Instead of the people competing with each other, they shall help and co-operate with each other. Here, they shall relearn the superior morality of the ancients."[47] Although the territory has been home to the condoled Bear Clan chief Karonhiaktátie, Kiotenhariyo said that the Condolence Council and the installation of a new chief were and are not necessary for territorial government; the people can and do govern themselves with a Clan Council.[48] Judy Delaronde believes that in founding Ganienkeh, she "learned a lot about being traditional."[49] Ganienkeh spawned another reclamation in 1993 when Tom Porter, a Mohawk chief who grew to maturity with the history of the prophecy of Mohawk return, heard about a piece of land along the Mohawk River coming up for auction. He bought it, founding the Kanatsiohareke Mohawk Community near Fonda, New York.[50]

However, the history of the "New York" Cayuga exemplifies that it can be hard to return home. In treaties made with either the State of New York or the U.S. government—in 1784, 1789, 1790, 1795, and 1807—the Cayuga ceded all their lands. Some Cayuga decided to head west to join kinsmen and women who had moved to Sandusky, Ohio, in the mid-eighteenth century.[51] Others chose to become the guests of the Seneca at Buffalo Creek. Some traveled to Six Nations in Upper Canada in order to investigate the possibility of joining the Haudenosaunee there. This delegation included Waowawanaonk (Peter Wilson, a Cayuga chief), six other Cayuga, and representatives from other "New York" Haudenosaunee. According to Waowawanaonk, this precipitated the first reunion of the League of the Six Nations since the break over the War of 1812. Wilson and the other "New York" Haudenosaunee declared that they would sooner reunite with their kinsmen at Six Nations than relocate west. However, after conferring, the chiefs refused to allow the homeless "New York" Cayuga to relocate to Grand River. They reminded them that they made common cause with the "Bostonians" in 1812, and while they regretted that the Cayuga had made such a poor alliance, the covenant had been broken then and could not be mended.[52] Some "New York" Cayuga found this response especially objectionable, as they believed it had been the "Canadian" Cayuga who had sold the bulk of their homelands in 1795.[53]

Meanwhile, the Cayuga people who had immigrated to Sandusky suffered grievous losses. When the last Cayuga chief was near death, he sent for a young man and charged him with preserving the two treaties that the diasporic Cayuga had carried with them. They constituted the "evidence," he supposedly said, "of the indebtedness of the State [of New York] to our nation." He died, and in the summer of 1847, this unnamed Cayuga man, along with the other surviving Sandusky Cayuga, arrived at Cattaraugus Seneca Territory in western New York and met with Waowawanaonk, who proposed to the young man that they purchase a tract of land in New York and reconstitute the Cayuga. The young man agreed but felt he should first consult with the "Canadian" Cayuga at Six Nations.

He crossed the border with the two treaties and headed to Grand River, where he died. These two treaties thus came into the hands of the "Canadian" Cayuga of Grand River, who then used them to claim a share of the annuity New York paid to the tribe from its 1795 and 1807 cessions. The state called a hearing in 1850 in which both "New York" and "Canadian" Cayuga made their cases before the assembly. Waowawanaonk reminded his Cayuga kin of the rebuff the "Canadian" Cayuga of Six Nations had given them. He employed his eloquence to convince state officials to exclude the "Canadian" Cayuga from sharing the annuities. "I am a Cayuga. I was born a Cayuga," he said. "If . . . you will decide against us . . . and give . . . our small annuity to a foreign people," just remember that "if perchance . . . an Indian shall call at your door for bread, do not, I beg you, in the name of the Great Spirit, do not ask to what tribe he belongs, but relieve his necessities and save him from starvation, for he may answer you, I am a Cayuga."[54] The State of New York ruled in favor of the "New York" Cayuga, and they continued to receive the entirety of their annuity payments.

After securing the exclusive control of their annuity payments, the New York Cayuga pursued legal avenues for the reclamation of some of their lands in New York. They cited the unconstitutionality of treaties the State of New York had made with them (article 1, section 8 of the U.S. Constitution stipulates that Congress has the sole right to make treaties with Indians) as the basis for their proposed reclamations. In 2000, 150 years after Waowawanaonk had defended the "New York" Cayuga's financial claims on the State of New York, the Cayuga Nation of Indians received a $248 million settlement in compensation for the unconstitutional treaties the state had made with them. However, in spite of this success, a federal court of appeals overturned the decision, and in 2006 the U.S. Supreme Court refused to review the case. In 2010, when traveling through western New York, I saw roadsides dotted with signs that read "No Cayuga Land Deal!" and "No Sovereign Nation. No Reservation."[55] The Cayuga Nation of New York's attempt to return home remains in limbo. Like Deskaheh, they are stuck in the imperial interstices of two settler nations.[56]

Haudenosaunee history encompasses deep time, and over this *longue durée*, Haudenosaunee territoriality has changed—namely, in the breadth and scope of its claims. At the same time, challenges to Haudenosaunee sovereignty and actual land-takings also have long histories and are ongoing as well. In 2010 the Iroquois Nationals lacrosse team became stranded in New York on their way to the World Lacrosse Championships because the British government refused to recognize their Haudenosaunee passports. They ended up not attending the event and returned home.[57] More recently, Tadodaho Sid Hill was waylaid in La Paz, Bolivia, where he and a Haudenosaunee delegation had been attending the World People's Climate Forum at the behest of Evo Morales. The Canadian government refused to recognize the Haudenosaunee passports they traveled on and tried to force them to take Canadian passports. With the intercession of the United States, they were allowed to return home.

It can never be assumed that Haudenosaunee people are secure in their lands in New York or anywhere else. Rapaciousness and greed should be considered baseline personality traits of the U.S. and Canadian settler states. How else to explain their assiduousness in undermining the very Indigenous sovereign right of movement they were forced to grant? Containment, removal, and enclosure are traditions as old as the commons against the poor in Europe and the poor and Indigenous in colonized locations. Nevertheless, it may be that settler greed only serves to burnish the tattoo of Haudenosaunee boundaries even more permanently into the land. "In the last thirty years or so," the Cayuga Nation of Six Nations Grand River Territory believes, "confrontations between the Iroquois and the governments of Ontario and New York have increased ... the unity of the Iroquois nations," not lessened it.[58]

Whether for the purposes of reuniting with clan members or for the aim of returning home, these border-crossing stories demonstrate that Etinoëh, the League's widest expression of spatial sovereignty, continues to be the basis from which Haudenosaunee people exercise their rights to freely move in their cultural space. Deskaheh declared in his last recorded oration on March 10, 1925, "I am the speaker of the Council of the Six Nations, the oldest League of Nations now existing." The other League of Nations accorded him neither the audience he requested nor the respect he was owed. He was unable to return home. Fifty years later, another Haudenosaunee leader, Sotsisowah, John C. Mohawk, from Akwesasne, spoke to an audience of non-governmental organizations of the United Nations in Geneva, Switzerland, under the authority granted to him by "the Iroquois Confederacy." He spoke on Indigenous sovereignty.[59] Spatial survivance requires Indigenous people to engage in such persistent showing up physically to reiterate the expansiveness of their boundaries over and against the expansive tendencies of settler nations.

Notes

1. Hill, *Clay We Are Made Of*, 229.

2. In 1926, the League of Nations convened a passport conference to formalize the passport as we know it today. Thank you to the anonymous reader of this chapter for this valuable insight. Peterson, review of *The Passport in America*; Robertson, *Passport in America*.

3. Hill, *Clay We Are Made Of*, 214–15, 230.

4. Both Lee and Hernández explore how the Border Patrol, established in 1924, and border policy in both the U.S.-Mexico and U.S.-Canada borderlands became the means of creating and defining state power. Hernández, *Migra!*, 20, 29; Lee, "Enforcing the Borders," 84.

5. Vizenor, *Survivance*, 1.

6. In Canadian conquest history, *la survivance* describes the persistence of an agrarian and Catholic Quebec culture under Protestant anglophonic rule. Cook, *Watching Quebec*, 38–49. *Survivance* is an old word of French origin, referring to when an incumbent or officeholder nominates a successor before his death: e.g., "Anne holds the title of CEO in survivance." *Webster's Third New International Dictionary* (1986), s.v. "survivance."

7. Smith, *Decolonizing Methodologies*, 146.

8. For a superb discussion of the first three, see Hatter, *Citizens of Convenience*, 11, 13; Spence, "Canada Thistle."

9. King George III, "Royal Proclamation"; Hatter, *Citizens of Convenience*, 178.

10. Library of Congress Online, "Jay's Treaty"; Boos, Fathali, and McLawsen, "History of the Jay Treaty," 35–66. Hatter argues that the more restrictive commercial convention, which the United States and Great Britain negotiated in July of 1815, should be included in analyzing the significance of the Treaty of Ghent. Hatter, *Citizens of Convenience*, 179–90; United States of America and Great Britain, Peace and Amity (Treaty of Ghent).

11. In this conception, a borderland is neither a syncretic zone nor a transformed "borderland land" à la Aron and Adelman. It is a place in stalemate: an Indigenous homeland with a line running through it representing settler dominion claims. Adelman and Aron, "From Borderlands to Border," 815.

12. For an analogous case from the border between Mexico and the United States, see Schulze, "We Are Lost between Two Worlds," 135.

13. The League of the Haudenosaunee was a confederation of—at first—five and later six Indigenous nations: the Mohawk, Oneida, Onönda'geh, Cayuga, Seneca, and Tuscarora (adopted in 1723). Euro-American scholars can agree on no firm date for the origins of the League. But they commonly agree that the League formed in reaction to the arrival of Europeans. Parmenter, like many scholars, keys the founding of the League to the arrival of Europeans around 1600. Parmenter, *Edge of the Woods*, 16–17. Fenton dates it at the early 1500s. Fenton, *Great Law and the Longhouse*, 69, 125. Mann and Fields say it was the twelfth century. Mann and Fields, "Sign in the Sky." Bardeau says it was the early nine hundreds. Bardeau and Cardinal, *Definitive Seneca*, 206.

14. Thank you to my editors and especially Alex Finkelstein for this and many other insights that contributed to this essay.

15. Website for the Indian Defense League of America, accessed September 15, 2010, https://bordercrossingidla.weebly.com/.

16. "Activist Roots Still Thrive in Canada Border Crossing," *Indian Country Today*, accessed September 15, 2010, http://www.indiancountrytoday.com/archive/28212089.html; Taylor, *Divided Ground*, 407.

17. Now the Grand Council advises Haudenosaunee to acquire special identity cards lest they be prepared "to not travel outside the country," and they still have no resolution from Canada on the question of honoring Jay's Treaty. Haudenosaunee Confederacy, "Haudenosaunee Documentation Committee"; Fletcher, "Death of History in the Roberts Court's Indian Law Jurisprudence."

18. Tadodaho (Grand Council chief) Sid Hill reaffirmed these more expansive boundaries as recently as 2015. Sid Hill, "My Six Nation Haudenosaunee Passport Is Not a 'Fantasy Document,'" editorial, *Guardian*, October 30, 2015, http://www.theguardian.com/commentisfree/2015/oct/30/my-six-nation-haudenosaunee-passport-not-fantasy-document-indigenous-nations.

19. Greer, "Commons and Enclosure in the Colonization of North America," 376, 381–86.

20. The Mohawk people inhabited the drainage made by their eponymous river, with flatlands to cultivate, the Catskills and Adirondacks rising on either side, and perched strategically at the Mohawk River's confluence with the Hudson. The Oneida people could retreat to safety in the Adirondacks, monitored a dynamic pinch point between the headwaters of the Mohawk River and Lake Ontario, and had ample access to resources in the forest flats around Lake Oneida. The Onönda'geh and Cayuga Nations cultivated well-watered and fertile lowlands and lived along waterways that enabled them to move up into the Appalachian highlands in times of

danger and patrol movements from the headwaters of the Delaware and Susquehanna Rivers toward Lake Ontario. O'Callaghan, *Documents Relative to the Colonial History of New York*, 99; Reynolds, "Weekly Historical Note"; Bardeau and Cardinal, *Definitive Seneca*, 77.

21. Bardeau and Cardinal, *Definitive Seneca*, 269.

22. Parker and Newhouse, *Constitution of the Five Nations*, 65–71, 83, 111. Fenton concludes that "Huronia and Iroquoia may be considered one cultural province." Fenton, *Great Law and the Longhouse*, 3, 86–98; Richter, *Ordeal of the Longhouse*, 15; Bardeau and Cardinal, *Definitive Seneca*, 209; Tanner, *Atlas of Great Lakes Indian History*, map 5.

23. New York State, "Jikonhsaseh"; Bardeau and Cardinal, *Definitive Seneca*, 224; Mann, *Iroquoian Women*, 36–39; Bilharz, "First among Equals?," 108; Fenton, *Great Law and the Longhouse*, 4, 101.

24. Cusick, *Sketches of Ancient History of the Six Nations*, 22–23; Fenton, *Great Law and the Longhouse*, 81; Ka-Hon-Hes, Akwesasne Notes, and Fadden, *Kaianerekowa Hotinonsionne*, 184. The *Kaianerekowa Hotinonsionne* document carries a heading stating that no date for its origins was recorded. The Peacemaker took Jegöhsahse:' with him when he confronted the terrifying Onönda'geh shaman named Tadodaho. She lifted the ceremonial antlers of the white-tailed deer onto Tadodaho's head and then repeated this action for the forty-nine other national chiefs, becoming the Mother of Nations. Bardeau and Cardinal, *Definitive Seneca*, 265; Morgan, *League of the Ho-Dé-No-Sau-Nee, or Iroquois*, 259–60; Richter, "War and Culture," 544.

25. Dennis, *Cultivating a Landscape of Peace*, 8, 63, 65–67, 105.

26. One example of this was when the Haudenosaunee extended their political authority over the nations at the Forks of the Ohio with the Treaty of Fort Stanwix of 1768. Wallace, *Death and Rebirth of the Seneca*, 154. This distinction also accords more accurately with the stretched Longhouse of today, where Etino'ëh spans thousands of miles and includes at least nineteen separate homelands, and with many Haudenosaunee ritually returning to Iroquoia on an annual basis. Haudenosaunee linguistics mirror this expansiveness. The "Lake Iroquoian" language group includes people on both sides of the lake: the so-called Huron peoples and the Five Nations. Linguist Wallace Chafe has remarked that of all the Northern Iroquoian languages, the Onöndowa'ga:' have been the most "exuberant" in adopting words and expressions from other languages, reflecting, in part, the open and welcoming Western Door of the Haudenosaunee. Chafe and Seneca community members, *Grammar of the Seneca Language*, 1, 6; Grey, "Personal Communication with Sue Grey," 3.

27. Brooks, *Common Pot*, 4; Jordan, *Seneca Restoration*, 28–29; Hill, *Clay We Are Made Of*, 42.

28. "We are in the middle of the forest! We are at the shore!" Head, *Forest Scenes and Incidents*, 342. Shannon, Smardon, and Knudson had the same assessment. Shannon, Smardon, and Knudson, "Using Visual Assessment as a Foundation for Greenway Planning," 358.

29. Sylvester, "Not Guilty."

30. Congress of the United States of America and Tribes of Indians Called the Six Nations, Treaty with the Six Nations; Morris, United States of America, and Seneca Indians, "Treaty of Big Tree."

31. Tonawanda, Buffalo Creek, Cattaraugus, Allegany, Oil Springs, Canadea, Gardeau, Squawky Hill, Little Beard's Town, Big Tree, and Canawaugus. Graymont, *Iroquois in the American Revolution*, 118; Fenton, *Great Law and the Longhouse*, 211, 382; Taylor, *Divided Ground*, 129; Campisi, "National Policy, States' Rights, and Indian Sovereignty," 99–100; Harring, *White Man's Law*, 35–61.

32. Hauptman, *Seven Generations of Iroquois Leadership*, 164–65.

33. Peter Wilson, the Cayuga chief, was the son of Young King, which was how he heard this story. Wilson, *Speech of Dr. Wilson in No. 130*; Onönda'geh chief Colonel Silversmith corroborated this story in the summer of 1849 in front of the New York State Senate's Committee on Indian Affairs. *No. 64*, 64.

34. Riley, 1845, in Tuscarora & Six Nations, "Legends, Traditions, and Laws of the Iroquois."

35. "Red Jacket's Burial," *Milwaukee Sentinel*, October 10, 1884.

36. Fenton, *Great Law and the Longhouse*, 207, 709.

37. Edmund and Mitchell, *Apologies to the Iroquois*, 170.

38. Ganondagan, "Ganondagan-Canandaigua Treaty Commemoration Day."

39. *New York History*, "29th Annual Iroquois Indian Festival."

40. Free Library, "Iroquois Confederacy Re-unification Begun."

41. Ramirez, *Native Hubs*, 1.

42. It may be that, as historian and Six Nations resident Deborah Doxtator (since deceased) believed, "New York" Haudenosaunee could more credibly lay claim to the idea of homeland because they held on to original pieces of their national territories. Doxtator, "What Happened to the Iroquois Clans?," 336.

43. Michael James and Neal Boenzi, "Mohawks Invade Upstate Area, Assert Treaty Gives Them Land," *New York Times*, August 17, 1957, 39; Wilson and Mitchell, *Apologies to the Iroquois*.

44. "Indians Get Land Grant," *New York Times*, March 6, 1958; "50 Mohawks Defy Order to Break Camp Upstate," *New York Times*, February 16, 1958; "Indians Defy Eviction," *New York Times*, January 18, 1958.

45. "Interview with Louis Hall," *Lake Placid News*, July 22, 1976; Greg Horn, "Ganienkeh Celebrates 25th Anniversary," *Native Canadian*, May 17, 1999. http://www.nativecanadian.ca/Kanienkehaka/Ganienkeh_vol_8_num_15.htm.

46. Doran, "Ganienkeh."

47. Ganondagan, "Ganondagan-Canandaigua Treaty Commemoration Day."

48. Thus, the land-right underpinning Ganienkeh territory is one based on a location of Mohawk culture but also one where the Condolence ritual led to the reification not of a new chief but of the return to what was considered to be a more traditional governmental structure based on the clan and a reclamation of land for all Indigenous North Americans. Kiotenhariyo of Ganienkeh, telephone interview by the author, September 14, 2010.

49. Horn, "Ganienkeh Celebrates 25th Anniversary"; Six Nations of the Grand River, *6 Miles Deep*; Haudenosaunee Confederacy, *Sewatokwa'tshera't*; Abler, "Kansas Connection," 87, 89. In 1974, the three Oneida tribes banded together and sued New York State and two counties for the return of 250, 000 acres of land. In 1980, the Cayuga of New York and the Seneca of Oklahoma filed suit against the state and a group of private landowners for the return of their lands, evictions of non-Indian residents, and $350 million compensation. The Onönda'geh Nation sued the State of New York, the City of Syracuse, Onondaga County, and five corporations in 2005 for illegal land-takings and damage inflicted on central New York's environment. All three claims are still pending. Shattuck, *Oneida Land Claims*; Cayuga Nation, "Land Claim History"; "Onondaga Land Claim Argued in Federal Court," *Indian Country News*, October 2007, http://indiancountrynews.net/index.php?option=com_content&task=view&id=1662&Itemid=109.

50. Porter formed a group that included John Mohawk, Ron LaFrance, and Mike Mitchell, who had been influenced by Ernest Benedict and his activism. Hauptman, *Seven Generations of Iroquois Leadership*, 168; White, Kanatsiohareke Mohawk Community Manager, telephone interview with author, December 29, 2007.

51. Indian Claims Commission, "Statement of Finding in Strong et alia v. The United States of America," August 9, 1973, 97–117; "Cayuga Indians (Great Britain) v. United States (1926)," in United Nations, *Reports of International Arbitral Awards / Recueils des Sentences Arbitrales*, vol. 6 (New York, 2006), 173–90.

52. Wilson, *Speech of Dr. Wilson in No. 130*, 10.

53. Cayuga Nation, "Land Claim History."

54. Wilson, *Speech of Dr. Wilson in No. 130*, 12–16.

55. Upstate Citizens for Equality, "Cayuga Indians and Their Land Claim"; Cayuga Nation, "Land Claim History."

56. Fletcher, "Death of History in the Roberts Court's Indian Law Jurisprudence"; Wilkinson, *Blood Struggle*, 252; The Oneida and Onönda'geh Nations also filed suits based on the same unconstitutional treaties. All three claims are still pending. "Onondaga Land Claim Argued in Federal Court." The Supreme Court said that Haudenosaunee land-rights had been dissolved by "generations [of] non-Indians [who] have owned and developed the area that once composed the Tribe's historic reservation"; therefore, the Oneida "cannot revive its ancient sovereignty, in whole or in part."

57. "Iroquois Passport Dispute Raises Sovereignty Issues: Team Forfeited Games and Headed Home," *Indian Country News*, accessed September 15, 2010, http://indiancountrynews.net/index.php?option=com_content&task=view&id=9646&Itemid=76; Joanna Smith, "Six Nations Passport More than Travel Document, Say Users," *Toronto Star*, July 15, 2010, https://www.thestar.com/news/canada/2010/07/15/six_nations_passport_more_than_travel_document_say_users.html.

58. Tuscarora & Six Nations, "Cayuga Nation."

59. Akwesasne Notes, *Basic Call to Consciousness*, 11, 21, 41–54.

Bibliography

Abler, Thomas S. "The Kansas Connection: The Seneca Nation and the Iroquois Confederacy Council." In Foster, Campisi, and Mithun, *Extending the Rafters*, 81–93.

Adelman, Jeremy, and Stephen Aron. "From Borderlands to Border: Empires, Nation-States, and the Peoples in between in North American History." *American Historical Review* 104, no. 3 (June 1999): 814–41.

Akwesasne Notes, ed. *Basic Call to Consciousness*. Summertown TN: Native Voices, 2005.

Bardeau, Phyllis Eileen, and Jare Cardinal, eds. *Definitive Seneca: It's in the Word*. Salamanca NY: Seneca-Iroquois National Museum, 2011.

Bilharz, Joy Ann. "First among Equals? The Changing Status of Seneca Women." In *Women and Power in Native North America*, edited by Laura F Klein and Lillian A. Ackerman, 101–12. Norman: University of Oklahoma Press, 2000.

Boos, Greg, Heather Fathali, and Greg McLawsen. "The History of the Jay Treaty, and Its Significance to Cross-Border Mobility and Security for Indigenous Peoples in the North American Northern Borderlands and Beyond." In *The North American Arctic*, edited by Dwayne Ryan Menezes and Heather N. Nicol, 35–66. Themes in Regional Security. London: University College London Press, 2019.

Brooks, Lisa Tanya. *The Common Pot: The Recovery of Native Space in the Northeast*. Minneapolis: University of Minnesota Press, 2008.

Campisi, Jack. "National Policy, States' Rights, and Indian Sovereignty: The Case of the New York Iroquois." In Foster, Campisi, and Mithun, *Extending the Rafters*, 95–109.

Cayuga Nation. "Land Claim History-Cayuga Nation of New York." Accessed June 26, 2023. https://web.archive.org/web/20170527235711/http://www.cayuganation-nsn.gov/LandRights/LandClaimHistory.

Chafe, Wallace, and Seneca community members. *A Grammar of the Seneca Language*. Vol. 149. Linguistics. Berkeley: University of California Press, 2015.

Congress of the United States of America and Tribes of Indians Called the Six Nations. Treaty with the Six Nations (Treaty of Fort Stanwix). October 27, 1784. University of Oklahoma, Digital Collections. https://dc.library.okstate.edu/digital/collection/kapplers/id/25856/rec/7.

Cook, Ramsay. *Watching Quebec: Selected Essays*. Montreal: McGill-Queen's Press, 2005.

Cusick, David. *Sketches of Ancient History of the Six Nations: Comprising First, a Tale of the Foundation of the Great Island (Now North America), the Two Infants Born, and the Creation of the Universe (1825)*. Lockport NY: Cooley and Lathrop, 1828.

Dennis, Matthew. *Cultivating a Landscape of Peace: Iroquois-European Encounters in Seventeenth-Century America*. Ithaca NY: Cornell University Press, 1993.

Doran, Kwinn H. "Ganienkeh: Haudenosaunee Labor-Culture and Conflict Resolution." *Project Muse: American Indian Quarterly* 26, no. 1 (Winter 2002). http://muse.jhu.edu/journals/american_indian_quarterly/v026/26.1doran.pdf.

Doxtator, Deborah Jean. "What Happened to the Iroquois Clans? A Study of Clans in Three Nineteenth Century Rotinonhsyonni Communities." London: University of Western Ontario, 1996.

Fenton, William N. *The Great Law and the Longhouse: A Political History of the Iroquois Confederacy*. Norman: University of Oklahoma Press, 1998.

Fletcher, Matthew. "The Death of History in the Roberts Court's Indian Law Jurisprudence." Presented at the Western History Association Annual Meeting, Lake Tahoe NV, October 16, 2010.

Foster, Michael K., Jack Campisi, and Marianne Mithun, eds. *Extending the Rafters: Interdisciplinary Approaches to Iroquoian Studies*. Albany NY: SUNY Press, 1984.

The Free Library. "Iroquois Confederacy Re-unification Begun." Accessed September 13, 2010. http://www.thefreelibrary.com/Iroquois+Confederacy+re-unification+begun.-a030564615.

Ganondagan. "Ganondagan-Canandaigua Treaty Commemoration Day." Accessed June 26, 2023. https://www.ganondagan.org/Events-Programs/Canandaigua-Treaty-Event.

———. "Seneca Art and Cultural Center." Accessed October 6, 2016. http://www.ganondagan.org.

Graymont, Barbara. *The Iroquois in the American Revolution*. 1st ed. A New York State Study. Syracuse NY: Syracuse University Press, 1972.

Greer, Allan. "Commons and Enclosure in the Colonization of North America." *American Historical Review* 117, no. 2 (April 2012): 365–86.

Grey, Sue. "Personal Communication with Sue Grey." Seneca Nation of Indians, April 28, 2014. http://www.sni.org.

Harring, Sidney L. *White Man's Law: Native People in Nineteenth-Century Canadian Jurisprudence*. Toronto: Published for the Osgoode Society for Canadian Legal History by University of Toronto Press, 1998.

Hatter, Lawrence B. A. *Citizens of Convenience: The Imperial Origins of American Nationhood on the U.S.-Canadian Border*. Charlottesville: University of Virginia Press, 2017.

Haudenosaunee Confederacy. "Haudenosaunee Documentation Committee." Official Website of the Grand Council of the Haudenosaunee Confederacy. Accessed February 16, 2021. https://www.haudenosauneeconfederacy.com/departments/haudenosaunee-documentation-committee/.

———. *Sewatokwa'tshera't: The Dish with One Spoon*. DVD. Haudenosaunee Confederacy, 2007.

Hauptman, Laurence M. *Seven Generations of Iroquois Leadership: The Six Nations since 1800*. 1st ed. Syracuse NY: Syracuse University Press, 2008.

Head, Sir George. *Forest Scenes and Incidents, in the Wilds of North America: Being a Diary of a Winter's Route from Halifax to the Canadas, and during Four Months'*

Residence in the Woods on the Borders of Lakes Huron and Simcoe. London: J. Murray, 1829.

Hernández, Kelly Lytle. *Migra! A History of the U.S. Border Patrol*. Berkeley: University of California Press, 2010.

Hill, Susan M. *The Clay We Are Made Of: Haudenosaunee Land Tenure on the Grand River*. Winnipeg: University of Manitoba Press, 2010.

Jordan, Kurt A. *The Seneca Restoration, 1715–1754*. Gainesville: University Press of Florida, 2008.

Ka-Hon-Hes, Akwesasne Notes, and Ray Tehanetorens Fadden, eds. *Kaianerekowa Hotinonsionne: The Great Law of Peace of the Longhouse People*. Berkeley CA: Oyate, 1999.

King George III. "A Royal Proclamation." Gilder Lehrman Institute of American History, October 7, 1763. https://www.gilderlehrman.org/history-resources/spotlight-primary-source/proclamation-1763-1763.

Lee, Erika. "Enforcing the Borders: Chinese Exclusion along the U.S. Borders with Canada and Mexico, 1882–1924." *Journal of American History* 89, no. 1 (2002): 54–86. https://doi.org/10.2307/2700784.

Library of Congress Online. "Jay's Treaty, November 19, 1794: A Century of Lawmaking for a New Nation: U.S. Congressional Documents and Debates, 1774–1875." http://memory.loc.gov/cgi-bin/ampage?collId=llsl&fileName=008/llsl008.db&recNum=129.

Mann, Barbara Alice. *Iroquoian Women: The Gantowisas*. New York: Peter Lang, 2000.

Mann, Barbara Alice, and Jerry L. Fields. "A Sign in the Sky: Dating the League of the Haudenosaunee." *American Indian Culture and Research Journal* 21, no. 2 (1997): 105–63.

Morgan, Lewis Henry. *League of the Ho-Dé-No-Sau-Nee, or Iroquois*. Rochester: Sage & Brother, 1851.

Morris, Robert, United States of America, and Seneca Indians. "Treaty of Big Tree," or Agreement with the Seneca Made by Robert Morris and the Chiefs and Sachems of the Seneca Indians, September 15, 1797. Indian Affairs: Laws and Treaties. Vol. 2. Accessed December 2, 2011. https://dc.library.okstate.edu/digital/collection/kapplers/id/29362/rec/5.

New York History (blog). "29th Annual Iroquois Indian Festival." August 31, 2010. http://www.newyorkhistoryblog.com/2010/08/29th-annual-iroquois-indian-festival.html.

New York State. "Jikonhsaseh: New York Historical Marker, Victor NY." Waymarking .com, 2006. http://www.waymarking.com/waymarks/wm1ax7_Jikonhsaseh.

No. 64: Report of the Committee on Indian Affairs on the Memorial of Peter Wilson, a Cayuga Chief, in Respect to the Law of 1848 Providing for the Distribution of the Cayuga Annuities. March 9, 1849. Documents of the Senate of the State of New York. 72nd session, vol. 2. Albany NY: Weed, Parsons, 1849.

O'Callaghan, Edmund Bailey. *Documents Relative to the Colonial History of New York*. Vol. 9. 15 vols. Albany NY: Weed, Parsons, 1853.

Parker, Arthur Caswell, and Seth Newhouse. *The Constitution of the Five Nations.* New York State Museum Bulletin, no. 184. Albany: University of the State of New York, 1916.

Parmenter, Jon. *The Edge of the Woods: Iroquoia, 1534–1701.* East Lansing: Michigan State University Press, 2010.

Peterson, Derek R. Review of *The Passport in America: The History of a Document*, by Craig Robertson. Special issue, *Kronos*, no. 40 (2014): 297–99.

Ramirez, Renya K. *Native Hubs: Culture, Community, and Belonging in Silicon Valley and Beyond.* Durham NC: Duke University Press, 2007.

Reynolds, Nicholas. "The Weekly Historical Note: The Oneida Carrying Place." Oneida Indian Nation, August 1, 2009. https://oneida-nsn.gov/wp-content/uploads/2016/04/16-09.08.31-Oneida-Carrying-Place.pdf.

Richter, Daniel K. *The Ordeal of the Longhouse: The Peoples of the Iroquois League in the Era of European Colonization.* Chapel Hill NC: Published for the Institute of Early American History and Culture, Williamsburg, Virginia, by the University of North Carolina Press, 1992.

———. "War and Culture: The Iroquois Experience." *William and Mary Quarterly* 40, no. 4 (1983): 528–59.

Robertson, Craig. *The Passport in America: The History of a Document.* New York: Oxford University Press, 2012.

Schulze, Jeffrey M. "We Are Lost between Two Worlds: The Tohono O'odham Nation." In *Are We Not Foreigners Here?*, 132–62. Indigenous Nationalism in the U.S.-Mexico Borderlands. Chapel Hill: University of North Carolina Press, 2018.

Shannon, Scott, Richard Smardon, and Melinda Knudson. "Using Visual Assessment as a Foundation for Greenway Planning in the St. Lawrence River Valley." *Landscape and Urban Planning* 33, nos. 1–3 (1995): 357–71.

Shattuck, George C. *The Oneida Land Claims: A Legal History.* 1st ed. The Iroquois and Their Neighbors. Syracuse NY: Syracuse University Press, 1991.

Six Nations of the Grand River. *6 Miles Deep: A Film about the Land Reclamation Movement near Caledonia on Six Nations Grand River Reserve.* 2009.

Smith, Linda Tuhiwai. *Decolonizing Methodologies: Research and Indigenous Peoples.* 2nd ed. London: Zed Books, 2012.

Spence, Taylor. "The Canada Thistle: The Pestilence of North American Colonialisms and the Emergence of an Exceptionalist Identity, 1783–1837." *Agricultural History* 90, no. 3 (Fall 2016): 511–44.

Sylvester, Nathaniel B. "Not Guilty: An Historical Account of a Murder in Herkimer County a Century Ago." In *Historical Sketches of Northern New York and the Adirondack Wilderness.* Troy NY: William H. Young, 1877. Reprinted in *North Country Life: A Digest for Northern New Yorkers*, Spring 1947. Library and Archives Canada, Ottawa.

Tanner, Helen Hornbeck. *Atlas of Great Lakes Indian History.* Norman: University of Oklahoma Press, 1987.

Taylor, Alan. *The Divided Ground: Indians, Settlers and the Northern Borderland of the American Revolution*. 1st ed. New York: Alfred A. Knopf, 2006.

Tuscarora & Six Nations. "Cayuga Nation." Accessed September 12, 2010. http://tuscaroras.com/index.php/legends-traditions-and-laws-of-the-iroquois-or-six-nations-and-history-of-the-tuscarora-indians.

———. "Legends, Traditions, and Laws of the Iroquois, or Six Nations, and History of the Tuscarora Indians-Sketches of an Iroquois Council, or Condolence." Accessed June 26, 2023. http://www.tuscaroras.com/index.php?option=com_content&view=article&id=37&Itemid=263&limitstart=26.

United States of America and Great Britain. Peace and Amity (Treaty of Ghent). Pub. L. No. 8, Stat. 218. Treaty Series 109 (1815).

Upstate Citizens for Equality. "The Cayuga Indians and Their Land Claim." Accessed September 12, 2010. https://web.archive.org/web/20081009234107/http://www.upstate-citizens.org/cayugaclaim.htm.

Vizenor, Gerald Robert, ed. *Survivance: Narratives of Native Presence*. Lincoln: University of Nebraska Press, 2008.

Wallace, Anthony F. C. *The Death and Rebirth of the Seneca*. New York: Vintage Books, 1969.

Webster's Third New International Dictionary of the English Language, Unabridged. Springfield MA: G. & C. Merriam, 1986.

Wilkinson, Charles F. *Blood Struggle: The Rise of Modern Indian Nations*. 1st ed. New York: Norton, 2005.

Wilson, Edmund, and Joseph Mitchell. *Apologies to the Iroquois*. Syracuse, NY: Syracuse University Press, 1992.

Wilson, Peter. *Speech of Dr. Wilson in No. 130: Report of the Commissioners of the Land Office*. March 12, 1850. Manuscripts and Archives, Sterling Memorial Library, Yale University.

PART 3

Institutions

NINE

Growing Up American

The Children's Aid Society and the American West

COURTNEY E. BUCHKOSKI

In 1853, a young minister named Charles Loring Brace lamented the squalor he saw in New York City. He complained that the city's ethnic enclaves were filled not with the "good—sober, hard-working people, who have spread over the country and become mingled with our population"—but with the worst kind of immigrant, who "settled and stagnated," falling victim to laziness and vice. The more Brace observed these impoverished communities, the more he believed them dangers to the nation. He predicted that immigrant parents, used to the hierarchical structures of the Catholic Church, would fail to teach their children the duties of republicanism, thus leading them to blind obedience to a demagogue. Brace warned his fellow Protestant elites that street urchins would "poison society" if no one intervened to reform them. Those who were "too negligent, or too selfish to notice them as children," Brace predicted, would "be fully aware of them as men." As Brace repined the regression of the city, he envisioned the West as an upstanding, moral alternative to the East.[1]

Overcrowding was the root of all urban woes, Brace decided as he traversed the neighborhood Charles Dickens once compared to the slums of London, calling them similarly "loathsome, drooping, and decayed." The solution to New York's tribulations was uniquely American and lay in the West, where Brace saw a veritable outlet for the city's population. Brace's Children's Aid Society (CAS) sought to reduce overcrowding in New York, Americanize the "dangerous classes," and sustain farmers in need of labor by moving immigrant children into western foster homes. From 1853 until 1929, the CAS sent approximately two hundred thousand children west, placing them with Protestant families who agreed to raise them in exchange for their labor.[2] The children the organization "placed out" included orphans, "half orphans," and some who were not orphans at all.[3] All of the children were, according to Brace, "at the turning point of their lives" and could still be saved through his intervention. Transplanting them would improve New York, with "much expense lessened to courts and prisons" and "much poisonous influence removed from the city."[4]

The process would also Americanize immigrants, Brace promised. Instead of growing up in urban poverty, where children were likely to become dependent on wage labor and political machines, a childhood in the West would transform them into republican citizens. The West, Brace declared, offered a unique combination of "immense space of arable land and practically unlimited demand for labor, especially children's labor." Juvenile labor was valuable to the farmer, who need not pay the child wages, only provide room and board. Placing-out would therefore assist in the long-term development of the West, as it would reinforce nascent Protestant colonies there.[5] The "great mass" of children sent from New York, Brace concluded, would "become honest producers on the Western soil instead of burdens or pests here."[6]

Nineteenth-century emigrant aid companies like the Children's Aid Society demonstrate that regions were not merely geographic but the result of imaginary boundaries drawn by a population anxious about sectional division.[7] As northern cultural elites worried about the rapid expansion of their cities and the South's commitment to slavery, they imagined an Edenic West that could promote sectional cooperation and the nation's Protestant majority. Their fantastical West could cure any person of their immorality and destroy the very possibility of disunion.[8] Brace envisioned the West as the safety valve by which he could eliminate threats to the Union, including foreign immigration, overcrowding, the expanding influence of Catholicism, machine politics, and slavery. In doing so, Brace believed he would preserve the North and create a more Protestant West that would reflect the nation's founding values.

Emigrant aid tied westerners to eastern political and religious debates, as middle-class cultural elites such as Brace used their investment to influence where emigrants settled and how they grew up. The CAS tried to tether the distant West to cultural centers in the East and create a Union that supported northern values over southern ones.[9] Emigrant aid companies were forums for eastern elites and western emigrants to debate their visions of regionalism, as they imagined the future of both the West and the nation. These debates helped define the American idea of the West as a region while also connecting it to national concerns. The northern vision of the West as a safety valve, an open and inviting sanctuary, would be contested by westerners as they formed their own regional identity.

Reforming the East

Brace began his public ministry in 1852 at the Five Points Mission, located in one of New York's poorest Catholic neighborhoods. The Irish who settled there were some of the most destitute and least educated immigrants in America. Only 12 percent knew a trade, and only 2 percent were merchants or professionals, leaving the majority qualified only for low-wage labor. By 1850, the Irish constituted a quarter of the city's population. By 1860, the number of Irish-born adults outnumbered native-born in fifteen of the city's twenty-two wards. German immigrants also proliferated, increasing from 60,000 in 1851 to 140,000 in 1853. Brace watched suspiciously as Italian immigrants joined the ranks of the growing Catholic population. As the Protestant majority fearfully observed their declining supremacy, they pointed to the truancy of immigrant children as evidence of societal decline. Chief of Police George W. Matsell estimated that ten thousand children, many of whom had "evil propensities," were roaming about the city unsupervised. Alarmed by these statistics and his own observations, Brace bemoaned the tragedy of "ten thousand children growing up almost sure to be prostitutes and rogues!"[10]

Determined to allay the immigration problem, Brace founded the CAS in 1853 as part of a wider evangelical reform movement. As reformers worked to eradicate vice, crime, and poverty, Brace was an early adopter of scientific charity. An enthusiast of Charles Darwin's *On the Origin of Species*, which he read thirteen times, Brace saw children as products of their environment rather than doomed by their lineage. The children of the poor, he reasoned, were actually "more vigorous than children of the higher classes" because only the strong persisted. The struggle of survival, however, reduced these children to an animal-like state, with their "sensual tendencies exaggerated to the extreme, and their intellectual and moral faculties weakened." If he could change the children's material circumstances and "draw them under the influence of the moral and fortunate classes," Brace believed that they would "grow up as useful producers and members of society."[11]

The CAS would save these children by removing them from perilous environments. Brace advocated removal for young children especially, since there was still "hope of a speedy improvement under family influence." The state aided in this endeavor by relinquishing problems of juvenile delinquency to charitable agencies such as the CAS. Using a state truancy law passed in 1853, the CAS arrested children between the ages of five and fourteen years. "On the final neglect of the parent," the statute stated, it became the duty of a municipal authority to provide them housing, employment, and education "until indentured or discharged." The law allowed the state to subsume parental rights if it were in the "best interests of their offspring, and the public safety." These ambiguous guidelines authorized the CAS to remove children without parental permission and with no other justification than their own interpretation of civilized living.[12]

After the CAS removed children from the dangerous influence of their parents, the society provided them a brief education in how to be proper Americans before sending them west. Located in the hearts of immigrant neighborhoods, CAS industrial schools taught children to read, worship, and perform their gender roles in accordance with the Protestant mainstream. The CAS taught girls middle-class standards of cleanliness. Housemothers enforced personal hygiene and employed girls "in scrubbing, cleaning, cooking, ironing or sewing." Wardens taught boys independence through financial management, using mock savings banks where they were "induced to leave their money" to gain small amounts of interest. The society claimed that these skills taught the "sharpness and self-reliance" necessary to thrive in the West.

The CAS declared that influencing a child's "religious future" was their "strongest and profoundest impulse." Evangelical theology, therefore, was a vital pillar of the CAS curriculum, which the society reinforced by removing children from their Catholic parish networks. This training in proper society ensured, according to the CAS, that children would not replicate the city's disorder in the West but contribute to its Americanization.[13]

CAS's annual reports to donors relayed tales of placing-out's success, emphasizing the superiority of agrarianism, the danger of the city, and the program's mutual beneficence to the East and West. The society reported that in the West, good Christian families provided the structure necessary to complete the reforms initiated in industrial schools. The West "absorbs them," Brace wrote, "honest occupation employs their energies, and all the Christianizing and humanizing influences of the rural districts continually elevate them." CAS promotional tracts argued that the "peculiar warm-heartedness of the Western people and the equality of all classes" gave the region the unique character needed to reform children.[14]

Brace praised the West's environment, claiming that adolescents would be healed physically and spiritually by the unpolluted air. The West, he declared, was "the nursery in whose genial soil the little plants and twigs plucked from the crowded streets and filth-reeking lands of our great city have taken root, and are blossoming with the promise of rich fruit." The CAS estimated that in the city, 50 percent of children would die before they were seven years old. The West was where their health would be "invigorated," their "minds strengthened," and their "principles fixed." Brace fervently believed that the very act of changing a child's environment would ensure they became "healthy and useful in the pure, free air of the West."[15]

Placing-Out in the West

Before the Civil War, the CAS had little trouble convincing westerners to take in children, who they advertised as good investments. CAS circulars promised that adopting a child would cost less than hiring an extra hand because the society's contracts stipulated the children work for board and clothing. The family would only owe the child wages if he or she stayed past the age of eighteen. The CAS put juveniles younger than twelve under stricter guidance, instructing families to treat them "as one of their own children in matters of schooling, clothing, and training." The child, in turn, would earn something more valuable than money—the chance to become a true American.[16]

The destinations of CAS orphans changed over time alongside the society's vision of regional boundaries. The company equated the West with areas populated by emigrants from New England and New York. In the 1850s, the West included Illinois, Indiana, Michigan, Ohio, and Wisconsin. Eventually, the society's "West" also included states such as California, Colorado, Iowa, Kansas, Nebraska, and even western Canadian provinces. Despite these shifts, their primary consideration remained finding rural homes for children dissimilar to the temptations of the city.[17]

When the CAS "orphan train" arrived at its western destination, crowds of farmers gathered at the station to compete for the best children. The next day, prospective parents met the company at a church or town hall. There, a CAS agent explained the "benevolent objects" of the society, hoping that the sight of the children's "worn faces was a most pathetic enforcement" of his arguments. A committee consisting of prominent town members, including ministers and city officials, then reviewed the applications and assigned children to couples. Just as CAS agents in New York enforced middle-class standards by deciding who to send west, the CAS trusted established elites in the West to vouch for families.[18]

By the time children arrived in these rural communities, many had already rejected the society's behavioral expectations. The trip west did not improve their character or make them obedient. When CAS agent E. P. Simon took a group of forty-six children to Michigan in 1856, he reported the difficulty of maintaining order. During a layover in Albany, Simon watched the children carefully, fearful that they would return home. The children also faced moral danger on the journey. When the group boarded a lake boat, Simon lamented that they spent the night in "washing, smoking, drinking, singing, sleep, and licentiousness." After the boat landed, the children scattered, coming back to the hotel with pilfered peaches, pumpkins, corn, acorns, and apples. Children also disturbed the town by standing on the road, trying to entice the richest-looking passersby to adopt them. Despite the group's moral failings, their labor remained valuable, and Simon had fifteen applications by the end of the day and placed out all the children over the next week.[19]

The training children obtained in industrial schools did not seem to improve their behavior either. Western parents regularly complained about their orphans' disobedience. Mrs. John Bacon became so frustrated with Mary Dudgeon's propensity to steal that she sent her back to New York, declaring her "awfully profane and a notorious liar." Ellen Maury befell a similar fate when her inclination to spit made Charlotte Otis claim, "Your girl is not capable of morals." Henry displeased his family with his tendency "to scoff at everything of a religious character." When Henry left for good, the family was happy but requested "another boy in his place that can wear his clothes."[20]

Children likewise grumbled that westerners were not as virtuous as the CAS advertised. Rural indenture, it turned out, could be just as cruel as a life of pauperism in the city. A boy named P. J. wrote the CAS to report that his family forced him to walk a mile barefoot each morning to tend to the cows. In the fall and winter, when the weather was cold, he was furthermore not allowed to warm his feet by the fire. P. J. also accused the family of lying because his parents claimed P. J. as their first adopted child, when he was, in fact, their third. When P. J. escaped and found refuge with a different family, the CAS demanded that he return, labeling him "A Stubborn Case."[21] Despite the society's shortcomings in the antebellum era, their methodology remained popular among evangelicals and thousands of children filtered out of New York.

Disunion

The outbreak of the Civil War in 1861 proved a fertile testing ground for the society's claims about placing-out and its importance to national unity. The CAS promoted former orphan train riders as the protectors of the Union who kept the West connected to national concerns. Finding their former charges now serving in the Union army was ample proof, the society claimed, that they had transformed the rebellious street urchins into true patriots in a "striking illustration of the elevating and Christianizing operations of our Republican Institutions." The CAS propagandized the Americanizing effects of placing-out. In 1862 the society reported that four hundred CAS boys were "offering their lives, if need be to sustain a Government, under which many of them were not born." They printed the account of a young German boy who proclaimed, "This has been a good country to me, and it is my duty to do something to defend its institutions; and I pray God, if I fall in battle, I shall not die like a coward, but like a brave man." To which the CAS report resounded, "An army of such men are invincible!"[22]

The CAS used the narratives of orphans' wartime service to reinforce their vision of the West as a region that could heal even the most broken child. Society reports overflowed with tales of CAS boys who lived in Confederate prison camps, died in hospitals, and "returned to tell of brave deeds and hair-breadth escapes." The CAS bragged that their orphans were officers and claimed that not one of the hundreds in the field had committed a disgraceful act. They published the letter of "D.M.," who helped another young soldier escape the "temptation of his constant accessibility to intoxicating drinks." Another wrote of the Confederate troops who succumbed to vice. He relayed the "sufferings of the forsaken families in the rebel States" at the hands of southern troops, who pillaged settlements of everything "fit to eat or wear, regardless of the entreaties of women and children." The society also used tales of death to dramatize their orphans' commitment to the Union. In one story, the CAS tracked down the birth mother of a slain orphan train rider. When a society agent came to the residence, he found a "den of the vilest sort." The CAS celebrated that a child who started in such squalor died a martyr for the Union. The CAS lauded these reports as evidence that dangerous children had quickly transformed into defenders of temperance and respectability.[23]

The work of the CAS was not complete, however, as rebellious immigrant factions continued to congregate in the city. The draft riots of 1863 proved to Protestant elites that while placing-out had mitigated some of the risks of immigration, they were far from eliminating the problem. The New York City draft riots began on July 13 when white working-class men gathered to protest Congress's conscription laws. Instead of going to work at railroads, machine shops, shipyards, and construction projects, workers marched to the site of the draft lottery, holding signs that read "No draft." They resisted conscription because of its inequity—wealthy men could avoid it by paying three hundred dollars or providing a substitute. The protest turned violent as rioters cut telegraph poles, used crowbars to uproot rail ties, and attacked police officers. The protest evolved into a race riot as poor white workers, many of whom were Irish immigrants, attacked their perceived competitors, free Black laborers. Rioters targeted Black homes for destruction, and the majority of the 120 people killed by mob violence were African American. The riot ended when President Lincoln diverted troops from the Battle of Gettysburg to the city.[24]

Brace pointed to the riots as evidence of the class divisions still present in the city, calling for further supervision of youth and immigrant populations. "These sackers of houses and murderers of the innocent," the 1863 report proclaimed, "are merely street-children grown up." The society concluded that the incident was only the first of many such violent outbursts that would be perpetuated by the city's ignorant classes, who cared little about the Union's stability. Conversely, the CAS argued that their emigration movement contributed to the restoration of law and order. They reported that two of their placed-out children participated in the draft riots not as protestors but as the keepers of civil order. The company report boasted that the boys came back to New York as part of a Wisconsin regiment to quell the violence "in which undoubtedly some of their old companions had part." The CAS interpreted the riots as proof of the city's continued problem with immigrant children and their success in teaching orphans the virtues of republicanism.[25]

Such efforts made the Civil War years most productive for the society—they received record numbers of individual donations along with an increase in orphaned children. On average, the society placed out about seven hundred children a year, but from 1861 to 1865 they averaged over one thousand. In the five years after the Civil War, the CAS performed even better, placing out 12,013 children and averaging around 2,400 emigrants a year. The war led to more orphans and fewer available wage workers in the West, which made the CAS message all the more pertinent to its donors. As the 1863 report advertised, despite the effects of war, "the West has never contributed so liberally to our charity, or has called for so many children."[26]

Postbellum Challenges

The postbellum years led to the gradual decline in the public's acceptance of Brace and his placing-out methods as regional attitudes about the Union shifted. The North continued its quest to cohere the nation under its principles, but sectional alliances increasingly formed over an urban-rural divide, aligning the West and South against the North.[27] While some northern urbanites considered Brace's work essential, westerners rejected his attempts to export New York's poverty abroad. Brace also faced the decline of the reform era in the North. In what historians have described as moral exhaustion, the end of the Civil War splintered the evangelical political and cultural hegemony that characterized the antebellum era.[28] White Protestants turned away from radical reform and instead organized for more conservative causes like the protection of family, the end of sexual oppression, and temperance. These more conservative reformers accused the CAS in the *Journal of Commerce* of "drawing off the best of our poorer youth for the West, and thus leaving in the City only its vicious, lazy and destitute children." This "process of unnatural selection" drained New York of "the flower of her youth."[29]

As the demographics of the city shifted to reflect the accumulating numbers of Catholics, Brace and his cohort of evangelicals also faced the opposition of Catholic reformers. Catholics blamed Protestants for the draft riots, claiming that the CAS policy of breaking up families exacerbated class antagonism and pushed the poor to violence. They believed that instead of child removal, the city should focus on subsidizing urban childcare institutions. Catholics worked to diminish public funding to the CAS and created their own welfare system to minimize Protestant interference. They found an ally in William Tweed, who began pouring state money into Catholic organizations and immigrant voters. Catholics used their newfound political influence to establish the Society for the Protection of Destitute Roman Catholic Children in the City of New York, known in short as the Protectory. The Protectory charter promised to care for poor Catholic children until they could find permanent refuge in the city. The Protectory's first president, Levi Sillman Ives, declared that in doing so, the organization would finally defeat the "doughty foe of the Pope of Rome," Charles Brace. The Protectory hoped to provide a safety net for Catholic poor and guard young souls against Protestant enemies.[30]

The Protectory did not see emigration as its primary focus but instead hoped to keep children within their own familial and parish networks. In 1868, the society housed 1,079 children but only indentured 371—around 35 percent. By 1877, this number had decreased to 332 children of 3,322—about 11 percent. The society instead focused on teaching children trades that they could use to find work in the city. When the Protectory did "collect poor and vagrant children," it vowed to send them only to "'carefully-selected homes' in the West."³¹

The evangelical interest in the West also changed with moral exhaustion. The West remained a concern of the reform movement, but as evangelical authority diminished, so did the ability of reformers to influence western politics. As westerners established their own political section, they no longer relied on eastern emigrant aid companies and charitable networks. Emigrant aid companies faced popular scrutiny for their methods, as voters became suspicious that companies were fronts for land speculation.

Westerners increasingly resisted the CAS as an undue regional intrusion, accusing the society of transplanting the problems of the East into the West. In 1876, at the National Prison Congress meeting in New York, several men argued that the CAS was "crowding the Western prisons and reformatories." CAS representatives denied these charges and sent agent Charles P. Fry to examine the prisons, houses of refuge, and reformatories in Illinois, Indiana, and Michigan. Fry concluded that of the ten thousand children sent by the CAS to these three states, "not a single boy or girl from this Society could be found in all their prisons and reformatories." The CAS responded that if the society was "scattering the seeds of vice and crime," there "would have arisen from the whole West, an united groan of opposition" to the placing-out system.³² Nevertheless, westerners continued to insist that their charitable organizations could better serve their own populations.

Brace continued to promote the placing-out method as a legitimate way to reform both New York and the West while realizing that he needed to adapt to postwar conceptions of regionalism. Brace replaced his vision of the West as an uncivilized territory waiting for influence with the acknowledgment that even small western communities faced problems of juvenile truancy. In 1880, Brace outlined a plan by which reformers across the nation could replicate New York's experiment in child saving. He admitted that the mere existence of a rural western community could no longer maintain the morality of children, as "each well-to-do and Christian family will naturally know in their town some semi-vagrant and half-criminal family, living on the outskirts of the village." Brace suggested, as he had in the 1850s, that this issue could not be fixed by mere charity but would require an adherence to the principles of free labor, mainly that money had to be righteously earned. He encouraged benevolent people to "gradually make the children self-supporting" by making every donation dependent on the child "doing some little job of work." Brace maintained that breaking up families and removing children from the influence of "bigotry and superstition" remained the principal goal of placing-out. Societies could feature reading rooms, educational facilities, lodging houses, and summer homes for sanitary rejuvenation, but the primary "object of the benevolent helper should be to endeavor to break up the vicious family."[33]

Brace's efforts to promote placing-out over other forms of charitable work did not have the desired impact on western philanthropists.[34] CAS branches in the West adopted Brace's ideas piecemeal, prioritizing needs other than removal. In 1870, Elizabeth Parrish built a branch of the CAS in Salem, Oregon. A Methodist missionary from New York, she thought the home could "be governed by Christian women and mothers." Unlike its New York counterpart, the Oregon CAS established clear legal boundaries for parents to voluntarily give up their children. Several organizational branches ensured the supervision of children, including a committee on discipline and discharge, which the society tasked with "inculcating principles of religion, sobriety, and honesty." The committee attended to all discharges from the house, "whether by adoption or indenture," maintaining a trial period of six months during which time the orphan or parent could rescind the arrangement. The Oregon CAS did not indenture children who were illiterate or under the age of twelve and vowed to correspond with each child twice a year.[35]

In the urban West, CAS branches focused on exposing poor children to nature rather than placing-out. In San Jose, California, the CAS established a sanitarium on the land of wealthy bachelor E. Searles. In St. Louis, the CAS built a sanitarium in a park overlooking the Mississippi River, where they secured a mansion to hold eighty infirm children. The same society sent children to country homes, but rarely for adoption, "on a plan similar to the Children's Aid Societies of New York, Boston, and other large cities." One division in Albuquerque, New Mexico, did organize to rescue "children in immoral environments" and did the "aggressive work" of placing children in "homes for adoption or by contract." Their leaders, however, eschewed any relation to the CAS, claiming to be "wholly independent" of Brace.[36]

Western middle-class reformers took the mantle of social control from easterners. Much as the CAS in New York set out to impose specific standards of order, western philanthropists levied their own visions of acceptable household management on the poor. In Duluth, Minnesota, the local CAS branch made it their mission to remove the sons of a local ne'er-do-well named Mr. Baldwin. "A large number of philanthropic ladies" decided that Baldwin's sons were "being abused and needed the help of the society." The CAS declared Baldwin a "worthless character" who was "bringing up his young boys in the same way and resents all efforts to better their condition." When Baldwin refused to accept CAS standards of childcare, the society partnered with the county to remove his children into foster homes.[37]

In Omaha, the Nebraska Children's Aid Society found a child living in a house of ill repute, under the care of a grandmother. A member of the society, Mrs. Quivey, decided to broker the release of the child, which she did in writing. Per CAS rules, this gave the society the "right to dispose" of the child "as it sees fit." The CAS placed the minor in a new home, until the mother, Laura Thompson, sued for the child's freedom. Because the unmarried Thompson became pregnant at the age of fourteen, Quivey believed that the child needed protection "from contaminating influences," and the CAS maintained custody.[38]

Westerners, broadly defined by their association with the process of expansion, continued to criticize the New York CAS at annual charitable conferences, claiming that New Yorkers had no right to export their worst residents to the West. At an 1883 delegation, westerners charged that New York boys remained unsupervised by CAS agents. Other westerners argued that placed-out children were hereditary criminals who would poison the West. Brace retorted that the children were the descendants not of criminals but "simply of poor laboring people and others who have become unfortunate." At a later conference of charities held in Omaha in 1887, the charge persisted that the society failed to look after children that it placed out. The Wisconsin State Charities Board tested whether the society regularly checked in with its charges. It claimed that the very first child it investigated failed the inspection. A man accepted a child five years earlier and died one year into the adoption period. Four years later "the society was evidently ignorant of the changes." The Wisconsin State Charities Board also found that people "frequently did not like the children after they got them and then placed them in almshouses." In conclusion, the report stated, "the Wisconsin people are highly indignant, and say that much dissatisfaction exists in other parts of the West."[39] As this critique grew, the organization shifted to a model much closer to modern foster care, focusing more on local placements than distant removals.

After the Civil War, westerners asserted their authority over their own region's residents. Although the CAS tried to reinforce its placing-out mission, westerners instead focused on local concerns. When Brace started the CAS, Protestant reformers believed that they could eradicate the problems of poverty, crime, and immorality. When reformers failed to eliminate these sins, volunteerism gave way to state activity. Charity became more scientific, secular, and professional. New York established a state board of charity in 1867, and by 1900, sixteen other states had followed suit. The labor disputes of the late 1870s, including the Great Railroad Strike, underscored the rising divisions between capital and labor. The class conflicts that Brace foretold in the draft riots came to fruition, and many northerners replaced their anxiety about disunion with fear of socialism and organized labor. They suspected that the breakups of families were to blame for class tensions. Experts also increasingly viewed children under fourteen as sentimentally valuable rather than as economic assets. By the end of the nineteenth century, adopting a child merely for his or her labor was no longer respectable.[40]

By the time Frederick Jackson Turner declared the western frontier "closed" in 1893, the region no longer wanted or needed scores of child laborers from New York. Facing their own crises of poverty, western cities rejected plans to import more children. In 1895, Michigan refused to accept out-of-state children unless the organizing party paid a bond guaranteeing that children would not become public charges. Similar laws passed in six western states. Brace's vision of the West, which would never run out of room for children, no longer existed. While placing-out would continue in fits and starts, its heyday had passed.[41]

The story of the CAS demonstrates the gradual process of region building in relation to those "back East." The West did not emerge as a functioning white, Protestant hierarchy from the moment of colonization. Instead, it went through iterations and manipulations, including those by the northern reform movement. This movement, so often remembered for its antislavery and temperance arguments, also impacted colonization through its funding of emigrant aid ventures. The emigrant aid function of the CAS strengthened Protestant families, who obtained nearly free farm labor. The CAS also used child removal to enforce an acceptable standard of living among New York's poor. The boundaries between East and West were dictated not by geography but by ideology. Brace and his fellow reformers sent children into a West that they imagined would cure immorality and bind the budding region to the Union. As the Union shifted and changed, so too did this vision of the West.

Notes

1. "First Annual Report of the Children's Aid Society," February 1854, RCAS, box 1, folder 25; Brace, *Dangerous Classes of New York*, 322.

2. The figure of 200,000 is an estimate based on company reports. It does not account for children who went west multiple times after return trips or fully account for the work of branch societies, which also used the placing out method.

3. The term *half-orphan* refers to a child who has one living parent and one dead.

4. Dickens, *American Notes*, 62; "First Annual Report of the Children's Aid Society," February 1854, RCAS, box 1, folder 25; Brace, *Dangerous Classes of New York*, 225.

5. Several historians describe regional aspects of the placing-out system. See Gordon, *Great Arizona Orphan Abduction*; Holt, *Orphan Trains*; O'Connor, *Orphan Trains*; and Langsam, *Children West*. While these accounts elaborate on aspects of the placing-out system, this essay highlights the connections and debates between the East and West about child saving.

6. "Fifteenth Annual Report of the Children's Aid Society," February 1868, RCAS, box 2, folder 5; Brace, *Dangerous Classes of New York*, 242.

7. For more on the American fear of disunion before the Civil War, see Gallagher, *Union War*; and Varon, *Disunion!*

8. See Deverell, "To Loosen the Safety Valve."

9. For more on how twentieth-century western writers came to define the East as a separate political sphere, see Flannery Burke's essay in this volume.

10. Anbinder, *City of Dreams*, 149, 189; Matsell, *Semi-annual Report*; Charles Loring Brace to Emma Brace, February 15, 1850, in Brace, *Life of Charles Loring Brace*, 82–83.

11. O'Connor, *Orphan Trains*, 80; "Eighth Annual Report of the Children's Aid Society," February 1861, RCAS, box 1, folder 32; Brace, *Dangerous Classes of New York*, 8–9.

12. "First Annual Report of the Children's Aid Society," February 1854, RCAS, box 1, folder 25; "Fifth Annual Report of the Children's Aid Society," February 1858, RCAS, box 1, folder 29; "An Act to Provide for the Care and Instruction of Idle and Truant Children Passed April 12 1853," reprinted in American Female Guardian Society, *Twenty-First Annual Report of the American Female Guardian Society 1853*, 11; New York Association for Improving the Condition of the Poor, *Twenty-First Annual Report of the New York Association for Improving the Condition of the Poor*; "Eleventh Annual Report of the Children's Aid Society," February 1864, RCAS, box 2, folder 2.

13. "Fifth Annual Report of the Children's Aid Society," February 1858, RCAS, box 1, folder 29.

14. "Eighth Annual Report of the Children's Aid Society," 1861, RCAS, box 1, folder 32; "Tenth Annual Report of the Children's Aid Society," February 1863, RCAS, vol. 19; "Fourth Annual Report of the Children's Aid Society," February 1857, RCAS, box 1, folder 28; "Sixth Annual Report of the Children's Aid Society," February 1859, RCAS, box 1, folder 30; Children's Aid Society, *Thirteenth Annual Report of the Children's Aid Society*, 8; Letter from F. L. Sessions to Charles Brace, RCAS, box 46, folder 4.

15. "Twenty-Third Annual Report of the Children's Aid Society," February 1875, RCAS, box 2, folder 7; "Twelfth Annual Report of the Children's Aid Society," February 1865, RCAS, box 2, folder 3; "Fourteenth Annual Report of the Children's Aid Society," February 1867, RCAS, box 2, folder 4.

16. Brace, *Dangerous Classes of New York*, 228; "Terms on Which Boys Are Placed in Homes," RCAS, box 45, folder 4.

17. For a discussion on the power of regional "mental maps" created by promotion, see Jimmy L. Bryan Jr.'s essay in this volume.

18. Brace, *Dangerous Classes of New York*, 231–33.

19. "Third Annual Report of the Children's Aid Society," 1856, RCAS, box 1, folder 27.

20. Mrs. John Bacon to Children's Aid Society, April 13, 1861, RCAS box 46, folder 4; Margaret David to Children's Aid Society, May 16, 1861, RCAS, box 46, folder 4.

21. "Eleventh Annual Report of the Children's Aid Society," February 1864, RCAS, box 2, folder 2.

22. "Ninth Annual Report of the Children's Aid Society," February 1862, RCAS, box 2, folder 1; "Tenth Annual Report of the Children's Aid Society," February 1863, RCAS, vol. 19.

23. "Ninth Annual Report of the Children's Aid Society," February 1862, RCAS, box 2, folder 1; "Tenth Annual Report of the Children's Aid Society," February 1863, RCAS, vol. 19; "Eleventh Annual Report of the Children's Aid Society," February 1864, RCAS, box 2, folder 2.

24. Bernstein, *New York City Draft Riots*, 18–19; Wilentz, *Chants Democratic*.

25. "Eleventh Annual Report of the Children's Aid Society," February 1864, RCAS, box 2, folder 2.

26. "Tenth Annual Report of the Children's Aid Society," February 1863, RCAS, vol. 19; "Ninth Annual Report of the Children's Aid Society," February 1862, RCAS, box 2, folder 1.

27. Historians have noted this shift in sectional alliances during Reconstruction. Elliott West coined the term "Greater Reconstruction" to describe the federal effort to build a new racial order in both the West and South. Nicolas Barreyre and Heather Cox Richardson have demonstrated the impacts of fiscal sectionalism and political alliances between the West and South. Richardson, *West from Appomattox*; Barreyre, *Gold and Freedom*; West, "Reconstructing Race," 6–26.

28. Blum, "'To Doubt This Would Be to Doubt God,'" 244.

29. "The Children's Aid Society. Charity that Never Faileth," *New York Herald*, February 22, 1874; "Twenty-Second Annual Report of the Children's Aid Society," February 1874, RCAS, box 2, folder 12; "Twenty-Seventh Annual Report of the Children's Aid Society," February 1879, RCAS, box 3, folder 4.

30. Fitzgerald, *Habits of Compassion*, 105; Brown and McKeown, *Poor Belong to Us*, 17; New York Catholic Protectory, *Thirteen Annual Reports with the Charter and By-Laws of the New York Catholic Protectory*, 8–9.

31. New York Catholic Protectory, *Seventeenth Annual Report of the New York Catholic Protectory*, 32; New York Catholic Protectory, *Report of the Rector of the Male Department of the New York Catholic Protectory*, 318–19.

32. "Twenty-Fourth Annual Report of the Children's Aid Society," February 1876, RCAS, box 3, folder 1; "Tenth Annual Report of the Children's Aid Society," February 1863, RCAS, vol. 19.

33. Brace, *Best Method of Founding Children's Charities in Towns and Villages*, PC, 1–3.

34. For more on the rise of western charity and maternalism, see Pascoe, *Relations of Rescue*.

35. "Children's Aid Society: A History of this Important State Institution," *Oregonian*, November 12, 1887; "Signed Agreements for Child Custody," January 14, 1884, OCAS, box 1, folder 1. Oregon Children's Aid Society, *Third Annual Report of the Oregon Children's Aid Society*, 12–13.

36. "Deeds Property to the Poor: Wealthy Bachelor Gives Farm to Children's Aid Society," *Evening News* (San Jose CA), November 23, 1904; "Children's Aid Society, Establishment of a Sanitarium in O'Fallon Park-Excursion Tuesday," *St. Louis Republic*, July 14, 1889; "Children's Aid Society, a Good Work Commenced—What Can Be Done to Help the Poor Boys and Girls," *Evening Bulletin* (San Francisco CA), March 18, 1874; "Children's Aid Society Doing a Great Work: Many Homes Have Been Found for Helpless Little Ones and Organization Is Now on Fine Basis," *Albuquerque Morning Journal*, July 23, 1908.

37. "Not As They Should Go: Children's Aid Society to Set Aright the Trend of Three Young Boys," *Duluth News-Tribune*, April 8, 1893.

38. "Kidnaped a Little Girl: The Nebraska Children's Aid Society Becomes Too Enthusiastic in One Case," *Omaha World Herald*, June 27, 1894.

39. "Children's Aid Society: A Reply to Attacks upon Its Work," *New-York Tribune*, March 27, 1883; "Philanthropy Astray: Some Practical Criticism of the Children's Aid Society," *New York Herald*, September 25, 1887.

40. Katz, *In the Shadow of the Poorhouse*, 89; Zelizer, *Pricing the Priceless Child*.

41. Trammell, "Orphan Train Myths and Legal Reality," 3–13.

Bibliography

American Female Guardian Society. *Twenty-First Annual Report of the American Female Guardian Society 1853*. New York: William Osborn, 1853.

Anbinder, Tyler. *City of Dreams: The 400-Year Epic History of Immigrant New York*. New York: Houghton Mifflin, 2016.

Barreyre, Nicolas. *Gold and Freedom: The Political Economy of Reconstruction*. Charlottesville: University of Virginia Press, 2015.

Bernstein, Iver. *The New York City Draft Riots: Their Significance for American Society and Politics in the Age of the Civil War*. New York: Oxford University Press, 1990.

Blum, Edward J. "'To Doubt This Would Be to Doubt God': Reconstruction and the Decline of Providential Confidence." In *Apocalypse and the Millennium in the American Civil War Era*, edited by Ben Wright and Zachary W. Dresser, 217–52. Baton Rouge: Louisiana State University Press, 2013.

Brace, Charles Loring. "The Best Method of Founding Children's Charities in Towns and Villages." Paper presented at the National Conference of Charities, Cleveland OH, June 29, 1880.

———. *The Dangerous Classes of New York, and Twenty Years' Work among Them.* New York: Wynkopp & Hallenbeck, 1872.

Brace, Emma. *The Life of Charles Loring Brace.* New York: Charles Scribner's Sons, 1894.

Brown, Dorothy M., and Elizabeth McKeown. *The Poor Belong to Us: Catholic Charities and American Welfare.* Cambridge MA: Harvard University Press, 2000.

Children's Aid Society. *Thirteenth Annual Report of the Children's Aid Society.* New York: Wynkoop & Hallenbeck, 1866.

Deverell, William F. "To Loosen the Safety Valve: Eastern Workers and Western Lands." *Western Historical Quarterly* 19, no. 3 (August 1988): 269–85.

Dickens, Charles. *American Notes for General Circulation.* London: Chapman & Hall, 1842.

Fitzgerald, Maureen. *Habits of Compassion: Irish Catholic Nuns and the Origins of New York's Welfare System, 1830–1920.* Champaign: University of Illinois Press, 2006.

Gallagher, Gary. *The Union War.* Cambridge MA: Harvard University Press, 2011.

Gordon, Linda. *The Great Arizona Orphan Abduction.* Cambridge MA: Harvard University Press, 1999.

Holt, Marilyn Irvin. *The Orphan Trains: Placing Out in America.* Lincoln: University of Nebraska Press, 1992.

Katz, Michael B. *In the Shadow of the Poorhouse: A Social History of Welfare in America.* 2nd ed. New York: Basic Books, 1996.

Langsam, Miriam Z. *Children West: A History of the Placing-Out System of the New York Children's Aid Society, 1853–1890.* Madison: State Historical Society of Wisconsin, 1964.

Matsell, George Washington. *Semi-annual Report of the Chief of Police from May 1 to October 31, 1849.* New York: City of New York, 1850.

New York Association for Improving the Condition of the Poor. *The Twenty-First Annual Report of the New York Association for Improving the Condition of the Poor.* New York: Trow & Smith, 1853.

New York Catholic Protectory. *Report of the Rector of the Male Department of the New York Catholic Protectory: Tenth Annual Report of the New York Catholic Protectory to the Legislature of the State, and to the Common Council of the City.* West Chester: New York Catholic Protectory, 1873.

———. *Seventeenth Annual Report of the New York Catholic Protectory to the Legislature of the State and to the Common Council of the City.* West Chester: New York Catholic Protectory, 1880.

———. *Thirteen Annual Reports with the Charter and By-Laws of the New York Catholic Protectory.* West Chester: New York Catholic Protectory, 1876.

Oregon Children's Aid Society. *Third Annual Report of the Oregon Children's Aid Society.* Salem: Oregon Stateman Job Print, 1870.

Oregon Children's Aid Society Records (OCAS), 1866–1960. Oregon Historical Society, Portland OR.

O'Connor, Stephen. *Orphan Trains: The Story of Charles Loring Brace and the Children He Saved and Failed.* Boston: Houghton Mifflin, 2001.

Pascoe, Peggy. *Relations of Rescue: The Search for Female Moral Authority in the American West, 1874–1939*. New York: Oxford University Press, 1990.

PC. Pamphlet Collection. Wisconsin Historical Society, Madison WI.

RCAS. Records of the Children's Aid Society, 1836–2006. New-York Historical Society, New York.

Richardson, Heather Cox. *West from Appomattox: The Reconstruction of America after the Civil War*. New Haven CT: Yale University Press, 2007.

Trammell, Rebecca S. "Orphan Train Myths and Legal Reality." *Modern American*, Spring 2009, 3–13.

Varon, Elizabeth R. *Disunion! The Coming of the American Civil War, 1789–1859*. Chapel Hill: University of North Carolina Press, 2008.

West, Elliott. "Reconstructing Race." *Western Historical Quarterly* 3, no. 1 (Spring 2003): 6–26.

Wilentz, Sean. *Chants Democratic: New York City & the Rise of the American Working Class, 1788–1850*. New York: Oxford University Press, 1984.

Zelizer, Viviana A. *Pricing the Priceless Child: The Changing Social Value of Children*. Princeton NJ: Princeton University Press, 1985.

TEN

Where the East Peters Out

*Dallas, Fort Worth, and Regional Branding
in the Great Southwest*

JIMMY L. BRYAN JR.

By the 1960s, geographers had learned the lessons that Texas taught about regionalism. As D. W. Meinig finds, attempts to define the state as a single "culture area" relied upon "a uniformity which could not possibly exist over so large and varied a country." Terry Jordan agrees, describing the futility of delimiting regions like Texas as "a fool's errand," adding that "attempts to define total, *formal* regions can only result either in gross statistical distortion—or departure from reality."[1] As Meinig and Jordan imply and as Flannery Burke and Lawrence Culver demonstrate in their essays in this volume, regions do not evolve organically from some confluence of unique geographies with unique people. Instead, they develop from human invention and represent mental and emotional cartographies intentionally drawn by specific groups to seize control of their worlds. Although imaginary, these "perceptual" or "vernacular" regions, as Jordan terms them, function as powerful engines of culture, commerce, and exclusion.

The scholarly quest to recover natural or empirical regions abets this project of exclusion. The geographer, the historian, or other investigators who attempt to locate a distinct region must draw its boundaries—lines that emphasize division and otherness. They must name it. They must determine who belongs within and who remains without.[2] This sorting most often falls along ethnic divides and results in decreasing the significance of a group based on the degree of their minority. In doing so, that scholar often reinforces the work of those who invent region as a tool to consolidate economic, political, and cultural power at the expense of their neighbors.

As a state that defies categorization, Texas illustrates this fantasy of defining objective regions. During the first two decades of the twenty-first century, historians have engaged in a discussion—serious, if not always sober—about whether Texas belongs to the U.S. South or the U.S. West. As the editors to this volume in their introduction and Sarah Miller-Davenport in her essay note, Oklahoma and Hawaiʻi—and likely most other states—exhibit similar contradictions that trouble scholars of region. In the Texas example, this argument reduces the state's complex cultural legacies to preformed categories of region and hinges on the presumption that the state must fit within, or divide evenly between, one section or the other. Some have offered that Texas is southern by birth and western by choice, but the notion of a "birth" erroneously suggests something natural, original, or entitled. It excludes the many Native cultures that thrived there for over ten thousand years or the Tejanos who resided within the province a century before the encroachment of southern enslavers. This privileging of Texas southernness as more authentic confirms the subjectively selective methods that underlie many studies of region. It also attests to the artificiality of Texas westernness, further suggesting that the process of region creation left a historical record that solicits investigation.[3]

Examining that record of region formation, William Cronon, Elliott West, David Wrobel, and other scholars have shown how boosters used branding to define and promote the U.S. West. In this context, branding refers to both product identification as well as claiming ownership. Cronon and West underscore the crucial role of cities in defining specific versions of the West. In their view, civic, business, and media leaders worked together to brand hinterlands from which to funnel profits into their cities.[4] Marketing historian Stephen V. Ward further argued that place promotion originated in the U.S. and Canadian Wests, where "new 'upstart' cities appeared in the newly colonized agricultural lands" and desired to "attract people and investment as rapidly as possible."[5] The boosters of Dallas and Fort Worth engaged in this kind of marketing, and the history of their efforts locates the centrality of economic aggrandizement in the formation of regional identity. This branding provided the means to achieve hinterland domination by forging consumer loyalty.

A review of the development of Dallas and Fort Worth provides an opportunity to better understand the ways that civic boosterism and the pursuit of hinterlands artificially created regions. The two cities sit astride the cultural, environmental, and economic crossroads that defy scholars' efforts to categorize Texas. Both communities reflected the "born southern" argument, and both endeavored to replace that history with western mystique. Their proximity to each other, however, nurtured a century-long rivalry that magnified both insecurity and aggression. Such magnification brings into focus the components of region formation by identifying its creators, deconstructing their mechanisms, and understanding their motivations.[6]

From the 1870s, when Dallas and Fort Worth emerged from the Civil War as competitors for railroad routes, to the 1970s, when they forged a cooperative identity as the Metroplex, their respective boosters persistently used similar toolkits to claim and brand their region as "the Great Southwest." Commerce and the ambition for profitable hinterlands provided the impetus. Transportation networks, in the form of railroads and later air travel, facilitated the movement of goods and commodities to landlocked cities like Dallas and Fort Worth. Communication fostered civic coordination and disseminated information through media like newspapers and later radio and television. Finally, the adoption of trademarks and other cultural representations by local advertisers offered a metric to assess the efficacy of this kind of brand loyalty.

Claiming the Great Southwest

Spared the physical devastation of military conflict, business, civic, and media leaders of Dallas and Fort Worth rebounded from the Civil War with optimistic and expansive visions of their futures.

Situated on the western edge of the fertile Blackland Prairie, Dallas served as a supply and market center for cotton and wheat farmers, while Fort Worth—thirty-four miles to the west—functioned as a waystation for as many as one million cattle that passed along the Chisholm Trail between 1866 and 1873.[7] The boosters of the towns recognized the utility of region for creating and branding hinterlands that funneled wealth to the metropolis. Each group adopted the same trademark, selling their cities variously as the "gateway," the "gem," "the queen city," or the "metropolis" of "the Great Southwest."[8]

Dallas and Fort Worth, however, did not draw on natural or preexisting geography. Since the 1830s, "the Great Southwest" label shifted with a temporal creep that did not follow an orderly east-to-west progression. By attaching "Great" to their region, the early boosters of Nashville, Memphis, New Orleans, and other locales evoked expansiveness and opportunity.[9] By the 1870s, Dallas and Fort Worth consciously vied for the trade of and title to "the Great Southwest" with established, more-eastern cities like St. Louis, New Orleans, and Kansas City or with emerging railroad hubs like Omaha and Sedalia. They also competed with Texas locations like Galveston, Houston, and San Antonio as well as closer upstarts like Denison and Waco.[10]

Fort Worth staked its claim as early as 1873. That year Buckley B. Paddock's *Fort Worth Democrat* published an essay entitled "Enterprise" that established the essential toolkit for the construction of region. The commercial desire for market control over vast spaces inspired his appeal to Fort Worth business leaders, calling on them "to foster schemes calculated to draw trade to our doors." As the presumed author, Paddock wrote at a time when Dallas and Fort Worth anticipated the completion of the Texas and Pacific Railroad, confident in the boom times that this new technology promised. The newspaper article illustrated how mass communication disseminated information and shaped ideas about region. It also revealed how media assisted in coordinating civic action, "a combined, continued and persistent effort to promote public enterprises." In adopting the term "great Southwest," Paddock initiated the process of creating a brand loyalty and implied that the construction of region required conscious and deliberate invention. He warned Fort Worth, "And while the golden sands of time are... running their course, the golden opportunities offered them are certainly passing from their control," and he implored them "to put their shoulders to the wheel and push forward the car of progress."[11]

Early Dallas and Fort Worth entrepreneurs focused on railroads to achieve their dreams of regional dominance, and they rose to Paddock's challenge for action. By lobbying the legislature and offering subsidies, they enticed rail companies to build to their towns. The first locomotive arrived in Dallas on July 16, 1872, on the north-south Houston and Texas Central, greeted by crowds and self-congratulatory speeches. Thirteen months later, the east-west Texas and Pacific officially opened its line from Marshall to Dallas, intersecting with the Houston and Texas Central, which had continued northward to connect with the Missouri-Kansas-Texas at Denison. The *Dallas Herald* later recalled this event as the moment when their city "entered the race for precedence among the cities of the Southwest."[12]

While Dallas celebrated, Fort Worth could only anticipate. In the summer of 1873, as construction of the Texas and Pacific progressed westward toward the Tarrant County line, Fort Worth promoters extolled their glorious prospects. "With this magnificent future, shortly to be realized," Paddock assured in June, "the citizens of Fort Worth have greater cause for congratulation than any other place in the South-west." The real estate firm of Brewer and Waterman commissioned a map that projected the convergence of chartered railroads at Fort Worth. Paddock used it to illustrate an August feature that promoted the county and the city as the region's railroad hub. The "tarantula map" depicted nine lines radiating out from Fort Worth, and it would become an enduring emblem of the town.[13]

Despite the confidence, the Panic of 1873 stalled Fort Worth's aspirations. The depression forced the Texas and Pacific to cease construction at Eagle Ford, about six miles west of Dallas. As the *Democrat* later recalled, Fort Worth "was peopled . . . with men

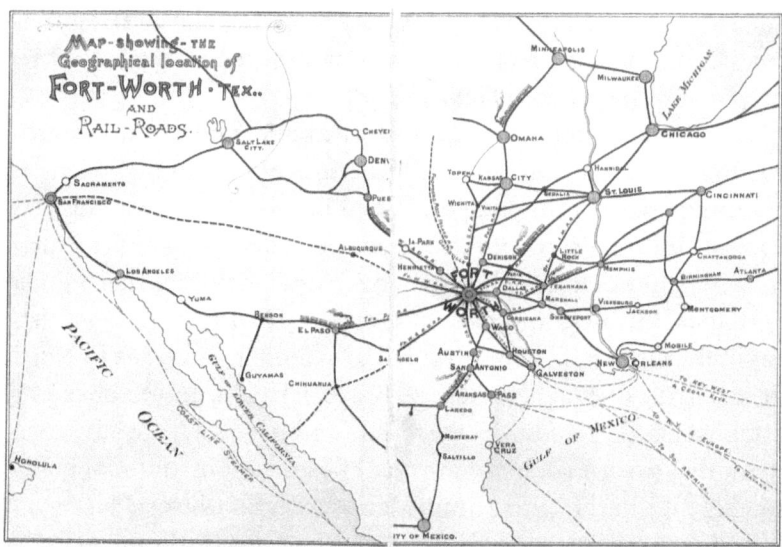

FIG. 6. By 1888, Fort Worth achieved the dream foretold by the "tarantula map." Unknown artist, *Map Showing the Geographical Location of Fort Worth, Texas, and Rail-Roads*. Chromolithograph by J. L. Ketterlinus, Philadelphia. From Edward J. Smith, *The Capitalist; or, The City of Fort Worth (The Texas Mikado)* (Fort Worth: Fort Worth Board of Trade, 1888). Cartographic Connections, University of Texas at Arlington Libraries.

who understood that cities"—and by extension regions—"are the work of man and not of chance." By the end of 1875, business leaders had chartered the Tarrant County Construction Company to assist and subsidize the Texas and Pacific. That effort and pressure from the state legislature succeeded, and on July 19, 1876, the first train rolled into Fort Worth.[14]

Over the next decade, Dallas and Fort Worth zealously pursued additional rail lines, fulfilling the prophecy of earlier developers. In 1880, the *Herald* boasted that Dallas "sits enthroned an imperial mistress of the trade and wealth of the great southwest" and the next year published its own version of a "tarantula map" that depicted the city at the "center of all this splendid region, and the entrepot and outlet for its trade and commerce ... [t]o the north, to the south, to the east and to the west." The *Fort Worth Daily*

Gazette responded by coronating Fort Worth as "the Greatest Railroad Center in the Great Southwest," with seven trunk lines, three of which it shared with Dallas.[15]

The intersection of local boosterism and railroad promotion further revealed the essential function of communications in claiming and defining region. When highly organized and well-capitalized media corporations entered the Dallas–Fort Worth markets, they deliberately pursued regional identities that aligned with local business and civic interests. A. H. Belo & Co., publishers of the *Galveston News*, decided to extend its coverage to North Texas. They dispatched George B. Dealey, who in October 1885 established the *Dallas Morning News* and issued a large advertisement that described the venture as "the greatest medium of public intelligence in the entire limits of the great Southwest."[16]

In Fort Worth, Amon G. Carter enjoyed less institutional backing. He was born to a modest farming family in Wise County, Texas, and after his mother's death, he left home to find work. Invested with a big personality and an apparent instinct for opportunity, Carter early honed his sales skills and learned how to build relationships and amass capital with other people's money. In 1905, he joined the Fort Worth *Star* to oversee their advertising department. Three years later, when the newspaper verged on failure, Carter bought it at a discount, and with the backing of several wealthy merchants, he merged with a rival newspaper to create the *Fort Worth Star-Telegram*. In its inaugural headline, Carter branded the daily with the proclamation that the *Star-Telegram* would set "a New Mark in the Southwest," announcing his intention to contest Dallas's claim to the region.[17]

With the arrival of new technologies, Carter and Dealey applied the old techniques of pursuing regional trademarking. In 1922, Carter and the *Star-Telegram* erected WBAP, the area's first radio station, and they used it to position their city as the wellspring of regional distinctiveness. On May 19, WBAP broadcasted its first program with "greetings to the Southwest." Fittingly, Carter chose William Massie, president of the Fort Worth Chamber of Commerce, to

FIG. 7. Newspapers collaborated with civic and business interests in the claiming and branding of regions. Cargo (*left*) and passenger (*right*) trains, skyscrapers, and smoking factories signified Fort Worth's prosperous modernity, and its position as a livestock, grain, and jobbing hub confirmed it as the "Gateway to the Southwest." *Fort Worth Record & Register*, October 16, 1910.

deliver the first message received by North Texas radio audiences. "Fort Worth is the geographical center of this vast area. It is, so to speak, its heart," Massie claimed. "In listening to this message tonight, of what we are doing in Fort Worth, it may not be too great a stretch of the imagination to suggest that the Southwest is listening to its heartbeat." Later that year in October, Dealey and the Belo Company dedicated WFAA as the first station in Dallas, "a gift to the American public and especially to the great Southwest." Fort Worth repeated this process in September 1948, when the Carter group broadcast the first test signal from WBAP-TV, announcing its regional intent: "Television for the Southwest has arrived."[18]

Massie's 1922 radio address further illustrated how active trade and booster organizations contributed to the shaping of the Great Southwest as a market. In 1874, after local merchants pooled together subsidies for the Texas and Pacific Railroad, they established the Dallas Board of Trade. Fort Worth organized its version two years later, and both groups charged themselves with disseminating information about their cities to the outside world. In 1890, Fort Worth established its chamber of commerce, which continued that work. The Dallas Commercial Club (chartered in 1893) focused on promotion, while the Dallas Trade League (chartered in 1900) worked to attract retail merchants to purchase from the city's wholesalers. Through at least 1911, the "Merchant's Meeting" became a regular event, with the league placing large advertisements calling buyers from Louisiana, New Mexico, Oklahoma, and Texas to place their orders in Dallas, "The Market of the Great Southwest."[19]

Although media groups supplied the lexicon of regional claiming, its adoption by local businesses in their advertising confirmed the efficacy of those promotional efforts. As early as 1882, famed Dallas merchant Sanger Brothers incorporated the language of region when it declared itself "the GREATEST RETAIL DRY and FANCY GOODS HOUSE of the Great Southwest." Other retailers followed, like Reinhardt and Company (1886) of Dallas or G. Y. Smith (1907) of Fort Worth. Banks in both cities promised to meet the financial needs of their branded region, while various industries from automobile manufacturers to skin product companies appealed to their customers' southwesternness. In the 1936 centennial edition of the *Texas Almanac*, published by the Belo Corporation, no less than fourteen Dallas-based companies advertised with specific references to the Great Southwest, including a full-page notice for the Dallas Chamber of Commerce that declared, "The Southwest—Land of Opportunity."[20]

Repressing the New South

By the 1920s, the Great Southwest emerged as the preferred territorial branding for Dallas and Fort Worth. Although both claimed preeminence as the metropolis, their chief rival was not the other city but another regional trademark. Like their fellow Confederate cities, Dallas and Fort Worth emerged from the Civil War and Reconstruction eager to join the industrialization of the United States. To achieve that goal, they needed northern investors, so they shed their Old South quaintness by marketing themselves as part of the New South. For the sake of economic progress, the regional branders of Dallas and Fort Worth evaded their Confederate past while they simultaneously preserved white superiority.[21]

Although trailing established southern cities like Atlanta and Memphis, Dallas and Fort Worth boosters used their geographic position to reorient and rebrand the New South to their advantage. In an 1886 letter to the *Gazette*, former Tarrant County judge and former Confederate soldier C. C. Cummins argued that African American freedom burdened the South, but he exempted his part of it: "I do not mean Texas, for she is the new South. I mean the old slave states.... They cannot ... keep up with the march of new ideas." In this view, the Southwest represented the best parts of the South and the West. Fort Worth—according to a local poet—lay at its epicenter "in the sunny land of Dixie, as it borders on the West." In its 1920s promotions, the Fort Worth Chamber of Commerce used "South" and "Southwest" interchangeably and adopted the motto "Where Golden West and Sunny Southland Meet."[22]

The glossy pamphlets produced by the Fort Worth Chamber of Commerce in the 1920s—with their subtext that the Southwest, as South and West, offered a haven for white Americans—belied a hard edge of racial violence that preserved this haven. By that time, both Dallas and Fort Worth had witnessed lynchings of African Americans and adopted Jim Crow laws, creating deeply segregated communities. A 1909 stage adaptation of Thomas Dixon's novel *The Clansman* played in Fort Worth, and Amon Carter's *The Fort Worth Star and Telegram* sponsored an essay competition to which "hundreds of children" responded with quaint paeans to the "ghosts of former masters." In 1911 and 1913, white mobs attacked Black citizens of Fort Worth. In both cities, the Ku Klux Klan rose to prominence, with political and business leaders openly joining its ranks. These Southern legacies tarnished the Southwest with the shame of slavery, the humiliation of Confederate defeat, and the stench of modern-day white supremacy.[23]

Some local leaders and scholars, referring to Dallas and Fort Worth's citizens and their "Southern" behavior, warned that the New South would falter as a brand. In October 1924, literary scholar Jay B. Hubbell and the English Department at Southern Methodist University took over publishing responsibilities of the *Texas Review* from the University of Texas and renamed it *Southwest Review*. As editor, Hubbell contributed an essay to the first number entitled "The New Southwest," referring to the journal's reframing as well as the region's. He conceded that the Southwest "is Western as well as Southern," but where the West evoked images of cowboys, oil wells, bluebonnets, and railroads, the South evoked religious fundamentalism, corrupt state government, cotton, and the Ku Klux Klan. He lamented that Southern literature "pandered to sectional prejudice" and stifled originality. The "New Southwest," by contrast, was youthful and embraced its skyscraper modernity.[24]

Another Southern Methodist University scholar, Henry Nash Smith, agreed with Hubbell that the current "renaissance" in Southern literature could not contain the Southwest. In 1928, years before the release of his influential *The Virgin Land* (1950), Smith shared his thoughts on region in the *Southwest Review*. He noted that "an observer from west of the Sabine" would describe much of Southern culture as old or unfamiliar: "I despair of conveying to an Easterner or even to a Virginian the sense of strangeness with which a Southwesterner visits New Orleans." Smith nevertheless reinforced the old myth that regional distinction germinated organically, and his method of omitting Southern elements despite their conspicuous presence in the Southwest epitomized the scholarly sins of arbitrary selection when defining region.[25]

To Be or Not to Be Cowtown

The 1930s and 1940s maturation of the Dallas–Fort Worth version of the Southwest away from southernness and toward westernness partly originated in the commercial rivalry between the two cities and, more specifically, in Fort Worth's sense of inferiority toward Dallas. By any measure of prosperity and growth, Fort Worth had always trailed Dallas. To counter this disparity, Fort Worth relied upon regional branding by fabricating a western persona as Cowtown and deflating Dallas as odiously eastern.

Initially, Fort Worth business leaders viewed the term *cowtown* as a disparagement because it connoted backwardness and rudeness. When Amon G. Carter launched the *Fort Worth Star-Telegram* in 1909, he happily assumed the mantle of booster-in-chief from Buckley B. Paddock. In early issues, he and his allies wanted to show that their city was no longer "merely a cowtown," yet they wanted to capitalize on the romance of its cattle-trail past and the prosperity of its ranching and meatpacking present.[26] In a 1910 essay, the *Star-Telegram* welcomed new residents to the "cultured cowtown of the Southwest." Two years later, when the Advertising Men's Clubs of America met at Dallas, the Fort Worth chapter invited the delegates to visit their city "to see what most of them knew by reputation as a 'cowtown.'" The hosts played upon their guests' expectations by regaling them with chuckwagon cuisine and a Wild West show while they transported them on an electric interurban, shuttled them in automobiles, and toured them through industrial meatpacking plants.[27]

By 1918, Cowtown reemerged as a moniker for Fort Worth in the slang used by area sports writers, but in 1924, when the name started to appear on local automobiles, the Ad Club, the chamber of commerce, and the Automotive Traders Association reacted with revulsion and formed a committee to stop it. They declared that the decals were "insinuating, vulgar and profane and calculated to do the city of Fort Worth more harm than good." In November 1927, the chamber commissioned William J. Reilly of the University of Texas to conduct a market survey, and he recommended dropping the name. Paraphrased by the *Fort Worth Record-Telegram*, Amon Carter's morning daily, Reilly argued that the city lost revenue because "its traditional status as a 'cow town'" redirected potential customers to other markets.[28]

Reilly's report, however, failed to appreciate the linkage between Cowtown and the cowboy culture associated with the romance of the West. Those who supported the nickname understood this connection. Responding to Reilly's proposal, "a West Texan" wrote to the *Record-Telegram* expressing affection for the term and, at the same time, confirming how the media, shared economies, and cultural affiliation forged regional bonds between the metropolis and its hinterland: "Out in West Texas . . . , we look to Fort Worth as our best friend, we read your papers. . . . We come often to Fort Worth, and . . . the very name of Fort Worth calls to mind romance—romance of the frontier, now so far gone." The *Record-Telegram* embraced the popular view: "We were born 'Cowtown' and as 'Cowtown' we will become immortal." The author, perhaps

Carter, also recognized the marketing potential that Professor Reilly failed to grasp: "When the world thinks of 'Cowtown' every time it thinks of Texas, Fort Worth will be getting 100 per cent 'pull' from our advertising."[29]

Carter's support of Cowtown revealed an emerging strategy to market his city as the capital of western mystique. As various groups debated the nickname, Carter and other leaders adopted the motto that proclaimed Fort Worth as the place "where the West begins." The phrase originated in a 1911 poem written by Arthur Chapman, a columnist for the *Denver Republican*. The motto occasionally appeared in Fort Worth newspapers as early as 1921, but it did not become a formal declaration until May 1923, when the West Texas Chamber of Commerce held its fifth annual convention at San Angelo. With dueling claims as the leading regional center, Dallas and Fort Worth each sent 150 delegates. Carter lent the airwaves of his new radio station, WBAP, and George Dealey delivered a special "Airplane Edition" of the *Dallas Morning News* to San Angelo aboard a "new Curtiss flying machine." The issue included a full-page advertisement illustrated by John Knott. It featured a West Texas dude—broad-brimmed hat, bushy mustache, smoldering cigar, cattleman's vest—and copy reminding its readers that "the News has toiled shoulder to shoulder with the people of its vast Western territory." In response, Cowtown's delegation visited fifty-four West Texas communities. They participated in parades and barbecues and displayed a large banner carried by twelve men that proclaimed, "Fort Worth 'Where the West Begins.'" On August 15, Carter placed the motto in the masthead of the *Star-Telegram*, and it would remain there until 1966. Through the 1930s and 1940s, the Fort Worth Chamber of Commerce consistently featured the phrase in its promotional literature.[30]

The rivalry between Dallas and Fort Worth attained national attention during the 1936 Texas Centennial celebration. When the state selected Dallas as the host of the official fair, Carter and other Fort Worth leaders responded by sponsoring a competing Frontier Exposition. The cameras for the *March of Time* newsreel series recorded Carter addressing a crowd of supporters. Standing

FIG. 8. Contesting the West Texas hinterland with Fort Worth, the *Dallas Morning News* published a special "Airplane Edition" for the 1923 West Texas Chamber of Commerce meeting in San Angelo. It included this advertisement, with which the *News* claimed "its vast Western territory." John Knott, "A Greeting and a Pledge," *Dallas Morning News*, May 21, 1923.

behind a large pair of longhorns as the head of steer peered down from above him, he blustered, "You'd think Dallas invented Texas just because they bid higher for the Centennial than any other city. But we're going to put on a show of our own and teach those dudes over there where the West really begins."[31]

In contrast to the educational approach of the Texas Centennial, Carter wanted to out-western Dallas by giving the Frontier Centennial audiences a rowdy good time. He hired Broadway producer Billy Rose to put on the extravaganza. Operating on a fraction of the Dallas budget, Rose relied on the less expensive "pelvic-machinery" of showgirls. His productions included a Sally Rand burlesque in *Casa Mañana* and the "wild and whoopee" romp of *The Last Frontier*. The Board of Control contracted a printer to deliver five hundred thousand posters, banners, and other advertising material that featured images of "nude-y cowgirls" by local pinup artist Jewel Brannon Parker, enticing folks to Fort Worth—"Where the fun begins." Dallas countered with the Rangerettes, young ladies outfitted in western garb who served as hosts and ambassadors for the Centennial Exposition.[32]

The 1940 world premiere of Metro-Goldwyn-Mayer's *The Westerner* permitted Fort Worth another opportunity to enhance its westernness at the expense of Dallas. The souvenir program included ample use of the "Where the West Begins" slogan, but it also permitted the chamber of commerce to emphasize the city's twentieth-century progress—"From Trail Station to Modern Metropolis." In another advertisement, a real estate group emphasized "The Modern Spirit of the West," depicting a cowboy with his lasso looped around a trio of skyscrapers. Apparently, the celebration also granted Carter the chance to famously refine his city's motto. In a nationally syndicated column, Hollywood reporter Robbin Coons quoted the publisher gloating that if Fort Worth is "Where the West Begins," then Dallas is "where the East peters out."[33]

FIG. 9. Led by tireless booster Amon G. Carter, Fort Worth put on the extravagant Frontier Exposition that rivaled the official Texas Centennial celebration in Dallas. Jewel Brannon Parker's "nude-y cowgirls" promised fairgoers a "wild and whoopee" romp in Fort Worth—"Where the fun begins." *Billy Rose Presents The Last Frontier* (1936). Digital Archives, Fort Worth Public Library.

Air Battles

As superficial as the battle between nude-y cowgirls and pretty Rangerettes might seem, it reinforced the importance of regional branding as a crucial strategy of cultivating big-business opportunities. Fort Worth kept up with Dallas with aggressive railroad promotion and by taking the lead in developing integrated media—booster-oriented newspapers and the region's first radio and television stations—but with the emerging importance of air travel, Fort Worth trailed Dallas. Amon Carter's line that "Dallas is where the East peters out" received wide publicity in September 1940—at the same moment that the U.S. Civil Aeronautics Authority (CAA) recommended that the two cities share a regional airport. Although the timing might have been coincidental, Carter's comment illustrated how over the next twenty-five years, Fort Worth would leverage its regional branding to compel Dallas to cooperate in building an international airport.

Both Love Field in Dallas and Meacham Field in Fort Worth originated as Great War–era installations and served the cities during the early days of commercial air travel, but in 1940, with another world war looming, the CAA determined that a joint regional airport would better serve national defense. Both cities rejected the plan. In 1941, however, the CAA reached an agreement with the city of Arlington to build an airport near the Dallas-Tarrant county line. This gambit forced the rival cities to concede, and they drew up plans for the new Midway Airport, which located the administration building at a central location on the north end of the property. As a publisher, or as someone serving on numerous civic committees, or as a board member of American Airlines, Amon Carter actively pursued Fort Worth's interests in the regional airport, and he likely contributed to the CAA's decision to relocate the administration building to the west side of the property and orient it facing away from Dallas.[34]

In the spring of 1943, when they first learned of the building's relocation, Dallas officials yowled in protest. The *Morning News* published an editorial cartoon by John Knott depicting "Fort Worth" as a Carteresque westerner, milking the "Airport" cow that stood astride the "Midway" fence with its snout stuffed in the bucket of "Dallas Business." The *Star-Telegram* replied with a cartoon that caricatured Dallas mayor Woodall Rogers as a top hat, coattails-wearing easterner, whining his complaint about the Fort Worth "bully" to the CAA. Felix R. McKnight, writing for the *Morning News*, termed the underhanded scheme to relocate the building "Catermandering" and called to his readers, "Gather closely, suckers, and hear the incredible tale of the disappearance of a giant airport. When last seen, it was being carted away in the direction of Fort Worth." Although the fight over the building's location may seem silly, McKnight warned that it signified a serious threat: "If the fraud is permitted to stand, Fort Worth is destined to become the air transportation capital of the Southwest." In March 1943, Dallas pulled its support for Midway, and the U.S. military operated the field for the duration of the world war.[35]

Love Field continued as the primary commercial airport in the region, and its dominance, Fort Worth boosters understood, could stymie their city's postwar prosperity. In 1947, the city council voted to purchase and expand Midway Airport, and in 1950, they renamed it Amon G. Carter Field—calculated to annoy Dallas. The first passengers arrived in 1953 aboard an American Airlines DC-6. They received "a Wild West hello" and feted with barbecue, but the landing portended future problems for both Carter and Love fields. The DC-6 was a propeller-driven aircraft, and within five years, carriers began using jetliners that required longer runways and expended much more fuel. Most flights that landed at Carter stopped first at Love, and the new technology rendered such city-hopping routes impractical.[36]

In 1961, Dallas requested funds to expand Love Field to better accommodate jet aircrafts, but they would not find an ally in the new Federal Aviation Agency (FAA). The recently installed chief, Dallas native Najeeb E. Halaby, denied his support. He suggested that Dallas and Fort Worth cease their bickering and formulate a strategy to build a regional airport with the capacity to accommodate modern air travel. In 1962, he testified before a

Senate committee that he would halt federal dollars for Love and characterized Dallas's obstruction as "a pure, unadulterated case of childish civic pride, costing the federal taxpayer many millions of dollars." Building on this support, the Fort Worth city council approved funds for additional expansion at Cater and recommended another name change to "Greater Southwestern International Airport—Dallas-Fort Worth Airfield," using the familiar branding to wrest symbolic control of the region.[37]

Fort Worth leaders, however, knew that expansion and name changes would not break the dominance in air travel that Dallas enjoyed, but they employed these tactics to coerce their neighbors to share in the benefits of that crucial means of transportation. In 1964, Fort Worth continued its pressuring maneuvers by convincing the Civil Aeronautics Board (CAB) to determine if Love or the Greater Southwestern should serve as the regional airport. On April 7, the CAB ruled that neither would receive the designation, and on September 30, it further declared that if Dallas and Fort Worth could not cooperate and agree upon a plan to develop a regional airport with 180 days, then the CAB would make the decision for them.[38]

The CAB's threat worked. On January 7, 1965, the city councils for Dallas and Fort Worth agreed to form a joint airport commission. In September, the commission selected a twenty-thousand-acre site immediately north of the Greater Southwestern Airport. They broke ground in 1968, and by the time that the first American Airlines flight touched down in 1974, the $700 million Dallas–Fort Worth International Airport (DFW) boasted four passenger terminals and two twelve-thousand-foot runways that could accommodate supersonic aircrafts. Serving two cities, it would become one of the busiest airports in the world.[39]

The Southwestern Metroplex

In the nine years between the initial 1965 agreement and the opening of the international airport in 1974, Dallas and Fort Worth demonstrated that their leadership could work together for mutual prosperity. The success of that endeavor convinced them that they should also cooperate in regional branding, which they had so long contested. In that effort, Dallas and Fort Worth used many of the same yet modernized tools that they had employed since the 1870s—declaring hinterlands, developing transportation networks, and using integrated media to deploy branding strategies.

Like their nineteenth-century counterparts, Dallas–Fort Worth boosters of the 1960s and 1970s recognized that region creation did not occur naturally. For example, the gathering of demographic data and marking statistical trends by the U.S. Census Bureau might appear objective and free of outside influence, but in 1950, the bureau artificially established Standard Metropolitan Areas (changed to Standard Metropolitan Statistical Areas—SMSAs—in 1959) to measure the postwar emergence of suburbs that extended economic connections beyond city limits and county lines. The bureau had assigned Dallas and Fort Worth separate SMSA designations, but in 1969, the chambers of commerce for both cities petitioned for a merger. As Harry K. Werst, president of the Fort Worth Chamber of Commerce, confirmed, they were less concerned about statistical accuracy and more concerned about "improving the image of North Texas" by making it seem larger.[40]

Anticipating the SMSA merger and the opening of DFW Airport, local chambers coordinated their marketing efforts for the region. "We had been telling a City of Dallas story which isn't competitive in some areas with a city like Houston," Edgar "Gar" Laux of the Dallas chamber explained. "But when you talk about the Dallas-Fort Worth area it is. And if a business moves to Irving or Fort Worth, it still helps Dallas." On April 30, 1971, Dallas and Fort Worth, with six area chambers, agreed to form the "North Texas Commission" (NTC) and to sponsor a joint $4.5 million advertising campaign to promote the airport and attract new businesses to the region using print media, excursion trips, and other familiar strategies.[41]

To assist in the rebranding of the region, the NTC hired the Dallas-based marketing firm Tracy-Locke Company in December 1971. In the new year, the group announced a slogan: "North Texas—The Good Land." Although area boosters had consistently used "North Texas" for over a century, the firm discovered that the term confused people outside the state. Tracy-Locke polled ninety-four executives and found that only 38 percent located North Texas as the Dallas–Fort Worth area. The region needed a new name, and according to local lore, Harve Chapman of Tracy-Locke suggested "Metroplex," a portmanteau of "metropolitan" and "complex."[42]

Although Chapman may have borrowed the term from Eugene I. Johnson—who applied it as early as 1952 in San Bernardino, California—its selection represented a deliberate choice made by Tracy-Locke and the NTC to rebrand the Dallas–Fort Worth region. In late January 1972, they purchased two-page advertisements in *Fortune* and *Business Week* that touted "the Southwest Metroplex"—coupling the old and familiar with the new and modern. Within weeks, area businesses deployed the term in their advertising, and by the end of the year, the *Morning News* and the *Star-Telegram* regularly used it in their copy and headlines. In November, WBAP-TV Channel 5—the station launched by Amon G. Carter—declared, "We're the Metroplex Station." In the next year's telephone directory, eight businesses appeared with "metroplex" in their names, increasing to 127 within six years.[43]

Local business and media leaders eagerly adopted this rebranding of Dallas and Fort Worth as a single regional identity, but the Southwest Metroplex did not survive unscathed. For one, it failed to achieve any recognition beyond the area. In 1975, Harve Chapman reflected, "The acceptance of the word has been amazing, especially on the local and regional level rather than on the national level where it was intended." As Channel 5's 1972 advertisement indicated, users more often omitted references to the Southwest, and as pervasive as the "Metroplex" became, the term received derision as an awkward word that, at best, described "nowhere" and, at worst, metastasized like "a tumor on the language."[44]

For a century, Dallas and Fort Worth leaders battled over a symbolic and economic hinterland. Situated upon the Texas regional crossroads, they co-opted the Great Southwest to funnel profits to their cities, and to achieve that goal, they employed similar tactics of railroad development, partnering with coordinated media and promoting regional branding. Both groups experimented with the New South trademark, but by the 1910s, they chose to repress the memories of slavery and Confederate defeat, yet they reconfigured white supremacy and white prosperity within their western fantasies. To distinguish themselves from Dallas, Fort Worth boosters adopted their Cowtown persona, and both cities fought the battles over a regional airfield with western imagery. By 1965, compelled by the CAB, Dallas and Fort Worth formed a partnership to build an international airport, and together they used the familiar toolkit of region invention when they promoted the joint brand of the Southwestern Metroplex.

The Dallas–Fort Worth example illustrates how North Texas boosters consciously and deliberately engaged in region invention. The evolutions from the Great Southwest, the New South, and Cowtown to the Metroplex reveal the flexibility and intentionality of marketing. That story also shows the fallacy of claiming that regions form organically and achieve distinctiveness from specific and unique intersections of landscape and human activity. When Dallas and Fort Worth hired a professional advertising firm to promote their new Metroplex trademark, they did not implement some modern innovation. Instead, they relied on tactics proven after a century of regional branding.

Notes

1. Italics in the original and hereafter. Meinig, *Imperial Texas*, 91; Jordan, "Concept and Method," 8–24. See also Jordan, "Perceptual Regions," 293–307.

2. For examples of scholarly region building, see Kolchin, *Sphinx on the American Land*; Woodard, *American Nations*. See also Ayers et al., *All Over the Map*.

3. Meinig, *Imperial Texas*, 90–109; Buenger, "Texas and the South," 308–25; Campbell, *Gone to Texas*, 207; Ely, *Where the West Begins*, 3–11; Cantrell, "Bones of Stephen F. Austin," 39–74; Cashion, *Lone Star Mind*, 25–45; McLemore, *Inventing Texas*, 81–93; González, *Border Renaissance*, 6–11, 29–66; Cummins, "History, Memory, and Rebranding," 37–57; Schiller, "Don't Sell Texas Short!" 389–416.

4. Jordan, "Perceptual Regions," 300; Cronon, *Nature's Metropolis*, 23–54, 264–80; West, *Contested Plains*, 108–13, 176–90; Wrobel, *Promised Lands*, 19–74; Abbott, *How Cities Won the West*, 1–30, 74–87; Wardle and Boehme, "Introduction," 5–35;

Neumann, "Reforging the Steel City," 582–602; Cummins, "History, Memory, and Rebranding," 41.

5. Stephen V. Ward also notes, "The rapid settlement of the North American continent left a boosterist legacy" (31) that significantly informed the global field of place marketing that emerged in the later twentieth century. Ward, *Selling Places*, 1–31. Ward, with coeditor John R. Gold, defines place promotion "as the conscious use of publicity and marketing to communicate selective images of specific geographical localities or areas to a target audience" (2). Gold and Ward, introduction to *Place Promotion*, 1–11.

6. Meinig, *Imperial Texas*, 75–76, 107.

7. Hill, *Dallas*, xxvi–xxiv; Rich, *Fort Worth: Outpost*, 1–12.

8. FWD, May 31, 1873; FWDD, September 9, 1876; FWG, May 6, 1891; DMN, January 1, 1889; January 11, 1895; Anonymous, "B. B. Paddock"; Rich, *Fort Worth: Outpost*, 11–12.

9. For examples of "the Great Southwest" as a market label, see William Hendricks, remarks in the Senate, February 23, 1836, *Appendix to the Congressional Globe for the First Session, Twenty-fourth Congress* (Washington DC: Globe Office, 1836), 162; *Weekly Courier and Journal*, December 14, 1838, 1; *Daily Picayune*, July 15, 1843, 2; *Nashville Union*, February 27, 1844, 1; *Journal of the Proceedings of the South-Western Convention*, 3–5, 7.

10. FWD, May 31, 1873; *Galveston Tri-Weekly News*, October 10, 1870; DDH, December 29, 1875; DWH, January 1, 1878; Graff, *Dallas Myth*, xix. By the late twentieth century, few scholars would include North Texas as part of a Southwest that centered around Arizona and New Mexico. Lavender, *Southwest*; Burke, *Land Apart*; Weber and deBuys, *First Impressions*.

11. FWD, May 31, 1873.

12. DH, June 11, 1870; July 20, 1872; DDH, August 10, 1873; December 29, 1875; April 5, 1877; FWDG, January 25, 1889; Paddock, *Early Days*, 4–6; Hill, *Dallas*, 3–4; Graff, *Dallas Myth*, 92–93, 148; Rich, *Fort Worth: Outpost*, 4, 15–21, 43–44; Campbell, *Gone to Texas*, 306. For the significance of railroads in place promotion, see Ward, *Selling Places*, 10–27; West, *Contested Plains*, 126–33; Wrobel, *Promised Lands*, 19–24, 48–68.

13. FWD, June 7, 1873; Knight, *Fort Worth*, 62–63; Rich, *Fort Worth: Outpost*, 15. The map first appeared in the *North Texas Epitomist*, July 24, 1873. FWD, July 26, 1873; August 2, 1873. *Fort Worth Daily Gazette* later incorporated a similar image into its banner. FWDG, January 11, 1887.

14. FWD, October 25, 1873; FWDG, July 20, 1876; April 19, 1886; Paddock, *Early Days*, 7, 11–12; Knight, *Fort Worth*, 73–76.

15. DDH, October 29, 1880; DWH, June 23, 1881; DMN, July 5, 1886; FWDG, Extra Edition; Paddock, *Early Days*, 12–13; Rich, *Fort Worth: Outpost*, 43–44.

16. DMN, October 1, 1885; October 12, 1885; Hill, *Dallas*, 5; Northrup, "George Bannerman Dealey," 19–21. For a case study on the role of newspapers in the "creation and promotion of . . . greater regional attachment" (211) in Roanoke, Virginia, see Myers-Jones and Brooker-Gross, "Newspapers as Promotional Strategists," 195–211.

17. FWST, February 1, 1909; December 10, 1911, Annual Edition; Cervantez, *Amon Carter*, 24–26.

18. FWST, May 20, 1922; September 16, 1948; DMN, October 1, 1922; June 9, 1929; September 22, 1929; Northrup, "George Bannerman Dealey," 136–37.

19. DDH, September 19, 1874; November 10, 1874; *Daily Fort Worth Standard*, October 25, 1876; FWDG, April 16, 1890; DMN, July 22, 1904; July 25, 1909; August 6, 1911; *Fort Worth, Texas: The Gateway*; *Fort Worth: The New Metropolis*.

20. DDH, January 1, 1882; November 11, 1886; DMN, January 1, 1907; *Fort Worth Telegram*, April 18, 1907; FWST, October 21, 1917; November 11, 1923, Jubilee section; *Texas Almanac*, 2, 25–26, 33, 35, 489–90, 495, 498.

21. For the New South, see Ayers, *Promise of the New South*; Humphreys, "New South Historiography." For Texas and the New South, see Campbell, *Gone to Texas*, 306–10; Garrett-Scott, "Hope of the South," 139–66. For the Texas shift from southern to western identities, see Buenger, "Texas and the South," 308–25; McLemore, *Inventing Texas*, 81–93; Cantrell, "Bones of Stephen F. Austin," 39–74; Cummins, "History, Memory, and Rebranding," 37–57.

22. C. C. Cummins to the editor, April 12, 1886, FWDG, published April 13, 1886; "C. C. Cummins," 7; Brashear, "Vine Clad Bohemian Nest," 1; *Fort Worth, Where Golden West and Sunny Southland Meet*; Cervantez, *Amon Carter*, 7, 27–28, 70–71. Early iterations of the Fort Worth stock shows emphasized the city's southernness rather than its westernness. Olsmstead, *Frontier Centennial*, 16–17.

23. *Fort Worth Star and Telegram*, January 1, 1909; Hill, *Dallas*, 100–106; Rich, *Fort Worth: Outpost*, 64–65, 134–35, 160–62; Phillips, *White Metropolis*, 77–101; Rich, *Fort Worth between the World Wars*, 54–74; Buenger and Buenger, *Texas Merchant*, 63–66; Campbell, *Gone to Texas*, 325–26; Cervantez, *Amon Carter*, 31–32.

24. Hubbell, "New Southwest," 91–99.

25. Smith, "Note on the Southwest."

26. The cattle-drive era ended for Fort Worth when the railroads arrived during the 1870s, but the cattle industry remained crucial to the city as the center of a ranching hinterland, as attested by the establishment of the Fort Worth Stock Yards (1893), the Southwestern Exposition and Livestock Show (1896), the Swift and Armour Meat Packing Company (1906), and others. Rich, *Fort Worth: Outpost*, 39–53, 88, 106–18.

27. FWST, September 20, 1910; December 15, 1912, Annual Development Edition, part 12.

28. DMN, July 7, 1918, part 1; FWST, August 24, 1919; August 27, 1924; FWR, August 28, 1924; FWRT, November 30, 1927.

29. FWRT, December 3, 1927; December 5, 1927.

30. While some detractors pointed out that other cities like Denver and Omaha used the same motto, Fort Worth's claim had always been more about market competition with Dallas. DMN, May 21, 1923, Airplane Edition; FWST, May 27, 1923; August 15, 1923; July 26, 1966; *Fort Worth, Where the West Begins* (1936); *Fort Worth: Where the West Begins* (1939); *Fort Worth: Where the West Begins* (1945); Sampsel and Puscher, "Out Where the West Begins"; Schiller, "Don't Sell Texas Short."

31. De Rochemont and de Rochement, *March of Time*; Ragsdale, *Centennial '36*, 54–61, 208–13; Graff, *Dallas Myth*, 150; Olsmstead, *Frontier Centennial*, 10–11.

32. Billy Rose's reference to "pelvic machinery" quoted in Cohen, *Not Bad for Delancey Street*, 99; FWST, May 2, 1936; May 9, 1936; *Billy Rose Presents The Last Frontier*, ephemeral program issued for the Frontier Centennial (Fort Worth TX: Fort Worth Centennial Board of Control, 1936), 3; Morang, *Texas Centennial Highlights*; Ragsdale, *Centennial '36*, 145–47, 217, 282–83; Cummins, "History, Memory, and Rebranding," 37–52; Olsmstead, *Frontier Centennial*, 113–97; Rich, *Fort Worth between the World Wars*, 141–50.

33. DMN, September 6, 1940; September 12, 1940; FWST, September 18, 1940; *Samuel Goldwyn Presents The Westerner*, ephemeral program handed out at premier, Fort Worth TX, 1940.

34. FWST, September 2, 1941; September 16, 1941; June 8, 1952; DMN, January 5, 1942; January 8, 1942; January 11, 1942; Cervantez, *Amon Carter*, 159–61.

35. DMN, February 28, 1943; March 2, 1943; FWST, April 1, 1943.

36. FWST, October 30, 1947; November 5, 1947; February 12, 1948; Jul 9, 1950; June 8, 1952; April 26, 1953; DMN, October 31, 1947; November 1, 1947; November 5, 1947; September 24, 1948.

37. FWST, May 12, 1961; May 13, 1961; June 14, 1961; August 15, 1962; November 1, 1962; November 5, 1962; DMN, May 12, 1961; August 10, 1962; November 2, 1962; November 6, 1962.

38. FWST, April 7, 1964; DMN, April 8, 1964; October 1, 1964.

39. DMN, January 7, 1965; January 13, 1974; FWST, January 16, 1966; December 12, 1968.

40. FWST, December 4, 1969, 2-A; DMN, December 6, 1969; June 11, 1971; Gardner, "Changes in Metropolitan Area Definition, 1910–2010"; Bauer, "Metroplexed."

41. DMN, May 1, 1971; June 11, 1971; January 23, 1972; FWST, January 28, 1972.

42. DMN, December 28, 1971; January 23, 1972; January 29, 1972; December 9, 1979; FWST, January 28, 1972; Bauer, "Metroplexed"; Rogers, "Don't Call It the Metroplex." The work of the NTC and Tracy-Locke anticipated the field of city or place marketing that emerged in the late 1970s and early 1980s. Ward, *Selling Places*, 1–3.

43. *Sun*, August 27, 1952; November 16, 1955; April 19, 1958; Johnson, *Community Education Project*; Johnson, *Metroplex Assembly*; DMN, January 29, 1972; March 5, 1972; December 9, 1979; FWST, November 19, 1972.

44. DMN, November 17, 1974; December 9, 1979; Bauer, "Metroplexed"; Rogers, "Don't Call It the Metroplex"; Jordan, "Perceptual Regions," 299–300.

Newspapers

Daily Fort Worth Standard.
Daily Picayune, The. New Orleans.
DDH. *The Dallas Daily Herald.*
DH. *Dallas Herald.*

DMN. *The Dallas Morning News.*
DWH. *The Dallas Weekly Herald.*
Fort Worth Star and Telegram, The.
Fort Worth Telegram, The.
FWD. *The Fort Worth Democrat.*
FWDG. *Fort Worth Daily Gazette.*
FWR. *Fort Worth Record.*
FWRT. *Fort Worth Record-Telegram.*
FWST. *Fort Worth Star-Telegram.*
FWWD. *The Daily Fort Worth Democrat.*
Galveston Tri-Weekly News.
Nashville Union.
North Texas Epitomist. Fort Worth.
Sun, The. San Bernardino CA.
Weekly Courier and Journal, The. Natchez MS.

Bibliography

Abbott, Carl. *How Cities Won the West: Four Centuries of Urban Change in Western North America.* New Haven CT: Yale University Press, 2008.
Anonymous. "B. B. Paddock." *Bohemian* 1, no. 1 (November 1899): 5–6.
Ayers, Edward L. *The Promise of the New South: Life after Reconstruction.* New York: Oxford University Press, 1992.
Ayers, Edward L., Patricia Nelson Limerick, Stephen Nissenbaum, and Peter S. Onuf. *All Over the Map: Rethinking American Regions.* Baltimore: Johns Hopkins University Press, 1996.
Bauer, David. "Metroplexed." *D Magazine*, January 1975. http://www.dmagazine.com.
Brashear, J. P. "The Vine Clad Bohemian Nest." *Bohemian* 1, no. 1 (November 1899): 1.
Buenger, Victoria, and Walter L. Buenger. *Texas Merchant: Marvin Leonard and Fort Worth.* College Station: Texas A&M University Press, 2008.
Buenger, Walter L. "Texas and the South." *Southwestern Historical Quarterly* 103, no. 3 (January 2000): 308–25.
Burke, Flannery. *A Land Apart: The Southwest and the Nation in the Twentieth Century.* Tucson: University of Arizona Press, 2017.
Campbell, Randolph B. *Gone to Texas: A History of the Lone Star State.* New York: Oxford University Press, 2003.
Cantrell, Gregg. "The Bones of Stephen F. Austin: History and Memory in Progressive-Era Texas." In *Lone Star Pasts: Memory and History in Texas*, edited by Gregg Cantrell and Elizabeth Hayes Turner, 39–74. College Station: Texas A&M University Press, 2007.
Cashion, Ty. *Lone Star Mind: Reimagining Texas History.* Norman: University of Oklahoma Press, 2018.
"C. C. Cummins." *Bohemian* 1, no. 1 (November 1899): 7.

Cervantez, Brian. *Amon Carter: A Lone Star Life*. Norman: University of Oklahoma Press, 2019.

Cohen, Mark. *Not Bad for Delancey Street: The Rise of Billy Rose*. Waltham MA: Brandeis University Press, 2018.

Cronon, William. *Nature's Metropolis: Chicago and the Great West*. New York: W. W. Norton, 1991.

Cummins, Light Townsend. "History, Memory, and Rebranding Texas as Western for the 1936 Centennial." In *This Corner of Canaan: Essays on Texas in Honor of Randolph B. Campbell*, edited by Richard B. McCaslin, Donald E. Chipman, and Andrew J. Torget, 37–57. Denton: University of North Texas Press, 2013.

de Rochemont, Louis, and Richard de Rochemont, prods. *The March of Time*. Volume 2, episode 6, "Texas Centennial." New York: Time, 1936.

Ely, Glen Sample. *Where the West Begins: Debating Texas Identity*. Lubbock: Texas Tech University Press, 2011.

Fort Worth, Texas: The Gateway to the Great Southwest. Fort Worth TX: Chamber of Commerce, 1912.

Fort Worth: The New Metropolis of the Southwest. Fort Worth TX: Chamber of Commerce, 1919.

Fort Worth, Where Golden West and Sunny Southland Meet: The Agricultural and Industrial Center of the Southwest. Fort Worth TX: Chamber of Commerce, 1922.

Fort Worth: Where the West Begins. Fort Worth TX: Chamber of Commerce, 1939.

Fort Worth: Where the West Begins. Fort Worth TX: Chamber of Commerce, 1945.

Fort Worth, Where the West Begins: Life Is Worth While in Fort Worth. Fort Worth TX: Chamber of Commerce, 1936.

Gardner, Todd. "Changes in Metropolitan Area Definition, 1910–2010." U.S. Census Bureau Center for Economic Study research paper CES 21-04, February 2021.

Garrett-Scott, Shennette. "'The Hope of the South': The New Century Cotton Mill of Dallas, Texas, and the Business of Race in the New South, 1902–1907." *Southwestern Historical Quarterly* 116, no. 2 (October 2012): 139–66.

Gold, John R., and Stephen V. Ward. Introduction to *Place Promotion: The Use of Publicity and Marketing to Sell Towns and Regions*, edited by John R. Gold and Stephen V. Ward, 1–17. New York: John Wiley & Sons, 1994.

González, John Morán. *Border Renaissance: The Texas Centennial and the Emergence of Mexican American Literature*. Austin: University of Texas Press, 2009.

Graff, Harvey J. *The Dallas Myth: The Making and Unmaking of an American City*. Minneapolis: University of Minnesota Press, 2008.

Hill, Patricia Everidge. *Dallas: The Making of a Modern City*. Austin: University of Texas Press, 1996.

Hubbell, Jay B. "The New Southwest." *Southwestern Review* 10, no. 1 (October 1924): 91–99.

Humphreys, James S. "New South Historiography." In *The New South*, edited by James S. Humphreys, 7–36. Kent OH: Kent State University Press, 2018.

Johnson, Eugene I. *The Community Education Project: A Four Year Report*. San Bernardino CA: n.p., 1957.
———. *Metroplex Assembly: An Experiment in Community Education*. Brookline MA: Center for the Study of Liberal Education for Adults, 1965.
Jordan, Terry G. "The Concept and Method." In *Regional Studies: The Interplay and People*, edited by Glen E. Lich, 8–24. College Station: Texas A&M University Press, 1992.
———. "Perceptual Regions in Texas." *Geographical Review* 68, no. 3 (July 1978): 293–307.
Journal of the Proceedings of the South-Western Convention. Memphis TN: n.p., 1845.
Knight, Oliver. *Fort Worth: Outpost on the Trinity*. 1953. Reprint, Fort Worth: Texas Christian University Press, 1990.
Kolchin, Peter. *A Sphinx on the American Land: The Nineteenth-Century South in Comparative Perspective*. Baton Rouge: Louisiana State University Press, 2003.
Lavender, David. *The Southwest*. Albuquerque: University of New Mexico Press, 1980.
McLemore, Laura Lyon. *Inventing Texas: Early Historians of the Lone Star State*. College Station: Texas A&M University Press, 2004.
Meinig, D. W. *Imperial Texas: An Interpretative Essay in Cultural Geography*. Austin: University of Texas Press, 1969.
Morang, Frank, dir. *Texas Centennial Highlights*. Newsreel. Dallas: Jamieson Film, 1936.
Myers-Jones, Holly J., and Susan R. Brooker-Gross. "Newspapers as Promotional Strategists for Regional Definition." In *Place Promotion: The Use of Publicity and Marketing to Sell Towns and Regions*, edited by John R. Gold and Stephen V. Ward, 195–212. New York: John Wiley & Sons, 1994.
Neumann, Tracy. "Reforging the Steel City: Symbolism and Space in Postindustrial Pittsburgh." *Journal of Urban History* 44, no. 4 (2018): 582–602.
Northrup, Cynthia L. Clark. "George Bannerman Dealey: A Study in Persuasion, Perseverance, and Progressivism." PhD diss., Texas Christian University, 2002.
Olsmstead, Jacob W. *The Frontier Centennial: Fort Worth and the New West*. Lubbock: Texas Tech University Press, 2021.
Paddock, B. B. *Early Days in Fort Worth: Much of What I Saw and Part of Which I Was*. Fort Worth TX: n.p., n.d.
Ragsdale, Kenneth B. *Centennial '36: The Year America Discovered Texas*. College Station: Texas A&M University Press, 1987.
Rich, Harold. *Fort Worth between the World Wars*. College Station: Texas A&M University Press, 2020.
———. *Fort Worth: Outpost, Cowtown, Boomtown*. Norman: University of Oklahoma Press, 2014.
Rogers, Tim. "Don't Call It the Metroplex." *Texas Monthly*, February 2013. www.texasmonthly.com.
Sampsel, Laurie J., and Donald M. Puscher. "'Out Where the West Begins': The Denver Song That Became a Western Classic." *American Music Research Center Journal* 22 (2013): 35–57.

Schiller, Joseph. "'Don't Sell Texas Short!': Amon Carter's Cultivation and Marketing of West Texas Nature." *Southwestern Historical Quarterly* 121, no. 4 (April 2018): 389–416.
Smith, Henry. "A Note on the Southwest." *Southwestern Review* 14, no. 3 (1928): 267–78.
The Texas Almanac and State Industrial Guide. Dallas TX: A. H. Belo, 1936.
Ward, Stephen V. *Selling Places: The Marketing and Promotion of Towns and Cities, 1850–2000*. New York: Routledge, 1999.
Wardle, Marian, and Sarah E. Boehme. "Introduction: Brandings." In *Branding the American West: Paintings and Films, 1900–1950*, edited by Marian Wardle and Sarah E. Boehme, 5–35. Norman: University of Oklahoma Press, 2016.
Weber, David J., and William deBuys. *First Impressions: A Reader's Journey to Iconic Places of the American Southwest*. New Haven CT: Yale University Press, 2017.
West, Elliott. *Contested Plains: Indians, Goldseekers, and the Rush to Colorado*. Lawrence: University Press of Kansas, 1998.
Woodard, Colin. *American Nations: A History of the Eleven Rival Regional Cultures of North America*. New York: Viking, 2011.
Wrobel, David M. *Promised Lands: Promotion, Memory, and the Creation of the American West*. Lawrence: University Press of Kansas, 2002.

ELEVEN

Local Identities and National Highways

How Roads Deepened and Diluted Historical Regionalism

ALEXANDER FINKELSTEIN

After returning from service in World War I, Lieutenant Colonel Dwight D. Eisenhower, along with nearly three hundred other U.S. Army personnel, undertook a sixty-two-day journey across the country, sponsored by the military. The War Department, according to the *New York Times*, proclaimed two goals for this trip: "It will be a demonstration on behalf of the government to show the need of an improved road system of national highways, and, second, it will illustrate the efficiency of the army's transport system."[1] Automobile, gasoline, and tire companies supported the Transcontinental Motor Convoy with funding and publicity to reinforce the need for federal investment in road infrastructure and build a nationwide market for their brands and products. Soldiers, reporters, and company representatives embarked on a trip that helped map the country and its infrastructural development by emphasizing material conditions across various geographic locales. The Transcontinental Motor Convoy constitutes one important moment in the long project of mapping and constructing the nation while continuing to protect regional spaces.

On July 7, 1919, the members of this convoy began their journey outside the White House with a ceremony to dedicate the "Zero Milestone." The Zero Milestone, the point from which all the nation's highways would be measured, established the infrastructural center of the United States at the seat of political power. After the ceremony, the eighty-one-vehicle convoy departed Washington DC toward its final destination in San Francisco. Over the course of the 3,251-mile trip, they averaged about 5½ miles per hour and suffered 230 road accidents, "or instances of road failure and vehicles sinking in quicksand or mud, running off the road or over embankments, overturning, or other mishaps."[2]

The reports from the trip offer a glimpse into how these soldiers defined region and nation as products of infrastructure, development, environment, and culture. In Maryland, Pennsylvania, Ohio, and Indiana, the convoy traversed concrete and macadamized, improved roads. Eisenhower reported that after Illinois, "practically no more pavement was encountered until reaching California." If the Mississippi River on Illinois's western border signaled a new region without improved roads, then Nebraska's dirt roads and sandstorms marked another distinct region within the arid and undeveloped West. From Nebraska through California, the roads, culverts, and bridges were poor, ungraded, and at times impassable, yet this space was not uniform: the sand drifts and lack of water throughout Nebraska, Wyoming, Nevada, and Utah exacerbated the poor conditions of the roads.[3] The soldiers recognized regional differences in the conditions of the roads and cultures of the people encountered, but they refrained from submitting a conclusion on whether they attributed the differences to sparser populations, climate, history, or the various federal and state tax and appropriation structures.

Despite the conditions of the roads, the troops arrived at their terminus in California, where the Willys-Overland Company hosted a celebratory banquet. The banquet's commemorative program declared, "So in this journey of yours across plain, desert and mountain trail, you, too, have blazed new trails—the trails of Commerce, Highways, Mechanical Achievement, and Protection of the Flag."[4] This trip did more than identify the infrastructural and environmental status quo; it sought to erase the borders and obstacles between regions that hindered continental development, nationwide industry and market, and national identity.[5]

The nationwide highway system and its development represent the complexities of U.S. federalism and offer a paradigm for understanding the evolution, importance, and use of regional categorization throughout twentieth-century U.S. history. Just as the Transcontinental Motor Convoy's experience shaped the participants' understanding of space and landscape, the broader contours of early road development rearranged conceptions of place and nation. Highways are both lenses through which historians can assess broader patterns of regional change over time and catalysts of regional change through environmental, urban, political, economic, social, and migratory shifts. As the roads changed definitions of regional constructions, regionalism changed the road system. Historical regionalism is a category of analysis that reveals ways in which individuals and associations claimed identity and power in relation to others and how these constructions of place and space changed over time. While the United States promotes nationalistic belonging based on a coherent idea and practice of cultural *Americanness*, regional association offers opportunities for political and social division and competitiveness within the unified nation.

Highways, maps, and travel guides offer insight into the construction of regional imaginaries and the implications of regional association. Regional identities are manifestations of accepted—by those within or those outside—interests, peculiarities, and narratives that reveal systems of power locally, nationally, and globally. The fact that these associations are accepted and recognized by some does not preclude dissent by others. While individuals may emphasize and claim competing regional constructions, regional association is defined in relation to other regions by both insiders and outsiders.[6] Regional association requires external validation, and such identity is built on competition. Historical regionalism by nature constituted a project that was contested, yet the project employed seemingly disconnected systems and processes to cement regional—often exclusionary—power structures.

Technological developments and political movements regarding the highways generated new regional awareness and national phenomena. Full understanding of these regional constructions and shifts demands methodological inquiry that transcends historical subfields and singular analytical approaches. The highways constitute tools by which regions were constructed and contested and also lenses through which to see complementary and simultaneous regional ideologies and practices. This chapter demonstrates that the study of historical regionalism compels diverse methodological inquiry because it bridges histories of infrastructure, capitalism, culture, politics, law, migration, technology, memory, and state development.[7] Historical regionalism mandates wide-ranging approaches to sources, people, and material. While this type of analysis reveals how actors considered themselves part of regional alliances and projected their understanding of regional identity, it also shows that historians can find connections between peoples that transcend space. Regional projects, although sometimes geographically discontinuous, emerged to define spaces and were recognized by others as tied together by collective material and imaginary goals. Regionalism throughout the twentieth century cemented as a reaction to the highway's project of national homogenization, as a symbol of pride in one's ideology and space, and in opposition to efforts by others to claim power and identity.

A Nation of Roads

The debates of the first decades of the twentieth century pitted a federally controlled highway system against a road system overseen by localities and states. On the one hand, the early development of the road system represents a move toward a more centralized and standardized American experience through road engineering specifications and the projection of a singular map. On the other hand, a unified road system across the country challenged regionalist boosters to conjure representations of their locales as unique parts of the United States. This national road system, for instance, potentially would usurp locally named roads and tourist promotion efforts. The development of regional identity presented outlets for dissent and difference while contributing to a nationwide body politic.

The early development of the road system destabilized constructions of the local and regional. The popular embrace of the automobile—from 8,000 registered in 1900 to 944,000 in 1912,

10 million in 1921, 20 million in 1925, and 30 million in 1937—changed Americans' routines and how they associated with space.[8] The automobile's ubiquity required roads, laws, maps, and travel guides. The construction of improved roads materially erased the regional bounds that the Transcontinental Motor Convoy found so glaring, but the material and structural uniformity inspired declarations of uniqueness based in localized cultures, historical narratives, and political pragmatism.

Understanding how roads and cars fractured and cemented regional identities and geographies forces us to turn to the earliest divisions that split road system stakeholders, and this division reveals a regional split that has been perpetuated ever since in highway policy. Between the 1880s and the passage of the first federal aid highway act in 1916, the Good Roads Movement engendered cooperation between diverse interest groups and stakeholders. But this diverse coalition for good roads was not inevitable. The Good Roads Movement's "exceptional" alliance of diverse interests overcame distinct and competing interests to bring together the many "common interests [of] rural famers, city drivers, and automobile industrialists."[9] The earliest rivalry of the roads movement pitted urban motorists against rural farmers, and this urban-rural division manifested beyond road improvement. While motorists used country roads as playgrounds to see rural places and enjoy the pleasures of the new technology, farmers detested the noise, dust, and costs. While some farmers favored local roads to transport goods to the closest rail station, urban motorists sought long-distance routes. Roads contributed to these divisions as defined by space throughout the twentieth century, which represented a new form of geographically disconnected regionalism.[10] Highways provided the infrastructure for this split to regenerate throughout the century.[11]

Early good roads advocates worked to bridge the gap between rural and urban communities. Isaac B. Potter's *The Gospel of Good Roads: A Letter to the American Farmer* (1891) crystallized the formation of an argument for a specific geographic population. "The road question is far and away the most important one to the

American farmer to-day," and Potter concludes that the farmer should be interested in good roads because of the financial benefits of the new and easier means of transporting goods to market.[12] Good roads advocates couched their argument in the uplift of rural communities: better education, more religious opportunity, community-building programs, and access to the market to sell goods. Farmers had rejected these improved roads because they seemed unnecessary for farming ventures, disproportionately benefited urban motorists, and left farmers bearing the costs of the road improvement and the nuisance of loud and dusty automobiles. As advocates reached out to farmers with one message, they also lobbied urbanites to invest in good roads with a different message: pleasure roads, sightseeing opportunities, cleaner cities, and national defense.[13] Early good roads advocates conceptualized two distinct regions within the nation with divergent interests.

Although geographically discontinuous, urban and rural coalitions formed around their identities and interests. The regional association divorced from geographic space challenges the vision of region as "place" confined by clear borders.[14] The early divergent interests of rural and urban factions in road development history illuminates how these entities became distinct regions with political and social competition.[15] Because of the recognition of different political needs for rural and urban peoples, we see both self-identification and identification by outsiders. Both urban and rural communities, moreover, continued to see themselves as part of the nation. This formulation of regions as geographically discontinuous yet competitive, allied, and recognizable undermines conceptions of region that rely on geographic continuity and political conformity. Urban and rural regions were organized for specific material interests, which were rooted in their connections to their constructions of space.

As a national coalition of interest groups, which included rural and urban stakeholders, overcame these early competitive interests and coalesced into the Good Roads Movement throughout the 1910s, debates raged over how roads would be built, where they would be built, and who would fund them. With the proliferation of the automobile in the early 1910s, the Good Roads Movement reached a fever pitch. This coalition forced legislators to respond, and the federal government formed a national road-building program with the Bankhead-Shackleford Bill of 1916 and the Phipps Act of 1921. While supporters of the federal aid system touted local control and a balanced state-federal partnership as the primary benefits of that model, supporters of the national highway system argued that centralized control of the nation's highway program provided uniformity, equity, and safety across the country.[16]

Lobbying by the diverse Good Roads Movement ensured that politicians across lines of party, geography, and ideology voted for the Bankhead-Shackleford Bill. This 1916 act appropriated $75 million over five years for road construction and an additional $1 million per year over ten years for roads in national parks and forests. States had to match federal funds and were responsible for maintenance. For the states to receive the appropriated funds, they had to establish a highway department that satisfied the Secretary of Agriculture, and with the $75 million carrot, states quickly assented to this federal control. The national aid system meant that the federal government funded state projects. Politicians opted to pursue a national aid system instead of a national road system in deference to local control over roads and maps. This local and state control proved nominal. The national aid system, in practice, consolidated federal power because of a strict federal bureaucracy, active private associations that monitored road development, and the organization of a uniform engineering profession with consistent standards.

Road construction eroded regional distinctions by reshaping the nation materially. With the power to approve or reject plans, the Bureau of Public Roads (BPR) ensured that states' highways conformed to a national framework. BPR engineers articulated national standards for bridge construction, material composition, road grade, curve maximums, and road signage style, among other engineering methods and processes. Throughout the course of a project, a BPR engineer conducted between twelve and sixteen site inspections. After completion of the road, the BPR inspected the road at least twice a year to ensure states' compliance with the maintenance requirement.[17] A nationwide campaign for uniform engineering education cultivated a "fraternity of experts" whose membership established information exchange networks across diverse entities and supported nationwide standards.[18] Working with colleges, Logan W. Page, the director of the Office of Public Roads, helped shape and implement a universal curriculum that relied on standard course texts.[19] By 1917, 76 colleges and universities offered courses in road building, and four years later, 112 of the 127 total engineering schools did so.[20] Historian Bruce Seely argues that the "foundation of the [BPR's] influence was expertise."[21] The professionalization of highway planning and engineering, paired with BPR oversight, guaranteed nationwide safety, durability, and uniformity.

As bureaucrats, engineers, and politicians began interpreting and implementing the 1916 highway legislation, the United States entered the Great War. The lack of progress on domestic highways during the war spurred the 1919 Transcontinental Motor Convoy to drum up support. The war cemented the government's role in national development by contrasting the failure of transportation systems in Europe with the success of U.S. strategic centralization.[22] This development and contrast also fed into a form of nationalism that the government cultivated in the context of World War I.[23] In the years following the war, the Bureau of Public Roads coordinated with the War Department to draw a strategic defense map. The BPR commissioned Army General John J. Pershing to identify the roads most important to national defense. Pershing and his military staff, in partnership with experts from the United States Geological Survey, drew up a seventy-eight-thousand-mile system of national highways of primary and secondary importance in cases of war.[24] This map reflected the military's view of this country: industrial and border (especially the U.S.-Mexico border) regions were worthy of investments because they served national defense purposes, while regions with neither industrial capability nor a land border proved unworthy of investment.

This strategic defense map became integrated into the BPR's nationwide road map because of another landmark piece of highway legislation. The 1921 Phipps Act upped the government's financial commitment to $75 million for fiscal year 1921–22, and it placed more stringent requirements on highway departments to conform to federal standards. With advice from individual states, the BPR would designate 7 percent of a state's road mileage to be improved, with 3 percent designated as "primary or interstate highways" and the other 4 percent as "secondary or intercounty highways." All federal aid went to the primary and secondary highways as part of the federal government's investment in a coherent national highway. These strictures guided funding to interstate travel rather than to many local concerns, such as linking farms to towns.

At the beginning of the map-planning and approval process in 1921, Thomas MacDonald informed his engineers that "local conditions should not be allowed to crowd out other considerations."[25] Although state highway commissions submitted maps for approval, BPR officials took seriously their duty to modify and approve these routes. Finally, in November 1923, the Department of Agriculture approved and published a complete map of the imagined federal aid highway system.[26] This map represented the federal highway administration's vision, and it included many of the Pershing Map's recommendations. As President Harding argued, "Our highways are built by and under the States, with such Federal participation as is calculated to assure continuity and articulation." This cooperation, Harding continued, was "set up to accomplish certain definite Federal objectives and purposes."[27]

America's Road Map

"The automobile road map," geographer James Ackerman argues, "was America's national blueprint."[28] Maps produced by the BPR's engineers and motoring organizations' cartographers represented visibly the ways in which highways reflected and exacerbated regional differences. The maps, for example, reinforced existing conceptions of regionalism as measured by population size, urban density,

FIG. 10. In 1926 the United States Department of Agriculture (USDA) adopted the American Association of State Highway Officials's proposed map as the official numbered highway map of the United States. *Source:* U.S. Highway Map 1926, folder 4, Maps of Highway System, RG 30, National Archives and Records Administration.

historical alignment, infrastructure development, and productive capacity. The map rendered visible the political and infrastructural importance of cities. While the map reinforced notions of space-based regionalism, it also helped transcend regional and state distinctions while showing how regionalist power dynamics changed over time.

The adoption of a new map and uniform numbering system enshrined the nationwide infrastructure-based landscape. In the early years of roadbuilding, private organizations often led local and regional pushes to build highways and roads, and they named these roads. By the mid-1920s, local boosters had named over three hundred roads. Many of these road names had regional or heritage implications.[29] These named roads—such as the Lincoln Highway, Dixie Highway, Jefferson Davis Highway, and Old Trails Road—boosted identities reflective of local, oftentimes racialized power structures. These names often wrote racial supremacy into the map by explicitly honoring figures such as Jefferson Davis or by implicitly honoring the processes of colonization and conquest. In 1925, the American Association of State Highway Officials, a private interest group made up of public officials and businessmen, proposed a new map that switched from the disjointed, localized system of named and numbered roads to a universal numbered system. The numbered map was adopted in 1926. By standardizing signage, landscaping, construction material, and engineering requirements, federal officials helped provide safe roads across the country. A legible and simplified map helped the federal state in producing standard space and promoting national identity.[30]

The numbered highway system made travel easy and predictable. The highways contributed to the rise of what historian Marguerite Shaffer recognizes as "national tourism," which "extended from and depended on the infrastructure of the modern nation-state."[31] National tourism contributed to the modern form of American cultural citizenship: boosters marketed the ritual of tourism to a new canon of attractions that linked national identity to engagement with the landscape. Americans embedded meaning into the landscape, and the highway became the vehicle to engage with space and citizenship.

Beyond engraining a new practice of nationalism as a form of civic engagement, the roles of the automobile and highway changed another aspect of citizenship: the protections of rights across the United States. Legal historian Sarah Seo argues that Fourth Amendment jurisprudence evolved to accommodate police discretion as the regulatory apparatus built around cars led to the policing of the "everyman." The automobile, which was private property, traveling on roads, which constituted public space, challenged the public-private distinction in Fourth Amendment jurisprudence and produced a standard of policing deferential to law enforcement agents.[32] The roads generated new forms of nationwide citizenship by simultaneously defining American identity through engagement with the landscape and restricting individual protections by allowing for a new model of policing and authority that crossed jurisdictional bounds. The policing of the open road inspired the "automobile paradox" between the automobile as the most policed aspect of everyday life and the imagined democratization of the automobile that promised freedom and independence.[33]

Although some involved in the named roads complained that the government was substituting names that connoted national identity for meaningless numbers, the government recognized the scenic and historical interest in many of the original routes. In the 1920s, the Bureau of Public Roads produced tourist guides that followed the legacy of private organizations' guidebooks in explaining points of geological, historical, cultural, or environmental interest. These BPR guides perpetuated the work of named road associations that sought to craft an ideal of nationalist belonging through highways, landscape, history, and experience.[34] Although automobile touring has been hailed as democratic, Shaffer argues that prior to World War II, touring was a "popular pastime for native-born, white, upper- and middle-class Americans."[35] Despite the reality of unequal access to and treatment on roads, advocates of good roads emphasized the transcontinental roads that introduced an accessible, unified geography that defined American nationhood.

Despite the assertion of motoring as democratic and a nationalist education program through the roads, local and regional groups continued to employ roads, signage, and naming to propagate exclusive identities, directly challenging and co-opting the numbered highway system. These identity projects reflected social power, and they generally elevated a view of region that privileged those already in power. Indeed, road naming and tourist brochures helped perpetuate a racialized order, such as with how the United Daughters of the Confederacy (UDC) used the roads and tourism to uplift the values of the "Old South," a South defined by white supremacy.[36] For example, the UDC mapped, marked, publicized, and claimed a transcontinental Jefferson Davis Highway that imposed its racialized view of history on the country, "stretching from coast to coast" as "the only physical memorial that preserves continually before the traveling public a reminder of the traditions and glorious history of the South and the eternal devotion of its women to its history and ideals."[37] Regionalism attempted to shift national public consciousness by emphasizing certain contributions in the competitive united system, and these efforts often came at the detriment of marginalized or minority communities. National signage forced boosters to redouble their efforts to promote a regionalist vision. Those who promoted regionalism turned to maps, signs, guidebooks, and travel experiences. Historian David Wrobel's study of western promotional materials and pioneer reminiscences shows how "they were imaginative efforts to bring places into existence or to hold on to earlier incarnations of places that had since changed."[38] Boosters of identity used the nationalistic focus on tourism to create images of places and people that are memorialized in power structures, experiences, stereotypes, and assumptions.

In the 1930s, the federal government amplified certain regional and local identities as part of the New Deal response to the Great Depression. During the Great Depression, Franklin Roosevelt, like many state leaders, recognized the potential for road construction to put people back to work. The road system continued to thrive with New Deal investment.[39] The Works Progress Administration completed over 650,000 miles of improved roads, and other federal funds from the Emergency Relief and Construction Act (1932), National Industrial Recovery Act (1933), and Agricultural Adjustment Act (1933) led to complementary road building efforts. Automobiles had become nearly ubiquitous during the preceding decade. By 1929, there was one automobile for about every five-and-a-half people in the United States, with over twenty-three million automobiles registered. While the number of registered automobiles dipped in the first years of the 1930s, they rebounded to over twenty-five million in 1937 and nearly thirty million in 1941.[40] Public investment reoriented the U.S. political and economic systems, and it dramatically expanded the road infrastructure.

As the government invested in building roads, it also carried on the task of interpreting the roads and ideas of national belonging. The Works Progress Administration (WPA) tourist guides amplified certain regionalist identities. The American Guide Series was a set of guidebooks on the forty-eight states, Alaska, Washington DC, and some cities. WPA director Harry Hopkins believed the Federal Writers' Project of the WPA achieved the New Deal's "ambitious objective of presenting to the American people a portrait of America."[41] The guides opened with essays on the state and general information and history, then they turned to information on cities and towns, and they closed with guided automobile tours. These tours took up over half of most volumes, and they show how authors used highways and road trips to define identity both as Americans and as citizens of a region. Although the federal office had the final editorial say over the guides, each state's editorial team delegated creation of the tours to various local employees. By elevating the states' identities and culture in these state-based road trips, the federal government both fostered and frayed identity formations. On the one hand, promoting state identities and characteristics undermined efforts at constructing a national identity based in space, environment, and culture. On the other hand, the emphasis on state-level culture and experience reinforced a national identity by offering an opportunity for Americans to learn about the constituent elements that made up the United States. "The WPA volumes," historian Christine Bold notes, "were floated as guidelines to cultural citizenship in modern America."[42] The roads tied together disparate peoples and events within the American story—a project that emphasized divergent histories and ideologies as vital components of the national fabric.

Though each guidebook presents slight variations regarding regional identity, historians can offer general summaries about the regional categorizations presented through the tours of each of the five regions that the New Deal administrators used to carve up the map. Favoring Confederate and plantation history, for example, the Southern guides reinforced a Lost Cause narrative that took the reader through an ethically unambiguous narrative that idealized the Old South and took the traveler to many Confederate sites from the "War between the States." The Southwestern guides highlighted Native American history and culture, epitomized by Oklahoma's celebration of past Indigenous heritages led by the guide's editor Angie Debo. The guides to the West celebrated rugged individualism, the outdoors, and a pioneer spirit, bringing the traveler to many sites of frontier settlements, particularly the overland trail and gold rush. Following California's Tour 5, for example, reveals how "the mark of man" is present still in this automobile tour: "Forests thinned by lumbermen, carved mountainsides and piles of tailings left by miners, lakes created in hydroelectric developments."[43] The Middle West guides presented a melting-pot America with a long history of European immigration and agricultural dependence, showing off, for example, the varieties of historical windmills and wells with roots in diverse European traditions. The Northeast guides largely brought the traveler into the settling of the continent and the making of the United States, providing a history in which they claimed the roots of Americanism.[44] One Massachusetts tour, for example, takes the driver through "country closely connected with Colonial and Revolutionary history."[45] These five regions, which the government employed to organize the country, reflect local identity. Yet these regions derived by the government beg for more complexity. These articulated regional differences that conferred legitimacy to a united whole constituted a project of reifying a positive and progressive historical narrative of trials and triumphs against people, nature, and institutions to propagate a regionalist vision. The New Deal guides represent the culmination of an accepted and cooperative positive vision of regionalism that flourished prior to World War II.

A National Highway System

As World War II broke out in Europe and the United States tried to remain ostensibly neutral, the importance of a nationwide system of highways reemerged with the need for national defense and effective movement of materials and troops. In 1938, the Bureau of Public Roads studied Roosevelt's idea for a national superhighway network with three north-south routes and three east-west routes. In April 1939, Roosevelt conveyed his recommendation to Congress: a "system of direct interregional highways, with all necessary connections through and around cities, designed to meet the requirements of the national defense and the needs of a growing peacetime traffic of longer range."[46] This plan explicitly called for federal and state cooperation on a unified plan as a requirement for military security and peacetime quality of life. The context of increased public spending during the Great Depression and World War II spurred this nationalist conception of infrastructure development. This initial proposal led to another report released in 1944, *Interregional Highways*. This report championed expressways throughout the country, cutting across nine BPR-defined regions. Indeed, the 1944 report explained, "These regions are composed of contiguous States grouped together by the United States Bureau of the Census because of generally similar population and economic characteristics."[47] Although the similar populations and characteristics remained ambiguous, this organization of regions employed state boundaries as arbiters of regional associations. These plans elevated the region as the organizing element of travel and connection and primed the country for a car-dependent postwar landscape.

This postwar version of highway federalism and automobile dependence developed as an outgrowth of World War II, the early Cold War years, and the Marshall economy. In these years, political and racial elites wielded highway development as a symbol of American exceptionalism—a nationalist symbol around which they could cohere a vision of the country. This postwar consumer society, as Lizabeth Cohen demonstrates, was deeply segregated, fractured along racial, gender, and class lines.[48] The New Deal project of state building primed the United States for development and investment in the World War II economy and beyond.[49] A buoyant wartime economy and rising tide of patriotic sentiment propelled a nationwide system of consumerism, tourism, migration, and infrastructure development. World War II privileged the "language, imagery, and cultural logic" of Americanism that encapsulated competing claims of national belonging and local pride.[50] During the war, the federal government expanded in size, extended the scope of its authority, and inaugurated new

FIG. 11. The proposed interregional highway route from 1944 based on the nine regions defined by the Bureau of the Census (Pacific, Mountain, West North Central, West South Central, East North Central, East South Central, Middle Atlantic, New England, and South Atlantic). *Source: Interregional Highways: Message from the President of the United States, Transmitting a Report of the National Interregional Highway Committee, Outlining and Recommending a National System of Interregional Highways* (Washington DC: U.S. Government Printing Office, 1944), 7.

forms of state financing. This system primed the government for investing in infrastructure after the war as a global symbol of modernization and progress. Domestic infrastructure projects represented a vision of American exceptionalism that linked culturally diverse elements and peoples, while U.S. infrastructure development abroad, based on prewar and wartime domestic experience, boosted "liberal modernization" with American political and economic goals.[51] The continued crisis of the Cold War perpetuated state and infrastructure development. Road building, motivated by the dual concerns of nationalistic exceptionalism and fears of foreign threats against the American way of life, continued in pursuit of a nationalist usurpation of regional and local dissent.

The postwar system sought social homogeneity, and a nationwide road project was one way to achieve an integrated nationwide system. Yet this system simultaneously perpetuated segregation. At the end of World War II in 1945, the United States had few of what historian Christopher Wells calls "car-dependent landscapes." These urban and suburban landscapes were spaces in which residents required and depended on cars rather than walking or public transit. In the years after World War II, "car-dependent landscapes became central to the basic administrative, financial, and growth strategies of several powerful sectors of the American economy."[52] The new car-oriented development entailed reordering both local and national spatial arrangements. The dependence on cars, paired with changing tax and race structures, generated a suburban interest that pushed the bounds of the city and informed a new quasi-urban interest group.[53] The reorganization of rural and urban demographics, in part spurred by white flight, led to a clash of postwar liberal traditions that culminated in two political movements represented by new racialized regions: a tax revolt in the white suburbs and a Black Power movement in the Black urban centers.[54] On a national scale, the highways stimulated mass migrations across the United States. As part of the program to demobilize while maintaining economic prosperity in the postwar years and build an infrastructure system to support national defense, Congress passed the Federal-Aid Highway Act of 1944, which provided $1.5 billion for three years to road construction. Interstates dominated federal and state budgets. This was one step toward *Interregional Highways*'s interest in transcontinental superhighways, which culminated in the 1950s.

Eisenhower first discovered the importance of roads when he took a slow and bumpy transcontinental trip after World War I. In the years following the trip, the state acted on the military's advice. The United States built and improved millions of miles of roads. American federalism, however, ensured that the federal government remained nominally subordinate to states. Yet federal engineering standards, conditions tied to federal aid funds, and the public works projects of the New Deal all built the central government's power and influence. During and immediately after World War II, the United States cultivated an ideal of national belonging and support for state building. Eisenhower, too, learned from his experience in World War II that the German autobahn allowed easy and efficient movement of troops and material: "The old convoy had started me thinking about good, two-lane highways, but Germany had made me see the wisdom of broader ribbons across the land."[55]

Eisenhower assumed the presidency in January 1953, and by July 1954, his administration asked the country's governors to help realize a national system of highways. In 1955, Eisenhower submitted a $27 billion plan to Congress for a 40,000-mile interstate system. With his report, Eisenhower told Congress, "Together, the uniting forces of our communication and transportation systems are dynamic elements in the very name we bear—United States. Without them, we would be a mere alliance of many separate parts."[56] Congress rejected Eisenhower's plan because of a financing issue. The next year, the Senate and House almost unanimously approved a bill that offered an alternative financing proposal. The interstate highway system would use the Social Security Trust Fund as a model for a Highway Trust Fund, with highway taxes used exclusively for the Highway Trust Fund and increase of the federal gas tax to three cents per gallon. The 1956 act authorized $25 billion to construct the 41,000-mile "National System of Interstate and Defense Highways." The federal government would bear 90 percent of the costs of the system.

The Eisenhower Interstate Highway Act of 1956 codified and formalized many of the structures that had given the federal government direction over road construction. The 1956 law, Sarah Jo Peterson argues, "turned what had been a federal funding *program* into a de facto *project*."[57] This project represents the culmination of infrastructural uniformity and nationwide connection, and the project included federal deadlines, oversight, and budgets. While regionalists still boosted their identities and interests through media such as road signage and tourist guides, the new funding and planning scheme solidified the national bureaucracy that pushed regionalist boosters to find other methods by which to define, articulate, and propagate their regionalism. The legislation expanded uniform highways, signage, directions, roadside amenities, and engineering. The AASHO (American Association of State Highway Officials) and BPR settled on design standards that would dictate the system's construction, including crossroads going under or over the routes, twelve-foot lanes, and fourteen feet of vertical clearance. By the end of the year, the pace of planning, bidding, and constructing proceeded so rapidly that the executive and Congress agreed on a position of a federal highway administrator that would oversee highway policy and the interstate program. By the end of Eisenhower's presidency, the government expended over $10 billion on highways so that travelers could cross more than ten thousand miles of the interstate system marked by the standard red, white, and blue interstate shield. Yet this program exacerbated segregation and inequity. Complementing the rise in white suburbia made feasible by highways connecting the suburbs, the construction of the highways led to displacement of families, often low-income and families of color, who stood in the path of the proposed infrastructure.[58]

Throughout the United States, since the Eisenhower Interstate System was built, highways have looked virtually identical regardless of their environmental, cultural, or economic context. From the early twentieth century onward, centralization and standardization dominated. Engineering standards, signage, maps, and tour guides promoted a system of highways that bolstered nationhood and nationalism. Challenging and co-opting this system of nationwide highways, regional actors found opportunities to produce meaning in space through local identity promotion that amplified historical narratives and region-defining attractions. They embedded in the road system narratives that defined themselves and their role in the larger nation. While centralization proceeded and regional repurposing of this nationwide system occurred, the highway system defined new forms of regional blocs. Regions, regardless of spatial continuity, defined themselves in relation to their material interests, competitive needs, or imagined cultural associations.

Notes

1. "Motor Truck Caravan to Cross Continent," *New York Times*, July 6, 1919, 11.
2. "Principal Facts Concerning the First Transcontinental Army Motor Transport Expedition, from Washington to San Francisco," comp. William C. Greany, p. 9, PPF, NAID #12005074, box 967.
3. Lt. Col. D. D. Eisenhower, "Report on Trans-Continental Trip," November 3, 1919, p. 4, PPF, NAID #1055071, box 967.
4. "A California Dinner in Honor of the Officers and Men Who Made up the First Transcontinental Convoy of the Motor Transport Corps, U.S. Army over the Lincoln Highway, Washington to San Francisco," July 7–September 7, 1919, USATC, NAID #12165975, box 1.
5. E. R. Jackson, report on First Transcontinental Motor Convoy, October 31, 1919, pp. 10, 29–30, USATC, NAID #12165976, box 1.
6. On competitive regionalism, see Ayers et al., *All Over the Map*.
7. The U.S. highway system and its relation to regionalism requires analysis from a breadth of histories, and the following examples provide a nonexhaustive sample of how highways have been analyzed and elucidated important phenomena. For an example of a political history of highways, see Gutfreund, *Twentieth-Century Sprawl*; a cultural history of the impact of the automobile and highways, see Bailey, *From Front Porch to Back Seat*; an environmental and social history of a car-dependent landscape, see Wells, *Car Country*; the ideological and imperial consequences of highway projects, see Ekbladh, *Great American Mission*; the legal changes wrought by highways, see Seo, *Policing the Open Road*; a historical and cultural geography of space and identity, see Akerman, *Cartographies of Travel*.
8. United States Department of Transportation—Federal Highway Administration, *Highway Statistics 1984*, accessed December 6, 2017, 50, https://rosap.ntl.bts.gov/view/dot/8338.
9. Ingram, *Dixie Highway*, 15.
10. The urban-rural divide in the late nineteenth century generated a competitive regionalism that manifested across racial, economic, and political divides. For an example of how agrarian politics and the Mountain West's sociopolitical identity informed a unique form of radicalism, see Berman, *Radicalism in the Mountain West*.
11. The urban-rural/suburban regional division persisted throughout the twentieth century, and scholars have noted its appearance, for example, in racialized housing policy and the geography of state investment through penal infrastructure: Self, *American Babylon*; Gilmore, *Golden Gulag*.
12. Potter, *Gospel of Good Roads*, 9.
13. Wells, *Car Country*, 29; Oliff, *Getting Out of the Mud*.
14. Walter Prescott Webb articulated this place-based definition of regionalism for the Great Plains: Webb, *Great Plains*, vi.
15. Ayers et al., *All Over the Map*, 8.

16. This debate was an explicit fight over state versus federal power, and politicians in the 1920s sought a compromise in which they could stand behind the principles of balanced federalism. For petitions as examples, see the letters from 1918 through 1921: "FAS—Dec. 1921 to Dec. 1925," folder, RG30, 530/22/23/6 box 1955.

17. "U.S.—Congress. (67th congress.) Federal aid in the construction of roads," item, RG30, 530/24/22/1 box 6.

18. This process is parallel to the technological "fraternity of experts" who used their expertise and planning to realize a national grid. Cohn, *Grid*, 27. This process was a means by which the government worked "out of sight" to influence planning and development while enlarging the purview of the state to ensure safety standards in construction. Balogh, *Government Out of Sight*.

19. The Office of Public Roads was one of the agencies that preceded the Bureau of Public Roads. Byrne, *Treatise on Highway Construction*; Baker, *Treatise on Roads and Pavements*; Table of Colleges and Responses, "Old Public Roads Corres.–Hwy Engr. Circ. Letters to Colleges 1909," folder, RG30, 530/21/23/3 box 90.

20. American Automobile Association, *Highways Green Book*, 390.

21. Seely, *Building the American Highway System*, 99.

22. Kennedy, *Over Here*.

23. Capozzola, *Uncle Sam Wants You*.

24. Paper on coordination between the BPR and War Department, n.d., THMC, box 6, folder 20, series 1: Personal.

25. Memorandum to all district engineers, "Memoranda to District Engineers May 5, 1921–Jul 24, 1922," July 11, 1921, RG30, 530/24/21/5 box 2.

26. "Annual Report to Congress, Required by Sec. 19–Act of Nov. 9, 1921, for Fiscal Year 1924," item, RG30, 530/B/1/3 box 1.

27. "Correlating State and National Highway Programs," paper from the Convention of Chambers of Commerce of Kansas, January 23, 1925, THMC, box 6, folder 61, series 1: Personal.

28. Akerman, *Cartographies of Travel*, 153.

29. This essay employs Jakle's category of "heritage implications" for road names that connote some historical significance beyond historically significant people, such as the Old Spanish Trail (which connected areas of Spanish or Mexican colonial implication). For simplification, however, this essay includes Jakle's category of highways named for celebrities in the broader category of heritage implications. Jakle, "Pioneer Roads," 1–22.

30. Scott, *Seeing like a State*; Lefebvre, *Production of Space*.

31. Shaffer, *See America First*, 3.

32. Seo, *Policing the Open Road*.

33. Seo, *Policing the Open Road*, 12.

34. White and Limerick, *Frontier in American Culture*, 53.

35. Shaffer, *See America First*, 161, 364n76.

36. Cox, *Dixie's Daughters*.

37. Minutes of the Sixty-First Annual Convention of the United Daughters of the Confederacy Incorporated Held at Roanoke, Virginia, November 7–11, 1954, Missouri Printing, Mexico, 191. See also Finkelstein, "Politics of Space and Memory," 73.

38. Wrobel, *Promised Lands*, 3.

39. Smith, *Building New Deal Liberalism*.

40. Federal Highway Administration, "State Motor Vehicle Registrations, by Years, 1900–1995," https://www.fhwa.dot.gov/ohim/summary95/mv200.pdf.

41. Quoted in Wrobel, *Global West, American Frontier*, 142.

42. Bold, WPA *Guides*, 18.

43. American Guide Series, *California*, 501.

44. Though the author has attempted to draw conclusions based on historical regions in the guides, these generalizations do not hold up under critical scrutiny. Though the broad contours are relatively consistent throughout the regions, a full picture ought to include local variations and complexities that complicate broader ideals and norms. See Wrobel, *Global West, American Frontier*, 142–80, for subregions and cross-state comparisons.

45. American Guide Series, *Massachusetts*, 442.

46. Quoted in Weingroff, "Federal-Aid Highway Act of 1956."

47. National Interregional Highway Committee, *Interregional Highways*, 6.

48. Cohen, *Consumers' Republic*.

49. Smith, *Building New Deal Liberalism*.

50. Sparrow, *Warfare State*, 4.

51. Ekbladh, *Great American Mission*, 113.

52. Wells, *Car Country*, 254.

53. Self, *American Babylon*; Lassiter, *Silent Majority*.

54. Self, *American Babylon*.

55. Eisenhower, *At Ease*, 167.

56. "Message to Congress Regarding Highways," February 22, 1955, White House Office, Office of the Press Secretary to the President, press releases, PPF, NAID #16857605, box 4.

57. Emphasis in original. Peterson, "Myth and the Truth about Interstate Highways."

58. For an example of the impact of interstate highway planning as a project of "urban renewal" in Syracuse, New York, see DiMento, "Stent (or Dagger?) in the Heart of Town."

Bibliography

Akerman, James R., ed. *Cartographies of Travel and Navigation*. Chicago: University of Chicago Press, 2006.

American Automobile Association. *Highways Green Book*. 2nd annual edition. Washington DC: Andrew B. Graham, 1921.

American Guide Series. *California: A Guide to the Golden State*. New York: Hastings House, 1939.

———. *Massachusetts: A Guide to Its Places and People.* Cambridge MA: Riverside, 1937.
Ayers, Edward L., Patricia Nelson Limerick, Stephen Nissenbaum, and Peter S. Onuf. *All Over the Map: Rethinking American Regions.* Baltimore: Johns Hopkins University Press, 1996.
Bailey, Beth L. *From Front Porch to Back Seat: Courtship in Twentieth-Century America.* Baltimore: Johns Hopkins University Press, 1989.
Baker, Ira Osborn. *A Treatise on Roads and Pavements.* New York: J. Wiley & Sons, 1906.
Balogh, Brian. *A Government Out of Sight: The Mystery of National Authority in Nineteenth-Century America.* Cambridge: Cambridge University Press, 2009.
Berman, David R. *Radicalism in the Mountain West, 1890–1920: Socialists, Populists, Miners, and Wobblies.* Boulder: University Press of Colorado, 2007.
Bold, Christine. *The WPA Guides: Mapping America.* Jackson: University Press of Mississippi, 1999.
Byrne, Austin T. *A Treatise on Highway Construction, Designed as a Text-Book and Work of Reference for All Who May Be Engaged in the Location, Construction, or Maintenance of Roads, Streets, and Pavements.* New York: John Wiley & Sons, 1908.
Capozzola, Christopher Joseph Nicodemus. *Uncle Sam Wants You: World War I and the Making of the Modern American Citizen.* Oxford: Oxford University Press, 2008.
Cohen, Lizabeth. *A Consumers' Republic: The Politics of Mass Consumption in Postwar America.* Vintage Books ed. New York: Vintage Books, 2004.
Cohn, Julie A. *The Grid: Biography of an American Technology.* Cambridge MA: MIT Press, 2017.
Cox, Karen L. *Dixie's Daughters: The United Daughters of the Confederacy and the Preservation of Confederate Culture.* Gainesville: University Press of Florida, 2003.
DiMento, Joseph F. "Stent (or Dagger?) in the Heart of Town: Urban Freeways in Syracuse, 1944–1967." *Journal of Planning History* 8, no. 2 (2009): 133–61.
Eisenhower, Dwight D. *At Ease: Stories I Tell to Friends.* New York: Doubleday, 1967.
Ekbladh, David. *The Great American Mission: Modernization and the Construction of an American World Order.* Princeton NJ: Princeton University Press, 2010.
Finkelstein, Alexander. "The Politics of Space and Memory: The Jefferson Davis Highway in the West." In *Contested Commemoration in U.S. History: Diverging Public Interpretations*, edited by Klara Stephanie Szlezák and Melissa Bender, 73–93. New York: Routledge, 2020.
Gilmore, Ruth Wilson. *Golden Gulag: Prisons, Surplus, Crisis, and Opposition in Globalizing California.* Berkeley: University of California Press, 2007.
Gutfreund, Owen D. *Twentieth-Century Sprawl: Highways and the Reshaping of the American Landscape.* New York: Oxford University Press, 2004.
Ingram, Tammy. *Dixie Highway: Road Building and the Making of the Modern South, 1900–1930.* Chapel Hill: University of North Carolina Press, 2014.

Jakle, John A. "Pioneer Roads: America's Early Twentieth-Century Named Highways." *Material Culture* 32, no. 2 (2000): 1–22.
Kennedy, David M. *Over Here: The First World War and American Society*. New York: Oxford University Press, 1980.
Lassiter, Matthew D. *The Silent Majority: Suburban Politics in the Sunbelt South*. Princeton NJ: Princeton University Press, 2006.
Lefebvre, Henri. *The Production of Space*. Translated by Donald Nicholson-Smith. Cambridge: Cambridge University Press, 1991.
National Interregional Highway Committee. *Interregional Highways: Message from the President of the United States*. Washington DC: Government Printing Office, 1944.
Olliff, Martin T. *Getting Out of the Mud: The Alabama Good Roads Movement and Highway Administration, 1898–1928*. Tuscaloosa: University of Alabama Press, 2017.
Peterson, Sara Jo. "The Myth and the Truth about Interstate Highways." *Metropole: The Official Blog of the Urban History Association* (blog), April 5, 2021. https://themetropole.blog/2021/04/05/the-myth-and-the-truth-about-interstate-highways/.
Potter, Isaac B. *The Gospel of Good Roads: A Letter to the American Farmer*. New York: League of American Wheelmen, 1891.
PPF. President's Personal File: DDE's Records as President, Dwight D. Eisenhower Presidential Library and Museum, Abilene KS.
RG30. Record Group 30: Records of the Bureau of Public Roads, National Archives and Records Administration, College Park MD.
Scott, James C. *Seeing like a State: How Certain Schemes to Improve the Human Condition Have Failed*. Yale Agrarian Studies. New Haven CT: Yale University Press, 2008.
Seely, Bruce E. *Building the American Highway System: Engineers as Policy Makers*. Philadelphia: Temple University Press, 1987.
Self, Robert O. *American Babylon: Race and the Struggle for Postwar Oakland*. Princeton NJ: Princeton University Press, 2005. http://www.myilibrary.com?id=545523.
Seo, Sarah A. *Policing the Open Road: How Cars Transformed American Freedom*. Cambridge MA: Harvard University Press, 2019.
Shaffer, Marguerite S. *See America First: Tourism and National Identity, 1880–1940*. Washington DC: Smithsonian Institution Press, 2001.
Smith, Jason Scott. *Building New Deal Liberalism: The Political Economy of Public Works, 1933–1956*. Cambridge: Cambridge University Press, 2006.
Sparrow, James T. *Warfare State: World War II Americans and the Age of Big Government*. New York: Oxford University Press, 2011.
THMC. Thomas H. MacDonald Collection, Cushing Memorial Library and Archives, Texas A&M University, College Park TX.
USATC. U.S. Army Transport Corps, Transcontinental Convoy: Records, 1919, Dwight D. Eisenhower Presidential Library and Museum, Abilene KS.
Webb, Walter Prescott. *The Great Plains*. Lincoln: University of Nebraska Press, 1981.

Weingroff, Richard. "Federal-Aid Highway Act of 1956: Creating the Interstate System." *Public Roads* 60, no. 1 (Summer 1996). https://www.fhwa.dot.gov/publications/publicroads/96summer/p96su10.cfm.
Wells, Christopher W. *Car Country: An Environmental History*. Seattle: University of Washington Press, 2012.
White, Richard, and Patricia Nelson Limerick. *The Frontier in American Culture*. Edited by James R. Grossman. Berkeley: University of California Press, 1994.
Wrobel, David M. *Global West, American Frontier: Travel, Empire, and Exceptionalism from Manifest Destiny to the Great Depression*. Albuquerque: University of New Mexico Press, 2013.
———. *Promised Lands: Promotion, Memory, and the Creation of the American West*. Lawrence: University Press of Kansas, 2002.

CONTRIBUTORS

Jimmy L. Bryan Jr. is a professor of history and director of the Center for History and Culture of Southeast Texas and the Upper Gulf Coast at Lamar University in Beaumont, Texas. He is the author of *The American Elsewhere: Adventure and Manliness in the Age of Expansion* (University Press of Kansas, 2017) and editor of *Inventing Destiny: Cultural Explorations of US Expansion* (University Press of Kansas, 2019) and *The Martial Imagination: Cultural Aspects of American Warfare* (Texas A&M University Press, 2013).

Courtney Buchkoski is an assistant professor of history at Doane University, where she studies the American West, the Civil War era, religion, and empire.

Flannery Burke is an associate professor in the Department of American Studies at Saint Louis University. She is the author of two books. Her third, entitled *Back East: How Western Writers Imagined the Eastern United States*, will be published by the University of Washington Press.

Mickell Carter is a PhD student in the department of Africana Studies at Brown University. Her research interests include Black internationalism, twentieth-century social movements, and the intersections between culture and politics. Mickell has written for the African American Intellectual History Society's (AAIHS) award-winning blog *Black Perspectives*, the American Historical Association's *Perspectives* magazine, and the *Washington Post*. She is also a host of the New Books Network's African American Studies podcast.

Lawrence Culver is an associate professor in the Department of History at Utah State University. He received his doctorate at UCLA. His research interests include U.S. environmental, climate, cultural, and urban history. He is the author of *The Frontier of Leisure: Southern California and the Shaping of Modern America* (Oxford University Press, 2012).

Alexander Finkelstein teaches at Western Colorado University. He earned his PhD in history at the University of Oklahoma focusing on western and environmental history.

Sean Parulian Harvey earned his PhD in history from Northwestern University in 2020. He teaches tenth- and eleventh-grade history at an independent school in Phoenix, Arizona. Harvey is currently working on a history of the War on Poverty in the United States.

Anne F. Hyde teaches history at the University of Oklahoma. She is editor of the *Western Historical Quarterly*. Her most recent book is *Born of Lakes and Plains: Mixed-Descent People and the Making of the American West* (W. W. Norton, 2022).

Jon K. Lauck is the author of *The Lost Region: Toward a Revival of Midwestern History* (University of Iowa Press, 2013), *From Warm Center to Ragged Edge: The Erosion of Midwestern Regionalism, 1920–1965* (University of Iowa Press, 2017), and *The Good Country: A History of the American Midwest* (University of Oklahoma Press, 2022) and serves as editor in chief of *Middle West Review*.

Sarah Miller-Davenport is a historian of the twentieth-century United States. Her book *Gateway State: Hawaiʻi and the Cultural Transformation of American Empire* was published by Princeton in 2019. She is currently the graduate program director at the Committee on Global Thought at Columbia University.

Jennifer Ritterhouse is a professor of history at George Mason University and the author of *Growing Up Jim Crow: How Black and White Southern Children Learned Race* (University of North Carolina Press, 2006) and *Discovering the South: One Man's Travels through a Changing America in the 1930s* (University of North Carolina Press, 2017).

Taylor Spence researches, writes, and makes art about the history and legacies of U.S. colonialism in North America. A Fulbright Fellow, he holds an MFA from the School of Visual Arts and a PhD from Yale University. He currently lives in Albuquerque, New Mexico. www.taylorwyoming.com.

INDEX

Page numbers in *italics* refer to figures.

abolitionism, 155, 157, 158, 162, 164n18
African independence, 85, 89. *See also* apartheid; Black communities; decolonization; imperialism
African National Congress (ANC), 88, 99–101
agriculture, 113, 118, 156; irrigation, 121–25, 131n19, 138; western paradise, 125, 127, 204, 218
air travel and airports, 226, 236, 240–43
alcohol, 24n1
All Over the Map (Ayers), xii, 6
American Association of State Highway Officials (AASHO), 263, 272
An American Daughter (Thompson), 39, 41–42
American Federation of Labor (AFL), 146
American Indian Movement (AIM), 187
Americanization. *See* assimilation
analytical category, region as, x–xi, xii, xiv, xvii, xx, 58–59, 77, 255. *See also* feminism; immigrants; intersectional identities; race
annexation, 116, 122, 155; Hawai'i, 61–63, 76. *See also* statehood; territory
annuities, 184–85, 188–89
apartheid, 85, 87–90, 93; Artists United Against Apartheid, 91–96, 99–102, 103; U.S. and, 88–90, 95–97. *See also* segregation
Appalachia, 3, 161, 182, 193n20
army. *See* military; *individual wars*
Artists United Against Apartheid, 91–96, 99–102, 103

Asia, 59, 61, 182; "bridge to," 58, 71, 73–75
Asian people, 58, 64–65, 69, 70, 71, 74
assimilation, 9, 73–74, 175, 178; Hawai'i and, 62–64, 68–71; placing-out and, 203–4, 207, 208, 211–12
autobahn, 271
automobiles: dependency on, 268, 270; nationalism and, 263–64; rise of, 256–57, 259, 265
Ayers, Edward, 6, 8

Bantus, 88, 93
Barkley Brown, Elsa, 5, 21–22
Bartlett, John Russell, 116–17
Bashore, H. H., 140
Bayonet Constitution, 62
binational land management. *See* territory: binational management of
"the Bitter Southerner," 3, 24–25n1
Black communities, 40–42, 45, 53n31, 85, 89; diasporic region, 92, 94–95, 98, 101, 102, 103; internationalism, 85–86, 92, 103. *See also* civil rights movement; *individual artists and intellectuals*
Black people, 53n45, 211; artists, 17, 39–45, 86–87, 90, 92, 100–101; feminists, 4–5, 12, 18–19, 21, 27n43; intellectuals, 12, 19–20, 24
Bliss, Robert, 121
boosters, 126, 225–26, 246n5, 263, 265; climate and, 127, 128, 130; Dallas–Fort Worth and, 232, 234, 239, 241, 243, 245; Great Southwest

boosters (*continued*)
and, 226, 227, 230, 231; Los Angeles and, 136, 143; roads and, 256, 262–63, 271
Bophuthatswana, 97, 99–101
borders, political, xiii, xviii, 51, 135, 145–46, 176–77, 191n4, 268; border-crossing rituals, 177–78, 185–86, 193n26; borderlands, 135–40, 142, 145, 147, 148, 192n11; nationalism and, 146, 254; policing of, 146–48, 176, 184, 191n4; U.S.-Canada, 176–79, 182; U.S.-Mexico, 123, 260
boycotts, 89, 99–102
Brace, Charles Loring, 203–6, 207–8, 211, 212–13, 214–15, 217–18
branding, regional, 225–26, 227, 228, 230, 243; businesses and, *231*, 232, 240, 244
Bread Loaf Writers' Conference, 33, 34, 53n36
British Empire, ix, 154, 175, 177, 191n10
Brown v. Board of Education (1954), 6, 16
Bureau of Public Roads (BPR), 259–61, 264, 267–68, 272, 274n19
Bureau of Reclamation (BOR), 139, 140, 144, 147
Bureau of the Census, 268, *269*
Burns, Jack, 71

Calhoun, John C., 117–18
California, 52n1, 125, 128–29, 130, 143; Hawai'i and, 63, 74–75
Canada, 175–76, 178–79, 184; French-Canadians and, 176, 191n6
Cárdenas, Lázaro, 141–42
cars. *See* automobiles
Carter, Amon G., 230–31, 233, 234, 235–38, *239*, 240–41, 244
Carter, Jimmy, 95
Cash, W. J., xi–xii, xvii
Catholics, 35, 116, 191n6, 203, 205, 207, 213–14
cattle industry, 129, 234, 235, 247n26
Cayton, Horace, 53n31
Cayuga people, 175, 187–89, 192–93n20
Chapman, Harve, 244
Chicago, 38, 40, 63; Black communities of, 40–41, 45, 53n31
child labor, 204, 208, 215, 218
children. *See* placing-out, of children; schools
Children's Aid Society (CAS), 203–4, 205, 206–12, 213, 214, 215–17, 218

Chinese Exclusion Act, 62, 64, 67, 74. *See also* immigrants
Christianity, 23, 61
Civil Aeronautics Board (CAB), 242
civil rights movement, 15, 16, 18, 26n32, 65, 72; anti-apartheid movement and, 88–90, 97; Black Power movement and, 75, 88–90, 270
Civil War, ix, 112, 157–59, 166n47, 210–13, 266. *See also* North and northerners; regions, relationships between
class, 69, 203, 206, 211–12, 213, 264; conflicts, 211–12, 217–18; middle-class standards, 207, 208–9
climate, 111–12, 114–16, 120, 123, 127–28; change, 124, 130; delusions, 112, 115, 117–18, 124–29; imperialism and, 111, 113, 121; technology and, 125, 129, 140
Cohn, Sarah, 42
Cold War, 16, 58, 71–73, 96, 268, 269
Colorado River, 123–24, 143
common struggles, 86, 90, 92–93, 97, 102, 103
communism, 73, 96
Communist Party, 15, 16, 20
Condolence Council, 185, 187, 194n48
Confederacy, 7, 12, 13, 14–15, 232, 266
Congress, 49, 125, 147, 189, 211, 270, 271, 272; statehood and, 63, 64, 70–71
conservationism, 33, 37–38, 45, 53n36, 140–41
consumerism, 226, 268
Cook, James, 60
cotton, 112, 156, 160
court cases, 16, 18, 157, 165n25, 183–84, 189, 195n49, 195n56
cowboys/cowgirls, 236, 238, *239*, 240
Cowtown, 235–36
Crenshaw, Kimberlé, 26n43
Crespino, Joseph, 9–11, 24
crossroads, regional, 226, 244; Chicago as, 38, 41
culture. *See* politics and culture

Dallas–Fort Worth: airports, 241, 242, 243; boosters, 232, 234, *239*, 241, 243, 245; cooperation between cities, 226–28, 242–45; East and, 234, 238, 240; railroads and, 228–30, *229*, 240; rivalry between cities, 228–30, 234–38, 240–42, 247n30; South and, 234

INDEX 285

Dallas Herald, 228, 229
Dallas Morning News, 230, 236, *237*, 240–41, 244
dams, 125, 133, 139, 140–41, 143
Daniels, Jonathan, 20, 21
Darwin, Charles, 206
Dealey, George B., 230–31, 236
decolonization, 58, 71, 73–74, 85, 87. *See also* imperialism
Democratic Party, 64–65, 158, 160
Deseret, 122
Deskaheh (Levi General), 175–76, 178, 190–91
DeVoto, Bernard, 32–39, 41, 51, 53n36
Diaz Ordaz, Gustavo, 133
Dickens, Charles, 203
Dixie, 9, 14–17, 19, 24, 42–43, 233, 262
Dixon, Thomas, 233
draft riots, 211, 213
Dred Scott v. Sanford (1857), 158
Drid, 183–84
Du Bois, W. E. B., 5, 7, 92

East and easterners, 31–32, 43, 48, 267; Easts, plural, 48, 51; as foil to other regions, 37, 40–45, 51, 153, 161, 218; Indigenous people and, 47, 49–51, 53–54n50. *See also* regions, relationships between
eastern dominance, xii, 37–38, 153; extraction of wealth, 42, 51, 53n24; intellectual and cultural life, 42, 48, 49, 161; political power, 48, 50, 214, 253; waning of, 212, 216; via wealth, 205, 214, 227
"The Easy Chair" (DeVoto), 33, 34, 35
Ebony magazine, 40, 102
economics, 144; construction of regions and, 61, 130, 226, 227; depressions and, 40, 144, 145, 228, 265; eastern dominance and, 42, 51, 53n24, 205, 214, 227; modernization and, 140, 142, 243, 269
education, 154–55, 156
Edwards, Laura, 12–13, 15
Eisenhower, Dwight D., 253, 254, 270–71
Erdrich, Louise, 38–39, 45–51
Etinoëh, 182, *183*, 184, 190, 193n26
Europe, 113, 260
evangelicals, 214
exceptionalism, 269; American, 7, 177, 268, 269; southern, 3, 7–10, 24

families, separation of, 43, 50, 93, 213, 215, 216, 218
farming. *See* agriculture
federalism, 254, 268, 270, 274n16
feminism, 18–19, 20; Black, 4–5, 12, 18–19, 21, 27n43
Florida, 52n1, 129, 130
Fort Worth, 229, *231*, *237*. *See also* Dallas–Fort Worth
Fort Worth Democrat, 227, 228–29
Fort Worth Star-Telegram, 230, 234–35, 236, 241, 244
Foster, Peter, 183–84
Frémont, John Charles, 119, 120, 126
Friend, Craig Thompson, 12
frontier, 31–32, 36, 38–39, 60, 111, 218, 239; Manifest Destiny and, 112–16, 125, 126, 128; Turner and, 111, 130n1, 153, 161, 218
Fugitive Slave Act, 156–57, 165n25
funding, federal, 117, 123, 125, 259, 261, 271

General, Levi (Deskaheh), 175–76, 178, 190–91
Ganienkeh, 187, 194n48
geography, xviii–xix, 57–58, 59–60, 65; natural boundary lines, 66–67, 160, 161, 162; vs. politics and culture, xx, 5, 11, 47, 57–58, 61, 77–78, 181; roads and, 255, 270. *See also* regions, categorization of: geographic vs. ideological
Germany, xv, 271
Gilmore, Glenda, 5–6, 15–17
Gilpin, William, 126–28
Glover, Lorri, 12
Good Neighbor policy, 142, 148
Good Roads Movement, 257–59
Gourneau, Aunishenaubay Patrick, 47, 49–50
Great American Desert, 113, 114, 115, 118–19, 122, 126, 127, 129
Great Depression, 40, 144, 145, 265
Great Lakes, 159, 160, 182
Great Salt Lake, 121
Gresham, Walter Q., 137

Halaby, Najeeb E., 241–42
Harding, Warren G., 261
Harlem Renaissance, 17
Harmon, Judson, 134, 137–38
Harmon Opinion, 134, 137–38, 139

Harper's, 33, 35, 37
Haudenosaunee, 175, 177, 180, 185, 186, 192n17; League of, 178, 181–82, 191, 192n13; "New York" and "Canadian," 184–85, 187–89, 194n42; politics of, 178–79, 181–82, 189–90, 193n26, 195n49
Hawai'i, 57–58, 62–64, 68–71, 78n1, 225; annexation of, 61–63, 76; California and, 63, 74–75; legislation and, 61, 62; Native Hawaiians and, 60–62, 64, 70, 76–77; New England and, 61, 69–70; sovereignty of, 58, 60–63, 76–77; statehood and, 57–58, 64–73, 72, 76–77
Hawaii Statehood Commission, 66, 68–69
health, 78n6, 113, 121–22, 127, 203–5, 207–8, 209
highways, 255–56; as defining regions, 266, 272; interstates, 129, 261, 271–72; policies, 257, 259, 270–72. *See also* infrastructure; roads
Hill, Tadodahoh Sid, 190
Hillbilly Elegy (Vance), 3, 24n1
hinterlands, 226, 227, 237, 243, 244, 247n26
hip-hop, 93, 94–95, 97–98
historiography, xx, 4–5, 9–13, 20, 24, 26–27n43, 59, 179
Hoover Dam, 141, 143
Howard, John, 22–23, 24
Howells, William Dean, 163
Hubbell, Jay B., 233–34
Huronia people, 193n22
hydroengineering, 140–42, 267

Ickes, Harold, 143–46
immigrants, xvi, 59, 63, 156, 203; "morality" and, 205–6, 210, 211, 213; race restrictions for, 62, 64, 74, 146
imperialism, ix, 38, 57–59, 60–63, 77, 78n6, 87, 143; anti-imperialists and, 67–68, 92; Canada and, 177, 191n6; climate and, 111, 113, 121; distancing from, 67–68, 71, 161; national ambition and, 57–58, 61, 119, 126–27. *See also* frontier; Indigenous lands; Indigenous peoples; westward expansion
Indian Defense League of America (IDLA), 178
Indian Wars, 47, 126
Indigenous lands, 179–82, 192n11, 194–95n48, 195n56; expropriation of, 48–51, 60–63, 67, 76, 117, 175, 180, 182–83, 184, 186; maps of, *183*, *185*

Indigenous peoples, ix, 26n40, 43–44, 114, 175, 225; boarding schools for, 43, 50; East and, 46–51, 53–54n50; languages of, 77, 193n26; legislation and, 49, 177, 184, 186–89, 195n56; sovereignty of, 47, 49, 175–81, 184, 190; stereotypical representations of, 47, 179, *180*, 266. *See also* Hawai'i; *individual nations and peoples*
infrastructure, 115–16, 123, 133–36, 159–60, *231*, 253; centralization and, 141, 144–45, 256, 260–63, 271–72, 274n18; legislation and, 125, 259, 261–62; segregation and, 268, 270, 272; war and, 253, 260, 269, 270–71
International Boundary and Water Commission (IBWC), 134–35, 142, 144, 146–47
internationalism, Black, 85–86, 92, 103
International Water Commission (IWC), 139, 140
Interregional Highways (report), 268, 269, 270
intersectional identities, 4–6, 11–15, 19, 21–22, 24–25n1, 25n2, 26–27n43, 31; vs. binaries, 12, 20, 26n40; whiteness and, 5, 11, 13
Iowa, 157
Iroquoia, 182, 186, 193n22, 193n26. *See also* Haudenosaunee
irrigation, 121–25, 131n19, 138
Irving, Washington, 118–19
Ivy League schools, 35–36, 45

Jackson, Michael, 90
Jansson, David, 9
Japan, 53n45, 64, 65, 69, 70
Jay Treaty of 1794, 177, 178, 191n10, 192n17
Jegöhsahse, 181, 193n24
Johnson, Lyndon, 133, 147

Kaianerekowa Hotinonsionne document, 193n24
Kalākaua, King, 62
Kamehameha, Chief, 60
Kamokila Campbell, Alice, 70
Kansas, 157–58, 165n31
Kentucky, 153, 166n54
King, Martin Luther, Jr., 97
Ku Klux Klan, 233

labor unions, 146, 217–18
lacrosse, 190

INDEX

Lake Ontario, 181, 182
Lassiter, Matthew D., 9–11, 24
Lauck, Jon, xiii
League of Nations, 175, 190–91, 191n2
League of the Haudenosaunee, 178, 181–82, 191, 192n13
legislation, 211; Hawai'i and, 61, 62; highways and, 270, 271–72; Indigenous peoples and, 49, 177, 184, 186–89, 195n56; infrastructure and, 125, 259, 261; segregation and, 88, 96; slavery, 153, 156–58, 161, 165n25; statehood and, 70–71, 153
LGBTQ history, 22–24
liberalism, 9, 58, 65, 68, 71–72, 74, 75–76
Lili'uokalani, Queen, 62–63, 76
Lincoln, Abraham, 155, 158, 163, 211
literary culture, 31, 39–45, 46–51, 161–63, 219n9, 234
Little Steven (Steven Van Zandt), 85, 91, 101
Live Aid, 90–91, 94
Long, Stephen F., 118
Longhouses, 186–87, 193n26
Los Angeles, 136, 143
Lost Cause narrative, 7, 266
Louisiana Purchase, 157
luau, 74–75, 80n49

Mandela, Nelson, 88, 89, 97, 99
Manifest Destiny, 112–16, 125, 126, 128. *See also* frontier; imperialism
maps, 67, 119–20, *124*, *180*; Indigenous land, *183*, *185*; road, 256, 260–66, *262*, *269*; tarantula, 228, 229, *229*
marginalized groups, xviii, 4, 265; displacement of, 93, 272. *See also* feminism; immigrants; intersectional identities; race
Massie, William, 230–31
McKnight, Felix R., 241
McLane, George, 69–70
Mead, Elwood, 139
media, 230–31, *231*, 240, 244
the Metroplex, 226, 245. *See also* Dallas–Fort Worth
Mexican-American War, 116, 118, 122, 126, 155–56, 162
Mexico, 121, 133, 139–40, 142, 148; Nuevo Mexico, 118, 121

Midwest, 39–41, 43, 267; emergence of, 152–53, 162–63, 164n3; as "Middle West," 162, 167n67; reform movements of, 154–56, 164n18; writers of, 39–45, 46–50, 163. *See also* regions, relationships between
migration, regional, xii, xvi, 59, 129, 270
military: Union, 158–59, 166n47, 210–11; World War I, 253, 260; World War II, 65. *See also* individual wars
Minnesota, 45, 66, 216
missionaries, 60–61, 70
Mississippi River, 162, 166n50
Missouri Compromise, 155–57
modernization, 140, 142, 144, 145, 243, 263, 269
Mohawk people, 186, 187, 192n20; Nation of Akwesasne, 183, 191
Monroe Doctrine, 61
Mormons, 120–22, 131n19
Mother Earth. *See* Etino'ëh
music, 90–95, 103

nationalism, xiv–xv, 49, 57–58, 146, 254, 267; race and, 63–64, 68, 74, 112; vs. regional interests, 136, 255, 256, 261, 269; roads and, 263, 266–67; South and, 6–11, 45; unity and, ix, 45, 51, 205, 210. *See also* internationalism
National Organization for Women (NOW), 15, 18
Native Americans. *See* Indigenous peoples
natural disasters, 129, 130, 137–38; flooding, 139, 140, 147
Nebraska, 157–58, 216
New Conservation, 142, 144
New Deal, 141, 144, 145, 265–67
New England, xii, 37, 41, 46–47, 53n36, 159; Hawai'i and, 61, 69–70
New York City, 17, 41–42, 203–6, 208–9, 211, 213, 216–17
New York State, 179, *180*, 183, 189, 190, 195n49
The Night Watchman (Erdrich), 47–50
North and northerners, 43, 204–5, 212, 217–18; as the Union, 158–59, 166n47, 210–11, 212. *See also* Civil War; Confederacy; regions, relationships between
North Carolina, 17
North Dakota, 39, 40, 43, 45
Northeast, 267. *See also* East and easterners

North Texas Commission (NTC), 243–44
Northwest, 141, 182
Northwest Mounted Police, 175
Northwest Ordinance of 1787, 153, 156, 161

Oceania, 77–78
Offenburger, Andrew, 162
Office of Public Roads, 260, 274n19
Ohio, 153, 157, 163
Oklahoma, x–xi, 225
Oneida people, 184, 186, 192n20, 195n49, 195n56
Onönda'geh people, 184, 192–93n20, 193n24, 195n49, 195n56
Ontario, 175
Oregon, 215
orphans. *See* placing-out, of children
othering, 8, 9, 25n14
Ownby, Ted, 11, 14

Pacific islands, 57, 60, 74, 75, 77–78
Pacific West, 78n3, 141
Paddock, Buckley B., 227–28, 234
Pan-Africanism, 87, 99
paradises, 75
Parker, Arthur C., 179, *180*
passports, 175–76, 190, 192n17
Peace Corps, 73
the Peacemaker, 181, 193n24
Pearl Harbor, 61–62, 66–67
Pershing, John J., 260, 261
Phoenix AZ, 125
Pike, Zebulon, 118
placing-out, of children, 203–4, 210–14, 218, 219n2, 219n5; western response to, 205, 207, 208, 209, 214–18
plains, xiii, 113–14, 118, 127, 130n3
plantations, 59, 61, 64, 69, 156, 266
"A Plundered Province" (DeVoto), 33, 37
police, 88, 97, 146–48, 176, 184, 191n4, 263–64
politics and culture, ix–x, xvii–xviii, 23, 130, 262; eastern dominance over, 42, 48, 50, 161, 214, 253; vs. geography, xx, 5, 11, 47, 57–58, 61, 77–78, 181; literary culture, 31, 39–45, 46–51, 161–63, 219n9, 234. *See also* borders, political; Haudenosaunee; imperialism; Indigenous lands; Indigenous peoples; nationalism; regions, categorization of: political and cultural; statehood; territory; United States; *individual nations and peoples*; *individual wars*
Polynesia, 57, 60, 71
Porter, Tom, 187
postal service, 115–16
postcolonialism, 76
postmodernism, 12
poverty, 7, 205, 212, 213, 218
Powell, John Wesley, 123–25, 131n21
power, state, 144, 191n4
prairies, 39, 41, 42, 45, 114
presidential elections, 24–25n1, 160
Proclamation of 1763, ix, 177
Protestants, 23, 191n6, 203, 204, 206, 207, 212, 213, 218
Puerto Rico, 49

Quakers, 164n18

race, xvi, 14–15, 23, 39, 42–43, 51; "civilization" and, 119, 128, 129; mixed-race people, 43–44, 50–51, 53n45, 116; national identity and, 64–65, 68, 72–75, 112; regional categorization and, 65, 86, 220n27; unity and, 43–45, 86–87, 94, 98–99, 101, 103; whiteness and, 5, 11, 13, 42, 62–64, 69–71, 101, 129, 233. *See also* intersectional identities; slavery; white supremacy; *individual peoples*
racial liberalism, 58, 65, 68, 71–72, 74, 75–76
racism, 42–43, 75, 143, 146, 211; against Asians, 58, 62–65, 67, 69, 72, 74. *See also* immigrants
railroads, 117, 128, 159–60, 162, 226; Dallas–Fort Worth and, 228–30, 229, 240
Reagan, Ronald, 95
Reclamation, 123, 125. *See also* Bureau of Reclamation (BOR); irrigation
Reconstruction, Greater, 220n27
Reece, Chuck, 24n1
Reed, John Shelton, 3
reform movements, 14, 140–42, 213–14, 216; evangelical, 206, 212–14, 217, 218; midwestern, 154–56, 164n18
regions, categorization of, ix–x, xi–xii, xiii–xiv, 152, 254–55; distinctions as invented, 224–25, 228, 229, 234, 243, 245; geographic vs.

INDEX

ideological, 5, 17, 24, 49, 101, 218, 259–60; political and cultural, ix–x, 11, 14–16, 23, 43, 51, 61, 130, 262, 268; power dynamics of, xvi, xix, 224–25, 255, 262, 264–65; race and, 65, 86, 220n27; as shifting or slippery, xiii, 160, 208, 218, 224–25, 255, 275n44; states as defying, 57–58, 77–78, 225; urban vs. rural, 212, 257–58, 273nn10–11. *See also individual regions*

regions, relationships between, xii, 46, 167n67, 212; East, as foil to other regions, 37, 40–45, 51, 153, 161, 218; East vs. Midwest, 31–32, 36, 38, 40–45, 51, 153, 161–62; East vs. South, 48; East vs. West, 31–39, 40–46, 51, 203–4, 218; Midwest vs. South, 153–61; Midwest vs. West, 160, 162, 208; North vs. South, 8, 112, 153, 154–55; rivalries and alliances, xv–xvii, 46, 212, 220n27, 255, 257, 273n10; South as national foil, 6–10, 45; South vs. Southwest, 233, 234, 245; South vs. West, xi, 117–18, 162, 166n54, 225, 232; Southwest vs. West, 233–34, 245. *See also individual regions*

Reilly, William J., 235–36

religion, 15, 23, 156. *See also* reform movements: evangelical; *individual religions*

republicanism, 62, 67–68, 203, 204, 212

Republican Party, 158, 160, 163

Richie, Lionel, 90

Rickard, Clinton, 178

Riley, G. S., 185

Riley, James Whitcomb, 163

Rio Grande: borderlands, 135–40, 142, 145, 147, 148; river, 133, 134–36, 137, 138–40, 142, 143

roads, 253, 255; boosters and, 256, 262–63, 271; naming of, 262–65, 274n29; national defense and, 253–54, 267–68; white supremacy and, 262–65, 268, 270, 272. *See also* Bureau of Public Roads (BPR); highways; infrastructure

Roosevelt, Franklin D., 141, 265, 267–68

Royal Canadian Mounted Police (RCMP), 175

Salt Lake Valley, 121, 122

Sandusky OH, 187–88

schools: Indigenous, 43, 50; industrial, 207, 209

science, 111, 113, 119, 123, 127, 128, 131n21

segregation, 6, 15, 43, 72, 233; apartheid, 85, 87–90, 93, 95–97; legislation and, 88, 96; roads and, 268, 270, 272

Seneca people, 184, 185

settlers, white, 38, 60–61, 62–63, 177, 182; climate and, 111, 113, 121

Sharpeville Massacre, 88

Shoemaker, Nancy, xx–xxi

Shortridge, James, 167n67

Simon, E. P., 209

Six Nations Grand River Reserve, 184

slavery, 6–7, 87, 154; legislation and, 153, 156–58, 161, 165n25; westward expansion and, 112, 115–17, 155–56

Smith, Henry Nash, 234

Smithsonian Museum, 50

Smythe, William Ellsworth, 123, 125

Soja, Edward W., 86

Sousa, John Philip, 40

South and southerners, xi–xii, xvii–xviii, 3–4, 127, 212; abolition and, 154, 233; archetypes of, 7–9, 11, 13, 20–21, 232–33, 245, 264–66; "badness" of, 3, 6, 8, 22, 234, 264–65; Hawai'i and, 59, 64–65; as national foil, 6–10, 45; southern dissenters, 14–15, 16, 17, 26n29; southern exceptionalism, 3, 7–10, 24; Souths, plural, 5, 21–22, 25n5, 26n29; Texas and, 225, 226. *See also* Civil War; Confederacy; Dixie; North and northerners; regions, relationships between

South Africa, 85, 87, 90, 96, 100

Southwest and southwesterners, 129, 233, 246n10; archetypes of, 266; Great Southwest, 226–32, 231, 244; southern archetypes and, 232–33, 245; western archetypes and, 235–36, 241, 245. *See also* regions, relationships between

Southwest Metroplex, 244–45. *See also* Dallas–Fort Worth

Southwest Ordinance of 1790, 153

Southwest Review, 233–34

sovereignty, 135, 137, 144–45, 157; of Hawai'i, 58, 60–63, 76–77; of Indigenous peoples, 47, 49; spatial, 175–76, 178–81, 184, 190; territorial, 136, 177

Soviet Union, 71, 73

Spanish-American War, ix, 63, 67

spatial sovereignty and survivance, 175–81, 184, 190–91

Special Committee Against Apartheid, 100

statehood, 122, 157; Congress and, 63, 64, 70–71, 153; Hawai'i and, 57–58, 64–73, 72, 76–77; race and, 65, 68, 72–73, 75
Stegner, Wallace, 33–36, 38–39, 51, 126
St. Lawrence River, 181, 182–83
Stowe, Harriet Beecher, 157
strikes, labor, 89, 217
suburbs, 130, 243, 270, 272, 273n11
sugar, 62, 64
Sunbelt, xiii, 129, 130
Sun City, 102; *Sun City* record, 85–87, 91–93, 101, 103; Sun City resort and casino, 85, 93, 97, 99–102; "Sun City" song and music video, 91, 92, 93, 97–99, 101
surveyors, geographic, 61, 116–17, 119–20, 120, 123, 136–37
survivance, 176, 191n6; spatial, 176–77, 179, 184, 191

tariffs, 155, 160
taxes, 270, 271
technologies, regions and, xv–xvi
Tennessee Valley Authority (TVA), 141
territory: annexation of, 61–63, 76, 116, 122, 155; binational management of, 123, 133–39, 148; conceptions of, 79–82, 145–46; incorporated U.S. territories, 57, 58, 59, 63–70, 122, 162
Texas, 52n1, 116, 129, 130, 155, 224, 232, 237–38; as "born southern," 225, 226; North Texas, 243–44, 246n10; water rights and, 134, 138, 139, 140, 147; West Texas, 235, *237*
Texas and Pacific Railroad, 227, 228–29
thirdspace, 86, 87, 92, 97
Third World Liberation Front, 75
Thompson, Era Bell, 38–45, 51
Thurston, Lorrin A., 63, 68–69
Thurston, Lorrin P., 68–69
tourism, 257, 263; guides, 264, 265–67, 275n44
Tracy-Locke Company, 243–44
trade, 59, 61–62, 64, 159–60, 182, 231
Transcontinental Motor Convoy, 253–55, 257, 260, 271
transnationalism, xiv, 19, 86–87, 89–91, 93, 101
Treaty of Ghent, 191n10
Treaty of Paris, 182
Troyer, Howard, 152, 164n1
truancy laws, 206

Turner, Frederick Jackson, 111, 130n1, 153, 161, 218. *See also* frontier
Turtle Mountain Band of Chippewa, 40–50
Tuscarora people, 176, 184
Twain, Mark, 36
Tyler, John, 61

Uncle Tom's Cabin (Stowe), 157
The Uneasy Chair (Stegner), 33–34, 35, 41
Union. *See* North and northerners
United Daughters of the Confederacy (UDC), 264–65
United Nations, 95, 191
United States, 71, 88–90, 95–97. *See also* borders, political; exceptionalism; frontier; imperialism; Indigenous lands; Indigenous peoples; nationalism; statehood; territory; *individual nations and peoples; individual wars*
United States Geological Survey, 123, *124*, 260
University of Hawai'i, 73, 76
urban vs. rural, 203–4, 207–9, 247n26, 262; as regional division, 212, 257–58, 273nn10–11; South and, 23
USA for Africa, 90, 94
U.S. Senate, 135, 142–43, 148
Utah, 34, 36, 122, 125

Valley of the Sun, 125
Van Zandt, Steven (Little Steven), 85, 91, 101
Vietnam War, 73–74
Vizenor, Gerard, 176
voting, ix, 10, 62, 63, 64, 96, 160, 213

Wadkins, Lanny, 101
Walker, Alice, 21, 27n43
Waowawanaonk (Peter Wilson), 184, 188–89, 194n33
War of 1812, 177
Washington DC, 42–43, 49–51
Water Treaty of 1944, 123, 134–35, 142–44, 146, 148
Watkins, Jerry, 23
"We Are the World" (song), 90–91, 94
Webster, Daniel, 115–16, 156
West and westerners, 112–13, *124*, 212; as agricultural paradise, 125, 127, 204, 218; archetypes of, 38, 44, 207, 235–36, 241, 245, 267;

back East, 36, 50; Far West, 44, 126, 162, 208; health and "morals" of, 203–5, 207–8, 209; land as "worthless," 115–16, 117, 118–19, 121; placing-out and, 205, 207, 208, 209, 214–18; urban development, 215, 218; writers of, 32–33, 35, 40–51, 219n9. *See also* regions, relationships between

West Coast, 63, 74–75

westward expansion, 59, 120, 126–27, 208; slavery and, 112, 115–17, 155–56. *See also* frontier; imperialism; Indigenous lands

Whig Party, 158

white supremacy, 4, 17, 43, 69, 232–33; roads and, 262–65, 268, 270, 272; voting and, 62, 63, 96; water rights and, 143, 147

Wilkes, Charles, 61

Wilmot Proviso, 155–56

Wilson, Peter (Waowawanaonk), 184, 188–89, 194n33

Wisconsin, 217

wlôgan, 180–81, 182

womanism, 21, 27n43

Woodward, C. Vann, 6–11

Works Progress Administration (WPA), 144, 265–66

World's Columbian Exposition, 63

World War I, 87, 253, 260

World War II, 16, 53n45, 61, 65–69, 87

writers, 31; midwestern, 39–45, 46–50, 163; western, 32–33, 35, 40–51, 219n9

Young, Brigham, 121

www.ingramcontent.com/pod-product-compliance
Lightning Source LLC
Chambersburg PA
CBHW031904220426
43663CB00006B/767